16 cines LAD2008

Immigrants and the American City

IMMIGRANTS
AND THE
AMERICAN
CITY

THOMAS MULLER

A Twentieth Century Fund Book

NEW YORK UNIVERSITY PRESS
New York and London

The Twentieth Century Fund is a research foundation undertaking time-ly analyses of economic, political, and social issues. Not-for-profit and nonpartisan, the Fund was founded in 1919 and endowed by Edward A. Filene.

Library of Congress Cataloging-in-Publication Data

Muller, Thomas, 1933–
    Immigrants and the American city / Thomas E. Muller.
        p. cm.
    "A Twentieth Century Fund book."
    Includes bibliographic references and index.
    ISBN 0-8147-5479-1 (cl. : alk. paper)
    1. United States—Emigration and immigration—Economic aspects—History. 2. United States—Emigration and Immigration—History. 3. Cities and towns—United States—History. I. Title.
JV6471.M85 1993
304.8'73—dc20   92-8934
                                                                      CIP

Cover Design and Illustration: Claude Goodwin
Manufactured in the United States of America.

To Sharon, Steven, Beth, and Joseph, with affection

Foreword

America has been a work in progress for most of its history. Yet Americans always have been ambivalent about change. Almost from colonial times, there has been a yearning for a lyrical past, when we were a less diverse, simpler country. All highly industrialized nations, of course, have experienced immense shifts of population from rural to urban areas. But only the United States has achieved a farm efficiency that requires just 2 percent of the population to work the land. So, it is not surprising that there is a nostalgia for all the small towns that have been left behind. Moreover, modernization has altered America by the introduction of mass media and the dissemination of new notions about sex, family, and religion. These developments all create uneasiness and uncertainty.

In addition, in an important sense, Americans have and continue to live with an element of change that exceeds that of virtually any other nation. For the United States is the one state founded upon and, more or less, continuously willing to accept significant waves of diverse immigrants. Yet, while the idea of who is a "normal" American has altered with time, there is, paradoxically, a persistent strain of nativism that craves a return to a time when almost everyone was, so to speak, like "us."

Today, discussions of the nation and its future usually are in terms of economics and the post cold war. Our political and media leaders are relatively united in the view that future "threats" to the nation involve America's struggle to meet the challenge of increased international economic competition. Our new president, quite properly, has pointed to the need to invest in our people as a key determinant of our ultimate success in that struggle. But, there is an alternative and unpleasant strain of political rhetoric that often uses code words to blame our competitive decline on particular groups or on the changing composition of the population. The fact is that most Americans don't yet know what to make of the groups that have comprised the lion's share of immigration over the last generation.

Like other groups arriving throughout the twentieth century, the newest Americans have settled disproportionately in urban areas. The difference is that the economic future of many of our largest cities is much more in doubt than was previously the case. This uncertainty surely adds a new element to the uneasiness felt by many about the impact of recent immigration. Yet, despite the importance of this movement of peoples, serious research and discussion of the subject is still at a relatively early stage of development. No consensus about the effects of this new wave of immigrants on our cities and our nation has yet emerged.

With this fact in mind, the Twentieth Century Fund was pleased to commission Thomas Muller, a former staff member of the Urban Institute and a frequent consultant to government agencies, to research and write about immigration and the American City. We believe that Mr. Muller has succeeded in greatly sharpening our understanding of the changes being wrought in our cities by these newest Americans.

As Muller powerfully argues, we are, in fact, in the midst of one of the great waves of immigration in our history. While it is a commonplace to note the non-European origins of some of these groups, we are just beginning to realize that, like those who came before them, this group of new Americans is providing a wellspring of innovation and talent for our cities. What has changed, of course, is the cities themselves. For it is far from clear that our older urban centers will be reborn as the central engines of economic and political progress in the nation. Going forward, our capacity to understand and perhaps shape a policy response to these changes will be greatly enhanced by Muller's work. On behalf of the Fund's Trustees, I thank him for his contribution to scholarship in this area.

Richard C. Leone, *President*
The Twentieth Century Fund
November 1992

Acknowledgments

This book would not have been possible without the financial and other assistance provided by The Twentieth Century Fund. The late director M. J. Rossant gave the project initial guidance, and Beverly Goldberg, vice president, director of publications, applied her many talents to turn the initial draft into a final product. My thanks are also extended to two editors, Michael Massing, on behalf of the Twentieth Century Fund, and Steven Greenfield at the Fund, for their skillful editing, which enhanced the quality of the book. The favorable comments by Henry G. Cisneros, Leo F. Estrada, and Professor Nathan Glazer facilitated the approval of the project. Professor Kenneth Boulding reviewed the early manuscript, and his insightful suggestions, as always, were invaluable. Ms. Helen Arnold deserves praise for her infinite patience and library assistance. Finally, the typing skills of Ms. Virginia Murray assured a readable manuscript.

Contents

1

Introduction

For centuries, nations receiving immigrants have experienced a fundamental tension. On one hand, governments and business interests generally welcome aliens for the economic benefits they can generate. On the other, a large influx of foreigners can be highly disruptive, weakening a nation's sense of cohesiveness. Since the Middle Ages, nations intent on invigorating their economies have invited such enterprising ethnic groups as the Chinese, Jews, and Germans. Often, however, the economic success of these groups has stirred distrust and envy, leading to discrimination, oppression, and, in some cases, eviction. English sovereigns and American presidents seeking economic expansion have tended to favor the admission of aliens; native populations and their legislative representatives, perceiving immigrants as undesirable, have frequently sought to make them feel unwelcome.

The immigration policies of most Western nations, including the United States, reflected efforts to balance the economic gains derived from foreign workers against the popular discontent that their presence often provoked. During periods of rapid economic expansion, when a shortage of workers threatened to slow growth, entry restrictions were commonly eased. At other times, ethnic and racial concerns prevailed, resulting in the imposition of severe controls.

The conflicting perceptions of immigrants evident in earlier eras continue to influence policymakers in Western nations today. Following World War II, Western Europe recruited several million workers from the Mediterranean basin, and England accepted workers from its former colonies. But when economic stagnation in the 1970s caused increased unemployment, housing shortages, rising crime rates, and growing outlays for welfare, immigrants were widely blamed. As antagonism mounted against workers of Turkish and North African origin on the Continent, political pressures built for curtailing further immigration and even for expelling alien workers and their families. Today, hostility toward immigrants has emerged as a major political issue in numerous European nations, most notably France and Germany.

Since the first Congress debated the issue, immigration policy in the United States has been bound up with some of our most basic concerns—economic well-being, national identity, internal stability, and the American role in the world. Throughout two centuries, public opinion on immigration has been marked by ambivalence. Some see immigrants as productive workers who can be absorbed into the national mainstream without much disruption. Others take a much dimmer view, regarding immigrants primarily as economic competitors or as foreigners with alien values.

On a number of occasions since the first great wave of people arrived on our shores in the 1840s, Congress has passed measures aimed at restricting immigration, and the White House has regularly vetoed them. This disagreement has been molded less by philosophy than by political considerations. Most of our presidents, viewing immigration from a national perspective, attached considerable political and economic importance to the large urban centers in which immigrants concentrate. Legislators generally mirrored the parochial interests of their constituents, most of whom do not live in big cities and are typically uncomfortable with any change in the ethnic composition of their communities.

In recent years, the debate has entered a new phase due to the vastly expanded volume and diversity of information available on the subject. Television, in particular, has become a major shaper of opinion, but the images shown on our screens send conflicting messages. On one hand, immigrants are favorably portrayed as hardworking exemplars of the American dream. Thus, when the Statue of Liberty turned one hundred years old in 1986, television celebrated our national tradition of openness by extolling those who have come to take advantage of it. Programs lauded the contribution of second-generation Americans to business, technology, science, and the arts. The nation watched the centennial finale with a gigantic display of fireworks over the Manhattan skyline as Neil Diamond sang "Coming to America." Two years later, when Governor Michael Dukakis, the nominee of the Democratic party for the presidency, pointed with pride to his Greek heritage, "Coming to America" seemed closer to reality than anyone a generation earlier would have imagined.

Television offers other scenes as well, depicting America as a nation under siege. We watch as men and women scurry across the narrow strip separating two nations—the one prosperous and stable, the other poor and desperate. The Mexican-American border has become a new symbol, not of welcome but of futile efforts to control entry. Meanwhile, in places like Central America, the Caribbean, and Asia, the camera documents refugees fleeing war, poverty, and repression. Salvadorans seek asylum in American churches; Haitians elude our patrol boats; and Filipinos are crossing the virtually open northern border undetected. These scenes evoke contrasting emotions—many are moved by the plight of those searching for a new home, but fear that this nation cannot absorb all those eager to become part of it.

Joined to these images of poor masses pressing from without are pictures of homeless Americans huddled within—sleeping in the doorways of Los Angeles, seeking shelter in the subways of New York, freezing in the streets of the nation's capital. The increase in minority unemployment and urban homelessness at a time of rising immigration raises some sensitive questions. Would more Americans have jobs, a roof over their heads, and three hot meals a day if fewer immigrants entered the country? Are racial tensions in American cities being exacerbated by the continuing arrival of immigrants who compete for jobs with members of the underclass?

Overpopulation is another concern. Blessed with open space, the United States is, compared with most other nations, sparsely populated. However, growing affluence has reinforced the desire for privacy and support for preserving our natural resources. Environmentalists argue that the dry, fragile ecology of the western states cannot sustain further settlement. The deadly pollution, traffic chaos, and poverty in Mexico City loom as examples of what uncontrolled urban migration can cause. Los Angeles and Dallas, cities that had taken pride in their rapid expansion, now seek to limit new development. And in suburban areas across the nation, antigrowth sentiment, a predominantly middle-class phenomenon, mushrooms during periods of economic expansion. Congestion has replaced the weather as a major topic of casual conversation. Complaints about traffic proliferate, but, like the weather, it seems beyond our control. The nation seeks economic growth to satisfy material wants yet appears unwilling to deal with its adverse consequences—too many cars, too few places to dump the trash. National organizations are formed to support "zero-growth" policies. These associations oppose immigration as a means of braking population growth.

Whenever legislators consider revising immigration laws, dire predictions are issued regarding the economic and social consequences of accepting more aliens. These forecasts often turn out to be wrong. Two generations ago, restrictions were placed on the inflow of Eastern and Southern European immigrants on the grounds that they were "undesirable"; today, the nation proudly trumpets the achievements of these same groups. Indeed, Americans who favor continued immigration point reassuringly to the contributions of these earlier entrants and their children as evidence of our ability to assimilate the current wave of aliens. Others, however, view with unease the growing number of illegal immigrants, most of them from underdeveloped nations. They fear that America will not be able to cope, economically or socially, with the multitudes of poor and hungry eager to cross our borders. With the global population doubling every forty years, they see no end to the torrent of illegal immigrants. This fear extends to the countless refugees who flee their homelands when political repression becomes intolerable.

Interestingly, fewer express concern that the number of legal entrants is also growing, primarily as a result of family reunification. It is commonly believed that legal immigrants are somehow of better "stock" than those who lack documentation. The prevailing image of illegal aliens is that of Mexicans waiting to wade across rivers or climb broken fences when darkness descends. Such a perception, however, does not take into account that many illegal aliens are professionals or skilled workers who enter legally and overstay—sometimes permanently—their visas.

Unfortunately, opinions are often formed on the basis of fleeting newscasts or chance encounters with aliens in restaurants, taxis, and gas stations. For a fuller sense of how immigration affects American cities, we need to look at the forces that have shaped entry policies. We also need to assess the economic impact of immigration on Americans, particularly urban residents, past and present.

American immigration policy has passed through three phases. From the colonial era until the 1920s, the borders of the United States remained wide open to persons of European origin, primarily because both government and business believed that immigrants were needed to sustain rapid economic growth. During this initial period, economic self-interest overcame periodic, and occasionally violent, eruptions of antiurban, anti-immigrant sentiment. Although organized labor and other groups opposed unrestricted entry, they lacked the political power to influence immigration policy at a time when Congress was dominated by antilabor interests.

Beginning in the 1920s, this open-borders policy gave way to tight control. The new restrictions were largely unrelated to economic factors. Instead, public pressure for change came from widespread and virtually unchallenged acceptance of theories about racial inferiority that were promoted by followers of the eugenics movement. Concerns about the influx of non-Protestant immigrants led to public demand for entry limits based on national origin. Most business enterprises continued to favor the inflow of cheap labor regardless of ethnicity, but they bowed to the growing public clamor for curbs. For several decades, the United States successfully enforced strict limits on the number and ethnic origin of immigrants from nations outside the Western Hemisphere. By the middle of the twentieth century, immigrant population as a percentage of all residents fell to the lowest level since the early decades of the Republic.

The third phase of national immigration policy began with legislative initiatives in the mid-1960s that abandoned the concept of immigration quotas based on nationality. This reversal was attributable to gradual changes in attitude among the post–World War II generation, who were less willing to accept the thesis that differences in appearance, culture, or religion from the Northern and Western European–derived mainstream signify inferior status. Sympathy for displaced persons showed in the acceptance of refugees from Southeast Asia, Afghanistan, and Central America. This new mood of acceptance was also conditioned by a need for alien workers to maintain economic growth. Although global limits on the number of immigrants remain in effect, these limits are no longer a gauge of how many persons from other countries are absorbed. The growth in temporary admissions and clandestine border crossings has overwhelmed those responsible for enforcement.

There was no immediate backlash in response to this development. First of all, American xenophobia was largely a thing of the past, having peaked in the 1930s. Furthermore, most new arrivals, both legal and undocumented, were concentrated in large cities that had successfully absorbed earlier waves of immigrants. For most Americans, illegal immigrants were largely invisible. Not until the inflow accelerated and the news media focused on the "quiet invasion" across our southern border during the 1980s did popular concern heighten, leading Congress to consider measures aimed at slowing the illegal inflow.

The Immigration Reform and Control Act of 1986 focused on two issues: an amnesty program, for which many illegal entrants were not eligible, and employer sanctions, which at best were not expected to substantially reduce the number of illegal workers.

As demonstrated by the high rates of illegal entry during the early 1990s, this legislation did not present a serious barrier to clandestine residence. An ambitious person with modest funds who is determined to enter and remain in the United States will be able to do so. Numerous paths, legal and illegal, are available to those seeking to settle in the United States without waiting in line for a permanent visa. If one has a resident friend or relative, the chances of finding a job and remaining undetected are very high. All of this suggests that insufficient resources are being applied to ensure compliance. Unfortunately, larger budgets for patrols and inspectors alone cannot achieve success. Only more draconian measures—such as virtually sealing the borders, issuing national identity cards, and imposing stiffer penalties on both employers and undocumented workers—would be effective.

The objective of this book, however, is to examine the effects of immigrants on the native population without regard to their legal status. Any proposed change in existing legislation should be based on the public interest; that is, it should have clear benefits for a substantial portion of the population.

The open-door policy in effect until the 1920s had positive economic consequences for many. During this period, much of the nation—

particularly its industrial cities—benefited from large-scale entry. As immigrants took bottom-level jobs, employment opportunities for skilled native residents increased. The cities of the Northeast and Midwest that became world-class industrial centers during the nineteenth century owed much of their growth to these immigrants. In the decade following World War I, European immigrants comprised about one-fourth of the work force in America's burgeoning industrial centers.

Two cities exemplified the contribution of immigrant workers who, in the 1920s, comprised about half their labor force—Chicago and New York. Both reached their zenith of wealth and power during this decade. But not everyone benefited. In the rural areas of the South and Midwest, where few immigrants settled, economic gains were negligible. In the cities where immigrants did congregate, benefits among the native-born accrued largely to property owners, members of the middle class, and skilled workers. Unskilled workers, especially blacks, gained little. In fact, the flow of immigrants probably dampened the economic progress of blacks by slowing their exodus from the South. As the average income of American workers rose, the gap between rich and poor widened, fueling antagonism toward immigrants among citizens who were less well off.

When, beginning in the 1920s, restrictions were imposed on immigration, the impact was greatest in those cities with large immigrant populations. Natives who migrated to cities once the immigrant flow ceased appear to have contributed less to urban development than did the foreign-born population. Can the decline of America's large industrial cities, beginning immediately after World War II, be linked to the change in immigration policy?

The latest immigration surge, which began in the 1960s, has facilitated urban renewal by strengthening small businesses, providing low-wage labor, and maintaining the population base necessary to sustain a high level of economic activity. The new immigrants—unskilled workers, professionals, and entrepreneurs—have encouraged the flow of investment, furnished workers for factories and service industries, and helped revive deteriorating urban neighborhoods. This has been especially true in cities serving as gateways to other continents—Los Angeles, New York, Miami, and San Francisco—which, since the mid-1970s, have sprouted new office towers, added jobs—particularly in the service industries—reduced (until the downturn of the early 1990s) unemployment, and shown other signs of urban renewal. These cities have the highest concentration of new immigrants in the nation.

But the most striking evidence of urban transformation has been the changing racial composition of major cities. In the 1920s, 95 percent of the residents of the dozen largest cities were of European descent. Seven decades later, non-Hispanic whites have become a minority in most of those cities. Additional immigration will only hasten these changes.

Notwithstanding the contributions of immigrants, American central cities continue to face serious economic disruptions and social problems. The abandonment of massive public housing projects, many built on the foundations of tenements that housed earlier immigrants, stands as a constant reminder of our failed urban social policies. Violent crime is rising, drug abuse continues to take its deadly toll of the young, and neighborhoods that house the underclass remain plagued by unemployment, poverty, and despair. Residents of formerly "safe" neighborhoods now fear to leave their homes.

Economic and demographic changes have not been confined to the cities. While industrial urban centers have lost several million residents, vast tracts of woodland and farms have been opened up to suburban developments. Metropolitan areas have increased their populations threefold. A virtually solid belt of development extends from southern New Hampshire to Richmond, Virginia, and from San Francisco to the Mexican border. The once common argument that the United States needs immigrants to build its cities and people a vast continent has long been abandoned by even the most enthusiastic proponents of liberal immigration policies. Today, the overriding concern is that additional population will absorb more open land, overburden public facilities, and reduce the quality of life in urban areas.

Nonetheless, stemming the flow of young immigrants could exact an economic price. America's native population is aging, increasing the ratio of nonworkers to workers. And, as the base of the economy continues to shift from manufacturing to services, productivity gains in coming years are expected to be modest. Unless there is an inflow of new labor, particularly skilled workers, American living standards could drop.

The American economy is expected to face shortages at both ends of the occupational ladder following recovery from the downturn of the early 1990s. At one extreme, low-wage, entry-level jobs will again be difficult to fill. Contrary to popular belief, technological changes have not substantially diminished the demand for unskilled and semiskilled workers. Immigrant laborers may no longer be needed in the steel plants and slaughterhouses of the Midwest, but they are in great demand in the hotels, restaurants, and sweatshops of Los Angeles and Miami. A shortage of workers for entry-level jobs in the late 1980s slowed economic expansion in such sectors as tourism and restaurants. The demand for new workers slackened when the economy declined, but because of the demographic reality of fewer young people entering the labor force, the worker shortage is expected to reappear.

America is also experiencing a dearth of engineers and other highly trained technical personnel. Foreign-born students comprise half the enrollment of graduate engineering schools as fewer native students seek to obtain advanced degrees. Thus, industries are increasingly dependent on a foreign-born technical staff. This trend is expected to continue even though reduced defense funding is releasing numerous engineers to work on civilian products. A failure to develop a cadre of Americans trained in these skills could hinder the ability of the United States to remain competitive in high-technology industries.

A report of the National Commission for Employment Policy suggests that, in order to meet projected labor demands, the nation may need to encourage immigration during the 1990s. It seems unlikely, however, that any such encouragement will be necessary. No scholarly study is needed to confirm that the United States remains as attractive as ever to would-be immigrants. During the period of unconstrained immigration, more than thirty-four million Europeans crossed the ocean to settle in this country. While Western nations have erected barriers against immigration, even from Eastern Europe, the number of people seeking to leave their native lands has swelled. Many, perhaps a majority, are eager to settle in the United States. The issue, then, is not the supply of immigrants—it is virtually limitless—but the nation's ability to absorb new entrants without tearing its social fabric.

Were economic issues the only consideration, the proper course for policymakers would be clear. Immigration would be encouraged, with entry levels determined by the number of immigrants—both those who are highly skilled and those who are not—the economy could efficiently absorb. Undocumented workers would pose a problem only insofar as they displaced large numbers of American workers or placed unacceptable pressures on public services. But there is no evidence that illegal immigrants have caused an increase in the overall unemployment rate for Americans. Further, while families of aliens attend public schools and frequently require social services, the public costs involved are at least partially offset by their economic contribution to the private sector.

More importantly, higher immigration levels would be likely to increase the living standards for most middle- and upper-income Americans. Skilled native minorities, particularly women, would find better employment opportunities as increased immigration contributed to overall economic growth. The presence of highly trained immigrants enhances technological advances, and thus the ability of the United States to compete in international markets.

It should be added, however, that a substantial increase in immigration would not help native workers with marginal skills and limited education; indeed, some are likely to be hurt. As in the past, the middle class, especially property owners, would benefit most. Moreover, rising immigration—although only one of many factors affecting income distribution—would widen the gap between rich and poor.

A surge in immigration could also aggravate racial and political tensions. With the growth of the Asian and Hispanic populations in our large cities, blacks are experiencing an eclipse of their political power. Asians and Hispanics account for most of the employment gains in the three largest labor markets; concurrently, the black share of the labor force has declined. In several service industries, the new immigrants are filling positions traditionally held by blacks. These changes contributed to the growing enmity between racial groups evident during the riots in Los Angeles, Las Vegas, and other cities during 1992.

In general, public anxieties about aliens are not based on economic concerns. The current surge of immigrants, although modest by historical standards, has given rise to fears that the nation is being swamped by foreigners. There is concern that immigrants are once again concentrated in enclaves that are detached culturally and psychologically from the American mainstream. In these neighborhoods,

English is, at best, a second language; bilingual education has become a controversial issue across the nation. The congressional response to widespread perceptions of unacceptably high social costs of seemingly uncontrolled non-European immigration was the Immigration Reform and Control Act of 1986. Although it has not substantially reduced illegal entry, the measure appeared to signal a less permissive attitude toward aliens than has been the case in recent decades.

The nation will continue its search for legislation aimed at balancing the economic benefits to be derived from immigration with the perceived threat it poses to ethnic and cultural identities. In the mid-1980s, the scales were tipping in favor of concerns over ethnicity, but as the unmet demand for labor mounted and immigrant groups flexed their political muscle, pressure for more open entry laws emerged in Congress, culminating in the 1990 Immigration Act. This suggests that the third phase of American immigration history—limited entry controls—has not run its course. The public continues to hold easing entry in disfavor, but this majority view appeared too shallow to elicit organized opposition to softening the terms of the 1986 law.

Nonetheless, elements within the conservative movement, led by Patrick Buchanan, began in the early 1990s to capitalize on fears associated with the social consequences of nonwhite immigration. This nativist ground swell followed on the heels of electoral successes of the European far right, taking a cue from its anti-immigrant rhetoric. These concerns also surfaced at a time when the American public, facing economic uncertainty, discontent with the political system, and calls for restrictive trade policies, appeared to be turning inward. Notwithstanding unrest among the electorate sufficiently deep-seated to propel candidates outside the two-party mainstream, Buchanan's immigration stance failed to arouse sufficient interest to advance his candidacy.

Following the 1992 Los Angeles riots, there were calls for a moratorium on immigrant admissions to allow for a reassessment of American entry policies on the premise that native-born minorities were hurt by the alien presence. But the reality is that the severe economic dislocations in the early 1990s failed to ignite widespread "immigrant bashing" that would have provoked a legislative response to these concerns. In the absence of a major shift in immigration policies, the ethnic transformation of American cities as well as suburbs will continue unabated.

2

The Unending Debate

The Old Testament adage "there is nothing new under the sun" is particularly apt in regard to immigration. Each generation appears to rediscover the same positions and restate like arguments for and against the admission of aliens.

American immigration policy can be said to span four centuries, its roots planted in Elizabethan England before the first colonists arrived in the New World. During this period, some were eager to expel recent immigrants from the domain. Although the Crown supported their presence, the English populace remained intolerant of those of foreign birth.

The political leaders of the American colonies, and later of the new Republic, recognized the benefits of accommodating immigrants from various lands. Nonetheless, periodic, and occasionally violent, opposition to their presence erupted. The business community, ever mindful that economic development depends on people, supported the national leadership. Economic self-interest and confidence in its future and limitless space allowed the United States to pursue an open-door policy toward those seeking a better life or refuge from oppression for a century and a half.

American policies were not generous to all groups. We objected to the entry of freed slaves from the Caribbean at the end of the eighteenth century and stopped the flow of Chinese and Japanese when their numbers grew. The European influx continued unabated until scholars and groups opposed to non-Protestants persuaded the public

that these immigrants were undesirable. In response to public sentiment generated by the opponents of immigration, discriminatory laws
aimed at limiting entry of those from "undesirable" countries were
passed during the 1920s. These laws were repealed four decades later,
and more equitable immigration quotas were allocated among applicants. In recent years new issues surfaced. Illegal immigration has
grown, and steps to restrict the flow appear ineffective. The number of
refugees applying for admission has grown, and more temporary residents tend to stay for longer periods than their visas permit. Congress
must deal continually with these and related problems as part of the
ongoing debate on the merits of immigration.

The Colonial Era

Early American immigration policy was built on lessons drawn from
the English experience. Early Tudor monarchs, eager to apply innovation from the Continent, invited German, Italian, and Flemish artisans to England. Most aliens admitted in the second half of the sixteenth century were persecuted Protestants from the Continent who
sought shelter in London and nearby cities. Queen Elizabeth recognized the economic contributions of these exiled Flemish and French
and protected their interests. Local craftsmen and merchants, on the
other hand, decried "unfair competition" from the newly arrived foreigners and sought to evict them. In a March 1570 letter directed to
the residents of Norwich who, jealous of the exiles' prosperity, plotted
against them, Elizabeth gave an account of "benefits received by the
strangers in Norwich for the space of ten years."[1] Among the numerous benefits listed were jobs, not only for themselves but also for poor
native workers who would otherwise remain unemployed, the pay-
ment of taxes, occupancy and repair of abandoned housing, and introduction of new agricultural products. During Elizabeth's long reign,
which accomplished a great deal in laying the economic foundations
of modern England, fifty-five grants of monopoly for such products
as soap, leather, and glass were issued to advance these industries.
Foreigners or naturalized subjects received almost half of these grants.[2]

In the seventeenth century, English traders envied the economic
surge in Holland, where open entry and religious tolerance brought
the Netherlands new manufacturing skills, financial talent, capital, and

a network of personal relationships spanning Europe. Oliver Cromwell, in response to these developments across the English Channel, asked his council in 1655 to admit Jews, particularly those from Holland, to the realm. This proposal, aimed at encouraging commerce and helping finance Cromwell's ambitious plans for his country, would have lifted the ban on Jews expelled from England four centuries earlier. Although opposition to this request quickly surfaced among the populace, and naturalization laws remained unchanged, the economic gains associated with immigration were openly discussed.

Following the demise of Cromwell and the restoration of the Stuarts, the Crown asked the British Parliament to allow French Protestants to become naturalized British citizens. The Crown wanted to help a group that had suffered persecution in Catholic France, but it also had economic motives for its request. Huguenots previously admitted to England had contributed significantly to the nation's industry and commerce. The Crown's wish to ease the naturalization process for Huguenots and others initiated lengthy parliamentary discussions on the merits and costs associated with alien entry. Speeches made in Parliament foreshadowed those heard three centuries later in the U.S. Congress. Both legislative bodies faced a similar dilemma: although immigration was acknowledged to benefit the economy as a whole, some native workers may suffer. Both bodies also were concerned that the admission of persons from other cultures might adversely affect internal cohesion and national identity.

This dichotomy is apparent in what may be the earliest surviving speech on immigration in an English-speaking political forum. Sir John Holland, in the course of a parliamentary debate on immigration and naturalization in 1664, spoke of balancing the advantages of admitting immigrants—more commerce, increased trade, and rising property values—against the accompanying discontent and agitation over the presence of foreigners. Sir Holland concluded that there would be little long-term national benefit from immigration unless "the people have peace and contentment at home."[3] His view that the populace would not accept a foreign element prevailed. Parliament finally passed a liberal naturalization act in 1709, but this measure was immediately challenged. Arguments presented to the Parliament bore a distinct similarity to those that would later be cited across the Atlantic by opponents of unrestricted immigration.

Proponents of the new measure again listed the benefits of economic expansion. Stating that "the increase of people is a means of advancing the wealth and strength of a nation," they noted that earlier refugees established new manufacturing industries, improved others, and expanded trade. But opponents expressed concern that the new immigrants would be poor and would thus become public charges. They also feared that these unskilled arrivals would compete for jobs as laborers, driving down wages and hurting poor English families. Immigrants, it was said, would accumulate wealth at the expense of English citizens, and by shirking taxes they could undersell and undermine native merchants. No one questioned the obvious contradiction in these positions. Would immigrants remain poor and require charity, or become rich at the expense of others?

Some of the arguments against liberalized immigration were political in nature. For instance, it was argued that, if aliens were given the right to vote and become members of Parliament, England's traditional form of government could be threatened. But the decisive handicap against the measure was a social one—a fear that immigrants, through intermarriage, would "blot out and extinguish the English race." The weight of opposition arguments was enough to secure repeal of the naturalization bill within months of its passage, and the issue was not considered again for decades.[4]

This episode in British legislative history shows that the major arguments for and against immigration were formed and articulated well before America was founded. Legislators understood that national economic growth was stimulated by immigration. At the same time, wage depression, rising welfare costs, unfair competition, control of commerce by aliens, political and social instability—these concerns about immigration have remained constant for centuries.

There was, however, one important difference between Britain and America in those early years. Britain, unlike the colonies, was not economically attractive to those emigrating from the Continent. The island nation had a rigid social structure, poor living conditions, and little surplus land. Most who sought entry were searching for refuge, not economic gain. Understanding the evolution of immigration policies in America requires an appreciation of the almost unique attraction this country has had for foreigners seeking new opportunities.

Religious liberty was on the minds of many who crossed the Atlantic during the seventeenth century, but the impetus to undertake the perilous journey was poor economic conditions at home and the expectation of a better life in the New World. The historian Maldwyn A. Jones writes that "piety and profit" were the compelling motives for emigration in this period.[5] But for indentured servants, who comprised more than half of all white immigrants, the dominant incentive was monetary. Those who ventured to the southern colonies in particular were responding not to the prospect of religious tolerance but to the generous economic inducements planters granted to overcome the drawbacks of an unhealthy climate and the fear of slave uprisings.

Prior to the 1660s, most colonists came directly from England. Though subjects of the Crown, the early settlers adopted naturalization policies aimed at encouraging the entry of non-English-speaking immigrants. These laws differed from the severe restrictions that continued to be placed on foreigners in England wishing to become subjects of the Crown.[6] The colonial elite recognized, as did Adam Smith in his classic work, *The Wealth of Nations*,[7] that skilled and commerce-oriented aliens—particularly Flemings, Huguenots, and Jews—contributed to British economic expansion and would promote development in the colonies as well. Although emigration from England continued in the late seventeenth century and subsequent decades, Germans, Scotch-Irish, and other nationalities crossed the Atlantic in great numbers.

The need for foreigners with mechanical and other abilities must have been apparent, for the majority of British subjects arriving in the colonies, particularly the Scotch-Irish, were indentured servants with practically no training or education. After Parliament passed an act in 1717 to ship convicts overseas, not only paupers but several thousand criminals were transported to America. Thus, the arrival of literate French Protestants and German farmers should have been particularly welcomed.

Still, xenophobia periodically surfaced. One of the earliest manifestations occurred in Quaker Pennsylvania. Governor William Penn was among the first leaders in America to recognize that the need to populate the vast territory overrode any social fallout that immigration might cause. He therefore encouraged German immigration to his domain, promising both religious liberty and generous land allotments.[8] Nonetheless, as the numbers of non-English speakers grew, Pennsylvania's legislators, fearful that the colony might degenerate into a foreign province, passed in 1729 a hefty tax to be levied on all foreigners entering its domain. Although quickly repealed, the measure marked the first (albeit modest) wave of anti-immigrant sentiment in the New World.

More enduring was the anti-Catholic sentiment expressed by the early settlers, an outcome of the bitter struggle between Rome and England. The intolerance shown toward this religious minority manifested itself in colonial legislation limiting its rights. As noted by the historian Ray Allen Billington, "By 1700 Catholics would enjoy full civil and religious rights only in Rhode Island."[9] In Maryland, only the tolerant attitude of the governor prevented the passage of harsh anti-Catholic legislation. The first wave of religious bigotry within the colonies reached its crest following the passage of the 1774 Quebec Act extending religious tolerance to Catholics in Canada. The legislation was viewed by some Americans as an effort to extend Catholic influence across the border into the northern colonies. Only the aid given by Catholic France during the War of Independence and the passage of the First Amendment subdued, for one generation, fervent anti-Catholic sentiment.

For the most part, however, the demand for labor and the urge to encourage settlement overcame religious and ethnic concerns, leading the colonies to enact legislation favorable to immigration. Until the reign of King George III, in fact, the British government itself promoted foreign immigration to its American colonies while concurrently discouraging (but not prohibiting) emigration of all but felons, paupers, and other undesirables from England. Because colonies were seen as economically beneficial, Parliament provided mechanisms by which aliens settling in America could be naturalized without direct approval from Britain. Gradually, though, the Crown grew concerned that immigration was strengthening the colonies at its own expense. In response to these fears, Parliament began blocking liberal entry laws passed by the colonies. In response to these fears, Britain imposed a prohibitively high tax on those heading for America, bringing the flow to a virtual halt. A subsequent bill intended to secure the dependency of the colonies stated in its preamble that "the great increase of people in the said colonies has an immediate tendency to produce independency."[10]

The colonialists, eager for newcomers to settle their vast lands, were not pleased. In its listing of charges against George III, the Declaration of Independence included the following: "[He] has endeavored to prevent the population of these states; for that purpose obstructing the Laws of Naturalization of Foreigners; refusing to pass others to encourage their migration hither."

In seeking to expand their population base, the colonies could offer virtually free land—a highly prized commodity among the peasants of densely populated Germany and Scandinavia. Land in the eighteenth century represented not only material wealth but also social rank and political privileges such as voting. For those with nonagricultural skills, the colonies offered plenty of good jobs, and even unskilled laborers earned more than their counterparts on the Continent. The average worker in the colonies lived better than most people in England, where wealth was highly concentrated among the landed gentry.[11] America also offered immigrants the right to become citizens regardless of religion or previous class status—something denied aliens in England and most other Western nations.

The new country's hospitality was not boundless, however; it was hedged by strict racial limits. In the early days of the Republic, the question of black citizenship took on enormous political as well as ideological significance. The Naturalization Act of 1790, the first law Congress passed dealing with immigrants, limited citizenship to "free white persons" who had resided in the United States for at least two years. This clause was intended to appease slaveholding states and assure their white residents that no free blacks coming from the Caribbean would be entitled to citizenship.

America's Founding Fathers expressed some ambivalence on the immigration question, but their views were considerably more tolerant than those expressed by legislators in Britain or on the European continent. George Washington, for instance, declared in a speech to newly arrived Irish immigrants in 1783 that "the Bosom of America is open to receive not only the opulent and respectable stranger but the oppressed and persecuted of all Nations and Religions,"[12] and his extensive correspondence confirms a tolerant attitude toward aliens. Washington was also aware of the economic gains associated with immigrants. In a letter to Thomas Jefferson, he discussed measures to attract capital by inducing "wealthy men from other nations to our bosom by giving security to property and liberty to its holders."[13] He also favored offering financial assistance as a means of encouraging skilled and professional workers to emigrate from Europe. At the same time, he believed that aliens, were they to be concentrated in one region, would maintain their language and customs and could therefore prove difficult to assimilate.

Jefferson, like Washington, championed immigration as a spur to economic development. He was particularly eager to attract immigrants from the Mediterranean basin, believing that they would contribute more to the economy than would those coming from Northern Europe. Notwithstanding his generally liberal outlook, Jefferson did not favor a rapid inflow of immigrants, although he agreed that the nation could easily feed and clothe all who came. He expressed anxiety that aliens coming from nations ruled by absolute monarchs would have difficulty adjusting to a society governed by elected representatives. Jefferson opposed any restriction on immigration but questioned the need for financial assistance to attract more aliens.[14]

Among the new nation's outstanding statesmen, the young James Madison had the most positive outlook on immigrants. At the Constitutional Convention of 1787 he declared, "That part of America which has encouraged them [foreigners] most has advanced most rapidly in population, agriculture, and the arts."[15] The scholarly Madison rarely ventured far from his Virginia homestead and met few white persons not of English descent. Nonetheless, Madison's intellect and powers of observation enabled him to understand the benefits of attracting settlers from differing backgrounds, at least within the European context.

Immigration and the Young Republic

The early years of the Republic were marked by general tolerance for European immigrants of all stripes. Distinctions that would become important during the second half of the nineteenth century—Northern as opposed to Southern Europeans, Protestants versus Catholics versus Jews—held little significance in these early years. Only one division really counted—that between black and white. The tolerance expressed by the Founding Fathers toward non-English immigrants may be linked to their classical education, which viewed the Mediterranean basin as the cradle of Western civilization. Men well versed in the Old Testament, Greek philosophy, and the Renaissance would not be expected to perceive Northern Europeans as intellectually superior to those residing across the Alps. Their awareness of history and understanding of how immigrants can accelerate growth laid the intellectual foundation for unrestricted entry of Europeans, regardless of their religious or ethnic background.

A brief spurt of anti-immigrant sentiment arose during the mid-1790s, in the wake of the French Revolution and the instability it sowed throughout Europe. The possibility that political refugees from these upheavals might enter the United States cast suspicion on all potential immigrants. The term "alien menace" entered the political lexicon during this period. In 1798 the Federalist Congress, with John Adams's approval, passed the Alien and Sedition Acts, which authorized the president to expel aliens suspected of treasonable activities. Jefferson considered the legislation to be in direct violation of the Constitution, and, following his election as president in 1800, the measures were quickly repealed.

Jefferson may have had more than the Constitution on his mind. Immigrants supported him against the Federalists, considered by new French and Irish immigrants as anti-alien. Jefferson's Republicans opposed efforts to slow immigration, a policy that paid dividends. Historians believe the immigrant vote in New York carried the state for Jefferson in 1800. John Adams and Alexander Hamilton charged after the election that he was elected by foreigners. By the early part of the nineteenth century, the Federalists had lost power, fears about political agitation had abated, and the first wave of anti-immigration sentiment since independence receded.

Immigration to the United States slowed during the latter part of the eighteenth century and the early decades of the nineteenth. One explanation was an embargo on emigration by skilled labor that was mandated by the British Parliament. A number of trained workers, mostly from Scotland, managed to make it to the Northeast in any case. Bringing with them skills and techniques unavailable locally, they provided a boost to struggling new industries, particularly textile mills. The embargo remained in effect until the 1820s.

Another reason for the downturn was the armed conflict raging in Europe. The fighting made overseas travel more difficult, and nations tightened emigration controls to prevent young men from evading military service. Even more significant, the United States was drawn into these foreign conflicts, disrupting the economic growth that had made America an attractive destination. Political refugees still came from France and Ireland but in much smaller numbers than previously. Overall, the population more than doubled between 1790 and 1830, primarily due to natural increase. Dutch and German, widely in use prior to the Revolution, were rarely spoken except in parts of Pennsylvania where church worship remained German. The level of immigration was so low during this period—fewer than 400,000 aliens arrived—that America became more homogeneous ethnically and linguistically than at any time before or since.

During the 1830s, immigration reached 600,000. In the subsequent decade, a massive Irish influx driven by the potato famine and a sharp rise in German immigration resulted in 1.7 million arrivals—probably a higher number than had come across in the preceding century.

Opposition resurfaced with the upsurge in immigration, this time in vicious, often violent forms, mostly in northern cities along the Atlantic coast where the new Irish had settled. Beginning in the 1830s and for a century afterward, immigrants came to be identified with a host of urban ills—congestion, crime, and political corruption. As the nation remained predominantly agrarian, intolerance toward cities and immigrants became intertwined.

The mood of small-town America was perhaps best summed up by Alexis de Tocqueville, who wrote of American cities during the early 1830s:

> [They] contain a multitude of Europeans who have been driven to the shores of the New World by their misfortune or their misconduct and these men inoculate the United States with all their vices. . . . The population of cities has hitherto exercised neither power nor influence over the rural districts. Nevertheless, I look upon the size of certain American cities and especially the nature of their population as a real danger which threatens the future of the democratic republic of the New World.[16]

The attitude toward the emerging urban centers expressed by Tocqueville may have been a reflection of the anticity bias among the

French aristocracy—a major audience for his book—in response to the revolutionary frenzy that had gripped Paris four decades earlier. Not that he was the first to hold such a dour view of urban life. In the seventeenth century, the English Parliament passed a dozen or more laws attempting to restrict migration to London, for political reasons and, to a lesser extent, for fear of epidemics caused by overcrowded, unsanitary living quarters.

When Tocqueville visited the United States, immigrants were a tiny minority even in cities where they were concentrated. In only two of the numerous New York City wards in 1830 were immigrants a substantial share of the electorate. Had Tocqueville come to New York or Boston two decades later, he would have observed large immigrant enclaves and growing Irish influence in local affairs. But contrary to his prediction, political power at the state and federal levels was retained by nonurban residents well into the twentieth century.

Americans, too, began questioning the merits of what was seen as a tide of mostly poor immigrants entering the seaports along the eastern shore. Among those arguing that the nation's political structure could be damaged by the influx was Henry Duhring. In a lengthy article written in 1833 for the *North American Review,* he argued:

> If the social character (of the United States) is liable to be infected by the vices and miseries of other countries, from too rapid absorption of their redundant population, or our political institutions exposed to overthrow and corruption by the undue accession of unassimilating elements, how can it be other than wise to guard against a state of things which must prove ultimately so unfriendly to the best and perhaps last hope of the human family?[17]

His concerns paralleled those expressed by Jefferson half a century earlier. Like the eugenicists decades later, Duhring also linked the downfall of the Roman Empire to its absorption of alien groups and suggested that this fate could await the United States.

Duhring began his commentary on the economic consequences of immigration on a positive note, stating that "nothing could be more beneficial to all parties than the unobstructed immigration of persons from the Old World." Nonetheless, he questioned whether the country benefited from the emigration from Ireland, and blamed the miserable economic conditions in their homeland on flaws in the Irish character.

Only the Englishman, he stated, could easily adapt to the American way of life.

Duhring's views represented the intellectual arguments for nativism. He attacked moral corruption in cities but made no mention of the concentrated presence of the Catholic religion there. The response among some in the working class was less circumspect. A growing fear over competition for jobs, the prospect of low wages, and the spread of Catholicism stimulated the formation of groups opposed to open immigration. Anti-immigrant activism was aimed principally at Irish immigrants. Not only were they Catholics in a predominantly Protestant nation, but they were also considered rowdy and uncontrollable, in contrast to Germans or other English-speaking groups. Anti-Irish riots broke out in several cities, and in Boston the state militia was called to keep mobs from attacking Irish homes.

The anti-Irish mood was part of deeper discontent that swept the nation, particularly the urban Northeast. Not only Irish immigrants, but blacks and abolitionists became targets of the urban poor. A four-day riot between Catholics and Protestants over the use of Bibles in Philadelphia schools in the mid-1840s could only be quelled, as in Boston, by military force.

One culprit in the rise of anti-immigrant sentiment was a qualitative decline in the nation's leadership and religious tolerance. Philadelphia, founded on the Quaker principle of tolerance, witnessed no fewer than five antiblack riots between 1829 and 1850. Fundamentalist, anti-Catholic denominations were on the rise, particularly in the South, and the brilliant statesmen who had guided the nation in its early years were followed by a generation of more shallow politicians who generally lacked the capacity or courage to contest growing prejudice.

Although nativists gained considerable notoriety following the Philadelphia and other riots, their violent actions were probably counterproductive. Most Americans considered themselves, despite their fear of Catholicism, respectable citizens who shied away from mob rule and bloodshed.

The often violent response to Irish Catholics was not unique to the United States. Irish immigration to England produced strikingly similar reactions. England's industrial cities tolerated Irish workers, seen as troublemakers and drunks, in the early nineteenth century because they provided a pool of unskilled labor, enabling native workers to move further up the economic ladder. However, in contradiction, the Irish were also blamed for depressing the wages of English workers. A decade later similar charges against the Irish—that they were prone to violence and reduced the earnings of native residents—were leveled in Boston and New York.

Perhaps the most notable characteristic of Irish emigration during this period was the pull toward the United States. Men and women forced by poverty to leave Ireland had other choices—England and its colonies—but the vast majority of those leaving came to this nation. Needless to say, economic opportunity was the primary reason. The Irish believed, no doubt correctly, that the road toward economic advancement would be blocked in England, where they had an especially nasty reputation and were considered an undesirable if necessary minority.

The pressure for limiting immigration to the United States during the mid-nineteenth century was not driven exclusively by anti-Catholic attitude. The growing concern over emerging income disparities in America, suggested by the rise in the number of paupers, contributed to the view that the nation could not absorb more poor families. Until the 1820s, inequality was not much of a national issue. But as the gap between rich and poor widened, anti-immigrant sentiment spread, especially among the northern urban poor and residents of rural southern states.

The regional pattern of anti-immigrant sentiment was illustrated by the growth of the anti-Catholic, antiforeigner Know-Nothing (or American) party. This movement had a one-issue agenda—opposition to immigration. Its platform was to exclude foreigners (as well as native-born Catholics) from all government positions and to require that immigrants be residents for twenty-one years before becoming citizens. Intolerance and even hatred of immigrants could be found in northern cities, and the strength of the party was at first centered in New York and New England. Yet the political strength of nativists found a home in the predominantly rural South. At its peak in the late 1850s, the Know-Nothings elected twenty-three members to the House of Representatives, including nineteen members from the slave states—one-fourth of all congressional seats from that region. In the following Congress, the thirty-sixth, it claimed the allegiance of two senators and twenty-three representatives, all from the South. This region had the lowest proportion of immigrants in the nation, and most of the voters there had never even seen a foreign-born German, Scandinavian, or Irish Catholic. Yet they rallied to the Know-Nothing position that foreign-born workers were providing ruinous competition to native labor. In an attempt to strengthen their position, the Know-Nothings formed alliances with abolitionist Republicans, arousing bitter anti-Republican sentiment among Irish immigrants. In 1856 the Know-Nothings nominated former president Millard Fillmore as their presidential candidate; in a three-party race he received 22 percent of the vote—more than half of it from the South. Although Fillmore won only Maryland's electoral votes, he nearly carried Alabama, Arkansas, Florida, Kentucky, Louisiana, and Tennessee. Despite scoring some initial successes, the anti-immigrant forces never attained sufficient support in Congress to change the immigration laws. Slavery had already become the burning issue for all political parties. The Know-Nothing movement, divided on slavery, disintegrated into oblivion. But it did mark a phenomenon that would be repeated in subsequent waves of anti-immigrant emotion: the strongest opposition was usually found in the regions where the fewest aliens resided.

The southern sentiment against immigrants reflected, in part, opposition to institutions associated with the urban North. Prior to the outbreak of the Civil War, insightful southerners correctly perceived immigrants as contributing to the industrial strength of the North. They understood that the continuing attraction for foreign-born individuals of the dynamic labor markets of the northern cities was becoming a potential economic and political, as well as military, danger to the South. This recognition, combined with the religious persuasion of many immigrants and their general antislavery sentiment, provided the rationale for the southern opposition to liberal entry.

From Appomattox to the Great War

The Civil War ushered in—at least in the North—a period of goodwill toward immigrants unparalleled in American history. The increased demand for industrial labor during the conflict prompted President Lincoln and the Congress to promote and financially assist immigrants for the first—and only—time at the federal level. Congress established a fund to pay the passage of immigrants. (They were expected to repay the advance from their earnings.) This assistance enticed many foreigners to northern ports during the war.

The brisk economic growth that followed Appomattox tempered opposition to European immigration for a generation. In response to the postwar expansion, numerous northern and southern states established agencies to promote immigration. South Carolina appointed a commissioner of immigration one year following cessation of the war. Georgia, Louisiana, Tennessee, and Virginia were among the southern states to establish immigration agencies. In fact, whenever labor shortages appeared acute, planters, railroads, and industries pushed for state action to lure labor to the South.[18] Although these ill-conceived attempts attracted few aliens, the mere presence of the agencies signaled recognition within the business community that immigrants could benefit the region.

Anti-immigrant sentiment in the East was at a low ebb. Nativists found a new, more vulnerable target—Asians. The Chinese and Japanese were leaving their countries for the same reasons Europeans were leaving theirs—accelerating population growth, stagnating national economies, and an oversupply of agricultural labor. The Asians were pulled first to Hawaii and then to the continental United States by the availability of jobs and the possibility of owning land, a particularly appealing prospect for the land-hungry Japanese. Most disembarked and remained in California, where labor shortages were chronic.

The growing presence of Chinese workers prompted a violent reaction, especially by organized labor. Among the intellectuals spearheading the verbal assault against the Chinese was the leading reformer of the 1870s, Henry George. In public, he focused on economic issues, noting that American labor was being hurt by the inexhaustible supply of Chinese workers who, unlike Americans, did not mind living at subsistence levels. In private, he expressed racial motives for his actions, including a belief that the Chinese could not be absorbed into the American mainstream.[19] In both respects, the views of George were widely shared.

The arrival of Irish workers in the labor-saturated markets of the East had, no doubt, at least in the short run, depressed the wages of native unskilled workers, but the growing political strength of the Irish by the 1870s offered them a shield against attack. Not so the Chinese or the Japanese, who had no political representation and were taunted as barbaric heathens. The fear of rapid ethnic and cultural change combined with emerging theories of racial inferiority to shift attention from white to Asian immigrants.

The Chinese found a handful of supporters, mostly California businessmen. Railroad, ranching, and farm interests testified at congressional hearings that the Chinese were exceptionally good and trustworthy workers. Several religious groups with missionary activity among the Asians were also supportive, although most religious bodies, including the Catholic press, viewed the Chinese with disfavor if not outright hostility.[20]

By the late 1870s, the anti-Chinese clamor was so strong as to easily overcome business opposition. Newly organized California laborers, mostly Irish immigrants, argued in favor of legislation to exclude Chinese settlement on the questionable grounds that their jobs were threatened. In fact, the ground swell of opposition, evidenced by voting patterns in Congress, was totally unrelated to economic factors. Rather, the resentment—fueled by inflammatory press accounts—was rooted in the perception that the Chinese, and later the Japanese, could not be assimilated. This anti-Asian sentiment culminated in passage of the most discriminatory immigration statute in our nation's history—the Chinese Exclusion Act of 1882. Although Chinese immigrants were concentrated in northern California, the legislation had national support, particularly among eastern political reformers; the limited congressional opposition to its passage was centered in New England. The act was favored by virtually all constituents, especially in the South, where Chinese immigrants were all but nonexistent, assuring its passage over President Chester Arthur's veto. Only one senator and two congressmen from the South opposed the measure. The region's stance toward Asian immigrants was an early indication that the traditional prejudice felt toward blacks was being transferred to another racial group. There could have been a political motive as well for the South's support of the western states. Pressure for passage of Jim Crow laws to force secondary status on blacks was rising, and southern legislators might have hoped for western support were these practices challenged.

The post-Civil War period also brought an increase in immigration to the United States from all corners of Europe. Improved communications and lower travel costs encouraged the transatlantic movement. The booming economy meant that many more immigrants could be accommodated than in the antebellum period. Emigration from Great Britain and other West European nations slowed as the demand for industrial workers rose in those countries. However, the slack was taken up by the less-developed southern and eastern regions of the Continent, where increases in population and the collapse of traditional agriculture sent millions of Catholic peasants looking for an escape. Most found it in the United States.

As with the Asian influx, new arrivals from Southern and Eastern Europe were unduly regarded as inferior. Organized opposition in the late nineteenth century came from groups representing differing agendas. The Immigration Restriction League exclusively sought limits on alien entry, while the American Protective Association focused on "protecting" the nation against a perceived Catholic menace.

The League was formed in 1894 by descendants of prominent, well-to-do New England families, mostly young Harvard graduates. Their merchant families had benefited from the labor of native and foreign-born Americans; as noted by Barbara Solomon in her influential and thoughtful study of the League's founders and ardent supporters, "The League's conception of immigration peril was not a matter of economics."[21] Their fears were racial, but the organization sought the support of others, including organized labor, whose concerns were mostly economic. The League was not openly anti-Catholic, in part because its most powerful congressional voice, Henry Cabot Lodge, depended on the Massachusetts Irish vote for his Senate seat. In later years, the League quietly supported anti-Catholic groups and publicly expressed their anti-Semitic sentiments. By the turn of the century, the League had already waned, but the social status of its membership exerted a more lasting effect on the middle class.

The American Protective Association (APA) was organized in the 1880s, fomenting another wave of anti-Catholic hysteria. The APA leveled charges that Catholics were gaining control of government institutions, the same charges voiced by the early settlers, but its activities did not lead to the violent response of the 1840s. The Association gained strength in the Midwest and such western states as Colorado, Montana, and Washington. Its message was spread by distributing periodicals and pamphlets exposing various Catholic "plots." Unlike the Know-Nothing party, the Association failed to convert its beliefs into concerted political strength.[22]

In contrast to the League, the Association was not directly anti-immigrant or anti-Semitic. Immigration proponents charged that the restrictionist sentiment was the loudest where the two groups had their strength, but this was not always the case. Neither organization was strong in the South, nor did they attract—except in Boston—much attention in northern cities. Though the League and the Association quickly faded from the political scene, as did virtually all prior and subsequent one-issue movements in the nation's history, their ability to arouse and harness anti-Catholic and anti-immigrant sentiment was a signal that unconstrained immigration would be difficult to sustain.

In the 1890s, Congress passed a variety of modest measures aimed at curbing entry. Literacy test legislation was introduced periodically in Congress, with backing from southern and western legislators. But President Grover Cleveland, following a long tradition of presidential opposition to restrictions on newcomers, vetoed many of these measures. In explaining his position, he wrote, "Stupendous growth, largely due to the assimilation and thrift of millions of sturdy and patriotic adopted citizens, attests to the success of this generous and free-handed [immigration] policy. . . ."[23]

It was not until 1917 that Congress was able to muster enough votes to enact a literacy test over President Woodrow Wilson's veto. The measure had little impact on the postwar inflow. To the chagrin of those who argued that immigrants from Eastern and Southern Europe were inferior, the majority passed the test. In fact, there were fewer illiterate naturalized Americans in 1920 (6 percent) than illiterate whites in southern states (6 to 20 percent).

The failure of the literacy test to slow immigration from the eastern and southern regions of Europe gave birth to an alternative—limiting entry to the proportion of the U.S. population that each nationality formed as of a given date. The selection of a census year prior to mass immigration from these nations (such as 1880 or 1890) would severely curtail entry from Italy, Greece, Poland, and Russia.

Some of the most virulent opposition to open immigration from these regions of Europe, as reflected in congressional votes, newspaper editorials, and contemporary accounts, came from towns and rural areas, especially in the South.[24] However, as in the pre–Civil War era, no region had a monopoly on nativism. Boston was the political and intellectual center of the Immigration Restriction League, and anti-Catholic, anti-Semitic movements dedicated to restricting immigration from Eastern and Southern Europe were active in many northern states. What distinguished the South was the virtual absence of any opposition to these positions during the first half of the twentieth century. The League faced more than token opposition from academicians and ministers in Boston, but counterbalancing forces did not emerge in the South.

The political solidarity of southern legislators on immigration issues was already apparent during the vote on the Chinese Exclusion Act of 1882. The literacy test proposed by Senator Lodge in 1896 was favored by twelve southerners and opposed by five (an indication that some thought "desirable" immigrants from Northern Europe could be attracted to the region). But the 1913 literacy test (vetoed by President William Howard Taft) passed the Senate with only two of the eighteen dissenting votes coming from the region. In the House, the measure passed by a vote of 179 to 52, with sixty-eight southern votes favoring restrictions and only five opposing the measure.

Urban-rural and North-South differences in attitudes toward immigrants can be attributed to several causes. By 1910, the economic disparities between the North and South reached their greatest level. Although the South began to industrialize, four out of every five residents lived in rural areas, while almost two-thirds of the population in northern industrial states were urban dwellers. In the North, the existence of a large, unskilled, urban immigrant labor pool helped increase profits for businessmen and boost wages for the mostly native skilled workers. The economies of scale available through new techniques of mass production led to a drop in prices for manufactured goods, but still most southerners could not afford them because of a chronic depression in farm prices. What little industry existed in the South was generally controlled by northern investors. For the most part, living standards in rural areas remained pitifully low. A few southern planters and industrialists encouraged the entry of foreign labor, but the majority remained unconvinced that the economic benefits to be derived from an expanded population base would compensate for the social problems caused by the presence of immigrants. (These regional differences are explored further in Chapter 3.)

John Higham, a respected historian, offers a somewhat different explanation of the causes for what he viewed as "nativist eruption" in the South. Higham argues that after 1900 southerners began to see new immigrants "with their own eyes" for the first time. He also believes the Spanish-American War evoked nationalism in the South, which enabled white supremacists to vent their racial beliefs by attacking new immigrants.[25]

These may have been contributory causes, but the premise that nativism erupted only after 1900 cannot stand up to the considerable evidence that anti-immigrant sentiment was present for decades beforehand. Nor is there a basis for asserting that nativist feelings in the rural South, where few immigrants ventured, were less extreme than in New Orleans, Richmond, and other cities. The deep roots of anti-Catholic, anti-immigrant sentiment were not severed by the unsuccessful actions of business groups to promote immigration in the late nineteenth century.

Economic considerations may explain why southern and other rural areas did not favor a liberal immigration policy, but one must examine deeper social causes to understand the prevailing bias against foreigners. Most of the nation's rural population, and 98 percent of all southerners, were natives. Southerners typically traced their American roots to the colonial period, and most retained no links with the homeland of their ancestors. White southerners and the mostly Scotch-Irish Appalachian dwellers were often severely impoverished, isolated socially as well as physically from the national mainstream.[26]

Race dominated all aspects of southern life since the early eighteenth century, and immigration was no exception. The deeply ingrained antagonism toward blacks was gradually transferred, as we have seen, first to Asians and later to immigrants from Southern Europe. Italians from southern provinces had the twin liabilities of being Catholic and having swarthy complexions, the latter being taken as evidence of "black blood." So strong was the fear that the presence of outsiders would threaten white dominance that even Anglo-Saxon Yankees were held in suspicion. In an environment permeated by racial antagonism, it is not surprising that anti-immigrant sentiment flourished.

Southern nativists cleverly exploited antiblack sentiment to pursue their anti-immigrant agenda. One of their arguments was that the new immigrants would begin to settle in the South, displacing blacks, who would migrate to northern cities, creating slums and racial conflict there. In the words of one nativist writing in the *Atlantic Monthly*:

It cannot be denied that there is a distinct feeling of satisfaction in the South that the North will soon have its share of the negro burden brought to its own doors, and a hope that actual contact with the negro will modify some of the sentimental ideas (about the negro).[27]

The same article lashes out at Italians and other ignorant and penniless aliens who are "no improvement over the negro." That Italians were also Catholics did not escape the attention of southerners, as religion played an important, if secondary, role to race in their attitudes toward immigrants.

A substantial number of post–Civil War immigrants were Catholic, and their growing presence in northern states was taken as a threat to Protestant values. Except in Kentucky, 97 percent of church members in the South (east of the Mississippi) were Protestant. Between 1820 and 1863, however, the Catholic population in the North rose from less than 200,000 to nearly 3 million, fueling rumors of plots by the Vatican to seize political control of the nation. Nonetheless, religion lagged far behind race as a subject of southern concern.

Finally, forces supporting unrestricted immigration in the North— heavy industry seeking workers and ethnic associations representing European minorities—lacked political influence in Dixie. At the turn of the century, industrialization was at an early stage in the South and was feared by many as disruptive of the region's social structure. Recent immigrants were few in number, and those who settled in large southern cities maintained a low profile as not to antagonize the populace.

Although few southerners had encountered one, the immigrant was associated with such unsavory northern institutions as foreign investment, greedy bankers, and the trusts that held sway over the rural economy.

Two groups that generally opposed immigration on economic grounds, blacks and organized labor, were all but powerless in the South and had practically no influence on its congressional representatives. The issue of job competition did not arise in Dixie until the 1880s, when the first Italians were recruited to work in southern fields. The response of the black community, which considered farm work to be essential to its survival, was swift and fearful. Booker T. Washington, the leading black spokesman for several decades, preached that blacks, unlike the Irish and Italians, were teachable and trustworthy.

Blacks also resented the flow of Mexicans to the Southwest, even though few blacks lived in that region. Most rural blacks, struggling at a subsistence level, readily believed that European immigrants, Mexicans, and Chinese were willing to come south and work at even lower wages and in poorer conditions. Although few immigrants were actually willing to work on plantations, southern politicians used the threat of immigrants to maintain control over black agricultural workers. The result, predictably, was a rise in anti-immigrant sentiment among blacks.[28] The black press, a mirror of black public opinion, did not oppose all immigrants. Jewish immigrants to the South were looked upon favorably. Jews, who were few in number, were seen not as job competitors but as employers and occasionally as benefactors. Black leaders pointed to these Jewish immigrants as setting an example for poor blacks, showing how to succeed through hard work, saving, and helping one another.

The generally negative black response to immigrants, although motivated by fears of job competition, was also fueled by noneconomic perceptions. Black Baptists could identify with the anti-immigrant, anti-Catholic sentiment manifested by white fundamentalist Protestants. Resentment was heightened by the observation that olive-skinned Italians and yellow Chinese could ride in "white only" streetcars and trains. Thus, both economic concerns and social fears led black newspaper editors to support legislation aimed at restricting immigrants.

The all-white southern congressional delegations were also opposed to unrestricted immigration, not in response to black concerns—most could not vote—but to their own biases. In their arguments against immigration, southern legislators maintained that restricting aliens would protect domestic labor. At the same time, they opposed all measures to improve the working conditions of native workers.

Although some legislators saw European immigration as a potential threat to their political strength in Congress, public statements were aimed at their white constituents and appealed to fears that outsiders could alter the racial status quo. During the 1880s, Senator Zebulon B. Vance from North Carolina expressed the sentiment that the mass of European corruption would soon infect the South. Other members of Congress in the late nineteenth century also feared the admission of "unassimilable inferior races that would endanger southern life."

Their views were echoed a generation later by Senator John F. Williams from Mississippi, who in 1912 denounced new immigrants as a threat to southern society, although hardly any had settled in the region.

Whatever their motives, the southern white leadership and impoverished blacks shared one common position—immigrants were held in disfavor by both groups. When black Americans joined with these legislators, they may have fantasized that being American born gave them status as coequals, at least on this issue. But, as noted by the writer and playwright Florette Henri, the opposite was the case—they actually tightened the chains of racism around themselves.[29]

Attitudes toward immigrants in the West paralleled in some respects the prevailing views in the South. Most western settlers were native Protestants who saw themselves as true American pioneers fulfilling their nation's manifest destiny. These settlers had little need for the manufactured goods coming out of the cities of the East. Westerners associated corruption and greed with cities, whose tenements were teeming with strange foreigners unwilling or unable to withstand frontier hardships.

By 1920, thanks primarily to the Asian inflow, about 15 percent of the West's overall population was foreign-born—higher than the national average, but the number of European immigrants remained low. Westerners showed little bias toward most of the European immigrants who moved to the region, and some foreign-born citizens managed to rise to prominence. Even so, western legislators joined with those in the South and the farm belt to vote strongly in favor of legislation curbing European immigration.

The latent bias toward non-English-speaking immigrants came to the surface when Chinese workers arrived in large numbers in the 1870s. By the end of the decade, there were more than 150,000 Chinese in California, mostly young males, who accounted for one out of every four workers in the state. The negative image of Asians, particularly Chinese, illustrated in the white press was generally shared by the very small number of blacks who resided in the West. Both whites and blacks, frightened by Oriental customs, considered San Francisco's Chinese population depraved and immoral. For Irish workers, the Chinese temporarily replaced blacks as scapegoats until congressional legislation virtually halted all Asian immigration.

The most consistent and influential defenders of a liberal immigration policy at the beginning of the twentieth century, other than immigrants themselves, were northern industrialists.

The business community viewed immigrants as an asset, since most aliens coming to the United States during the first two decades of the twentieth century were young, providing a large pool of workers for the nation's factories.[30] In addition, the demand for manufactured products increased because workers were also consumers of these products. These basic economic principles were well understood by Andrew Carnegie, who proudly wore his status as a Scottish immigrant. "I would like to ask what this country would have been without immigration? Every immigrant is a consumer. Labor is one undivided whole, and every laborer, being a consumer, employs other labor."[31] His pragmatic view dominated the position of industrialists until World War I. Carnegie recognized the widespread antipathy toward Southern European immigrants and tried to mitigate it by noting, during a public debate on immigration policy, that it was the "mingling of different bloods that makes the American."[32] Unfortunately, his favorable opinions on Mediterranean immigrants, echoing those of Thomas Jefferson a century earlier, were becoming less acceptable as the current of racial bias gained momentum. The policy of open borders to Europeans that began during the colonial era was about to end.

Eugenicists, Progressives, and the Ku Klux Klan

It has been said that World War I, by propelling the United States into the international arena, ended American innocence. But the conflict and its aftermath inflicted other casualties: a campaign of repression directed first against German-Americans, followed by antiblack riots in northern cities, and finally the mass arrest of so-called radicals and anarchists. Unrestricted immigration, already under attack by groups opposing immigrants from Eastern Europe and Italy prior to the conflict, was doomed as the mood of the nation became increasingly xenophobic.

In Europe, the war displaced millions of people, while the Russian Revolution turned millions more into refugees. The redrawing of national boundaries after the war created new ethnic enclaves, which, in a continent gripped by nationalism, led to serious social and political tensions. On top of it all, Europe's economies were in a state of collapse.

The United States, meanwhile, was experiencing a postwar boom, especially in urban areas. Automobile production was expanding, sales of appliances were soaring, and construction activity was reaching new heights. Industry was seeking workers to meet the rising demand for new products and anticipated that Europeans would, as during earlier periods of economic expansion, be attracted to the steel mills and coal mines.

With Europe in ruins and the United States prospering, conditions seemed ripe for a resumption of the massive transatlantic migration that had brought nearly nine million aliens to our shores during the first decade of the new century. But it was not to be. In a revolutionary change in policy, the United States closed its doors to immigrants from Southern and Eastern Europe, leaving ready access only to those from the Western Hemisphere. Some historians, including Pulitzer Prize-winner Samuel Eliot Morison, have attributed the sudden restrictiveness primarily to economic factors. Morison points first and foremost to organized labor, which, he maintains, was concerned that the wage gains won during the war would not be sustained if immigration were to return to prewar rates.[33]

In fact, labor's role in influencing Congress on immigration issues was only marginal, and in the South, nearly nonexistent. Support for the restrictive measures came primarily from legislators who depended little on organized labor—who were actually antilabor. A look at the record indicates that the shift in immigration policy was largely unrelated to economic issues. After all, the 1920s (despite two downturns) were a relatively prosperous time. While those hostile to immigration cloaked their positions in terms of economic grievance, they were, at bottom, driven by ethnic and racial concerns. Understanding the interwar restrictive legislation requires a look at three parallel developments: the growing popularity of eugenics, the influence of Progressivism, and the rebirth of the Ku Klux Klan.

At first glance, these three phenomena might seem to have little in common, although support for eugenics and the Klan reached their zenith more or less concurrently with the passage of the restrictive immigration bills. The eugenics movement was founded by late-nineteenth-century intellectuals who believed that science could improve the quality of the human race.[34] Eugenicists quickly found adherents among respectable physical and biological scientists, sociologists, as well as members of the urban social elite. There was a predisposition among these professional groups to accept the concept that differences in individual intelligence and behavior were attributable to ethnicity and race.

The Progressives constituted a loosely based, middle-class movement that included socialists as well as conservatives. They attributed various social ills, including business monopolies and urban slums, to rapid growth and greed. Reforming institutions, fighting urban corruption, and increasing government involvement, they argued, were the means to restore lost social values. The strength of the movement peaked before World War I, but its position that more aliens should not be admitted until those already present were fully assimilated gained momentum after the conflict ended.

The reborn Ku Klux Klan (the movement erupted first in the South in the aftermath of the Civil War but waned a decade later) catered not only to southerners but also to the discontented lower-middle- and working-class elements in northern cities. Its strength was concentrated among groups that failed to progress economically and were searching for an outlet to vent their frustrations. Other adherents of the Klan were angered by social change they could not control. The Klan was able to build on the virulent anti-Catholicism that had given sustenance to the American Protective Association two decades earlier, the deep bias against blacks, and anti-Semitism. Blacks, Catholics, and Jews became the symbols of what the movement perceived to be the moral disintegration of the nation.

Despite the differences in class representation, these three groups shared several fundamental convictions. They all believed in the inferiority of blacks and, by extension, of all ethnic groups that were less than "pure white."[35] They all believed that America's cities had a corrupting influence, not only on their own inhabitants but on the nation as a whole. The Progressives blamed much of the rampant urban corruption of the era on the presence of an ignorant, foreign-born electorate that had no sense of democratic institutions and values. The eugenicists charged that cities were overcrowded and dirty because immigrants were breeding too rapidly and lacked compassion for their offspring. The Klan argued that urban violence was attributable to

Italians and other Catholics who were genetically prone to criminal activity and lacked the moral values of superior races. Taken together, these beliefs helped generate a shift in public opinion away from tolerance of immigration.

Of the three movements, the eugenicists promulgated ideas that had the strongest impact on immigration policy. The decadent Ku Klux Klan found new life in the pseudoscientific rationale for intolerance provided by the eugenics movement. Racism in the guise of science became acceptable to all strata of American society. The eugenicists broadened the definition of inferior races—at first limited to blacks and Asians—to encompass all groups other than Northern and Western Europeans. Immigrants from the Mediterranean basin, they maintained, were tainted by African blood and were thus "colored."

The concept of mixed blood first caught on in the South, but the tenets of eugenics gradually gained broad acceptance in other regions as well. The Immigration Restriction League in the years just prior to World War I adopted these beliefs. Some League members repeated the argument that southern Italians were undesirable because they were partially Negroid; others stated that Jews, for biological reasons, could not adapt to American life. The academic trappings of this pseudoscience appealed to educated members of the middle class, many of whom unhesitatingly accepted head measurements and other physical tests as proof of differing mental capabilities. Most disturbing of all, eugenics gained enthusiastic adherents among academicians who formed the vanguard of the Progressive movement at the nation's most respected institutions. Remarkably, this group included several well-known economists who, ignoring the economic consequences of immigration, used their academic prestige to promote questionable anthropological concepts.

Among the early advocates of what was hailed as the scientific approach to exclude "inferior" ethnic groups was E. G. Conklin, one of the nation's leading biologists at Princeton University, who wrote, "How insignificant are the considerations of cheap labor and rapid development of natural resources when compared with these (race-mixing) biological consequences of immigration?"[36] Francis A. Walker, an economist and president of the prestigious Massachusetts Institute of Technology, argued that the new immigrants represented "beaten races" whose willingness to work at low wages was responsible for reducing the birthrates of the superior races unwilling to compete on these terms.

An influential member of the Progressive movement, John R. Commons, professor of political economy at the University of Wisconsin, also sought to downplay the economic contribution of immigrants and emphasize their undesirable characteristics. For more than two decades, in lectures, articles, and a book, *Races and Immigrants in America,* Commons persisted in arguing that immigration to the United States had to be constrained.[37] He claimed that immigrants were not only depressing wages of American workers but were more likely to be paupers and criminals than were native-born residents. William Ripley, a Harvard economics professor, focused his attention on the concentration of immigrants in the nation's large cities. In a full-page Sunday *New York Times* article, he concluded that the hordes of new immigrants were "a menace to our Anglo-Saxon civilization."[38] Ripley observed that cities are producing a "swarthy and black-eyed primitive-type" population.

Edward A. Ross, a middle-class Progressive and respected sociologist at Wisconsin, also found, on the basis of observing new immigrants gathered on street corners and in churches, that pure and honest Anglo-Saxon blood was being diluted by "sub-common" elements from southeastern Europe (Greece and Italy). To save America from "race suicide," he claimed, immigration from Eastern and Southern Europe had to be restricted. His numerous magazine articles on the subject were followed by *The Old World in the New,*[39] first published in 1914 but reprinted in five editions. In this book, quoted on the floor of Congress as presenting scientific evidence for the need to revise immigration laws, Ross included a chapter on the adverse economic impact of new immigrants. The discussion of social consequences associated with undesirable foreign-born residents concludes with the questionable finding (asserted without supporting data) that congestion, segregation, and corruption are seen in cities like Pittsburgh and Fall River, less so in Nashville and Los Angeles where there are few aliens.

The low level of scholarship by these professors is apparent in the words and reasonsing of a study undertaken by Robert Foerster, a member of Princeton's economics faculty. Asked by the U.S. Department of Labor to investigate the effects of immigration from the rest of the Western Hemisphere, he traveled through Latin America and concluded, in a report published by the government in 1925, that broad entry by Latin Americans would "lower the [average of the] race value of the white population of the United States."[40]

The Ku Klux Klan effectively cited these men in its efforts to sway public opinion against immigrants. Speeches by Klan members were virtually indistinguishable in substance and language, if not in style, from the writings of many university professors.

Not all university faculty supported the racist notions that accompanied the Progressive and eugenics movements in the United States. The president of Harvard, Abbott Lawrence Lowell, for one, was a leading opponent of constraints on immigration that were based on biology. Herbert Jennings, a well-respected professor of zoology at Johns Hopkins, warned against the misuse of science by the eugenicists, as did the sociologist Lester Ward.[41] But the few voices of reason from the ranks of universities were overwhelmed by the many leading academicians who expressed eugenicist arguments that found their way into newspaper editorials.

Most of the mass-circulation press—the *New York Times* was among the notable exceptions—accepted the position of eugenicists and Progressives that urban corruption, vice, and crime were attributable to immigration. Many middle-class families relied on magazines for commentaries on national events, and prior to World War I influential publications, such as the *Saturday Evening Post, Harper's,* and *Scribner's,* provided varying opinions on the merits of limiting immigration. During the early 1920s, when the issue was debated in Congress, articles in these and other magazines, with the exception of the *Nation,* adopted more strident attitudes that generally followed theories promulgated by eugenicists.[42]

Groups such as employers that were not eager to have the entry gates totally shut recognized the futility of trying to convince the public that immigration was not solely responsible for urban woes. As an alternative to severe restrictions, they proposed the distribution of immigrants from coastal cities to the interior. Industry leaders also supported admitting only immigrants who could respond to labor needs, an idea rejected by legislators as unworkable. Business also initiated various Americanization programs with the support of private organizations, hoping to deflect anti-immigration sentiment by showing the public that aliens, once Americanized, could become good citizens.

Many Progressives were not persuaded by these programs. Ross, for one, viewed Americanized education with "half amused contempt" and stated that other sociologists shared his belief.

Progressives concerned with urban issues favored eugenicist theories because they offered an explanation for the maladies—perceived and real—afflicting American cities. The movement was haunted by the specter of a tide of immigrants and their hungry, homeless children overwhelming solid, middle-class families. As a counter, Progressives favored not only restricted entry from abroad but also birth control for poor urban families. But the movement could not control black migration to cities, and there was no legal basis for birth control legislation. Placing little faith in efforts to educate undesirable immigrants, they believed that cities could be saved by immigration control, the one measure they could influence in Congress.

The list of causes contributing to the outburst of anti-immigrant sentiment in the early decades of the twentieth century is extensive. The Ku Klux Klan, Progressives, and eugenicists were not alone. Organized labor feared a surplus of workers, and many Protestants, particularly in the South and Midwest, feared immigration would bolster Catholicism. Although business generally favored open immigration, the fear of labor radicalism eroded their support. Among these forces, the eugenics movement stands out as the most influential in shaping the national origins legislation. Each group opposing immigration accepted at least some of the genetic arguments. As local newspapers, the *Saturday Evening Post,* and other periodicals began to urge restrictions based on genetic differences, public opinion shifted from indifference to supporting controls. Subscribers were swayed by the apparently scientific conclusions of leading university professors that admitting inferior races would damage the nation. The impact of eugenics was most apparent at the political level. Eugenicists exercised considerable control over the activities of the House Committee on Immigration and Naturalization, which was given responsibility for the drafting of new immigration laws in the early 1920s. Its chairman, Albert Johnson of Washington, was also a member of the American Eugenics Society. An important leader in the movement, Harry Laughlin, became a staff member of the committee and its eugenics expert.

The movement's influence was also evident at the White House. While Presidents Cleveland, Taft, and Wilson vetoed immigration measures aimed at particular ethnic groups, Calvin Coolidge, as vice president, declared that "America must be kept American. Biological laws show . . . that Nordics degenerate when mixed with other races."[43] Warren Harding and Coolidge became the first American presidents to favor restricting European immigration based on ethnicity.

Undesirables at the Gate: An Era Ends

With bias against outsiders spreading to all classes, the ranks of those supporting unrestricted entry dwindled after World War I. Able to mount only token resistance to the new laws, these proponents sought mainly to avert the adoption of the most extreme measures.

Businessmen continued to look favorably upon immigration, although not from any sense of charity. They believed that immigrants not only helped keep wages low but also diluted the strength of organized labor. Furthermore, businessmen were convinced that the population growth induced by immigration increased the demand for goods and services, causing sales and profits to rise. Owners of urban land continued to benefit from immigration because the added demand for housing caused land prices and rents to escalate. Business interests, at first, continued to oppose congressional preference for the use of the 1890 census as the basis for national origin questions, since applying that base year would largely exclude laborers from Southern and Eastern Europe, a major source of unskilled manpower. Both the National Association of Manufacturers and the National Conference Board, an umbrella organization representing most of the nation's important industries, took this position at congressional hearings. The president of Bethlehem Steel argued that production could not rise unless more able bodies arrived from Eastern and Southern Europe.[44] However, as popular perceptions of these immigrants soured, the business community began to retreat from its earlier position. Following the Russian Revolution, fears that Communist agitators among the ranks of Eastern European immigrants would encourage strikes aimed at disrupting American industry further diminished the willingness of business to counter the anti-immigration surge.

Political support for unrestricted immigration during the 1920s was limited primarily to those northern urban areas in which most foreign-born persons lived. Aside from the industrialists and property owners who expected to gain economically from broad immigration, legislative constraints were opposed by groups like the National Catholic Welfare Conference, the American Jewish Congress, the Polish-American Alliance, and the American-Italian League. These associations also opposed the decision of the Immigration Committee to use the 1890 census as the basis for allocating the number of immigrants admitted from any nation, for the obvious reason that the proposal was aimed directly at their compatriots and coreligionists.

Labor organizations, most notably the American Federation of Labor (AF of L), which had a heavily urban membership, asserted their opposition to unrestricted immigration for the same reasons business supported it—immigrants would drive down wages and impair efforts to organize workers. The AF of L, representing conservative, craft-oriented unions, chose to ignore the fact that few immigrants would compete with their membership. The leadership was also aware that new immigrants were hostile because unions generally excluded aliens, but no attempt was made to recruit non-English-speaking workers. Although immigrants were probably no more extreme in their political views than native labor activists, the label of radicalism was pinned on them by the craft unions.

While organized labor was dead set against the entry of any Asian workers, it was not uniformly opposed to European immigration. Some city-based unions, including the International Ladies' Garment Workers' Union, actually encouraged immigrant membership. Prior to the New Deal, however, labor's voice was too weak even in industrial states to sway any significant number of legislators.

In 1924, following three years of bitter controversy, the House accepted the recommendation of its Immigration Committee that national origin quota systems be permanently adopted. Entry for the next five years would be restricted to 2 percent of the population each nationality formed in 1890. Limits imposed by the legislation on Eastern and Southern European nations were severe. Average annual immigration from Russia and Italy taken together in the first two decades of this century was 270,000; but the combined total for the two nations, applying the 1890 census, was only 6,000. Greeks were even more constrained. Although about 17,000 arrived annually before 1922, the annual quota was set at 100.[45]

Much to the consternation of eugenicists, the Immigration Act of

1924 did not limit entry from the Western Hemisphere. The powerful chairman of the House Immigration Committee, Albert Johnson, decided that votes of congressmen from the Southwest were needed to ensure passage of legislation to restrict European immigration. To alleviate the concerns of southwestern growers about the availability of Mexican agricultural workers, Johnson agreed to incorporate into the measure a provision allowing unrestricted entry from Latin America. Johnson explained his position in hearings held in 1921:

> The fact that this country comprises a large area and that our indus-
> try, including agriculture, must expand to meet a growing popula-
> tion makes imperative a similar increase in common labor. There is
> a dire and imperative need to permit Mexican labor to enter this
> country on easy terms.[46]

Many members of Congress saw in this a self-serving rationale that could apply to European laborers as easily as to those of Mexico. Despite public sentiment to limit Mexican immigration, though, the growers had enough economic clout to get their way, and no quota system was imposed on countries in this hemisphere. While administrative measures were put in place to limit entry across the Rio Grande, those who really wanted to cross the border were generally able to do so.

Johnson carried the day, and, with support from the Southwest assured, the measure passed the House by a margin of 323 to 71 (with 37 abstaining). Almost all the opponents came from eight northern urban states; nearly half the no votes came from Boston, Cleveland, Detroit, and New York. The South voted as a block in favor of the bill, without a single dissent. Again, the region with the fewest foreign-born residents most vehemently supported limiting their entry, although western support was also solid. The bill was hailed by the Klan as its most important (and ultimately only) triumph.[47]

By the time the 1924 act was passed, the nation had already recovered from a brief recession, the fear that the country would be swamped by millions of World War I refugees had receded, and business was once again searching for workers. Economic conditions, then, were conducive to immigration. What had changed, writes Robert Divine, was the injection of racial theories.[48]

The imposition of the national origin quota system had its desired effect: After 1924, immigration from Eastern and Southern Europe fell sharply. Many "undesirables" from these regions were literally stopped at the gates of American embassies. There was a final attempt in 1929 to postpone the application of the Immigration Act of 1924, better known as the "National Origins law." Despite vehement southern opposition (two-thirds of the negative votes came from this region), the postponement resolution passed the House, but the Senate failed to act on it.

Matters changed little in the 1930s and 1940s. During the Great Depression, Congress curtailed immigration further, going as far as denying cases involving family reunification. The eugenics movement remained strong, and the public feared swelling the rolls of the unemployed. Quotas were strictly enforced.[49] Even children facing death in their home countries were excluded on the nominal grounds that they would increase unemployment. During World War II, traditional European immigration routes were totally shut down, and laborers had to be recruited from the Caribbean basin and Mexico—areas unaffected by war and immigration controls. Overall, the combined effects of the quota system, the depression, World War II, and the nation's reluctance to admit refugees resulted in a drastic reduction in the number of entrants to the United States. Between 1930 and 1945, immigration to this country totaled fewer than 700,000, compared to 5.4 million the previous fifteen years.

At the end of World War II, the United States, now the undisputed leader of the Western world, passed the 1952 Immigration and Naturalization Act—better known as the McCarren-Walter Act, after its Senate and House sponsors—over the objections of President Harry S. Truman. In his veto message, the president noted that the measure, by reaffirming the national origin laws of the 1920s, continued to discriminate against friendly nations. He also pointed out that holding immigration to the levels first imposed in 1924 would produce a labor shortage that constrained economic vigor.

President Truman had to prod Congress to pass the Displaced Persons Act of 1948, which allowed 400,000 refugees to enter the United States. This new statute assumed that we had a responsibility to deal with the consequences of massive destruction and displacement caused by the war. The Refugee Relief Act, passed in 1953, established a new category of persons that could enter the United States—individuals persecuted for their political beliefs. The act, as applied, was in service of national foreign policy goals. Thus, many people were admitted from Hungary and Cuba not only because they were legitimate political refugees but also because they were fleeing Communist regimes.

The new legislation also established preferences for skilled workers; for the first time, the law recognized the economic benefits to be derived from selective immigration based on occupation. The concept of giving preference to persons with certain skills was common in Europe, and both Canada and Australia had applied this criterion for decades. Although the numbers admitted under this clause were small compared to those entering because they had relatives in this country, the principle of linking immigration with labor needs was established.

Otherwise, few changes were made in the immigration laws. Despite the horrors that were committed in the name of racial purity during the war, no preferences were established for residents of countries that suffered the most during the war. Another decade elapsed before the United States adopted immigration reforms more closely in line with the nation's traditional ideals—ideals abandoned in the 1920s.

Removal of Ethnic Barriers and the Rise in Illegal Entry

It was not until the 1960s that the national origins standard was repealed. As was the case with the 1920s legislation, the change came about primarily for noneconomic reasons. Although the quota concept was generally considered unjust, public attitudes had to change before Congress would approve legislation based on principles of racial equality. As a senator from Massachusetts in 1958, John F. Kennedy wrote *A Nation of Immigrants* to show the contribution of foreign-born residents in an effort to sway legislators to vote for immigration reform.[50] As president, he asked Congress to eliminate the injustice of the quota system and endorsed legislation to accomplish this objective in what would have been his 1964 State of the Union message. But with Kennedy's assassination, legislation to reverse the eugenics-derived principle that immigrants from other than West European nations were not desirable had to await the presidency of Lyndon B. Johnson.

The new Immigration Act of 1965 came at a time when postwar liberalism hit its zenith. With unemployment near an all-time low and economic prosperity at hand, the national mood was upbeat. The Vietnam conflict, still in its early stages, had yet to temper the climate of optimism. More critical for the immigration debate than the economic state of the nation, though, was the growing commitment to racial equality, evident in the passage of the Civil Rights Act in 1964.

Nearly all the congressional opposition to changing the status quo came from senators in southern states. Senator Allen Ellender (D.-La.) stated that the national origin principle should continue "because it attempts to continue the cultural heritage, political, and social traditions of this nation."[51] He also asserted that only Western and Northern Europe can provide the skilled and educated persons the nation requires. The American Coalition of Patriotic Societies, founded in 1929 and claiming a membership of close to three million, predicted that any increase in immigration was certain to raise unemployment. The group defended the ethnic quotas because they were "based on our own people." The American Legion echoed this position, as did, unsurprisingly, the Eugenics Society. Nonetheless, with labor organizations, Catholic groups, and the president backing the measure, the Senate voted 76 to 18 for immigration reform.

The legislation could hardly qualify as radical. Its most significant change was to eliminate the use of the 1890 census to determine entry from nations in favor of a measure constraining immigration to no more than twenty thousand from any nation, with an aggregate global limit. Under its provisions, a Korean citizen would have the same opportunity to enter the United States as one from England or Sweden, subject to the twenty thousand cap. However, as part of the political compromise, the bill no longer exempted the Western Hemisphere from numerical limits. With this change, all nations were given equal standing. To appease agricultural elements that had prevented the inclusion of Western Hemisphere nations in limits set during the 1920s, an amendment to the 1965 Immigration Act allowed employers to hire undocumented workers without penalty.

As with earlier measures, family reunification was a major goal of legislation, and immediate family members of U.S. citizens were given priority over others. Professional and other skilled workers were also given limited preference if the Department of Labor could certify a need for their occupation or training.

At the time of the Immigration Act's passage, few in Congress thought it would make for any fundamental adjustments in immigration patterns. In fact, the measure opened the way for a surge of immigrants from Asia. The number of immigrants from this region rose from about 150,000 in the 1950s to more than 2.7 million in the 1980s, while European immigration fell by more than one-third.

Looking back, Americans should not have been surprised by the rise of non-European immigration. In countries like Korea, Taiwan, Hong Kong, and India, population pressures and limited opportunities for the rapidly growing middle classes pushed many to leave. The United States already had well-established communities of Chinese, Japanese, and Filipinos, mainly in California, which attracted newcomers. As will be discussed in later chapters, these communities provided an essential economic and social link in the process for absorbing immigrants into their new environment. Meanwhile, few nations other than the United States were willing to accept Asian immigrants.

Immigration was facilitated by the trade that developed between the United States and the Far East beginning in the 1960s. Personal contacts were made, and job opportunities opened for those with language and business skills. The large number of students from Asian nations that streamed to American universities in the early 1960s created a core of foreign professionals well adapted to our customs and practices.[52] As the demand for personnel grew in technical, scientific, and medical fields, Far Eastern immigrants helped expand the available human resources.

In addition to the need for educated people, the American economy had openings for those with limited skills or no skills, and they came in ever-greater numbers from the Caribbean and Latin America. This Western Hemisphere inflow, like the increase from Asia, marked a major departure from earlier patterns of immigration. One would have expected immigration from these nations to slow considerably as a result of hemispheric limits that came into effect in the 1960s, but instead the number of those entering rose sharply during the 1970s.

During the 1950s, the 600,000 who came from Latin America and the Caribbean accounted for one in four aliens admitted. Three decades later, 3.5 million came from the Americas, with the regional share rising to 47 percent of all admissions. Were one to include illegal entry, well over half of all immigration to the United States was from the Western Hemisphere.

These data suggest that the 1965 act had an impact only upon the legal status of immigrants from the Americas, not upon their number.

The rise was a result of overpopulation, low living standards, and the inability of local economies to absorb new workers. Although these circumstances were manifest earlier, they intensified during the 1970s, contributing to a general sense of economic malaise. Political repression also has contributed to the flood of immigrants from several nations in Central America. The Central American refugee pattern observed is similar to what happened in the first three decades of this century, when 1.5 million Mexicans escaping political upheavals and economic chaos settled in the United States. This number accounted for 10 percent of Mexico's entire population at that time.

Those seeking to enter the country illegally have been abetted by improvements in transportation and communications. Until the 1960s, most immigrants (other than Mexicans) entered this country by ship. Immigration officials boarded vessels almost a full day before passengers disembarked, allowing ample time for careful inspection of documents. Airport controls are considerably more difficult to implement because of the millions of air passengers who arrive here every day; moreover, fares have declined to the point at which even an impoverished Caribbean farmer can afford to fly to the United States. Millions of foreigners enter the country on visitor permits, and several hundred thousand foreign students attend U.S. schools. Many simply fail to leave after their legal stay expires. Meanwhile, improvements in international communications have enabled villages in remote regions of the world to obtain up-to-date information on both job opportunities in the United States and the latest methods of clandestine entry.

Undoubtedly, though, the most important cause of the rise in undocumented migration was the nation's continuing demand for low-wage, unskilled labor. During the earlier open-door era, the demand for such workers was satisfied by two waves of European immigrants. When ethnic quotas were enacted, labor needs were filled by blacks moving from the rural South to the urban North and by Mexicans moving across the border into the Southwest. A reservoir of married women and surplus agricultural workers also came into the labor force during the 1940s and 1950s. Thus, during the five decades of controlled entry, the nation found several alternate sources of unskilled labor. By the end of the 1960s, however, this supply was nearly exhausted. Black migration from the South had virtually ceased,

the farm population had shrunk to only a few million, and the percentage of women in the labor force, although still rising, was expected to peak.

One contributor to the inflow of undocumented Mexicans was the cessation of the Bracero Program, which found temporary jobs for some 4 million Mexicans between 1942 and 1960, reaching a peak in the late 1950s. The program ended in 1964 in response to charges that the presence of these workers limited opportunities for American citizens.[53] The termination of the program had little impact on the demand for workers, although wages did rise in response to the shortage of agricultural labor. Many workers who previously were legally employed continued to filter across the border, joining other Hispanics seeking nonagricultural work. In a sense, then, the increase in undocumented immigration can be seen as a rational response to domestic economic needs. At the same time, it eroded the nation's ability to enforce its immigration laws. In some metropolitan areas, most notably Los Angeles, the number of aliens arriving illegally in the 1970s exceeded the number entering legally. The 1965 act succeeded in one of its aims—eliminating the inequitable distribution of entrants based on their places of origin. Another objective, maintaining a global annual limit on immigration, succumbed to population pressures in the third world, an inability to control the Canadian and Mexican borders, and job opportunities in the United States.

Since the 1970s, illegal immigration and nonquota legal entries have essentially reduced the global limit (including the higher limit permitted since 1990) to a symbolic number. This marked a new period in which most persons, regardless of national origin, who were strongly motivated to enter, live, and work in the United States, could do so without having to wait for years to be admitted legally. Poor persons with courage could enter illegally across the Mexican or Canadian border, while those with enough resources to enter legally on a temporary basis could remain with little risk of being detected.

The idea of overstaying one's visa is nothing new, of course. Thousands of visitors to the United States did so in the 1930s and 1950s. For the most part, though, these were affluent individuals who could not only afford the expensive fare to get here but also had the means to support themselves at a time when few jobs were available. The more recent and much larger influx is fed by all economic and social strata, taking advantage of low transportation costs, porous borders, and abundant job opportunities. Not only are chances of apprehension and deportation slim, but for those caught, the maximum penalty is, in essence, no more than the cost of their travel.

As the flow of illegal aliens grew, a backlash developed. Similar to what occurred earlier, opponents of immigration began to associate aliens with a host of problems—crime, poverty, the loss of jobs, and depressed wages. While the 1965 act helped restore fairness to our immigration policy, it failed to address directly the issue of illegal entry and residence. At the time, this was not perceived to be a critical matter, but within a decade the illegal-worker issue came to dominate the immigration debate.

The 1986 Legislation

By the mid-1970s, Congress recognized that the 1965 act fell short in the area of illegal immigration. The House passed a measure to fine employers for hiring illegal aliens, but a similar bill could not overcome opposition from the agricultural interests in the Senate and the measure languished. Frustrated by its inability to deal with the issue, Congress in 1979 appointed a blue-ribbon group, the Select Commission on Immigration and Refugee Policy, to evaluate existing laws and policies governing the admission of both immigrants and refugees to the United States.

The commission's report, delivered in March 1981, had numerous recommendations to overhaul immigration, including two dealing with the undocumented population. The commission favored legislation similar in form to that passed by the House in the late 1970s, making it illegal for employers to hire undocumented workers. A program to legalize undocumented alien workers residing in the United States prior to 1980 was also proposed. This idea was suggested earlier by President Carter and introduced in Congress, but it failed to pass.

The commission also proposed that the annual global ceiling on immigration subject to the quota be raised from 270,000 to 350,000. Consistent with the concept incorporated in the 1952 Immigration Act, another recommendation was to establish a "small, numerically limited category" to facilitate the entry of immigrants with exceptional qualifications.

The report, considered well balanced by both political parties, placed pressure on Congress, never eager to deal with immigration, to tackle the issue once more. Several developments also prompted legislators to act. The economy was lagging, with unemployment rates in 1982 reaching 10 percent. Close to eleven million people were out of work, the highest number since the Great Depression. The number of undocumented persons, based on such indicators as border apprehensions, appeared to be growing. The sense of crisis was heightened by the Mariel boatlift, which brought 125,000 Cubans into the country, and the dramatic arrival of the Haitian "boat people" on the beaches of Florida.

In March 1982, Republican senator Alan K. Simpson from Wyoming and Democratic congressman Romano L. Mazzoli from Kentucky introduced bills in each chamber that were generally consistent with the commission's recommendations. The bills called for sanctions against employers who hire illegal workers as the chief weapon to stem the transborder tide. Other measures, such as increasing patrols, were considered ineffective. To enlist the support of Hispanic and liberal groups, Congress would have granted amnesty to illegal aliens who entered the country prior to 1980.

The Senate passed the bill by a wide margin, but the House Democratic leadership balked. The objections of Speaker Thomas P. O'Neill were never stated, but the opposition of Hispanics and many liberals to employer sanctions was no doubt considered divisive among the Democrats. Having failed the first time, the bill's tortuous movement through the legislative labyrinth continued for several years.

To assist passage by focusing attention on the issue, joint congressional hearings were held in the early 1980s. The hearings provided a forum for civil rights groups, associations, and others with positions on immigration reform. These hearings paralleled those held in 1921. At that time, many of the groups supporting restrictions had disparate interests that came together on the issue of immigration. For example, conservatives and upper-class socialites favored restrictions to keep out left-wing labor agitators and others from "racially inferior" countries to preserve order and maintain labor peace. Socialists also favored restrictions, but for the *opposite* reason. They argued that American workers had to be protected from unfair competition by meek, servile immigrants unwilling to become organized.

The record of hearings held in 1982 yields an opportunity to examine informal alliances and compare positions taken by organized labor, business, and minorities over several decades. Because legislators expected a close vote in the House when the Simpson-Mazzoli bill was introduced again in 1984, some bizarre alliances were struck. Liberal congressman Barney Frank (D.-Mass.), observing the efforts to defeat the bill, noted facetiously, "Today is apparently the day the large agricultural owners joined the American Civil Liberties Union."[54] The liberal ACLU opposed employer sanctions because the measure could discriminate against minorities. Conservative growers also objected to sanctions, not to protect workers but because they could no longer obtain an ample supply of cheap labor without risking severe fines. Under the bill, employers would have to check Social Security or other identity cards to verify the legal status of the job applicant.

The business community, consistent with its earlier, active support for unconstrained immigration, now lobbied against employer sanctions. The Chamber of Commerce of the United States joined western and southern agricultural interests in leading the campaign. California's well-organized growers were particularly vocal in opposing any measure that would restrict the flow of illegal immigrants into their state. Working conditions were difficult, and growers feared their inability to find a large enough native-born work force to harvest the fruit and vegetable crops. An article in the *Wall Street Journal* (which editorially opposed the Simpson-Mazzoli bill) reported that "California's $14 billion agriculture industry owed its harvest to illegal labor almost as much as to the sun and rain."[55] The Chamber of Commerce's membership includes a great number of small businesses, and many of them, especially in the Southwest, employ undocumented workers. In both the House and Senate versions of the Simpson-Mazzoli bill, firms with fewer than four employees were exempted from employer sanctions; nevertheless, the Chamber of Commerce opposed the bill. Its opposition may have been due, in part, to deep-seated abhorrence of any constraints on the free flow of labor. The formal statement of the chamber criticized employer sanctions as "ineffective, unworkable, unreasonably burdensome and unduly expensive."[56] The chamber recommended that Congress provide additional funding to strengthen border controls, although no

doubt the group understood that such an approach could never stop the flow of illegal immigrants.

As usual, labor took a very different position from business. Most unions strongly supported employer sanctions as an effective means of reducing the flow of illegal workers. The premise of organized labor, as in the 1890s and 1920s, was that these workers would be difficult to organize. Lane Kirkland, president of the AFL-CIO, stated to Congress in 1982 that "millions of illegal workers . . . are a threat to minorities, women, and unemployed workers who are American citizens."[57] Kirkland, like other unionists, linked high unemployment in the United States during the 1980s to illegal immigration. While strongly backing employer sanctions, labor unions actively opposed a provision in the Senate version for admitting several hundred thousand temporary farm workers. Publicly, the unions expressed concerns about the possibilities for exploitation of farm workers, but what really worried labor was that alien workers would dilute its organizational strength.

Hispanic groups did not participate in the immigration debates of the 1920s. Six decades later, numerous well-organized associations unanimously opposed the Simpson-Mazzoli bill. The National Council of La Raza, a Hispanic civil rights organization and one of the most active on this issue, supported broad amnesty for undocumented persons already living in the United States but was greatly concerned about employer-sanctions provisions. Specifically, La Raza feared that the process to verify worker eligibility by employers would discriminate against Hispanics and others whose looks or language differed from most Americans. The La Raza stand was supported by the League of United Latin American citizens, the nation's largest Hispanic organization, and the Mexican-American Legal Defense and Education Fund, an organization focused on protecting the constitutional rights of Mexicans. These Hispanic organizations shared the view that the root cause of the undocumented worker problem is the vast difference in economic opportunity that exists between the United States and Mexico. As an alternative to sanctions, these groups proposed establishing labor-intensive economic programs in the "sending" countries, which, they argued, would reduce the motivation for immigration to the United States. Hispanic spokespersons stayed away from another sensitive point—the possibly adverse effect of undocumented immigrants on the job opportunities and wages of native Hispanics. Because of this issue, the broader Hispanic community had a less benign view of undocumented workers than its leadership. Nonetheless, many Hispanics opposed employer sanctions for reasons of potential discrimination.

Black organizations, meanwhile, played only a minor role in the immigration proceedings. For them, the issue presented a conflict between political and economic priorities. In 1982, Althea Simmons, director of the Washington bureau of the NAACP, set forth the organization's position: "We not only believe, we know that undocumented workers do have a disparate impact on unskilled, unemployed, and marginally employed blacks. . . . Many blacks are forced from employment rolls by the undocumented worker who is usually hired at a subminimum wage."[58] Employer sanctions were seen by the organization as a means to relieve high black unemployment. Five years earlier, the NAACP had adopted a resolution urging an immediate end to the use of all illegal alien labor. This position was consistent with the stance that black groups have taken on immigration since the turn of the century. However, the black community was by no means united on the issue. Despite the NAACP position favoring employer sanctions, the Congressional Black Caucus opposed the Simpson-Mazzoli bill in 1983 and 1984. The Caucus, conscious of growing Hispanic political power, was not eager to oppose a traditional ally in the struggle for minority rights on this emotional issue. The importance of the Mexican-American vote was also appreciated by the Rev. Jesse Jackson, who was gathering support for his "rainbow coalition." A few days prior to the 1984 House immigration debates, Jackson told Mexican groups in Tijuana and Southern California that he believed that undocumented Mexicans have no adverse impact on black workers.

Special constituencies like business, labor, and minorities received their fullest hearing in the House of Representatives, which, more than the Senate and executive branch, tends to be responsive to outside pressure groups. This was especially true in the case of Simpson-Mazzoli. The 1984 hearings on the bill took place only five months before the fall election, when legislators' sensitivities were at their sharpest.

Not surprisingly, then, House members expressed concern over the economic impact of undocumented workers. During the floor debate, proponents of the employer-sanctions provision in the bill often mentioned fears over job losses for American workers. Thus, Congressman Stan Lundine (D.-N.Y.) declared that "as many as 1.2 million jobs held by an alien could be filled by unemployed Americans."[59]

A few congressmen opposed the bill on the questionable premise that granting amnesty and allowing temporary workers in agriculture would hurt American labor. (It is naive to think that, in the absence of such a program, undocumented workers would pack their belongings and leave the country.) Several legislators stated that amnesty appeared to be accommodating unlawful behavior. Those uncomfortable with growing ethnic, cultural, and racial diversity may have opposed amnesty because the provision could be interpreted as implicitly endorsing a policy to tolerate the predominantly nonwhite illegals. These sentiments would not be stated publicly, but would more likely be expressed under the guise of "law and order." These legislators were willing to scuttle the measure with its employer sanctions simply because limited amnesty was included. Congressman Kent R. Hance (R.-Fla.) asserted, "For every job in the country now occupied by an undocumented worker, it costs the country. . . . Amnesty costs jobs for American citizens. It legalizes the theft of American jobs."[60] His views echoed those of C. M. Goethe, president of the Immigration Study Commission in 1930, who wrote that "the number of unemployed American whites just about equals the number of Mexican aliens in this country. Would not a solution to current unemployment be found in the deportation of Mexicans across the border until all white Americans are employed?"[61]

Another group of legislators opposed Simpson-Mazzoli for its sanctions on employers. A vote against sanctions could reflect two very different concerns: (1) that the civil rights of undocumented workers might be violated; and (2) that employers, especially growers, could suffer hardships. An influential and respected conservative member of the House, Jack F. Kemp (R.-N.Y.), voted against the bill. "Immigrants don't take jobs and wealth away from Americans," Kemp argued. "Immigrants create jobs and wealth. . . . Immigration is not a zero-sum proposition."[62] On this basis, Kemp opposed employer sanctions, a view shared by many liberal Democrats.

Congress voted separately on amnesty for illegal aliens and employer sanctions before taking up consideration of Simpson-Mazzoli as a whole. Legalization of undocumented aliens under the amnesty program passed the House by a comfortable margin, but the 1984 vote showed that geography continues to play an important role in defining attitudes toward immigrants. Half of the votes cast against amnesty came from the South. All House members from Alabama, North Carolina, and Mississippi, where practically no illegals are known to be working, opposed the provision, as did two-thirds of those from Florida and Texas. In all, 70 percent of southern representatives voted against the measure. Negative votes were also cast by legislators from such rural states as Idaho, Montana, and South Dakota. Support for legalization was concentrated in such heavily urban states as California, New York, and Illinois, where more than three of every four congressmen voted "aye."

The employer-sanction provision was challenged in states with heavy concentrations of Hispanics and growers. It was opposed almost unanimously by legislators from Arizona (17 percent Hispanic), California (20 percent Hispanic), and Colorado (15 percent Hispanic). These three states depend on Mexican agricultural workers. New Mexico, with the highest concentration of Hispanics in the country (37 percent), also opposed sanctions. The delegation from Texas, where one out of five residents is Hispanic, was split. By contrast, in the South (outside Texas) and Midwest, where nonimmigrant workers do most of the harvesting and fewer than 2 percent of the population is Hispanic, most congressmen voted for sanctions. Indeed, only six southern House members (again, outside of Texas) voted against sanctions. This indicates that, despite increased urbanization, rising incomes, and economic growth, southerners' traditional fears about immigration have not subsided.

To the relief of its sponsors, the House passed the Simpson-Mazzoli bill with amnesty intact by a razor-thin margin of 217 to 214 in June 1984. But the bill was ill fated—a conference committee to reconcile the House and Senate versions could not reach an agreement.

In 1986, the House was back at it, taking up an immigration bill similar to the one passed two years earlier. At this point, the differing perspectives on immigration in Congress and the White House, apparent so often in the past, surfaced once again. On the one hand, the Reagan administration's probusiness, free market philosophy placed it on the side of those who favored unlimited immigration as a valued source of labor. Thus, in

January 1986, the president's Council of Economic Advisers, in a draft of its annual report to Congress, stated that employer sanctions would reduce employment and output. The council also remarked that the difficulties associated with enforcement would represent a "labor market cost" that would hurt native minorities and youth the most.

Other currents in the administration, however, ran counter to such a position. The Department of Justice, with its law-and-order orientation, favored steps to assert greater control over the inflow of aliens. And the notion that the United States could not control its own borders clashed with the administration's effort to present an image of strength to the rest of the world.

In the end, the draft council report, which had been leaked to the press, was modified prior to delivery, and criticism of the immigration measure quieted. The White House lent its formal, if tepid, support to the bill. But in an effort to meet its various concerns, especially on the critical question of providing alien agricultural workers for growers, the administration entered a series of lengthy private discussions with members of Congress.

The ambivalence of the executive branch on the bill stretched back to the early years of the Reagan administration. The White House gave the Senate Republicans lukewarm support (primarily because Senator Simpson was well respected by the party leadership). The Office of Management and Budget (under White House control), however, expressed reservations about the measure because the agency calculated the cost of providing federally funded services to legalized aliens to be as much as $10 billion. Congressional testimony by this author and the Congressional Budget Office indicated that the OMB cost estimates were too high.[63] They were taken seriously by the White House, though, and there were "leaks" that the president, concerned about the high cost of amnesty to the Treasury, would veto the bill.

Compromises were eventually reached among competing interests, assuring passage of the measure in the House in October 1986, a few weeks before the election. The employer sanctions remained unchanged from previous bills. The measure also retained the controversial amnesty program for undocumented workers already living in the country prior to 1982.

Why did this "Rasputin of legislation," as Congressman Robert Garcia (D.-N.Y.) called it, finally pass after so many previous false starts? One key reason was the support of several influential Hispanic legislators who in the past had objected strenuously to the employer-sanction provisions as discriminatory; they now maintained that the revisions contained in the bill would reduce the danger of discrimination. More important, Congress believed that the growing national sentiment against the amnesty provision would doom any such program if the legislation were delayed further. Furthermore, rising unemployment in Texas in the wake of plummeting oil prices raised fears among some Hispanics that further illegal immigration could hurt their own job prospects. Paradoxically, improved economic conditions in other regions allayed the concerns of workers there that aliens receiving citizenship would provide stiff competition for jobs. Few editorials expressed concern over the jobs issue, and in Congress the rhetoric against amnesty was much more muted than during the floor debate two years earlier.

The powerful agricultural lobby, meanwhile, was placated with special provisions allowing entry of a sufficient number of Mexican workers to meet the labor needs of the Southwest. The proposal gave these workers some protection against exploitation. In the past, organized labor and most civil rights groups had objected vociferously to such a concession, but this time they agreed not to oppose the bill, fearing that the amnesty program would be in jeopardy. Finally, to placate states and localities fearful that the bill would saddle them with added expenditures for services to legalized immigrants, the measure provided for compensating payments from the federal government.

The Justice Department also lent a hand, although indirectly. In the weeks leading up to the congressional debate on the bill, the department was issuing almost daily press releases linking illegal entry to the rise in drug traffic from Mexico. Only days before the immigration bill came to the floor, Congress had passed a tough antidrug measure, and members would have found it hard to vote against an immigration bill that was perceived to offer a new weapon in the war on drugs.

On November 6, 1986—almost six years after the Select Commission on Immigration and Refugee Policy had submitted its initial report—President Ronald Reagan signed the Immigration Reform and Control Act of 1986 into law. The administration was not entirely enthusiastic over the law—it never actively lobbied for it—but a veto would have been unpopular, given the public clamor for employer sanctions and the bipartisan support for the measure in Congress.

As happened so often in the past, the 1986 law bore little relationship to economic realities. The catalyst for passage was not concern over jobs but unstated fears that millions of nonwhite aliens crossing our borders would ultimately change the character of the nation. However, the primary goal of the new legislation—to sharply curtail the illegal inflow—is not succeeding for the simple reason that the demand for low-wage workers remains high.

No sooner was the immigration bill passed than several members of Congress began drafting legislation to deal with the issues neglected in the 1986 measures. In 1987, Senator Edward M. Kennedy (D.-Mass.) introduced a bill to liberalize entry, essentially along the lines recommended by the 1981 Select Commission on Immigration and Refugee Policy; however, he could not garner sufficient votes for passage. In 1988, after lengthy negotiations with members of Congress, Kennedy introduced a modified bill, this time with the support of Senator Simpson, a conservative more likely to attract Republican votes.

The measure provided a dual preference system: one for family members, already in effect, and a second for so-called independent immigrants, those without close relatives in the United States. As Kennedy explained, this latter category was needed to rectify a situation in which only 1,852 applicants from Ireland qualified in 1986 for immigrant visas on the basis of family preference.[64] He was concerned that the Irish were entering illegally in substantial numbers because they could not obtain visas. An innovative approach introduced in the bill to deal with "independent" immigrants was to distribute fifty-five thousand visas based on a point system that included such considerations as educational attainment, English proficiency, and occupational demand in the United States among its criteria. The fifty-five thousand immigrants determined by the point assessment system would be in *addition* to the fifty-four thousand who qualify annually under the 1965 legislation based on their professions or skills.

An important provision of the bill was to place, for the first time in American history, a cap or maximum on the number of visas issued annually. Under current law, the limit is 270,000, and all immigrants who are close relatives or who qualify because of their skills are included within this limit. However, those defined as immediate relatives (spouses, children, and parents of U.S. citizens) are outside this numerical constraint. The Kennedy-Simpson bill would have represented a change in current policy by imposing a global cap of 600,000, *including* immediate relatives. The only exclusion from this limit would have been refugees, who are admitted under separate legislation.

The measure also curtailed the number of brothers and sisters who can enter under family preference by two-thirds, to twenty-two thousand, limiting entry to never-married brothers and sisters of citizens. Currently, married and single brothers and sisters can enter as part of the fifth preference category. Once these relatives enter, they can bring their spouses and, upon attaining citizenship, their children. This results in a continuing chain of immigrants forming an extended family, well beyond the concept of immediate family reunification that was the intent of Congress. Opposition to restricting this preference category came mostly from senators serving states with large immigrant constituencies—California, New York, and Texas. They criticized this provision as unfair to the million or more brothers and sisters of U.S. citizens currently waiting for entry.

The most controversial element in the new bill was a section that set aside some forty-eight hundred visas annually for persons who would each invest at least $2 million in the United States. Supporters of the provision held that each such investment would create ten jobs for Americans. But Senator Dale L. Bumpers (D.-Ark.) remained unconvinced, charging that this was a bribe to buy residency and that its beneficiaries would include drug dealers. He added, "I do not know how many people you can admit into this country before you sink the ship and everybody goes down."[65] Bumpers was joined in his opposition by such liberal senators as Alan Cranston (D.-Calif.) and Carl Levin (D.-Mich.); nonetheless, this section of the bill passed by 51 to 33.

Following inclusion of the investment provision, the measure passed the Senate by a lopsided vote of 88 to 4; three of the "nay" votes were made primarily in protest of the limit on the fifth (brothers and sisters) preference. As with earlier proposals to change immigration laws, the major battles would be in the House, which has been less eager than the Senate to amend them.

The Kennedy-Simpson immigration bill contained none of the more divisive provisions of its predecessors—no amnesty was offered, no sanctions imposed. The AFL-CIO supported the bill, and no organized opposition materialized. One group that may have challenged the bill was the Federation for American Immigration Reform (FAIR), an organization that lobbies against increasing the level of immigration. The group decided that the benefits of a "cap" on entry outweighed objectionable provisions. The most notable feature was its new but limited preference for those with job skills and an ability to speak English. Although the provision was aimed at encouraging emigration from Ireland and Great Britain, it would have benefited most those applicants from the former British colonies like India and Pakistan, as well as the Philippines, where educated people speak English.

The bill fared less well when it left the Senate chamber. The House was not in a mood to debate immigration, an unpopular topic, just prior to the November 1988 general election. Nor did the presidential candidates even acknowledge immigration as a national issue, in spite of Michael Dukakis's trading on his Greek heritage.

When the newly elected 101st Congress convened, immigration bills were introduced in both chambers. In the Senate, the Kennedy-Simpson Bill (S.358) reemerged with only minor changes from the 1988 version. But the full Judiciary Committee in the summer of 1989 changed two key provisions of S.358. Both married and single siblings would again be eligible for entry, restoring the language of the 1965 Immigration Act. The number of siblings to be admitted was also restored to the original level. This revision of the Kennedy-Simpson bill represented a victory for various minority groups, particularly Hispanics anxious to have visas granted to their families.

The committee also excluded English-language ability as one of the criteria to award points that would form the basis for determining independent immigrant eligibility. Senator Paul Simon (D.-Ill.), who spearheaded the opposition to this provision, argued that it would unfairly favor persons from English-speaking nations. The memory of the 1924 National Origins law bias toward Western Europeans disturbed Simon. In fact, the number of Irish or British likely to have been admitted had the language criterion remained would have been small. Millions of Indians, Jamaicans, Pakistanis, and other English-speaking non-Europeans would meet the eligibility criteria with or without language preference. Because those who qualify under the point system to receive visas are selected at random, the probability of selecting an English-speaking European applicant would have been small.

Conservative senator Jesse Helms (R.-N.C.) objected to both of the committee changes offered and, with Senator Richard Shelby (D.-Ala.), proposed an amendment during the brief floor debate on the bill restoring the original language of S.358. Helms noted that only one year earlier, the Senate had voted, with virtually no opposition, for the wording he wished to restore. But the Helms-Shelby amendment was rejected by a lopsided vote, with only twenty-seven votes favoring giving English speakers preference or limiting the entry of brothers and sisters to those who were unmarried. Nine of the "yes" votes came from the South, eight from the West, six from the Midwest, and from the Northeast, four. In every instance, senators favoring the amendment represented areas with few foreign-born residents. Senators from Alaska, New Hampshire, Idaho, Indiana, Kansas, and South Carolina all supported Helms. But only 1.3 percent of all recent immigrants settled in those six states. Senators from areas that absorbed the largest number of recent immigrants—California, Illinois, Florida, Maryland, New Jersey, New York, Pennsylvania, Texas, and Virginia—opposed the amendment.

Sponsors of S.358, having disposed of the Helms challenge, faced another hurdle—a floor amendment by Dennis DeConcini (D.-Ariz.) and Orrin Hatch (R.-Utah) to break the 600,000-immigrant cap. Essentially, the effect of the cap would have been to reduce the number of family connections in future years. Total immigration would have fallen below entry levels under the 1965 Act by the mid-1990s had this provision remained.[66] The sponsors of S.358 defended the original bill, with Senator Simpson charging that the DeConcini-Hatch amendment proponents "are asking for one thing only. They must want unlimited immigration to the United States."[67] All senators from Kansas, Maine, Montana, West Virginia, Mississippi, New Hampshire, and South Carolina favored maintaining the cap, as did, somewhat surprisingly, two from states with a large immigrant presence, Daniel Patrick Moynihan (D.-N.Y.) and Lloyd Bentsen (D.-Tex.). But their votes were insufficient. The Senate adopted the amendment by a margin of 62 to 36 and passed the modified bill by a vote of 81 to 17—solid support for higher immigration levels for both family members and independent immigrants.

The passage of the bill in the Senate marked a significant shift. In 1987 and 1988, Ted Kennedy lacked sufficient votes for the admission of independent immigrants without agreeing to an overall immigration cap—hence the cosponsorship with Senator Simpson, who insisted on a limit as the price for his support. The passage of the more liberal 1989 immigration bill in the Senate suggests the congruence of several events, most notably the growing political strength of Hispanics and Asians, who lobbied for removing the cap and the inability of those opposing changes in immigration law to arouse public opinion during a period of economic prosperity. Regional voting blocks have also weakened. Opposition to higher immigration levels continues to be concentrated in southern and rural states. Yet a Utah senator sponsored the amendment to increase immigration levels, and half of all senators representing the South supported the amendment.

Economic forces, internal migration, and shifts in racial attitudes have contributed to these changes. For example, Virginia, an economic stronghold in the antebellum era but long in eclipse afterward, emerged during the 1980s as one of the most prosperous states in the nation. Both the domestic migrant and immigrant populations have grown rapidly, with northern Virginia currently a major center for Asian enterprises. The state attracted very few immigrants in the nineteenth century but now ranks eighth in the admission of immigrants. The same forces of economic change that encourage immigration are also evident in Florida and Georgia.

Many congressional observers were convinced that the House would pass a similar measure during 1989, but, contrary to expectations, no action was taken until the end of the 1990 session when the Family Unity and Employment Act of 1990 (H.R.4300) finally came to the floor. The bill in its final form expanded annual immigration (other than refugees) from the current 540,000 to 775,000. The numerical rise was attributed primarily to boosting the number of legal entrants based on their skills from 54,000 to 188,000.[68]

Aiming to protect American workers, the bill required attestation (labor certification) by employers that they are unable to find persons with required skills at prevailing wages within the ranks of the domestic labor pool. A fee of $500 to $1,000 was to be levied on the employer for each alien worker, but employers with fewer than fifty workers would be exempt from this provision. As such, perhaps the majority of potential employers would not pay such a fee. The funds collected would be used to educate and retrain U.S. workers. The Bush administration objected to the fee provision because an additional burden would be imposed on private business.

Although the new bill would accelerate the previously time-consuming process for admitting needed workers, for those in occupations represented by collective bargaining the process may become more burdensome. Among the stipulations is that copies of the attestation certificate be provided to local unions. Representatives of these organizations could challenge at public hearings the attestation that no U.S. workers are available. One would expect, particularly when unemployment is rising, challenges to many applications by worker organizations intent on discouraging employers from hiring aliens. The process must try to balance protection of American labor with the admission of needed workers from other nations.

The notification process would not be necessary for some "priority workers" such as outstanding researchers. In response to requests by employers for persons meeting the necessary priority worker criteria, the Immigration and Naturalization Service would be required to consult with the aliens' peer group (researchers with similar professional backgrounds) to determine their qualifications.

H.R.4300 was debated on the floor for several hours on October 3 and October 4, 1990. The arguments against the bill were varied, although no one issue galvanized the opposition. Several members asserted that immigrants are a fiscal drain, and therefore admitting more would impose a greater financial burden on all levels of government. An amendment to compensate states and localities for the costs of social services, medical services, and education, however, had little support and was defeated by a three-to-one margin. Objections were also raised concerning the high numbers to be admitted. Congressman George Gekas (R.-Pa.) stated that he could only support a bill "that will not require opening the floodgates of immigration."[69] Several members questioned the view that the nation had a labor shortage, citing rising unemployment. Congressman John Bryant (D.-Tex.), a leader of the opposition to the bill, stated his objection to admitting more Europeans: "It is difficult to understand how bringing more [Anglo-Europeans] into the country would in any case increase diversity when [they are] the majority group."[70] Notwithstanding such speeches, those objecting to the bill failed to focus their attention on any particular provision, assuring its passage. The measure managed to satisfy business, labor, and various immigrant constituencies. The House of Representatives voted 231 to 192 in support, but because its version was more liberal than the Senate bill, the conference committee reached expected compromises.[71] The final bill enacted by Congress, retitled the Immigration Act of 1990, set the new level of immigration at 675,000 (700,000 for the first few years), almost exactly the midpoint between the House and Senate ceilings. About 140,000 visas were reserved for individuals (and their dependents) with needed job skills and talent. Employment-based immigration levels changed little, but the committee accepted the Senate labor certification processes. The "point system" for the 55,000 immigrants accepted for the sake of diversity (which the author opposed) was also dropped. The compromise agreement was the House version, which specified that visas for persons from historically low-admission countries should be distributed among those who filed applications by a random process (such as a lottery). The bill guaranteed Europeans about one-third of all visas and also legalized the status of undocumented Irish.

For proponents of higher immigration levels, the timing of the final debates and votes could not have been more apt. The "silent majority" of the American populace, which probably would have opposed the legislation if asked, had no organized voice. There was no barrage of telephone calls or telegrams from irate voters. Although elections were only days ahead, members of Congress did not fear a backlash. The attention of the nation was focused on the Persian Gulf (where war seemed imminent), the savings and loan scandals that threatened the integrity of the banking system, and early signs of an economic downturn. Most of the voters seemed unaware of higher immigration limits being set, levels that would not have been seriously considered only a few years earlier. Had the bill been delayed until 1991 or 1992, when the national economy was in a slump, opposition from regions with high unemployment would probably have materialized. When the bill reached the White House, President George Bush was receptive, and the measure was quietly signed into law while Congress was in recess.

3

Immigrants and the Prosperity of Cities

That part of America which has encouraged [the foreigners] has advanced most rapidly in population, in agriculture, and in the arts.

James Madison[1]

The rapid rise of America's cities from a few modest settlements along the Atlantic coast to the world's leading industrial centers cannot be separated from the saga of mass immigration. Nowhere else, in fact, have the economic consequences of transnational migration been more pronounced. Migration to cities is not a new phenomenon, of course. Since the dawn of civilization, peasants and farmers have moved to urban centers in search of refuge or better economic opportunities. In England and Western Europe, the Industrial Revolution triggered a continuous flow of landless peasants to burgeoning manufacturing centers. In these cases, however, the flow into cities took place entirely within national boundaries.

In the United States, by contrast, the migrants came from other countries, providing a unique source of strength. Immigration from the early part of the seventeenth century through 1772 enabled the colonies to achieve the economic base and the self-reliance necessary to revolt against the British Crown. From the 1830s to the 1920s, more than thirty-five million people landed on our shores. Many of these immigrants, particularly the young men, returned to their native lands, but many others remained. They and their descendants are thought to have accounted for fully one-half of total U.S. population growth between independence and 1920.[2] They were highly concentrated in northern cities. Indeed, as those cities became more and more industrialized, they grew increasingly dependent on a continuing flow of immigrants to expand their industrial base and replace those middle-income families who were leaving. The presence of the newcomers enabled northern cities to grow considerably faster than either rural areas or cities in other regions.

The halt in immigration brought about by the restrictive legislation of the 1920s initially had few adverse effects, perhaps because the 1930s were a time of general economic stagnation. After World War II, however, the impact on our northern cities became quite noticeable. In explaining why those cities underwent such a precipitous decline, analysts commonly point to the replacement of aging city plants by new factories elsewhere. The loss of city jobs, the argument goes, induced outmigration as workers followed jobs to their new locations. A less appreciated, but equally if not more important, explanation for the decline is the drop in immigration levels after 1924. Until the 1930s, immigrants replaced natives leaving the congested urban core. The post–World War II boom in suburban residential construction, fueled by rising income, allowed the middle-class exodus that was slowed by depression and war to resume. This time, however, there were few immigrants to take their place.

Aggregate national statistics mask the vast economic and social impact that mass immigration has had on city and country, North and South. This chapter examines the effects of changing levels of immigration on the growth of the nation's cities and on regional economic development.

The Regional Consequences of Unrestricted Entry

Young immigrants who crowded into city tenements supplied the cheap labor that accelerated industrialization, a process that expanded output and created substantial wealth for the established families, particularly urban property owners who traced back their American roots for several generations. However, the mostly rural South, where one out of every three Americans—one-third of them black—lived during the antebellum period, the rural Midwest, and the western territories were only marginally affected by the increased concentration of production, income, and wealth in northern cities. The rising economic dominance of cities no doubt contributed to the latent antipathy of the rural majority toward large urban concentrations and their seemingly unassimilated foreign-born residents. This antipathy was abetted by regional differences in wealth and culture, to which the foreign-born influx contributed. Deeply rooted distrust of urban life and the resentment of economic disparities between cities and rural areas were mirrored in the views of southern congressional delegates toward immigrants.

Urban-rural disparities were minor in the early years of the Republic. At the start of the nineteenth century, America was a largely agrarian nation. Only 3 percent of the population lived in cities. The largest of these, Philadelphia, had barely seventy thousand inhabitants. The pace of urbanization and economic growth remained slow through the first two decades of the century. To the extent that growth occurred, immigrants played only a minor role, for war, blockades, and restrictions on emigration in Europe prevented many from coming here. Population increase in cities was due mainly to high birthrates and falling death rates among native families. Immigration accelerated sharply during the mid-1830s, marking the start of the first wave. Most of the new arrivals settled in northern coastal cities, especially Boston and New York. Although the nation remained predominantly rural—in the 1820s, only one of every twelve persons lived in cities—massive immigration caused a surge in urban population. In 1850, the first year for which figures are available, 14 percent of the U.S. population outside the South was foreign-born; in large cities, however, immigrants accounted for 39 percent of all residents. Not coincidentally, industrial production soared and internal trade increased tenfold during the 1840s and 1850s.

The role of immigrants during this period is well summarized by the economist Douglas North: "In a society where the problem of relative labor scarcity was augmented by aspirations of the native born for independent employment, the supply of European labor provided a work force ready and willing to enter industrial employment."[3] Industrialization developed in northern cities primarily because of ready access to natural resources like iron ore and to the ports through which iron and other goods could be shipped. But labor was not readily available. Deteriorating economic conditions that plagued Ireland and Germany following the Napoleonic wars proved to be fortuitous for this nation. Two million

Irish, their plight worsened by the potato famine, came to the United States over the course of three decades. They were mostly unskilled and were willing to take any job, however harsh the working conditions. The Irish performed the backbreaking labor needed to build canals, railroads, and bridges across the nation. But the majority of men settled in northeastern cities and found jobs in factories, while women worked as housekeepers and maids. In Boston (and later other cities), revolutionary changes in production were made possible by low wages paid to the Irish masses who settled in the area during the 1840s.[4] Meanwhile, newcomers from Great Britain—the heart of the Industrial Revolution—poured in with their various skills. Just as Irish laborers made up the commoners of the American work force, so English and Scottish artisans formed its aristocracy. Nearly every industry begun in the United States prior to 1840 was "fertilized" by British skills.[5]

Native ingenuity, together with large-scale investment (both domestic and foreign), accelerated the growth of heavy industry. Newly realized economies of scale helped lower prices, which stimulated consumer demand. That, in turn, created new unskilled jobs, which were taken primarily by immigrants. The growing presence of immigrant households lifted population density in the Northeast, giving rise to a burgeoning market for consumer goods. Massive immigration provided a large enough population base to enable northeastern industry to thrive on the basis of domestic sales, without reliance on exports. By contrast, the South and West remained sparsely populated. Lacking an industrial infrastructure, these regions were dependent on the North for manufactured products and capital.

Within four decades following the Civil War, the enormous growth in population, labor force, and markets converted an essentially agrarian society to an industrial one to an extent that other nations took a century to achieve. Job opportunities in large northern cities mushroomed, attracting peasants, artisans, and adventurers from European towns and villages.

The American consumer market, unhampered by national boundaries that restricted trade within Europe, reached seventy-six million by the end of the nineteenth century, when the United States had overtaken England and Germany as the world's leading economic power. This remarkable progress was due to a number of favorable circumstances: the presence of abundant natural resources, striking

advances in technology, an expanding domestic market, political stability that attracted foreign capital, and the availability of almost unlimited manpower. Young workers from Southern, Eastern, and Central Europe
poured into this country, forming the second wave of mass immigration.
In 1920, when the tide began to ebb, 40 percent of white residents in the
North were either foreign-born or had both parents born overseas.

Thanks in no small part to the European influx, the population of the
United States grew from 17 million in 1840 to 106 million in 1910.
(While the country had fewer people than Great Britain at the start of
this period, it had well over twice as many at the end.) The growth was
most striking in the cities of the Northeast and Midwest. New York City
grew from 200,000 residents in 1830 to more than 1 million in 1860, reaching almost 7 million in the late 1920s when immigration constraints came
into effect. Chicago's growth was equally spectacular. The relationship
between urban economic growth and immigration is evident from the
proportion of the labor force in these cities that was foreign born.

At the start of the twentieth century, one-half of all male workers, and
only a slightly lower proportion of all female workers, in New York
City and Chicago—the nation's two largest cities—were immigrants.
Workers with native parents constituted only a small minority of the
New York work force, a fact that suggests not only a massive immigrant
flow into the city in preceding decades but also a sizable outward flow
of native households to the suburbs and the West. Other cities showed
the same pattern. In Detroit, almost half of all male workers were
immigrants; in St. Paul, one-third.

Between 1900 and 1920, four of five aliens at the time of entry to the
United States were between the ages of fourteen and forty-five, and therefore apt to join the labor force. By comparison, less than half of the native
population was in its prime working years. The typical native worker
at the turn of the century had two dependents; the immigrant, one or
none. Over time, of course, this gap narrowed, but it never closed
entirely.

On the Continent, urban population growth during the nineteenth
century was fed not only by high birthrates but by migration from
rural areas. Moreover, rural migrants consisted primarily of families,
whereas more than 60 percent of the emigrants from Europe were
men, most of them of working age. Because children under the age of
fourteen never accounted for more than one of every eight that took the

transatlantic journey, childbearing costs were largely absorbed by the nations from which the aliens came. Most of those who arrived in the twentieth century were healthy; those suffering from physical or mental defects deemed to limit their ability to become self-sufficient were refused entry. Ellis Island was the end of their journey to the United States.

The nation's cities became importers of human capital—adaptable persons willing and able to work from the day they set foot on the pavements of Boston, New York, or Philadelphia. But American cities were more than large concentrations of polyglot humanity crowded into slums. Chicago and New York became highly efficient economic units that surpassed their European counterparts in the production of goods and generation of income. The ease with which American cities outperformed those in other nations reflects both differences in migration patterns and a more rapid absorption of technology. The immigrant presence had a profound impact on several industries in these cities. Before the last decade of the nineteenth century, the United States, following Britain's example, imported much of its apparel goods from low-wage nations. With the sudden availability in the 1890s of Eastern and Southern European labor at wages below the native worker level, the cost of production was reduced substantially. This resulted in American-made clothing replacing imported goods.[6]

Technology had two distinct but interrelated effects on the nation's productivity. Technological progress in areas such as construction, transportation and sanitation enabled cities to house immigrants at high densities. Concurrently, the presence of a large and concentrated immigrant labor force provided factory owners with the opportunity to introduce more efficient mass production methods and reap economies of scale. Brinley Thomas commented, "The great injection of cheap labor from Southern and Eastern Europe after the turn of the century . . . enabled the country [the United States] to take maximum advantage of the technological innovations of that time, establishing the basis for its economic power."[7]

Among the earlier innovations quickly applied in Manhattan and Chicago were steel-frame structures. The first such building, a five-story factory in New York City, erected in 1849, reduced the danger of fire. Combined with a safe elevator, first installed by Otis nine years later, again in New York, this allowed for high-rise construction, a prerequisite for employing a large labor force within a small land area. With elevators facilitating vertical movement in high-rise buildings, these structures became concentrated in the downtown business districts from which streetcars radiated.

The introduction of rail enabled the work force to be distributed over a large geographic area and to commute to the urban core. The expansion of outlying residential areas helped reduce the terrible over-crowding within the inner city. New immigrants tended to live in tenements near factories, but native workers with higher earnings moved to the periphery.

The most striking relationship between economic growth and immigration is seen in income and wealth comparisons. By the 1920s, per capita income in the United States was the highest of any industrial country, but considerable internal disparities were present. In the ten most affluent states in 1920, one of every four residents was an immigrant (see Table 3-1). All but two of these states (Nevada and Wyoming) had an industrial base. The wealthy industrial states, which included Connecticut, Illinois, Massachusetts, New Jersey, and New York, attracted a high proportion of the second wave of Eastern and Southern European immigrants who became factory workers. New immigrants gravitated to states with high income, and surprisingly these states, after accepting poor immigrants, not only maintained their relatively prosperous position but in many cases improved it. New York State, which absorbed more immigrants than any other, increased its per capita income 3.7 times between 1880 and 1920. In 1880, the state ranked ninth in income; four decades later it led all states. Illinois, the state with the third-highest number of immigrants, increased its income by a factor of four and improved its ranking among states from fifteenth to seventh within the same period. Overall, the presence of foreign-born individuals correlated positively with higher income. Living standards for immigrants themselves also began to rise, benefiting from what might be called an ethnic agglomeration effect: the more members of an ethnic group gravitated to a city, the more job opportunities they created for members of that group. For example, once the number of Irish in a city reached a critical mass, their political influence became significant. Once this group gained control of Tammany Hall in New York, the city police department became almost all Irish. The availability of patronage jobs attracted still more Irish immigrants, further strengthening their political hold on the city. Similarly, the presence of Jewish- and Italian-owned shops and small factories in New York and other large cities created employment opportunities that did not exist in smaller communities for members of these groups.

By the turn of the century, most jobs taken by Jewish immigrants were provided by Jewish entrepreneurs. As described by one researcher, "The symbiosis of Jewish employers and employees created a curious interdependence marked by low wages, very low search costs, and low barriers to entry."[8] The clothing industry was concentrated in cities with large Jewish and Italian immigration,which induced additional alien settlement. Their presence created a highly efficient and competitive industry, developing a mass market for apparel goods across the country. The potential for employment, combined with the apparent difficulty immigrants faced breaking into the labor force in smaller cities, encouraged immigrant concentrations in such urban centers as New York, Philadelphia, and Chicago.[9]

The presence of larger ethnic enclaves—neighborhoods whose residents shared a common language or heritage—also enhanced the economic prospects for immigrant professionals. Italian-speaking

Table 3-1

Characteristics of States with the Highest and Lowest Per Capita Income, 1920

	Average Per Capita Income	% of all U.S. Immigrants	% of Population Immigrants	% of Population Black	% of Population Urbanized
10 Highest-Income States[a]	$882	53.4	23.7	2.0	76.3
Ten Lowest-Income States[b]	357	1.4	1.0	32.9	21.6
U.S. Average	650	—	13.0	9.9	51.2

Sources: Income statistics derived from Series C47, *Long-Term Economic Growth, 1860–1965*, U.S. Department of Commerce, 1966. Other data derived from the Bureau of the Census.

[a] In descending order, 1920: New York, California, Massachusetts, Nevada, Wyoming, Rhode Island, Illinois, New Jersey, Connecticut, Washington.

[b] In ascending order, 1920: Mississippi, Alabama, Arkansas, South Carolina, Georgia, North Carolina, Tennessee, Kentucky, Louisiana, Virginia.

physicians had no difficulty attracting patients in New York, and Polish-speaking lawyers found abundant clients in Detroit. The enclaves evolved into ethnic labor markets, in which immigrants established their own stores and personal services. These enterprises provided employment to the newest immigrants who spoke no English. As we will see in a later chapter, this phenomenon is again evident in recent times.

The striking economic and social effects of immigrant workers in the urban North become more apparent in contrast to the plantation-dominated South. The urbanization and industrialization that altered the face of the Northeast and Midwest during the first half of the 1800s spread little influence through most southern states. Of the 4 million foreign-born people living in the United States in 1860, only 500,000 lived in slave states (mostly in the border states of Missouri and Maryland). The lack of immigration to the Deep South prior to the Civil War has been linked by historians to both antislavery sentiment among aliens and the southern perception that immigrants were "white slaves" who could not be assimilated into the national mainstream. Yet many Germans who identified with the abolitionist cause flocked to slaveholding states, particularly Kentucky, Missouri, and Texas. Meanwhile, the Irish, although typically opposed or indifferent to abolition, rarely settled in the South. This suggests there were more causes for the regional imbalance than simply the slavery issue.

In fact, the main drawback discouraging unskilled immigrants from settling in the South was not the presence of slavery but the lack of job opportunities. Most of the Irish who entered this country, despite their rural background, had only rudimentary knowledge of farming and almost no capital. In the South, they could not have effectively competed for jobs with black slaves, and they lacked the wherewithal to become planters or shopkeepers. Germans, on the other hand, were typically independent farmers in their native land and frequently had the mechanical skills or capital needed to find a niche in the South.

The South's dearth of immigrants, together with its dependence on a slave-labor plantation economy, slowed the region's industrial development and urbanization. In 1810, Charleston, with 24,000 inhabitants, ranked fifth in the nation in population; a century later, with only 59,000 residents it did not rank even in the top one hundred. At the start of the Civil War, New Orleans was the only southern city that ranked among the nation's fifteen largest. That ranking was due, in part, to the presence of many foreign-born residents; a point of entry for many immigrants, the "Queen of the South" had substantially more of them than the combined total of the next five largest southern cities.

The South's unattractiveness to immigrants had significant demographic and, ultimately, political effects. In 1830, two of every five Americans lived in the South. By 1860, that ratio had dropped to one in three, and only one in five white Americans lived in the South. The consequences of this growing imbalance became evident during the Civil War, at a time when over 35 percent of the adult males in the North were foreign born. When Lincoln issued a call for volunteers for the Union army, immigrants enlisted in heroic numbers. Although exact figures have never been established, it is estimated that as many as one-third of all northern soldiers and one-half of all workers in northern factories were immigrants. The sizable, strongly abolitionist German immigrant population helped slave-owning Missouri remain in the Union. Some 200,000 German-born Americans fought for the North. So did an estimated 145,000 to 170,000 Irish-born soldiers; the Union army even had all-Irish regiments, some of which distinguished themselves in combat. Of 583 Union commanders, 45 were born overseas—an impressive sum given lingering nativist sentiment.

Northern leaders were well aware of the importance of immigrants to the Union effort. In 1863, the U.S. Consul in London employed a full-time agent to promote immigration. With the war draining northern factories of young men, Congress passed the Act to Encourage Immigration, enacted on July 4, 1864. Foreigners without adequate funds could pledge to repay their fares from the wages they would earn after arriving. Although relatively few took advantage of the pledge contract (most were able to pay their fares), the congressional action underscored the importance attached to immigrants during the war. When ships unloaded at Castle Gardens at the edge of New York Harbor, recruiting officers were standing by to offer the new immigrants inducements to enlist.[10]

The contribution of immigrants to the Union cause was appreciated by contemporary observers. One conservative Democratic party leader stated in 1861 that "at the first shot at our flag, we find the foreign-born rising, if possible, with more enthusiasm and patriotic self-devotion to defend the Republic than our own citizens."[11] Some later commentators even argued that immigrants were the decisive force in determining the outcome of the war. The Nobel laureate Simon Kuznets, in a clear understatement, concluded that immigration, in addition to promoting rapid growth, had noneconomic consequences as well. Immigrants, Kuznets states, helped tilt the balance of power against the slave-holding South.[12] Most military historians agree that the success of the North owed not to the quality of its military commanders or the combat capabilities of its soldiers but rather to the sheer quantity of the men and material at its disposal. Had the manpower resources of the two sides been more evenly matched, the superior military leadership of the southern forces could well have prevented a Union victory. At a minimum, had the North been unable to draw on immigrant manpower, the conflict would surely have been more protracted.

Immigrants were not totally absent in the South. The Irish constituted the largest foreign-born contingent on the Confederate side, but their number came to fewer than forty thousand. The few non-Irish immigrants contributed disproportionately to the southern cause. The Confederate cabinet included three Jews, and several German-born officers held important command positions. Outstanding individual contributions aside, however, the role of immigrants in the southern cause was predictably minor.

After the Civil War, the South continued to lag economically behind the rest of the nation. Total income during the 1920s in New York State —with 10 percent of the nation's population—exceeded that of all southern states combined (with the exception of Maryland). One reason was that blacks, the nation's poorest racial/ethnic group, continued to be concentrated in the rural South (more than one of every three southern residents in 1920). The most affluent states—New York, California, Connecticut, Delaware, Illinois, and New Jersey—included fewer than 600,000 blacks. A second and related factor was the dominance of a relatively unproductive agricultural economy. Almost four out of five southerners, both black and white, continued to live in rural areas in the early decades of the twentieth century, while most northerners lived in urban areas. Damage incurred during the war was another reason southern income fell in comparison to other regions, as was a precipitous drop in the demand for cotton, causing prices to tumble. Output declined as former slaves, observing little improvement from their pre-war conditions, worked fewer hours or withdrew from the labor market altogether. Because blacks made up at least one-third of the work force, this development adversely affected other economic sectors as well.

Poor economic conditions further decreased the South's appeal to new European arrivals. Immigration to the South, already slight, slowed to a trickle in the postbellum period. Continued, steady immigration to the North further widened the gulf between the regions. According to the historian Robert L. Brandfon, the lack of immigrants meant that "the South remained a second-class section [of the country], geared to the decisions of Northeast capitalists."[13] Brandfon was restating the position of southern business leaders during the post-Reconstruction era— that immigrants were needed to industrialize the South. In the absence of an industrial base, the region could not generate sufficient capital to lessen its dependence on northern institutions.

Efforts by forward-looking businessmen to recruit a share of nonnative labor were deflected by the two traditional roadblocks to settlement in the South: the limited economic opportunities that the region had to offer and the continued unwillingness of southerners to tolerate foreigners. There is no question that the demand for unskilled labor in the South was limited. Not only did blacks perform most unskilled jobs, but wages for both whites and blacks were low by northern standards. The hourly rates in southern mills—which employed only whites—were about 30 percent lower than the wages prevailing in New England for similar work, even though living costs were comparable. The disparity in wages for unskilled work was even greater. In addition, the continued concentration of capital in agriculture, the poor state of transportation, and the lack of skilled labor continued to limit industrial growth until the early part of the twentieth century.

However, the low level of wages and lack of job openings cannot fully explain the slow pace of postbellum immigration. Many immigrants came to America expressly to escape religious intolerance and class prejudice, but the South could only offer a history of racial strife. As for white southerners, most resented foreigners, especially those considered racially mixed. Though some Italians came to work on southern plantations in the 1890s, they met great hostility, and a number of them were lynched. Southern employers also considered immigrant workers problematic. In the words of one southern historian, "Immigrant labor proved too intractable for southerners used to a more malleable labor force."[14]

There were exceptions. Immigrants who found their way to the growing cities of Atlanta and Richmond were generally well received.

In 1870, for instance, the latter had some eleven thousand whites, slightly fewer blacks, and about one thousand foreign-born residents. Both cities offered native and immigrant workers considerable opportunities for job advancement. In contrast to northern cities, very few immigrants in the South held bottom-rung jobs because these were generally reserved for blacks. Aliens were pushed into work not accessible to blacks—as tradesmen, mechanics, or even peddlers. Because the energies of immigrants were channeled into occupations with considerable potential for advancement, antiblack bias actually helped immigrants to advance economically.

Some of the new arrivals to the South, particularly Jews of German descent, became leading merchants; the Irish became involved in local politics; and Germans advanced in industry. These minorities were accepted at least as readily as in the North, and they prospered. Outside the few urban centers however, the role of immigrants in the postbellum period remained insubstantial.

The economic gap between the industrial North and agrarian South remained large well into the new century. In 1920, true to the pattern evident since the end of the Civil War, the ten states with the lowest per capita income were all in the Old South (see Table 3-1). Generally speaking, the population of these southern states was poor, rural, overwhelmingly native, and disproportionately black. The region accounted for less than 1.4 percent of the nation's foreign-born population but more than 77 percent of its blacks.

The interregional income gap began to narrow only with the start of World War I. Until then, the surplus of black rural laborers working at minimal wages encouraged the South to maintain its agrarian economy at the expense of industrial development. Despite their abject poverty, few blacks moved to northern cities between 1870 and 1910, primarily because immigrants were available there to serve in such menial jobs as day laborers and servants. With the outbreak of World War I, however, European immigration to northern cities slowed. Northern industrialists, searching for an alternative labor supply, actively encouraged black migration from the rural South. The overdue outmigration of poverty-stricken southerners, together with stepped-up federal assistance to the South—beginning with the public works programs of the New Deal—and successful efforts to attract industry, had a positive effect. The South, considered the nation's poorhouse in the 1930s, began to catch up economically with the rest of the nation.

It is difficult to assess precisely the extent to which a more tolerant attitude among southerners after the Civil War would have attracted more immigrants and accelerated the pace of industrial development and urbanization. A larger influx of immigrants would undeniably have quickened the South's economic growth, but the racial status quo could have been upset by their entry. The southerner's perception of immigrants during this period cannot be isolated from the uneasy black-white relations in the South. In the absence of fundamental changes in racial attitudes (which were not in evidence for a century following the Civil War), large-scale immigration was not feasible.

The West was far more open to immigration than the South, although the increasing alien presence provoked outbursts of nativist hostility even amid the wide-open space. The development of the West was aided both by direct immigration and secondary movement of those displaced by immigrants in the East and Midwest. Well over half of all foreigners who came to the region gravitated to California. Chinese workers came first in response to labor shortages following the discovery of gold. Japanese, Filipinos, and smaller groups of other Asians arrived in the wake of the Chinese Exclusion Act, which exacerbated chronic labor shortages in the state.

The flow of Mexicans northward accelerated in the first decades of the twentieth century as conditions in their homeland deteriorated. The movement across the border numerically strengthened the already well-established Hispanic population. Most Mexicans in the Southwest worked in agriculture, but in California they held 19 percent of all industrial jobs.[15] Wages of Mexicans, as with earnings of foreign-born workers in the East, were below the earnings of native whites with similar skills. Their low pay and high productivity evoked favorable employer responses to a survey taken by the state of California; the majority of respondents were sufficiently impressed by Mexicans to rank these workers higher than whites or Japanese.

Eastern and Southern European immigrants were also attracted to California, although most did not come directly. Rather, the majority settled first in eastern cities, acquiring language and other skills. These immigrants expanded agriculture and contributed to the commercial development of what was to become, within a few decades, the most populous state in the nation. European-born Jews figured prominently in transferring the movie industry to the West Coast. By the 1920s, Los

Angeles, with over one-fifth of its population foreign born, and San Francisco, with nearly a third of its residents from other nations, became the thriving commercial centers of the West.[16]

Immigrants also contributed to western growth indirectly. Census data indicate a strong correlation between the number of new immigrants in a state and outmigration among the native population. The reasons for this are not well established, but at least one analysis can be offered: Unskilled native workers, concerned with competition from unskilled aliens in the labor market, believed that greater job opportunities were present in the western territories. The better-trained and professional workers had few such concerns, however; in fact, they would benefit by an immigrant presence that frequently complemented their skills and therefore tended to remain. As immigrants settled in eastern cities, less-skilled natives moved westward in search of new opportunities and free land. In the absence of the immigrant surge that encouraged migration to the West in the 1840s, it is unlikely that predominantly Hispanic California and the Southwest would have attracted sufficient population from eastern states to press for rapid absorption into the Union.

Open Immigration and the Well-being of Natives

While it is beyond question that the presence of immigrants in northern cities spurred overall economic expansion, it is not immediately apparent whether all benefited from that growth. Clearly, the immigrants themselves, coming from impoverished nations to a prospering America, bettered their own economic lot. And businessmen profited from the cheap labor that immigrants provided. But what about other, less well-off native inhabitants? Throughout the latter part of the nineteenth century and the first part of the twentieth, many Americans remained skeptical about the benefits they derived from immigration. Labor organizations believed that immigrants served primarily to keep wages low. The immigrant flow also concerned black leaders, who feared that the modest strides black workers were making in the North would be reversed and job opportunities for blacks in the South would be curtailed.

However, an examination of changes in per capita income during the century of rapid immigration (1830–1930) supports the position that the influx also improved the economic standing of native workers.

From 1800 to 1820, a time of negligible immigration, per capita income growth averaged only 0.5 percent per year. Between 1830 and 1860, a period associated with the first wave of mass immigration, the per capita average grew almost 2 percent annually.

Income growth rates were attributable to a higher percentage of the total population working, rising industrial productivity, and gains in agricultural production. Despite the huge inpouring of unskilled labor from abroad, the real earnings of all unskilled urban workers rose by 62 percent between 1820 and 1860.[17] The predominantly native skilled workers experienced an even higher growth rate in real earnings. The nation's ability to absorb several million aliens, including many from rural regions, into an industrializing economy and to sustain a rising living standard is impressive. The pattern of steep gains in income was evident again between 1872 and 1913. During this period, which roughly corresponds with the second major immigration wave, per capita income rose 2.5 times, and output per worker rose almost as rapidly.

It is worthwhile to compare the growth in output per worker in the United States with that in Great Britain and Germany, two nations at a similar level of technological development. By the start of World War I, the average American worker was producing 2.2 times as much as a counterpart was turning out in 1870; the German worker was producing twice as much; and the British laborer, only 1.6 times. The rise in American living standards was credited both to a rapidly growing labor force and to higher productivity. That is, industry was able to absorb unskilled immigrant workers and still sustain productivity gains that exceeded those of other nations with few immigrants.

A considerable part of the rise in per capita income can be attributed directly to the immigrant inflow because, as noted earlier, a high proportion of all immigrants were gainfully employed. For example, more than two-fifths of the total immigrant population in New York City in 1855 worked—a percentage not reached by the nonimmigrant population even a century later. From 1870 to 1910, the aggregate labor participation rate in American cities rose from 36.2 percent to 45.4 percent, primarily the result of young, foreign-born workers entering the labor force. Typically, in a city where 30 percent of the population was foreign born, immigrants accounted for about 45 percent of the work force.

The impact of immigration on income has been quantified by the economist Peter J. Hill, who finds that per capita income of native residents living in 1910 would have declined by up to 14 percent in the absence of immigration.[18] This analysis takes into account differences in labor participation and skill levels between immigrant and native-born residents. The decline, the author notes, could have been yet more severe. For example, the study assumes that immigrants had an adverse effect on production because their skills were below average. It would have been natural to expect productivity to drop with the absorption of presumably unskilled immigrant workers into the labor force. Rapid gains in output per worker would not be expected if most immigrants lacked skills or the ability to learn quickly. However, by the turn of the century, workers in large, immigrant-laden cities, particularly New York, were at least as productive as in other locales not inundated with immigrants. A likely explanation is that Eastern and Southern Europeans either brought with them or quickly acquired the skills needed in the vast and extremely productive New York garment industry and the Chicago meat-packing plants.

In New England industries, productivity rates in factories dominated by immigrants grew more rapidly than those in similar industries employing few foreign-born workers. Given that employees elsewhere had access to the same technology, the data suggest output per immigrant worker was higher. Of course, it would be difficult to control for all factors that affect productivity, but data generally support the contention that a foreign-born worker employed in the United States for a few years and a native worker were equally productive. But since a higher proportion of immigrants held jobs, their presence raised output and income.

Until the Great Depression, the majority of immigrants to the United States were male, and 80 percent were more than fourteen years old. But for every age group and for both sexes, as shown in Table 3-2, immigrants' labor participation rates in the 1890s were higher than those of native workers. The most pronounced differences were found among young workers; three times as many immigrant women between the ages of fifteen and twenty-four worked as did those with native-born white parents. The pattern glimpsed in the 1890s continued for decades. In 1930, as recent immigrants became integrated into the labor force, 47 percent of all native-born whites over the age of ten were gainfully employed. The corresponding figure for the foreign born was 56 percent. Immigrant employment rates exceeded those of native whites in every state.[19] With virtually all foreign-born adult males working, and their share of the industrial work force higher than other groups, the immigrant contribution to the national economy remained disproportionate to their numbers. The contribution of the foreign born was strengthened over time as their skills improved. By 1930, immigrants were more likely to be semiskilled and skilled than their predecessors working in the late nineteenth century.

The flow of young male workers (Italians, Slavs, and others) to the United States responded to an upswing in labor demand during periods of economic expansion, and this response itself generated additional development. That the well-being of natives correlated with the size of the resident immigrant labor force was suggested in Table 3-1, which juxtaposed state income and foreign-born population. But these statistics do not fully capture the linkage between urban income and immigration, as most of those born overseas lived in large cities. One of three residents of New York's three largest cities in 1920 was an immigrant; outside these cities, one of seven. Chicago's population was 30 percent foreign born; in the rest of Illinois the figure was closer to 10 percent. Income in these cities was higher than in less-urbanized areas with fewer immigrants.

So far, our discussion has focused on the economic effects of immigrants as industrial workers, with good reasons, since immigrants left their deepest imprint in manufacturing. From a practical standpoint, most of the available statistics relate to this sector. But immigrants had

Table 3-2

Labor Participation Rates by Age and Sex, 1890

Age	Native White, of Native Parents		Foreign-Born	
	Percent Male	Percent Female	Percent Male	Percent Female
15 to 19	50	16	82	59
20 to 24	89	20	97	45
25 to 34	97	11	98	20
35 to 44	96	10	97	11

Source: U.S. Department of Commerce, Bureau of the Census, *1890 Census of Population*

other positive, if subtle, effects on living standards. To distribute mass-produced consumer goods, a new class of immigrant merchants developed such innovations as department stores and, in rural areas, catalog sales, helping to increase competition and lower prices. New York remained the center of the nation's retail trade, but Jewish immigrant families became merchants in Boston, Richmond, and Phoenix. In Chicago and smaller midwestern cities, Greeks set up small candy stores and restaurants. By the end of the nineteenth century, Italians dominated not only New York's construction industry but also its entire fruit business, from wholesale produce to retail outlets. On the West Coast, Japanese entrepreneurs opened small businesses in ethnic neighborhoods.[20] Even before World War I, white merchants in Los Angeles were complaining that grocery stores, barber shops, and neighborhood restaurants were being taken over by the Japanese.

Despite the low wages paid to them in their entry jobs, immigrants were able to accumulate capital, an essential ingredient in sustaining a high level of economic expansion. Because many immigrants were without dependents, they had high propensities to save. Those with families were able to accumulate capital largely because there were typically two or more earners in the household. While some aliens returned with bulging pockets to their native lands, most remained. According to one analysis, by the year 1912 immigrants accounted for between 13 percent and 42 percent of all capital accumulation in the United States.[21] Thus, immigrants provided not only human capital—labor and skills—but also badly needed investment and business start-ups. Taken together, these contributions helped sustain economic expansion for a century.

At the same time, immigration probably brought about a more unequal distribution of wealth, particularly in the cities. During the eighteenth and early nineteenth centuries, the northern economy, dominated by small independent farmers, enjoyed a relatively even distribution of income, especially in contrast with the slave-driven plantation economy of the South, which had a rigid class structure. As northern towns grew and became bustling cities, however, wealth became more concentrated. In part, this has been attributed to the surge of low-paid immigrants.

Tax records for Boston and Brooklyn from the late 1830s and 1840s show a growing concentration of wealth in these urban areas. As the first mass wave of immigration subsided, the top 1 percent in Boston had more wealth than half a century earlier. While the community as a whole grew more affluent, the wealthy got richer more quickly. In 1840, the nation's forty thousand richest families owned about 7 percent of the total wealth; a half century later that figure had increased to about 17 percent.[22] To put it another way, in the first decade of the nineteenth century, 1 percent of all U.S. families controlled about one-fifth of the wealth; by the end of the century, their share had increased to between 26 percent and 31 percent.[23] The bottom four-fifths of the population held only 5 percent of the nation's wealth at the turn of the century.

Data on wealth by place of birth also implicate immigration in terms of disparities in wealth. Assets tend to accumulate from one generation to another, especially in the case of land, which in early America was a major form of wealth. One would expect wealth to be concentrated among families whose roots in America could be traced to the eighteenth century or earlier. In 1850, only 25 percent of all foreign-born males owned property, compared to 45 percent of native-born males.

During the next two decades, a period of relatively low immigration, the ownership gap between the two groups was reduced. Nonetheless, the average value of property owned by immigrants in 1870 was only $1,204, compared with $1,714 for the native-born. Probably because the Irish possessed the fewest skills, their average wealth ($965) was substantially below that of the more skilled English immigrants ($1,555).[24]

The presence of immigrants from Southern and Eastern Europe added to the wealth and profits of industrialists. During the 1890–1910 period, these immigrants received wages about 10 percent lower than those of their counterparts from Northern and Western Europe. Some researchers contend that these lower wages reflected lower productivity among the "less desirable" Southern and Eastern European immigrants, but most believe that they were simply "exploited"—that is, paid a lower wage for the same work.[25] Part of the variation in wages among ethnic groups could be explained by differences in length of residence, literacy, and fluency in English. Thus, such non-English-speaking groups as Italians and Poles initially received lower wages than Irish and Scots, but the differential decreased as length of stay in the United States increased.[26] But whatever the explanation for wage disparities, they resulted in huge profits for industry, which became increasingly concentrated after 1870.

Income statistics are less available than records of wealth because a tax on income was not levied until the 1860s and was discontinued within a decade, not to be reintroduced until World War I. Nevertheless, statistics from the 1860s suggest income inequalities of almost the same magnitude as wealth disparities in New York, Philadelphia, and Cleveland.

Immigration had an important effect on the distribution of income. This was most apparent in the widening gap in earnings between skilled and unskilled workers. Immigrants—most of them unskilled—could only find work in dangerous, dirty, and odorous occupations. These jobs paid little, and the constant tide of newcomers ready to take them ensured that wages would remain low. European immigrants monopolized jobs in fertilizer plants and the slaughterhouses of Chicago. In California, Mexicans dominated the canneries. There was, of course, no minimum wage during the period of mass immigration.

Meanwhile, the economic expansion that immigrants helped fuel increased the demand for skilled labor, professionals, and clerical workers—positions that were filled largely by native-born workers. At the start of the twentieth century, most high-status positions—engineers, lawyers, bankers, and brokers—were reserved for "old stock" Americans. New York City had a sizable population of foreign-born professionals, but even there the high-earnings jobs went mostly to natives with native parents. Given that immigrant women represented a majority of females employed in New York, one would expect foreign-born individuals to be heavily represented in such female-dominated fields as stenography and teaching, but, in fact, native women accounted for almost four of every five such jobs; they also held 77 percent of all female sales positions. Most immigrant women became servants or clothing factory workers, for which they were paid very poorly.

As noted earlier, the flood of immigrants into the northeastern cities appears to have caused many native unskilled workers to move west, where periodic gold and silver rushes sent wages for manual labor soaring. The cost of travel across the continent, however, meant that few European immigrants ventured to the frontier and beyond. Although some newcomers—mostly Germans, Czechs, and Scandinavians—settled on midwestern farms, their numbers remained small. Western lands were being opened and touted by the railroads as territories with boundless opportunities. Vast new reaches of western ranch and farmland produced a major spurt in food production. This westward movement was financed from profits generated by northern industries with cheap immigrant labor. Meanwhile, in the northern cities, wages for unskilled work did rise as the national economy grew, but earnings for the mostly native skilled workers increased more rapidly. In addition, native workers who elected not to move west had far more opportunities than the foreign-born to advance as supervisors, inspectors, and foremen.

A paradox developed. Because the demand for farm products—food and the raw materials for clothing—rises roughly in proportion to population, the prices for such products should have risen as the number of immigrants climbed. But the rapid settlement of the western territories—spurred in part by immigration—resulted in such rapid increases in production that supply quickly outstripped demand. During the 1840s, as immigration accelerated, food prices actually fell. Eastern farmers, who lacked the acreage of their western counterparts that encouraged efficiencies of scale, were especially hard hit.

So despite a substantial rise in gross farm output, income disparities between rural and urban areas widened after the Civil War. In the forty years after 1867, farm production rose at an average annual rate of 2.5 percent. However, only a fraction of this growth was due to productivity gains; most was attributable to the cultivation of additional land, available at a very low cost. During periods of rising demand, farmers cultivated virgin land, increasing production and driving prices down. Although total output increased, individual farmers dependent on farm workers did not benefit. As farm workers developed skills, many left to cultivate their own land, contributing to labor shortages.

Only one of five immigrants during the period settled outside cities. This imbalance is shown in labor participation rate differentials between cities and rural areas. In 1870, the proportion of the population working in rural areas was close to the urban average, but within four decades the rural rates fell to 74 percent of the urban level, a result of the high participation rates among immigrants in cities. The concentration of better-paid manufacturing jobs and high labor participation rates among immigrants in cities exacerbated urban-rural income disparities. In 1870, there were 1.8 million manufacturing-related jobs in cities and about the same number in towns and rural areas. With the second wave of immigrants, the number of urban manufacturing jobs grew to 9.1 million forty years later, but outside the cities, total manufacturing employment increased to only 2.6 million by 1910.

The income gap between urban and agricultural areas was further widened by circumstances unrelated to immigration. The value of farm products doubled in the last quarter of the nineteenth century, a respectable gain. But during the same period, the value of nonfarm goods increased fourfold. In Georgia, Mississippi, and South Carolina, farm income that was dependent on exports stagnated, causing the Deep South to fall behind other agricultural areas.

At the time, the link between large-scale immigration and depressed rural incomes was no doubt hard to perceive. The growing pressure for curbs on immigration was not spurred by any concern for the well-being of rural laborers. Few could have anticipated that the new restrictions would cause a profound change in the relation between rural and urban regions as well as in the racial composition of our nation's largest cities.

Immigrants and Blacks

Farmers were not the only group that failed to share in the rise in living standards brought about by the introduction of new technology, the growth in urbanization, and the presence of immigrant labor. Blacks, who remained concentrated in the rural South, did not derive much benefit from urban economic growth.

The level of personal contact between blacks and immigrants was low. Most immigrants did not find southern states hospitable; nor were they eager to compete with blacks for unskilled agricultural jobs. Blacks, too, were not ready to compete with immigrants, and during the period of rapid immigration following the Civil War, relatively few blacks moved to the North.

There were small black communities in northern cities in the antebellum period when the massive Irish influx began. The new immigrants placed some unskilled white workers at a disadvantage. But urban blacks were in a particularly difficult position to compete with the Irish, both before and after the Civil War. To understand their position, it is necessary to examine how immigrant ethnic groups in both the North and South interacted with black workers.

The onset of mass immigration in the 1830s placed blacks at an immediate disadvantage. With the rise of unskilled alien labor, white natives found it relatively easy to gain skilled positions, but native blacks, facing prejudice at every turn, had few such prospects. As Frederick Douglass observed, "Every hour sees the black man elbowed out of employment by some newly arrived immigrant."[27] The Irish, unskilled and seeking any available jobs, posed particularly stiff competition. Whenever blacks and Irish applied for positions as dockworkers and other such jobs, the latter invariably won. Before the swarms of Irish arrived, blacks in New York City commonly worked as bricklayers, waiters, and servants.

But the animosity of blacks toward the Irish seemed deeper than could be explained by economic competition. Because of their adherence to the Democratic party, the Irish were viewed by Douglass as representing the proslavery interests in the North. "The Irish were the most formidable enemies of the Negroes," commented one observer of working conditions during this period.[28]

For their part, the Irish asserted that blacks were a threat to their economic well-being. Antiblack hostility among the Irish populace erupted into violence in the 1830s and 1840s.[29] The fear that southern blacks, freed by the Emancipation Proclamation, would come to New York and take their jobs was the spark that ignited the vicious 1863 antidraft riots. Not unexpectedly, the response of the northern black community to Irish and other immigration was strongly nativist. But their criticism of immigrants was aimed primarily at a native white audience, in the naive belief that their anti-alien stand could bring them equal access to jobs and political rights.[30] By the mid-1860s, however, when one-quarter of New York's population was Irish born, Irish workers dominated many unskilled or lesser-skilled occupations.

Other ethnic groups presented similar problems. In the 1830s, blacks provided most of New York's barbers, but they were quickly supplanted by Germans and other immigrants. In general, blacks were no match for the better-organized, politically powerful white ethnic groups. Still, the number of people affected was relatively small. In the 1850s, there were no more than four thousand gainfully employed blacks in New York, roughly the same number in Philadelphia, and somewhat fewer in Boston. The total northern black urban population, in fact, was less than the annual immigrant flow. Through the end of the Civil War, most blacks remained as slaves on southern plantations.

The emancipation of southern blacks initiated a period of outmigration that lasted for a century. Most headed North, and those who came to the industrial centers of the Midwest during the 1890s encountered "second wave" Eastern and Southern European immigrants, particularly Poles and other Slavs. With the expansion of the region's economy, both blacks and immigrants were drawn to steel mills, mines, and slaughterhouses. Blacks who already held jobs believed that their kind should receive preference over newly arrived, non-English-speaking Slavs.[31] The Polish press, on the other hand, frequently described blacks as "scabs" attempting to steal jobs from immigrant workers (who, in contrast to the blacks, tended to be unionized). Poles, like the Irish before them, quickly came to see blacks as inferior. Polish-language newspapers reported attacks by armed black strikebreakers against Polish workers as evidence of their belief that blacks were the tools of the bosses.

These labor tensions were exacerbated as black communities expanded to the edge of immigrant enclaves. Growing fears that blacks would "invade" ethnic neighborhoods caused occasional riots. Animosity between immigrants and blacks continued well into the twentieth century, particularly in Chicago and Detroit. During World War I, southern blacks entered Chicago in numbers that doubled the city's black population in three years. Most found bottom-rung employment in meatpacking and other plants dominated by unionized immigrants—predominantly Irish and Slavs. The expansion of the overcrowded black ghetto into Irish-dominated neighborhoods, together with the perception of blacks as strike breakers, supplied the sparks that set off Chicago's bloody 1919 race riots.

Tensions also developed between blacks and Italians. In New York, blacks resented the presence of numerous Italian-owned stores in Harlem. (When Mussolini's troops invaded Ethiopia in 1936, local black leaders organized a boycott of Italian businesses.) Problems between the two groups arose even in the South. Some Italians had been lured there in the 1880s by planters dissatisfied with black labor. Small groups of southern Italians established their own communities in the Mississippi Delta, their proximity leading to the first serious immigrant-black conflicts in the South. Southern planters used the specter of immigrant labor to help keep blacks "in line." Although this was never a serious threat, blacks, economically insecure in the best of times, readily believed that Italians would accept lower wages and drearier working conditions than they themselves already had to endure. Echoing such concerns, the black press featured periodic attacks on the "dirty and ignorant sons of Naples." Booker T. Washington, the most respected black spokesman of the period, accused Italians of criminal activity and called the Mafia a threat to the South.[32]

For all the recrimination, the Italian population in the South peaked in 1910 at forty-six thousand, or 0.5 percent of the black population. Southern European immigrants found the working conditions in the region intolerable and the attitudes of white southerners humiliating. Natives, for their part, complained about the inability of Italians to adjust to the southern life-style. The staid southern evangelists were disturbed by the wine drinking, music, and dancing that reminded them of local blacks, and southern biases against the one group were quickly extended to the other.

Relations between blacks and other immigrants, such as Germans and Jews, were more benign because these ethnic groups—especially in the South—were more likely to employ blacks than compete with them for jobs. In Georgia, Mississippi, North Carolina, and South Carolina, one-fifth or more of all male immigrants, with Jews and Germans figuring prominently, were merchants, and many of them employed blacks as laborers.

Although most blacks remained in the rural South following the Civil War, small groups headed West, particularly for California, finding jobs as domestic and laundry workers—only to have new competitors. By 1876, there were eight thousand Chinese working as domestics and in laundries. Black women, who had earlier held a virtual monopoly on these jobs, feared that the Chinese, presumably willing to work at "coolie wages," would replace them (which they did in some cases). White employers, notably the Pullman Corporation, frequently threatened blacks with dismissal and replacement by Asians if they organized.

Job competition was the principal reason for the negative image of the Chinese in the black press, although others seem to have contributed to the animosity. Some blacks resented the economic success of Chinese restaurants and laundries. Although generally held in low esteem by both whites and blacks, the Chinese felt superior to blacks, and mutual distrust continued for decades. But because the black population in California remained small until the 1940s, the number of blacks displaced by Chinese or, in later years, Japanese workers was never substantial.

Black leaders and newspapers in the North and West linked the lack of black advancement to the inflow of low-skilled immigrants. For the most part, however, these views were based on anecdotes and unprovable assumptions. The occupational structure of black labor in northern cities with large immigrant populations varied little from that in cities of the South, where immigrants were scarce. Even a comparison of jobs held by blacks at the turn of the century in northern cities with few immigrants versus cities with large immigrant concentrations fails to uncover real disparities. In both places, blacks were concentrated in the same low-skill, low-wage categories. Everywhere, the same forces were at work—racism and lack of education. One would have expected that, in the absence of alien workers, southern factories would have hired blacks. But the proportion of blacks working in southern factories during the early decades of this century was only slightly higher than that in northern cities. Owners of the textile mills—the largest source of manufacturing jobs in the region—preferred to hire rural white men and women; through the end of World War II, blacks were systematically excluded from such jobs.

Although income statistics on urban blacks during the nineteenth and early twentieth centuries are spotty, data on occupational status obtained by census takers indicate that, economically, blacks progressed more slowly than immigrants. Consider the case of Philadelphia, a city that, by the start of the twentieth century, had a relatively large black population. While nearly half of the city's immigrants and white native workers in 1900 held jobs in manufacturing, three of every four blacks worked as either domestic workers or common (unskilled) laborers. Fewer than one of every three immigrants worked as laborers and domestics in 1900. (By 1930, that ratio had dropped by one-third, while the figure remained the same for blacks.) Only 4 percent of blacks worked as clerks or sales personnel, owners of businesses, or professionals.

The occupational breakdown in other cities followed the Philadelphia distribution. In 1930, fewer than 3 percent of all blacks in cities North and South were professionals. Similarly, the proportion of urban blacks who worked as servants showed little regional variation.[33] It seems safe to conclude, then, that the occupational distribution of blacks in the first three decades of the twentieth century was unaffected by the presence of immigrants.

Immigrants in the nineteenth and early twentieth centuries were far more likely than blacks (or native whites, for that matter) to be involved in the retail business. During the 1920s, there were more immigrants than blacks in business in all states even though foreign-born merchants made up only a small percentage of all merchants in the South. By contrast, almost one-half of the merchants in some northern cities were immigrants. As shown in Table 3-3, the fewest blacks were in business in those states where they made up the largest proportion of the population, that is, in the South. States with the highest percentage of immigrants also

Table 3-3

Rate of Male Retail Merchants per 1,000 Working Males by Race and Birth, 1890, 1910, and 1930

	States with Highest Proportion of Blacks[a]	States with Highest Proportion of Immigrants[b]	Other States	U.S. Average
1890				
Black	3	15	6	—[d]
Native white	34	56	41	—
Immigrant white	148	53	60	—
1910				
Black	5	8	8	—
Native white	36	42	40	—
Immigrant white	163	46	65	—
1930				
Black	3	10	—	6
Native white	43	38	—	30
Immigrant white	124	72	—	63

Source: Tabulations of Census data.

[a] Alabama, Arkansas, Florida, Georgia, Louisiana, Mississippi, North Carolina, South Carolina, Tennessee, Virginia

[b] Only states with considerable black population in 1890 are included here: Illinois, Massachusetts, New York

[c] Maryland, Missouri, Ohio, Texas

[d] Not available

had the highest proportion of blacks in business. The proportion of native whites that were merchants declined in extensively urbanized states with a large immigrant presence between 1890 and 1930. However, the proportion of black merchants, although low, remained three times greater in these urbanized states than in the South.

What explanation is there for the greater propensity for blacks to be in business in northern cities such as New York, where more than one-half of all merchants were immigrants, than in places with few immigrants? For one, the most meager business opportunities for blacks were in the impoverished Deep South, where there was no chance to accrue capital or to receive credit from banks. The rural white population actively discouraged blacks from self-employment. In northern cities, blacks had higher earnings from which to accrue savings, and there were fewer barriers to opening a store, particularly in black neighborhoods. It is noteworthy that black business activity was greater in New York City than in the rest of New York State, and greater in Chicago than in the rest of Illinois. The absence of immigrants in upstate New York and downstate Illinois appears not to have improved the chances of black enterprise.

More difficult to explain is the decline of black business in urban states. But blacks were not alone in their predicament; native-born white merchants were also gradually supplanted by immigrants from Eastern and Southern Europe. In 1890, native- and foreign-born whites in the northern urbanized states were equally likely to be in business. Forty years later, immigrants were twice as likely to be merchants. Many immigrants, frequently lacking the opportunities for advancement available to native workers, sought self-employment as a means to gain economic security and advancement despite the long hours and risks involved.

Sales in black-owned stores, regardless of region, were low. Retail sales in black-owned stores represented only 0.2 percent of total sales nationally by 1940, although black earnings were perhaps 4 percent of earnings overall.[34] Virtually all black purchases were from white merchants, whether native- or foreign-born.

White workers had options that were unavailable to most blacks. They could more easily move to the suburbs, to smaller cities, or to the West—places where competition from immigrants was almost nonexistent. Whites also had much more opportunity to acquire skills through apprenticeship programs. Thus, the economic adversity that immigration posed for unskilled white workers tended to be modest.

To the extent that the century-long period of mass immigration slowed black economic progress, it did so less by directly increasing job competition than by reducing mobility, discouraging migration to northern cities following the Civil War. Southern industrial employers, with a surplus of poor, rural whites, could manage without blacks or immigrants. In the North, employers preferred to hire immigrants rather than blacks, whom they generally held in low esteem. Only acute labor shortages would force northern employers to hire blacks. Had fewer immigrants lived in the North, more factory jobs would have opened for blacks. Even then, however, opportunities for blacks in the North would have remained limited, for a dearth of immigrants would have been accompanied by substantially lower rates of urban economic growth, lessening the demand for workers. As it was, massive black migration to the cities of the North did not begin until World War I, when economic expansion created new jobs just as the flow of immigrants was being curtailed.

The Consequences of Limiting Immigration

So far, this discussion has focused on the economic effects of unconstrained entry—the benefits it brought to northern cities, the regional and income disparities it fostered, the problems it caused for blacks. What about the impact of immigration curbs? Did they bring about the opposite effects, namely, a decline in the economic fortunes of large cities, a narrowing of regional differences and income distribution, and greater opportunities for blacks? In view of the current debate over the economic results of the immigrant tide of the 1980s, the answer to this question is of more than academic interest. Strangely, the vast literature on immigration in America is practically silent on the long-term effects of restricted entry. The respected historian Oscar Handlin was among the few to consider the social and economic consequences of an America with few immigrants.[35]

To assess the economic effects of immigration limits, it is necessary to estimate, however crudely, the level of net immigration that would have occurred in the absence of any statutory constraints. It seems reasonable to assume that the net inflow from Eastern and Southern

Europe (other than the newborn Soviet Union) would have continued at a level no lower than the net annual average between 1901 and 1914. On this basis, the nation would have received a total net inflow of about 6 million aliens during the 1920s, more than two-thirds of them between the ages of sixteen and forty-four. (This is, in fact, a conservative estimate, since the American economy was expanding and the pressures for emigration in Europe were mounting.) The actual net inflow during the 1920s was about 3 million, or half as many.[36] This translates as more than 1.5 million additional workers forgone. Like those who did come, most of these "phantom" immigrants would have settled in the cities of California, Illinois, Massachusetts, New Jersey, New York, and Pennsylvania.

In the absence of these workers, black farm workers, facing falling prices for cotton, headed to northern cities to take newly available unskilled jobs. This migration was facilitated by a relatively open housing market—thanks largely to the lessening of immigration. It was during the 1920s that the middle class began fleeing to the suburbs in large numbers, enabling earlier immigrants to move from tenements to better city housing and creating many housing vacancies in inner cities. Had immigration levels remained high, these vacancies would probably have been taken by newcomers from Europe. As it happened, blacks had a relatively easy time finding decent housing.

Native blacks may have derived some benefit from the fall off in immigration, but the economy as a whole suffered. The 1924 Immigration Act was part and parcel of an isolationist mood that spread through the land in reaction to World War I and events that accompanied the conflict (such as the Bolshevik Revolution) or came in its aftermath (hyperinflation and rising discontent in Central Europe). The protectionist Smoot-Hawley tariff barriers enacted by Congress in 1930 at the outset of the Great Depression complemented the new immigration restrictions: one aimed to exclude foreign goods, the other to keep out foreign labor and alien ideas and values. Tariffs were similarly raised in other industrialized nations, and the resultant interruption of free trade greatly aggravated the severity of the depression.

To be sure, the stock market crash of October 1929 was fed by many sources, including regressive fiscal and unsound monetary policies, corruption, and a drop in domestic demand for housing and durable goods, as well as the externally oriented policies concerning trade and immigration and the gathering global crisis of militarism and dictatorship. Among the domestic culprits, the slide in housing demand had an especially devastating effect on investment levels in the early 1930s. During the 1920s, construction had served as an important economic stimulus in urban areas; expenditures in this sector rose from $5 billion in 1920 to $10.7 billion six years later. Thereafter, however, the figure fell sharply.[37]

The drop was caused primarily by a slowdown in population growth and household formation, a phenomenon attributable in no small part to the cutoff of immigration. In one decade, the number of children under the age of five declined from 604 to 506 per 1,000 young women—the sharpest percentage fall in the fertility rate in American history. Between 1916 and 1928, the population of the industrial regions grew by 10 percent; after 1928, the rate of growth was down to 3 percent. The decline can be attributed to a rapid drop in birthrates and (not entirely unrelated, since many foreign arrivals were in their prime childbearing years) curbs on immigration. Taken together, these trends caused a deep cut in the national demand for housing and durable goods.

Brinley Thomas studied the relationships between immigration, emigration, and economic growth in Great Britain and the United States. Based on extensive statistical analyses, he found significant linkages between major inflows of immigrants and rises in capital investment during periods of rapid American economic expansion. Thomas also determined that the Immigration Act of 1924 had numerous repercussions on international capital flows, worldwide agricultural output, and capital goods demand. He concluded, "The action of the United States in blocking the natural flow of transatlantic migration was only one factor in a complex set of circumstances, but it played an important part in causing the cumulative process which ended in the world depression."[38]

The Thomas thesis implies that a rise in immigration leads to economic expansion. To help assess this relationship, it is worth examining the effects of immigration on other nations, as well as migration within the United States during the depression years. Many South American nations allowed relatively free immigration, despite the economic downturn, and with the imposition of restrictions in the United States, more than 600,000 Europeans headed for Argentina, Brazil, and Canada between 1925 and 1937. However, these immigrants constituted only a fraction of the total that would have come to the United States.

By all accounts, the Latin American nations benefited from the inflow, as new immigrants stimulated business activity, thereby helping to off-set the effect of the depression. Mexico City, Santiago, and Buenos Aires were among the cities that prospered from the entry of middle-class immigrants trained in the technical and medical professions. Until severe restrictions were imposed in Canada in the early 1930s, that country, too, received a steady supply from several European nations that had exhausted their entry quotas for the United States. Between 1921 and 1932, the total number of immigrants to Argentina, Brazil, and Canada exceeded the number entering the United States by a sub-stantial margin.

In the absence of large-scale immigration, internal migration played a more important role as an engine of development in United States. California was the only state during the depression to attract significant numbers of internal migrants as well as immigrants. Between 1935 and 1940, over 650,000 persons moved to California, primarily to the southern part of the state. The newcomers, who represented almost 10 percent of the state's population, increased the demand for housing, consumer goods, and services, both private and public. The state also benefited from massive government projects—federal and local—that were initiated to meet the tremendous demand of the mushrooming population for roads, bridges, and water and to relieve unemploy-ment. Throughout the 1930s, California outperformed the national economy in numerous categories, including housing construction, per capita income, output per worker, and investment per worker. Despite the depression, California absorbed large numbers of migrants without having its unemployment rate rise above the national average. Manufacturing employment, contrary to the national pattern, rose during the 1930s. This expanded labor pool helped California emerge as a major industrial center during World War II.

The newcomers were drawn to California's urban areas, especially Los Angeles, which grew by more than 250,000 during the depression. Most were able to find jobs, helping to stimulate economic activity, much as the arrival of immigrants in eastern cities had done in earlier decades.

With the exception of migration to the cities of southern California, movement from rural to urban areas virtually ceased during the depres-sion. Indeed, the period from 1935 to 1940 was the first in the nation's history in which the urban share of the population did not increase. This plateau was caused by both the lack of job opportunities in cities and the slowdown in immigration.

The effect of reduced immigration on the quality of urban life was vividly described in a bulletin of the Public Works Administration (PWA), one of the most successful New Deal programs:

> The blighted effects of slums and human lives was less acute during the period of immigration and rapid immigration growth than it is now. Newcomers sought the cheapest and therefore the worst housing, literally pushing out, and necessarily into something better, the last previous immigrant wave. They were able to afford to move because rapidly expanding population meant rapidly expanding jobs.... Living in slums was a temporary discomfort. Since immigration stopped, all that has changed.[39]

Immigration restrictions were not the only reason for the decline in the number of persons entering the United States during the depression. The lack of job opportunities was the primary cause for slowed immigration from England and Ireland, which did not fully utilize their generous quota allocations. Emigration controls, such as those imposed by Fascist Italy, also dampened departures from certain nations.[40] But a modest influx from Eastern, Central, and Southern Europe would nonetheless have continued in the absence of quotas. Most would have come to join relatives in the United States; otherwise, they had skills that would ease their search for jobs.

From 1935 onward, the political turmoil in Europe caused an accelerating outflow, consisting primarily of middle-class refugees. The vast majority of these refugees would have settled in the United States had immigration controls not been imposed. This uprooted, predominantly urban population was considerably more educated than earlier immigrants. Those who did manage to make it to the United States, mostly to its larger cities, included members of Europe's intellectual elite, people who had made important contributions to the professions, arts, and sciences.[41] We will never know, of course, how many more Nobel prizes this country would have won or how many more sick people would have been cured had entry requirements been relaxed. Clearly, though, additional newcomers would have immeasurably enriched our academic and cultural institutions, accelerated scientific knowledge, and stimulated the depressed economy. All in all, these middle-class entrants created substantially more jobs than they took.

The reduced alien inflow had a significant impact on the composition and direction of internal migration within the United States. During the New Deal era, southern blacks continued to move to industrial regions, especially New York City, despite depressed economic conditions. If work could be found, wages were three to four times higher in northern cities than in the rural South. At the same time, more than 800,000 whites left the North for the South and West between 1935 and 1940. Given the negative perception of black workers that many employers held, southern migration to northern cities would almost certainly have slowed if additional immigrant labor had been available. This movement was unintentionally furthered by the New Deal programs. The federal government provided minimum relief assistance to the most needy, but required no state matching funds. Southern states not only elected to provide zero supplement but insisted that federal funds were to be based on regional cost-of-living adjustments, further reducing payments. As a result of federal and state policies, a Kentucky family, for example, received $7 in relief per month in 1934; the same family in New York would receive $42. New York City was considered to have the most generous relief standard in the nation.[42]

Unskilled workers had other incentives to move North. The average Public Works Administration (PWA) employee received 63 cents per hour in New York, 30 cents in Mississippi. Southern states suppressed wages paid under relief programs to preserve wage differentials between relief and nonrelief workers, a policy that encouraged both black and white outmigration.

The nation began to recover its economic health with the start of World War II, when the demand for military hardware soared. The around-the-clock operation of factories, together with the loss of ten million men and women to the military, created severe labor shortages in industrial cities. Unfortunately, this growing demand coincided with a total cessation of immigration from Europe. Agricultural areas received some relief in the form of temporary workers brought in from Mexico and the Caribbean basin. For the most part, though, industry's demand for workers was met by massive internal migration. More Americans moved across state lines between 1940 and 1944 than in any other four-year period before or since. Many of the migrants were black. During the 1940s, 1.6

million blacks left the South, with 60 percent settling in one of four states—New York, California, Illinois, and Michigan—the same ones that had attracted 40 percent of all immigrants in earlier decades.

What if more liberal immigration laws been in effect throughout the 1920s and 1930s? The working-age population at the start of World War II would have been 2.5 million higher than it actually was. The armed forces would have absorbed perhaps 700,000 of these newcomers, with most of the balance going to work in defense and civilian industries. Additional military personnel and higher production—the nation was never short of raw materials—would probably have brought an end to the conflict sooner with fewer American casualties.

Postwar Expansion and Inner-City Decline

With the end of World War II, the nation entered a period of unexpected—and unparalleled—prosperity. The United States, with less than one-tenth of the global population, produced at this stage one-half of the world's output. This industrial dominance was fostered by a well-trained labor force, an abundance of natural resources, massive capital investment, rapid technological advancement, and political stability unshaken by the depression and armed conflict. While most of Europe and Asia was struggling to recover from the war, America was at the height of its economic and political power.

The postwar economic boom followed a twenty-year period of greatly restricted immigration, with little prospect of changing the entry laws soon. The nation's cities, experiencing a need for fresh manpower, had to draw upon several alternative sources. Blacks continued to leave the South in large numbers until the mid-1960s. Many young men and women left family farms to head for the excitement of the cities. And more and more women began entering the labor force. Cities were thus able to meet the needs of the expanding economy without immigrant labor. Meanwhile, the nation's inner cities were beginning to feel the effects of large-scale demographic and social changes. The rising living standards of the postwar period, together with substantial household savings accumulated during the war, enabled many families to purchase their first automobile and ended their dependence on the streetcar for transportation to work. The government embarked on a major highway construction program, which opened urban peripheries to commercial development and resulted in a heavy exodus to the suburbs.

The case of Newark, New Jersey, is typical. This industrial city, located in the shadow of Manhattan, was never very affluent, but during the early twentieth century it prospered with each new wave of immigrants. However, by the 1950s, one generation after the last major disembarkation of immigrants, Newark had already begun to deteriorate as middle- and lower-middle-class white families—mostly descendants of second-wave immigrants—moved out of the city. Within two decades, Newark became synonymous with urban decline, topping almost every list of distressed American cities. Blocks of older housing that had been occupied by immigrants in the first three decades of the twentieth century were, during the 1960s and 1970s, abandoned, torn down, or incinerated in accidental fires, arson, and rioting. If properly maintained, these predominantly two- and three-family frame buildings would have been far superior to the public housing units built to replace them. It was not until Portuguese immigration was renewed in the 1960s that some of these units were restored.

The movement to the suburbs that created Newark's inner-city problems was duplicated in other cities with large immigrant enclaves, including Chicago, Detroit, and New York. Had no migration in or out of the city taken place, the white population in these three cities would have risen by 1.5 million as a result of natural increase. In fact, the population declined by 1.5 million. This means that net outflow exceeded three million—almost one out of every three white residents. While the black population grew as a result of continuing migration and natural increase, without the help of new immigrants this gain did not keep pace with the white outflow. The population of central cities in the North declined.

The absence of new immigrants seems to have played a major role in the decline of the nation's inner cities. It is commonly believed that the move to the suburbs responded to a decline in job opportunities. However, demographic data suggest that the relationship worked in the opposite direction. Decline occurred because of the flight of middle-class residents, with few immigrants arriving to take their places.

The relocation of manufacturing jobs from northern cities is often cited as a cause of urban flight in the "Rust Belt." Yet manufacturing employment across the nation actually declined between 1968 and 1988 while employment in other sectors gained thirty-five million jobs. Some city factories went out of business, others moved to the South, and a few shifted some operations overseas. Although cities lost a disproportionate share of manufacturing jobs, the net employment gain in the suburbs was far too small to explain their attraction to the middle-class. Most of the jobs created in suburban areas have come in retail sales, wholesale activities, personal services, and related nonmanufacturing sectors that grew *in response to* expanding population. Many of those who moved to the suburbs continued commuting to the city at least until suburban jobs were generated later. Structural economic change, then, was not the primary cause of central city economic stagnation, only a contributor.

The flight to the suburbs can be traced to growing affluence. Rising incomes enabled apartment dwellers to purchase suburban homes and adopt a life-style that, prior to World War II, had seemed but a dream. Growing dissatisfaction with urban life—racial strife, rising crime, and all the rest—coincided with the availability of low-interest home financing to spur the mass movement from the cities. The movement took place not only between city and suburb; there was a steady stream of departures from established cities to younger metropolitan areas. Employment opportunities, particularly for professionals and skilled workers, in the South and West encouraged migration to these regions.

The gap left by these urban "refugees" was filled in part by blacks pouring in from the South and to a lesser extent by immigrants. Puerto Ricans flocked to New York, and Mexicans to Los Angeles. In addition, European immigrants arrived under the quota system, but in far smaller numbers than during the pre–World War II period. If newcomers were still finding reasons to move to the city, why were they seemingly less able to provide the economic stimulus, or attain the material success, associated with their predecessors? It is necessary to look first at two critical ingredients of immigrant success—strong family and ethnic bonds. Most second-wave immigrants came from Catholic or Jewish cultures, which placed emphasis on the coherence of the family unit. The proportion of female-headed households among these immigrants was lower than among native families. Families also depended on their bond with others of the same ethnicity to cope with their new, often unfriendly environment. The support networks and self-help organizations that emerged within enclaves were the products of strong family and ethnic identity.

Frequently, there was a hunger for success among these groups—driven by the favorable economic and social circumstances encountered in cities—that had been suppressed in their native lands. Class barriers were probably easier to cross in American cities (outside the South) at the turn of the century than perhaps anywhere on earth. Hard work and enterprise could propel a poor family into middle-class status within a decade. The system of free public education opened another route for those with ambition and talent to enter the middle class as professionals.

Although many failed in their quest for a better life, a sufficient number succeeded to encourage others. Less commonly recognized is that a substantial number of immigrants came to cities with training in crafts or industry. For example, 40 percent of all immigrants in the early decades of the twentieth century were skilled, a remarkable number particularly when compared to the 46 percent of the native-born work force that had similar skills.

Black society, particularly southern rural blacks who came to American cities after World War II, did not fare as well, in part because it lacked the ingredients that launched many immigrants into the American mainstream. The black rural family that moved to northern ghettos was typically large, frequently headed by a woman, and usually poor, with a working mother toiling to feed and clothe her children. Because the vast majority of blacks were unskilled and worked for whites outside the ghetto, opportunities for training and experience were absent.

The importance of the lack of earlier business experience is particularly evident in contrasting the relative success of Caribbean blacks (to be discussed in a later chapter) with the failure of most native blacks to become entrepreneurs. Rural black culture, in the face of endless deprivation, stressed immediate survival and had no tradition of saving money.

On top of everything else, blacks had to bear the ongoing burdens of racial prejudice. For those growing up after World War II, it is embarrassing and even painful to look back at the first half of the twentieth century and see the depth of openly expressed racial antagonism on the pages of newspapers and periodicals. Many white newcomers, although initially handicapped by their foreign appearance and poor command of English, could, through devoted labor, eventually melt into the mainstream; blacks, no matter how diligent they might be, were marked by their color. Overcoming this handicap usually required a professional education, unique talent, or other ability that could advance individuals in spite of their color.

But most blacks were thwarted by their lack of education. Segregated schools in the South produced limited opportunities at best. Schools were better in the North, but black families failed (as did Irish immigrants before them) to sufficiently emphasize the merits of education as a means to escape poverty. This hurt the black community when higher-paying jobs that required education developed in the 1950s and 1960s, a time of unique opportunity as discrimination barriers were at least partially removed. Slowly, more blacks completed higher education and achieved middle-class status; they, too, moved away from the inner core of cities. An underclass remained behind with fading hope for a better life that had stimulated immigrants.

Urban whites, although less overtly hostile to black progress than earlier generations, reacted to the black influx in two ways. Lower-middle-class whites who could not afford the more expensive suburban housing attempted to maintain all-white enclaves. The more affluent whites relocated. The white population in Chicago, Cleveland, Detroit, and Philadelphia began falling in the 1930s and again in the 1950s, well before the racial tensions of the 1960s. The black-white conflict that erupted in urban riots during the 1960s and the implementation of school desegregation plans in cities such as Richmond only accelerated white flight. Even cities with few blacks, such as Minneapolis, St. Paul, Salt Lake City, and Seattle, have been experiencing considerable outmigration. Thus, in all likelihood, even if black migration from the South had ceased in 1940, white middle-class families would nonetheless be moving, if somewhat more slowly, from the urban core to tract homes with front lawns.

The change in the demographic profile of the nation's cities had major consequences for their economic performance. Because most of the blacks migrating into the cities were poorer than the whites who were leaving, business activity declined and the local tax base shrank. Moreover, the new residents required more municipal services than those departing, creating growing fiscal pressures. The drop in the number of immigrants did have some positive effects for urban blacks. More immigrants could have meant fewer job opportunities for them. By moving from rural areas to cities, blacks gained not only better-paying jobs but also increased political power and access to municipal employment. And those fortunate enough to escape public projects were able to find solid housing stock in previously working- and middle-class white neighborhoods.

Overall, however, the cities that were most dependent on immigrant labor and enterprise—Chicago, Cleveland, Detroit, Newark, and New York—were, two decades after the imposition of immigration controls, among the most severely disadvantaged in the nation. Had enterprising immigrants replaced those members of the middle class bailing out of the urban core, the adverse economic effects of the exodus would have been cushioned. This is not to say that immigrants could have reversed technological advances and public policies that have weakened the economic well-being of inner cities. Nonetheless, their presence could have helped sustain commercial activity and small-scale manufacturing, strengthening the economic base of these cities. This conclusion bears directly on the current debate over the impact of immigration: many of our newest arrivals are settling in cities that were depressed in the 1970s.

4

The Immigrant Contribution
to the Revitalization of Cities

The richest regions are those with the highest proportion of immigrants. . . . Their industry, their skills and their enterprises were major factors in the economic development that made these regions prosperous.

President's Commission on Immigration and Naturalization, 1953[1]

Immigration has had its deepest and most sustained impact on what can be called "gateway cities." The most important examples of these are Los Angeles County, Miami/Dade County, New York City, and the city of San Francisco; Washington, D.C., and possibly Chicago qualify as second-tier gateways.[2] These cities share several important demographic characteristics. Their population growth since the 1970s is attributable exclusively to immigration. As shown in Table 4-1, the majority of the population in each city is some combination of Asian, black, and Hispanic, with only two of every five residents a non-Hispanic white. Immigrants have flocked to the cities for generations, and these urban centers have become dependent on their labor. In 1930 almost one out of four residents in the primary gateway cities was foreign-born, twice the national average. But six decades later, well over one in three are immigrants, almost five times the national average. Although the four areas account for less than 8 percent of the nation's population, nearly two-fifths of all recent immigrants have settled there.

Finally, 45 percent of the population speak a language other than English in their homes, three times the rate of the United States as a whole. Gateway cities also share several economic characteristics linked to immigration and international activity, as shown in Table 4-2. Two-thirds of all foreign bank branches in the United States are located in gateway cities, and gateway ports account for nearly two-fifths of all U.S. exports. In the central business districts (CBDs) of the four gateway cities, foreign investors in 1987 held office buildings valued at more than $12 billion, or 60 percent of total overseas investment in office real estate within the United States. Almost one-half of the office space in downtown Los Angeles, for example, is owned by foreign, mostly Japanese, groups. Conversely, international investors are practically absent from Baltimore,

Table 4-1

Demographic and Ethnic Characteristics of Gateway Cities

	Los Angeles County	Miami/ Dade County	New York City	San Francisco (city)	U.S. Total/ Average
Percentage of Total U.S. Population (1990)	3.6	0.8	2.9	0.3	100.0
Population Change (1980–90)	18.5	19.1	3.5	6.6	9.9
Percentage Non-Hispanic Black and Hispanic	48.7	50.7	49.4	24.5	21.1
Percentage Non-Hispanic White	40.0	30.2	43.3	46.6	75.6
Percentage Foreign-born:					
1930	22.1	11.9	33.1	24.1	11.6
1990	32.7	57.4	28.4	24.3	7.8
Percentage of All U.S. Immigrants:					
1988	13.7	5.9	14.5	2.8 [a]	100.0
1989–90[b]	27.3	2.4	10.7	2.1 [a]	100.0
Non-English-speaking (at home)	45.4	57.4	41.0	34.4	13.8

Sources: U.S. Department of Commerce, Bureau of the Census, *1930* and *1990 Census of Population*; U.S. Department of Justice, *Statistical Yearbook of the Immigration and Naturalization Service*, various years

[a] San Francisco Principal Metropolitan Statistical Area (PMSA).

[b] The two-year period reflects the impact of the amnesty program in Los Angeles.

Cincinnati, Phoenix, and other large urban centers with few immigrants. The prevalence of foreign bank branches, foreign investment, and immigrant-based commercial activity, together with the presence of many large domestic financial institutions, has helped integrate these gateways into a worldwide commercial network. In the four urban centers, household income in 1989 was substantially above the national average (with the exception of non-Hispanic white households in Miami/Dade County and Hispanic households in New York). Remarkably, income growth in these gateway cities during the 1980s was not slowed by massive immigration, which included the entry of well over a million aliens whose earning potential was low. Concurrently, earnings of black residents in each city expanded more rapidly than those of Asians, Hispanics, or whites.

The concept of gateway cities is related to the notion of "primary core world cities" used by urban planners and social scientists, but it differs

Table 4-2
Economic Characteristics of Gateway Cities[a]

	Los Angeles County	Miami/ Dade County	New York City	San Francisco (city)	Four cities	Total U.S.
Percentage of All Foreign Banks in U.S.[a]	11.6	5.4	42.9	6.9	66.8	100.0
Value of Imports as Percentage of U.S. Total in 1989[b]	13.1	1.4	17.0	5.4	36.9	100.0
Percentage of Foreign-owned CBD Office Space[c]	46.0	18.0	21.0	17.0	31.0	13.5[d]
Household Median Income as Percentage of U.S. Average (1989)[e]						
White	122.7	91.9	110.0	114.2	109.7	100.0
Black	130.7	104.3	120.6	110.0	116.4	100.0
Hispanic	119.9	105.9	84.5	123.4	108.4	100.0

[a] *American Banker*, February 23, 1987.

[b] U.S. Department of Commerce, Bureau of the Census, *Highlights of U.S. Export and Import Trade,* in 1989 FT (Foreign Trade) 990, 1990. Includes port activity, which may be located beyond the limits of central cities.

[c] "Coldwell Banker Commercial Real Estate Services Report" (mimeo), 1987. For summary of report, see Mark Memmott, "Foreigners Buy in USA's Downtowns," *USA Today*, August 18, 1987.

[d] Largest 15 U.S. downtown markets.

[e] U.S. Department of Commerce, Bureau of the Census, *1990 Census of Population,* special computer runs by the Population Division, September 1992. These percentages compare household income of each group in cities to the group's average income nationally.

in several critical respects. John Friedmann's list of "world cities"—Chicago, Houston, Los Angeles, Miami, New York, San Francisco, and a dozen others located outside the United States—overlaps with the roster of gateway cities presented above. However, Friedmann makes mostly negative assertions about those cities. He argues that world cities, by attracting so many internal migrants as well as immigrants, are growing at such a rapid rate that their social costs are outstripping their financial resources.[3] He also maintains that growth in corporate headquarters, international finance, and related commercial activities leads to the creation of low-wage service jobs at the expense of high-wage employment. Friedmann strongly suggests that these world cities will eventually collapse under the weight of the poor masses flowing into them. A similar view is held by Saskia Sassen-Koob, who believes that world cities require for their well-being the presence of a growing underclass.[4] The positive assessment registered in this book—that immigration to American gateway cities has contributed to their economic and social vitality—is partially attributable to the economic success of many recent arrivals, mainly non-European immigrants, as a consequence of the 1965 Immigration Act.[5]

The Immigrant City Anew

In the decades following the passage of the national origins legislation in 1924, the immigrant role in cities diminished as the aging foreign-born population and their children joined the exodus to suburbs. But after the 1965 Immigration Act became effective, the inflow of non-European legal aliens and illegal workers accelerated, with the result that numerous places—once the homes of the newest European aliens—again became immigrant cities. These places include not only the six gateway areas specified, but also other large and small urban centers that have been affected by the growing immigrant presence.

The net population increase in the United States due to immigration between 1970 and 1990 is estimated at well over 10 million and accounts for about a fourth of the overall population gain the nation has experienced over twenty years. This estimate does not fully incorporate the probable magnitude of illegal immigration that has taken place during the past two decades, which would increase the total by perhaps another two million. Over four-fifths of the newcomers to our shores settle in metropolitan areas—most of them in central cities. Of all immigrants arriving in New York State during the 1980s, almost 90 percent gave New York City as their destination; three of every five arrivals in Illinois listed Chicago. Overall, the majority of aliens choose to live in a handful of areas, with New York and Los Angeles in the lead, followed by Chicago, San Francisco, Washington, D.C., and Miami. The number initially settling in places like Buffalo, Indianapolis, Memphis, and Pittsburgh is negligible, although even these areas are being "penetrated" by Asian entrepreneurs and professionals.

The ethnic distribution of aliens in our major cities reflects historical patterns and geography. There are reliable figures only for legal entrants; of these, New York attracts about two-thirds of all Dominicans, one-half of all Russians, one-fourth of all Chinese, and one-third of all Colombians. But fewer than one in one hundred Mexicans settles in New York. They prefer Los Angeles County, where nearly four in ten residents enumerated in 1990 were Hispanic; the same is true of Koreans, Salvadorans, and Vietnamese. Chicago attracts more than one-fourth of all Poles, while Miami is a magnet for Cubans, Haitians, and Central Americans. San Francisco boasts the largest Chinese community in the nation; about three in ten residents of that city are Asian. As for illegals, Mexicans, Koreans, and Central Americans gravitate to Los Angeles, Chinese to San Francisco, and Caribbean nationals to New York. The latest among illegal entrants are the Irish, who, driven by a stagnating economy in Ireland that has failed to provide enough jobs for those leaving school, can be seen much as they were a century earlier, working on construction crews on the streets of New York.

The ethnic composition of immigrants has shifted from Europe to Asia and the Western Hemisphere since the 1950s, but the occupational patterns of aliens who enter legally (with the exception of Mexicans) has remained essentially stable. Professional and blue-collar positions continue to attract immigrants in greater proportions than among the native-born work force. The groups with the highest proportion of professionals are Indians, Filipinos, and Britons, with percentages well exceeding the average for urban natives; by contrast, Mexicans, Vietnamese, and Haitians tend to be blue-collar workers.

The growing presence of non-European immigrants, together with the high birthrates of new entrants and native minorities, is also affecting the size and ethnic distribution of the nation's labor force. To the envy of other Western nations, the United States gained twenty-three million jobs between 1977 and 1987. Hispanics, blacks, and Asians account for somewhat more than two of every ten residents but supplied four of every ten workers added during the decade. In central cities, both large and small, these three groups accounted for almost one-half of the growth in the labor force, mostly through immigration. The number of Hispanics in the work force more than doubled, while the number of Asians increased 134 percent during the ten-year span, to 1.9 million. Job gains for blacks have been somewhat higher than the national average. However, a substantial number of blacks gaining employment in New York and particularly Miami were recent immigrants. All in all, immigration is helping to bring about a change in the racial composition of the labor force unseen since the late seventeenth century, when black slaves became a critical component in the southern colonies.

Immigrants coming to live in the inner cities are now filling the void left by those moving to the suburbs. This process is by no means recent. In earlier periods it was rural migrants, blacks, and immigrants who flowed into the urban core. Today, those first two categories have run dry. America's rural agricultural population has been so diminished that only minimal outmigration can be expected in the future. And blacks are now more likely to be leaving rather than entering large cities. Moreover, in a period of low birthrates, natural increase cannot be expected to maintain a growing labor force. That leaves immigrants. A large enough number of recent immigrants have settled in inner cities to have a measurable effect on their population size, age distribution, and work force characteristics.

The effects of a shrinking population base on urban life have been amply chronicled. Schools grow empty, housing is abandoned, infrastructure crumbles. As more buildings are taken off the tax rolls, a city's ability to maintain services is further diminished. Abandoned buildings breed crime, which leads to a further deterioration in neighborhood life. Commuters come to work in downtown office towers but spend their earnings in the suburbs. So do many of the remaining inner-city residents, causing a drop in sales tax receipts.

Such was the experience of the gateway cities—and most others—during the 1970s. But the situation would have been far worse in the absence of immigration. For instance, New York, a city of more than

7 million residents, lost 700,000 persons during the decade; without immigrants, the decline would have exceeded 1.5 million. During the 1980s, the city officially gained 251,000 residents; were it not for the 854,000 legal immigrants who settled there, New York's downward spiral would have continued, although more slowly. Had legal and undocumented immigration ceased in the mid-1960s, the city would probably now have considerably fewer than 6 million inhabitants.[6]

In some circumstances, inner cities could benefit from reduced population. No doubt many New Yorkers, faced with crowded subway cars, clogged streets, and rising rents, would prefer a city of six million. If New York had been able to adjust to a lower population while also retaining a strong middle-class presence, its quality of life may well have improved. But in reality, population losses are selective. Outmigrants from cities tend to be better educated and more affluent than those remaining: New York had a net loss of 40,000 college graduates between 1975 and 1980.[7] In the absence of immigration, the city's share of middle-class families and active workers would have fallen further. Between 1975 and 1980 the vast majority of those leaving the city had household incomes between $25,000 and $50,000. The city's poor population, meanwhile, increased by 36,000.

Most residents of Los Angeles County, frustrated by traffic congestion and air pollution, would also favor fewer people. Similar to New York, the Los Angeles County population, which remained stable in the 1970s, would have declined by up to one million had no immigrants settled there. The county's population gain of 1,386,000 during the 1980s is primarily attributable to the immigrant inflow. The county has experienced no net migration from other parts of the nation since the early 1970s despite considerable economic growth. Without the alien contribution, the population in the two other gateway cities, San Francisco and Miami, would unquestionably have fallen.[8] The upturn in the number of immigrants during the 1980s reversed the population decline in Boston and San Francisco, although the economic health of these cities during the 1980s certainly aided their stability.

These population effects of immigration assume that the alien influx is unrelated to the departure of the middle class from cities. It may be that, in the absence of renewed immigration, more natives would have remained. During the 1980s the number of non-Hispanic whites declined by over one million in the four gateway urban centers combined, with the steepest fall (over 22 percent) in Miami/Dade county. Part of the outflow from Miami is attributable to immigration, but to what extent the losses in Los Angeles and New York are linked to the growing alien presence is difficult to assess. However, among the nation's twenty largest cities, Baltimore, Cleveland, Detroit, Milwaukee, and Philadelphia have attracted few immigrants and, not coincidentally, lost 5 percent or more of their population in the 1980s. This supports the thesis that the absence of immigration does not constrain the flight of middle-class residents to the suburbs. The inability of these industrial cities to attract immigrants has further weakened their economic base.

Achieving a stable population by itself adds little to a local economy. In fact, a population with a high proportion of children and the aged can actually weaken economic activity. However, fewer than 4 percent of recent immigrants are over the age of sixty five (compared to 11.5 percent of the total U. S. population), and the percentage under the age of eighteen is similar to the native-born population. Therefore, a high proportion of new immigrants are in the working-age category. In addition, immigrants also have higher labor force participation rates than the population at large. Since their rate of unemployment is only somewhat higher than average, immigrants are overall more apt to be in the work force than native residents.

Dishwashers and Engineers

New immigrants are most likely to be seen working at sewing machines in apparel factories, as engineers in high-technology industries, washing dishes in restaurants, and as shop owners in central- city ghettos. Such diversity should not be surprising since, conservatively, one of every five workers entering the nation's labor force in the 1970s and 1980s was a recent immigrant, and in central cities the proportion was much higher. If these workers—six million or more in all—had not come to our shores, would these jobs have been taken by others, remained unfilled, or created at all in the first place? This is a critical question because immigrants have been portrayed alternately as unwanted aliens taking jobs from Americans, as competitors causing wages to decline, or, more benignly, as laborers who accept jobs that natives shun. All these images have some validity. There is no doubt that some immigrants take jobs that would otherwise go to natives. And the wages paid to unskilled workers can be depressed by an immigrant-fed labor surplus. Many aliens, meanwhile, take on such unwanted jobs as dishwasher and hotel maid.

But immigration has also helped create new jobs—in some cases for members of the same ethnic group, in other cases for native workers. The chief effect of immigration on the urban occupational structure, from the perspective of native white workers, has been to supplant low-wage blue-collar and service jobs with white-collar and public-sector positions. Many new immigrants, particularly undocumented workers and Hispanics, accept work in hotels, restaurants, and low-wage manufacturing establishments that are unattractive to most natives. Their earnings stimulate employment in higher-paying jobs, including finance, utilities, and local government.

Before discussing the importance of immigrants in various economic sectors, it is worth pausing to note the characteristics of illegal, or "undocumented," workers. In Los Angeles, the number of illegal immigrants (prior to the legalization programs) exceeded that of legal entrants; in New York and Miami, illegals make up a somewhat lower but still considerable share of all employed immigrants. Contrary to common perceptions, the economic behavior of undocumented aliens in major cities does not differ from that of legal entrants. In fact, the two groups play markedly complementary roles in local economies. Among those that applied for legalization in the late 1980s, 60 percent were at the low end of the occupational spectrum—laborers and service workers. However, 14 percent were skilled workers, 10 percent performed clerical or sales jobs, and 4 percent held managerial or professional positions. Although undocumented workers are generally paid less than legal aliens, the difference is primarily due to length of stay in the country and the degree of social and economic integration. Immigration status and ethnicity are less important factors. But the 1986 Immigration Act may have brought about a further increase in wage disparities because employers willing to hire workers without proper documentation may attempt to offset the risk involved by paying them less.

The productivity of illegal workers, despite the absence of wage parity, is equal to—and perhaps above—the level of others performing similar tasks. So, although it is at times useful for statistical (and legal) purposes to distinguish among undocumented aliens, refugees, and properly documented entrants, these distinctions are generally irrelevant in terms of the labor market.

Almost one-third of all new immigrants in 1980 worked in manufacturing, a much higher rate than for nonimmigrants. Among undocumented workers, more than one-half are employed in the production of apparel and other manufactured goods.[9] Given that the number of manufacturing jobs (unlike jobs in other sectors) has remained stable since the late 1960s, immigrants are taking the place of domestic workers, especially those engaged in low-wage production jobs in cities.

The role of manufacturing in urban economic life began to recede after World War II. By the 1960s, with factories relocating first to other parts of the country and then overseas, most cities experienced a sharp decline in their manufacturing fortunes. Hardest hit were apparel, textiles, shoes, furniture, and electronics. Where immigrants were present, however, the trend was slowed. This was nowhere more apparent than in Los Angeles. Between 1972 and 1986, as manufacturing employment nationwide dropped slightly, it grew in Los Angeles County by almost 20 percent. This was due primarily to the presence of Hispanics willing to work for low wages. With the exception of high-wage sectors like aerospace, Hispanics had by the late 1980s become the backbone of the county's industrial work force.

In the Los Angeles furniture and fixture industry, wages have been rising more slowly than the national average. The majority of furniture workers are immigrants, but low wages and the use of undocumented workers did not prevent productivity gains from outpacing those in other furniture industry centers. In the food sector—where almost one-half of the production workers are immigrants—employment (again countering the national trend) increased, but wage gains in Los Angeles actually exceeded those in the rest of the nation. Employers could afford higher wages because value added per worker in the food industry rose more rapidly in Los Angeles than elsewhere, improving the competitive position of food processing in the region. The pattern that emerges in Los Angeles is one of immigrants, in industries where they comprise a large share of the work force, receiving lower wages than native workers, improving the area's competitive status and stimulating the demand for additional low-wage production workers. Concurrently, there has been a small rise in the number of white-collar workers, including supervisors, managers, and accountants, employed in these factories.

The Los Angeles shoe industry is also highly dependent on immigrant labor. Nationally, the proportion of imported nonrubber footwear has been rising steadily, from 12 percent in 1965 to 72 percent in 1984. In Los Angeles, however, the industry has maintained a foothold by concentrating on specialized women's shoes and by employing skilled Mexican immigrants.[10] Without these immigrants, who are willing to work for low wages ($5.16 per hour for the industry in California during 1982), local shoe manufacturers would find it difficult to survive in the world market. Unskilled blacks could not fill the role of these immigrants, who had extensive shoemaking training in Mexico and were accustomed to working for rock-bottom piece rates.

In New York, as in Los Angeles, immigrants have played an important role in the manufacturing sector, which has suffered for numerous reasons—foreign and domestic competition, a weak regional economy, the high cost of doing business in Manhattan, and obsolete facilities. The availability of immigrant labor in New York, although not enough in itself to reverse the loss of manufacturing jobs, has apparently slowed the rate of decline.

The importance of undocumented aliens in several manufacturing sectors is readily illustrated in statistics. In 1980, according to one estimate, 39 percent of all jobs in apparel, 37 percent in leather and footwear, and 36 percent in canned foods and vegetables across the nation were held by illegal workers.[11]

Apparel production in gateway cities is the sector most dependent on immigrant labor, and as such it demonstrates the impact of recent entrants on low-wage manufacturing. The high concentration of immigrants in the field is not a new phenomenon. At the turn of the century, workers from Eastern Europe and Italy in the Northeast and Chinese workers in San Francisco provided the low-wage labor force in this highly competitive industry.

Although apparel employment in the nation declined substantially between 1972 and 1987, there was a considerable increase in Los Angeles. A survey found that almost all of the 80,000 apparel workers in the region were female illegal aliens.[12] In 1979 undocumented workers in the local apparel industry earned only $2.75 per hour—considerably below the $3.68 earned by U.S. citizens.[13] Wages in Los Angeles

Table 4-3

Apparel Industry in Gateway Cities
1972 and 1987

City	Employment as a Percentage of U.S. Employment		Wages U.S. = 100		Value Added per Worker U.S. = 100		Capital Investment per Worker U.S. = 100	
	1972	1987	1972	1987	1972	1987	1972	1987[a]
Los Angeles County	4.5	8.8	102	94	107	114	109	111
New York City	15.1	9.7	114	108	144	156	104	92
Miami/Dade County	1.4	1.7	95	87	82	91	85	114
San Francisco	0.5	1.0	106	88	113	113	88	123
Total/Average	21.5	21.2	104	95	112	126	100	110

Source : U.S. Department of Commerce, Census of Manufacturers, 1972 and 1987

[a] Combined investment in 1982 and 1987.

for all apparel workers fell from 102 percent to 94 percent of the U.S. average between 1972 and 1987 (see Table 4-3).

Immigrant labor likewise enabled New York City to maintain its historically important role in the apparel sector, particularly women's clothing (although at somewhat reduced levels). During the 1970s and early 1980s, the rate of job loss in this industry in New York was only slightly more rapid than it was nationally. Employment in apparel and textiles in the borough of Queens rose modestly in the mid-1980s, suggesting that the industry has remained competitive. The growing use of low-wage immigrant labor did not appear to diminish the historically high productivity of the New York labor force in this sector; rather, productivity in New York remained above the national average, allowing the industry to maintain a presence in the area.

As shown in Table 4-3, in three of the four gateway cities—New York being an exception—employment in the apparel industry as a share of the U. S. total remained level or expanded. Wages exceeded the national average in 1972 but, probably as a result of immigrant labor, fell below the average during the 1980s. Nonetheless, despite lower wages and the use of (mostly illegal) immigrant workers, value added per worker, a key measure of productivity, remained the same or improved. This finding is significant because it contradicts the frequently expressed concern that the use of low-wage workers discourages capital investment and leads to lower productivity.[14]

Many employers could not have obtained, at prevailing wages, sufficient native workers in apparel and other low-wage industries to maintain profitable operations. Without such labor these jobs presumably would have been moved to other countries with lower labor costs. This would have resulted in higher imports and larger balance-of-payment deficits. Manufacturing jobs were also retained in industries supplying materials to apparel, furniture, and metal-products firms and other sectors dependent on alien workers.

Immigrants, undocumented workers in particular, are also represented disproportionately in service industries, especially in restaurants, hotels, hospitals, and as private household help. These are typically low-paying jobs that require only limited English-language or other skills. Undocumented workers comprise 80 percent of all Hispanics employed in Los Angeles restaurants. Hispanics, in turn, form the majority of all such workers in the city. Virtually every restaurant in Miami, New York, and San Francisco depends on immigrant dishwashers and busboys. Hotels in gateway cities are also dependent on immigrants to work in their kitchens, clean rooms, and maintain the grounds. Employment in restaurants and hotels doubled between 1970 and the late 1980s; such growth could not have been sustained without the alien presence. About 7 percent of all hotel and restaurant jobs in 1980 were held by illegal workers,[15] and that figure has increased during the 1980s to perhaps 10 percent or more of the total.

Although immigrants are popularly seen as holding the types of jobs discussed so far, others are skilled craftsmen and professional workers. Thus, it is not only through their willingness to perform undesirable tasks that immigrants contribute to urban economies; they also bring—or develop in the United States—badly needed skills. In the New York area, more than eleven thousand of those who arrived during the 1970s were employed as craft workers in manufacturing. A good example is the production of precious jewels. New York accounts for more than one-third of total national output, centered in the "Diamond District." The aging local labor force in cutting and setting jewels—many in the industry were refugees who arrived in the late 1930s—has been rejuvenated through the arrival of new immigrant craftsmen, mostly of European origin. The presence of foreign-born workers is similarly important in furs (Soviet Jews), wigs (Koreans), and other highly specialized fields.

The importance of skilled immigrant labor is not limited to the manufacturing sector. Since the late 1960s (repeating the pattern of the late 1930s), this nation has attracted many well-educated professionals from overseas. Most of them have settled in the large coastal cities of California and the New York megalopolis. In New York City, the percentage of recent arrivals who are professionals is considerably higher than that for the European immigrants who came prior to 1970. Among the city's recent Asian immigrants, the proportion of professionals is almost as high as that among the native white population.

For the most part, these professionals are concentrated in two fields—health care and engineering sciences. In many public hospitals in gateway cities, the majority of interns and other staff workers are foreign nationals. During the late 1970s, more than one-half of all interns in New York City municipal hospitals were Asians; in Brooklyn Hospital, a private, nonprofit institution, the percentage was even higher. Unfamiliarity with English often creates difficulties in communicating with patients, but without these immigrants, our nation's public hospitals—inside and outside big cities—would probably suffer a shortage of doctors.

In 1976, as enrollment in American medical schools climbed, Congress ordered a curtailment of immigrant physicians. At the moment, the United States has sufficient physicians to meet the demand for medical services; the problem is one of distribution. Most American doctors prefer to live in large urban areas and become private practitioners. Foreign-born and foreign-trained physicians typically have fewer options and are more likely to be found in inner-city hospitals, state facilities, or in small communities unable to attract native-born Americans. During a recent trip to a remote, economically depressed coal-mining region of Pennsylvania, the author found two Indian physicians working in a state hospital. The hospital administrator noted the difficulty in recruiting Americans because of the low pay and location. The two physicians and their families were the only recent immigrants and apparently the only non-Caucasians in the community.

Foreign-born engineers and scientists, meanwhile, have made an important contribution to the nation's technological standing. The 1980 census identified more than seventy thousand Asian-born engineers and natural scientists, 97 percent of them employed in metropolitan areas. Immigration statistics indicate that nearly one-third of the college-educated immigrants who arrived in the early 1970s held scientific or technical jobs. According to a National Science Foundation study, foreign-born individuals account for almost 20 percent of the scientific staff in the nation's largest firms. Electronics firms are likely to hire aliens because Americans with similar qualifications are not readily available. Usually located in urban areas, electronics companies have a large pool of immigrant professionals at their disposal. In 1982, noncitizens and naturalized citizens accounted for 26 percent of all engineers with master's degrees and 36 percent of those with Ph.D.'s.[16]

As is the case with the medical sciences, immigrant engineers are frequently found in the public sector. In the Tidewater area of Virginia, for instance, the heads of the engineering departments of several municipalities are of Asian Indian origin (probably because most native engineers prefer to work in the private sector). Typically, these foreign-born engineers are better educated—most have advanced degrees—than native professionals holding similar positions.

The National Science Board reports that there are three times as many Asian as black engineers, despite considerable growth in the number of blacks in this profession since the 1970s. Hispanics (most of them foreign-born) also outnumber blacks by a substantial margin. Almost one-fourth of all black scientists and engineers are foreign-born, even though immigrants represent only a very small minority of all black residents.[17] These data suggest that blacks and other immigrants are enriching the scientific and engineering community. While some American professionals have expressed concern that alien engineers are taking jobs from natives, there is no evidence to substantiate this. Indeed, there was, until the decline in defense procurement during the early 1990s, a constant demand for domestic engineers among firms working under contract for the U.S. government.

The economic value of attracting trained professionals from other nations can be calculated not only by their contributions to their occupations but by the cost of their education, paid in their country of origin. One estimate is that $500 million was saved by the prior education and training of physicians, engineers, and others who emigrated to the United States in 1971. This "brain drain" has had an adverse effect on countries of emigration by depleting their human resources. For this reason, some countries have adopted strategies to limit enrollment of their nationals in the U.S. universities. The Chinese, for example, curtailed the flow of their Ph.D. students in some scientific fields to the United

States—even prior to the May 1989 bloody upheaval in Beijing—because a large number never returned. These students are now being sent to Western Europe (the former Soviet Union is no longer favored), where they are less likely to find employment, permanent jobs, or social acceptance than in this country.

Immigrants who have come to the United States legally since the late 1960s have higher educational achievement levels than earlier entrants or native-born Americans. In 1982, 11.6 percent of recent immigrants had four years of college and 11.8 percent had graduate-level training.[18] Among natives, 10.6 percent had sixteen years and 7.9 percent had seventeen or more years of schooling. Recent entrants are overrepresented at both ends of the educational spectrum—with Hispanic immigrants below the American average, Asians above the average.

The Middle-Class Entrepreneurs

For centuries commercial activity has been a dominant feature in the growth and economic vitality of central cities. In fact, a city's economic health can be roughly gauged by changes in the number of its retail and service establishments. In the 1972–82 period, the number of retail stores in most industrial cities fell. Across the country the total count remained essentially unchanged, although retail employment rose. The national trend was shifting from small, family-operated businesses to larger operations, but the pattern in three of the four gateway cities countered the trend, thanks to the growth in Asian- and Hispanic-owned stores. Had that number of Asian businesses remained constant, both Los Angeles and San Francisco would have experienced declines in retail stores. Similarly, the absence of new Cuban enterprises in Miami would have reversed the growth pattern.

Between 1972 and 1982, the number of retail businesses in New York City actually declined, as did the number of jobs in stores. The sharpest decline came in establishments without payrolls, that is, mom-and-pop stores that employ only family members. This falloff reflected two developments—the loss of clients due to outmigration and the consolidation of stores into larger, more efficient units. In the following five years, however, New York retail trade recovered in response to modest population growth and a rise in income at a rate exceeding the national average. Paralleling this economic expansion, the number of

Asian and Hispanic retail establishments grew, and retail employment increased by 14 percent (though a weak regional economy in the early 1990s reversed the employment gains).

In gateway and other cities, immigrants have made an important contribution to retail growth. A disproportionate share of non-Hispanic immigrants work as entrepreneurs, and most favor retail trade or services. More than one-tenth of all recent immigrants are self-employed (a category that includes professionals and business owners); among Asians the rate is even higher. In fact, in 1987 Asians owned 4.1 percent of all retail stores across the nation, a percentage considerably in excess of their share of the population. This high rate of self-employment set Asian immigrants apart from blacks, who in that same year owned only 3.1 percent of business establishments (and comprised 12 percent of the population), as well as Hispanics, with one notable exception—about 20 percent of all Cubans are self-employed; another 30 percent worked for other Cubans. In the four gateway cities, two out of every nine Asian households owned a business enterprise in 1987.

Immigrant entrepreneurs are helping to revive the small neighborhood stores that were common in the nation's cities prior to World War II. Arabs in Detroit and Chicago, and Cubans and Nicaraguans in Miami, have helped confound the predictions of some economists that large corporations would take over the retail trade, forcing many independent merchants out of business.[19]

Nowhere is the proliferation of immigrant businesses more evident than in New York. Many Greeks own coffee shops; Koreans, fruit and vegetable markets; Dominicans, construction firms; Asian Indians, travel agencies; and Chinese, restaurants. In Los Angeles, Koreans are concentrated in the proprietorship of liquor stores, gasoline stations, and hamburger stands, while Indian immigrants own motels and dry cleaning establishments.

Much smaller in number but equally enterprising in their own way—and certainly more exotic—are recent African immigrants. The several hundred Senegalese peddlers who crowd the sidewalks of New York in their native garb are no doubt the city's most colorful self-employed group. Although many of these activities are not legal (because the peddlers lack licenses), their uncanny ability to materialize with umbrellas in the midst of unexpected downpours has elicited the appreciation of many a Manhattanite. These small-time black entrepreneurs purchase their goods from Chinese and Korean wholesalers in the city, thus further promoting ethnic business activity.[20]

No group better exemplifies the entrepreneurial spirit than Asians. Remarkably driven, they have grabbed an increasingly large, but by no means dominant, share of retail establishments in Los Angeles, New York, Houston, and other metropolises. Perhaps it should not be surprising that Houston, the embodiment of the freewheeling Texans, would be attractive to equally freewheeling entrepreneurs from the Far East. The Asian population in this city has risen from 2,500 in 1965 to 67,000 in 1990. Among the early Asian settlers was Lang Lee Woo, who left mainland China in 1949 and became one of the city's wealthiest individuals. Thanks to him, Houston can boast of being the first metropolis to have a suburban Chinatown, complete with pagoda-like structures selling western-wear clothing, built from a master plan.[21] In Houston's downtown, with its own, more genuine Chinatown, 39 percent of all commercial buildings are owned by foreign, mostly Asian, investors—the highest percentage of such ownership in the country, with the exception of Los Angeles. Asians are estimated to own (in the early 1990s) two out of five retail stores in Los Angeles County, and one-third in the San Francisco metropolitan area, although high-volume chain stores remain predominantly in white hands. There are a dozen or more Asian Indian, Chinese, and Korean businesses in every state, including the Dakotas, Maine, and Vermont.

Of all Asian groups, the Koreans have progressed most rapidly in the shortest period of time. The total number admitted to this country during the 1950s was only 6,000—mostly wives of American soldiers—rising to 35,000 in the 1960s, 268,000 in the following decade, and 334,000 in the 1980s. Remarkably, for every thousand Korean residents, there were more than one hundred Korean-owned enterprises in 1987. This means that every third Korean household owned a business—a rate much higher than that for other ethnic groups. In a five-year period (1982–87), the number of Korean businesses more than doubled, and sales tripled, as Koreans raced ahead of other Asians in Los Angeles, Chicago, and Washington, D.C. Moreover, the Korean stores tend to be highly profitable, although in New York the recession curtailed their expansion in the early 1990s. Korean sales-per-enterprise ratios exceed even those for stores owned by Japanese-Americans and

Chinese-Americans, many of whom arrived here a generation or more ago.

Why have the Koreans (who are concentrated in retail trade), Asian Indians (found mostly in services), and many other immigrant groups done well as entrepreneurs? Some point to cultural factors; immigrants, they say, come from ethnic backgrounds that incline them to self-employment. Others cite economic causes, maintaining that the structure of urban economies and limited opportunities for aliens in American business make self-employment one of the most direct routes to success. Examining how these explanations apply can help provide an answer to the pressing question of whether immigrants compete with or complement domestic workers.

In fact, both cultural and economic motivations are present and reinforce each other. For example, East European Jews were much more likely to be self-employed than others in the early part of the twentieth century. But they also brought with them extensive experience as small businessmen that was lacking in rural Catholics who emigrated from the same region. Today, a much higher proportion of Indians and Koreans are self-employed than Mexicans or native-born Americans. But a substantial number of Asians who own businesses were involved in some form of commercial activity prior to emigrating. Asian Indians have a long tradition of small-business ownership in African nations, and Chinese entrepreneurs have been active in Southeast Asia for centuries. Similarly, the business success of Cubans, and more recently Nicaraguans, in Miami can be linked to their commercial experience.

One common thread is that typically, new entrepreneurs, be they Korean, Cuban, or Indian, have a middle-class background. This is particularly evident among those from Korea. Most Koreans who purchased the first fruit and vegetable stands in New York had owned small businesses in South Korea. A hairstylist and a jewelry store proprietor in a small Maryland suburban shopping center were proprietors of similar establishments in Korean cities. Other entrepreneurs were able to transfer profitable wig-making operations from Korea to Los Angeles.

Emigration from Korea has been very selective; those who depart are particularly well educated, with a high proportion holding college degrees. It is not unusual to find Koreans holding two full-time jobs as a means of saving sufficient funds to purchase small stores. They also show exceptional willingness to locate in older, minority neighborhoods that American supermarket and other retail chains regard as too risky. In earlier generations such stores were run by immigrant Jews, Italians, and Greeks, but their sons and daughters showed little interest in carrying on the tradition. Undeterred by high crime rates, exorbitant insurance premiums, and stupendous levels of pilferage, Korean entrepreneurs eagerly bought stores that their previous owners, white and black, were only too happy to unload. Capital came from so-called *kehs*, a centuries-old Korean system of investment in which members of a group contribute a certain amount of their weekly earnings into a common pot, and individuals in turn take the total sum home. The money accrued by this process frequently supplements savings necessary to purchase a business, typically a cash transaction.

In Los Angeles County, Koreans, who made up less than 1 percent of the population, were by the early 1980s operating nearly 5 percent of all retail enterprises. By the mid-1980s about seven thousand stores were identified as Korean-owned. In the low-income south central Los Angeles area, one-third of all small markets and liquor stores and a majority of gas stations are in Korean hands. About two-fifths of all Korean household heads in Los Angeles are self-employed.[22] Across the continent, in Washington, D.C., Koreans are reported to control 54 percent of all dry cleaning establishments and 16 percent of all liquor stores. Virtually every shopping center in northern Virginia has one or more Korean-owned shops and markets.

Korean business acumen and willingness to work long hours have been widely reported in business journals. Articles profile young Koreans and other Asians who combine sixteen-hour days and shrewd investments to become wealthy within ten years of their arrival in America. Koreans appear to be moving more rapidly into the national mainstream than any other ethnic group in the past, including the Irish, Jews, and Italians. Most Koreans, unlike other Asian groups, belong to mainstream Protestant denominations, and their church-related activities facilitate their rapid absorption into American society.

The economic success of recent immigrants, particularly Asian entrepreneurs, is commonly attributed to their personal traits—relatively high levels of education, the mastery of important skills, high motivation for success, and a strong work ethic. Perhaps equally important, although often overlooked, is the existence of the ethnic enclave as an economic entity with elements resembling a medieval guild. An ethnic enclave is a geographic area that includes among its residents a high proportion of persons with similar ethnic backgrounds or native origins. As applied here, the term differs from the more negative "ghetto," which implies that residents are restricted to an area not by choice but by economic circumstances or prejudice. In the case of ethnic enclaves, many people reside there for the sense of belonging and security they provide.

Ethnic enclaves offer their residents several advantages. First, they provide cultural and language affinity, something most immigrants crave, be they Russians, Laotians, or Mexicans. Second, entrepreneurs within the enclave offer work to immigrants who have few other options. Many newcomers, lacking proficiency in English or legal status, or both, have difficulty finding work in the open market at wages commensurate with their abilities. Within the enclave, language and legal status take second place to performance and willingness to endure grueling conditions.

From the perspective of the ethnic entrepreneur, hiring from within the enclave through an interpersonal network offers several advantages. The employer can obtain detailed information on the background of prospective workers and use their families as a means to influence behavior. The employment of these people can help insulate ethnic firms from the economic forces operating in the outside labor market, such as labor shortages, union pressures, high turnover, and expectations of a formal, structured process for advancement.

Because of the symbiotic relationship between the ethnic employer and worker, labor codes, minimum wage standards, and overtime pay regulations are often ignored. The informal work relations that prevail in ethnic firms provide the edge these enterprises need to prosper in the highly competitive business world. Workers understand that, in exchange for their loyalty and willingness to accept lower wages and benefits than those working outside the enclave, they are ensured job security. Among the advantages of working for fellow ethnics is the opportunity for on-the-job training. Many young immigrants prefer to work within the enclave because their ambition is to become self-employed. This requires more capital than can be saved; they know they will be dependent on ethnic credit associations for loans, and access to these loans depends on a favorable reputation in terms of hard work within the enclave.

To an outsider the relationship between employers and employees might seem too casual, as federal and state labor regulations intended to protect workers from abuses are frequently ignored. But the relationship has to be viewed as being closer in spirit to the medieval guild practices than to the American business environment. The use of community elders to resolve disputes between owner and worker observed in Asian enclaves would not be acceptable to most Americans. Yet in today's highly successful industrial Japan, employers are expected to intervene in the personal lives of their workers if problems in their homes could affect work performance.

Much has been written about "Little Havana," the Cuban enclave in Miami.[23] A similar, more recent success story is "Little Managua," home to the 75,000 to 100,000 mostly middle-class Nicaraguans who came to Miami after the Sandinista takeover in 1979. Despite their previous status of relative affluence, only a minority of the Nicaraguans arrived with money; most had to accumulate capital by taking odd jobs or obtaining professional licenses. Within five years after arriving, these ambitious Central Americans had established an estimated six hundred businesses, from small shops to professional offices.[24] Their ethnic enclave is thriving, in part because coming to an area that already had a large Hispanic population facilitated their absorption, and in part because skills and entrepreneurial activities are transferable, be it from Europe, Asia, or Central America.

The economic viability of enclaves, regardless of ethnicity, depends on four conditions. First, capital must be possessed or accumulated within the enclave. Second, there must be a core of individuals with substantial business and financial skills. A labor force willing to work at lower wages, or under conditions that would not be acceptable outside the enclave, is essential. Finally, local merchants and professionals must depend on their fellow ethnics for a substantial share of their business.

Earlier immigrants—Jews, Italians, and Greeks—had few, if any, sources of outside capital. However, many middle-class Asians come to the United States with the specific objective of investing their funds. Similarly, numerous Cubans and Central Americans had their savings on deposit in Miami banks prior to emigrating. Other middle-class entrepreneurs accumulate capital by working outside the enclave as professionals. A high proportion of wives are also employed, as are teenagers (on a part-time basis) and other family members, who are expected to pool their earnings. In addition to using family earnings, Korean and Hong Kong expatriates also benefited from the real estate boom in their countries, and selling their property provided the capital to purchase businesses in the United States. Those who lack such initial capital, as noted earlier, join a *keh*. A conservative estimate is that, in the Washington, D.C., area alone, over $100 million is deposited in these clubs.[25]

Core groups of experienced entrepreneurs typically establish the first businesses in an enclave. As new immigrants arrive, with or without capital, they take jobs with these earlier entrepreneurs to accumulate business and language skills, and in later years many become independent. Ethnic businessmen in the construction or food-service industry, Korean greengrocers and wholesalers, and Chinese apparel producers offer their compatriots opportunities for on-the-job training. Buoyed by such experiences, workers in ethnic enclaves can often advance at a rate that they could never match in the general economy.[26]

The continuing economic success of the enclaves is critically dependent upon their ability to obtain a continuous supply of new immigrants. Our immigration laws, by emphasizing family reunification, facilitate the recruitment of kin as additional workers in family enterprises. However, obtaining entry visas from most Asian nations, particularly for brothers and sisters, may involve a wait of five or more years. So ethnic businesses, which are typically family rather than individual enterprises, must often look for workers outside their own family—or resort to illegal means.

The most efficient recourse is to hire undocumented workers, drawn from members of one's extended household, other relatives, or close friends. As a result, the pace of illegal entry into U.S. cities in recent decades for numerous ethnic groups has been closely related to work opportunities with others of the same nationality. If fewer jobs in traditional ethnic sectors had been available during the 1980s, the number of undocumented workers coming to our cities would have been substantially smaller. Moreover, had the immigrant population been less concentrated, the job opportunities available to undocumented workers would have been much greatly reduced.

The ethnic enclave provides employment opportunities for countrymen and women regardless of their skills. In front of one building in New York's Chinatown, an observer can see elderly Chinese laborers struggling to lift heavy cargo from trucks driven by other Chinese to fish markets and restaurants whose owners and employees are also Chinese. On the second floor are offices of Chinese physicians and dentists, while an importer of silk occupies the third floor. The building is a microcosm of a closely knit economic network involving all skills and ages. Chinese immigrants, unlike those from Korea or India, include large numbers of unskilled workers with little formal education.

Enclave businesses also benefit from the patronage of compatriots. Observations in the Chinese enclave in lower Manhattan, Vietnamese shopping areas in Orange County, California, and Cuban enclaves in Miami suggest that the vast majority of customers and clients (restaurants geared to tourists being an exception) are fellow ethnics. The prosperity of immigrant-owned enterprises within enclaves is particularly dependent on such familiar faces as consumers in gateway cities, where small business is highly competitive and requires aggressive measures to remain solvent. Ethnic consumers also include persons who moved from the immediate neighborhood to better housing as their incomes rose but return to shop in the enclave, seeking ethnic products not available elsewhere. The enclave also serves in the role of a social center for dispersed ethnic communities.

Sustained patronage is facilitated by hiring fellow ethnics, and the proportion of these employees in enterprises is high. In Atlanta, for example, 58 percent of all Korean stores have one or more paid Korean employees.[27] Such patronage makes these neighborhoods almost self-sufficient units.

Although the ethnic enclave benefits new immigrants and contributes to their economic advancement, its presence is not essential for success. The ability of numerous immigrants to advance as entrepreneurs outside the enclave suggests that it serves as more than a protective shield from external competition. The example of Bhaktars and Patels from the Indian state of Gujarat illustrates this point. Gujarat is located on the Indian Ocean and has been a trading center since the Middle Ages. Bhaktars and Patels, members of a small minority from this state whose religious teachings differ from the Hindu mainstream, established businesses in East Africa decades ago and have been among its most active traders. As a result of African nationalism, many were forced to leave the continent. In the early 1970s some settled in England, others in California, where they were joined by relatives coming directly from Gujarat. Because the Bhaktars and Patels who came first were typically professionals—many had engineering degrees—skilled jobs on the West Coast were not difficult to find. But many strove to become self-employed, following in their centuries-old tradition as traders.

Bhaktars began purchasing small motels along California highways in the early 1970s and owned two hundred motels in that state and more than four hundred in other states by the end of the decade. The Patels have done even better, apparently controlling one thousand of the six thousand motels in California. In the late 1970s some began to invest in the South, a region historically not receptive to nonwhite immigrants. A common pattern among Patels is for the men to work in industry, using their earnings to purchase motels to be operated by their wives and extended families.[28] By 1982 Indians owned more than 3,100 hotels and motels across the land, 8 percent of all such establishments in the nation. These entrepreneurs found an economic niche in small motels that, under their previous ownership, could not withstand the competition from chains. Many native owners were simply not willing to devote the long hours and hard work necessary to remain in business; most, in fact, were thrilled to find someone willing to take the motels off their hands.

Motels are considered good investments by Indians because the entire family can be utilized to run them and because they anticipate rising land values will cause the property to appreciate. Their interest in this sector may also arise from the experience of other Gujaratis who came to London in the 1960s and bought small hotels, accumulating capital that was later brought to the United States. But whatever the financial rewards, it is nonetheless difficult to imagine a well-paid American engineer asking his parents and children to live and work in a motel.

Korean businessmen also settled far beyond their base in Los Angeles, establishing enterprises in places as diverse as Pittsburgh, Salt Lake City, and Poughkeepsie. In these communities the Korean population is widely dispersed. In Reno and Tulsa most of the several hundred Korean-owned restaurants, stores, and service shops can be found in low-income neighborhoods. A similar phenomenon is apparent in the proliferation of Chinese restaurants in communities that have not attracted immigrants in large numbers for two centuries. New immigrants are leaving their entrepreneurial imprint primarily in retail sales and services, but a growing number also own factories, which make products as diverse as soaps and metalwork. The largest concentration is in the apparel industry, where Asian (primarily Chinese and Korean) entrepreneurs in 1982 employed over 7,000 workers, and more than 25,000 in 1987.[29]

Cities in a Competitive Market

American cities thrived for a century or more because they enjoyed several inherent advantages. The concentration of skilled and unskilled labor allowed the efficient production of goods and services. These production centers were the places where transportation networks were formed and converged. Their accessibility allowed downtown areas to become the dominant business districts in virtually every metropolitan region. In the post–World War II era older northern core cities became less competitive as demographic and other changes caused economic activity to shift to suburbs, the South, and the West. Since the 1970s international competition has further weakened the manufacturing base of cities, while suburban shopping malls have become the new climate-controlled downtowns.

Perhaps the most important effect of recent immigration has been the restoration of urban competitors in particular sectors. This has been achieved by immigrants in their roles as low-wage workers, professionals, and entrepreneurs who encourage and contribute investment. To evaluate immigrant workers' importance in the urban economy, their roles must be considered in the context of the larger labor market.

Economists frequently view the labor market as composed of two sectors. The first is the primary market where workers are subject to standard labor laws. A set of formal rules and regulations governs the relationship between employers and workers. Enterprises include the government, large corporations, and institutions that are frequently unionized, with wages negotiated through collective bargaining. This sector has been diluted by falling union membership in manufacturing, once the mainstay of organized labor, and by significant job cuts in large, service-oriented enterprises, particularly those in communications and finance in the early 1990s. Native workers are more likely than immigrants to be employed in the primary sector.

Characteristics distinguishing the secondary sector include a labor market that is not unionized, with few regulations and wages set by supply and demand. The majority of new immigrants, particularly undocumented workers employed within ethnic enclaves or toiling in restaurants and personal service businesses, are likely to be in the secondary labor market.

The presence of secondary-market workers has enabled cities to compete at two levels: with the suburban areas that have become the new centers of metropolitan commercial activity and with other nations that export their products to the United States. Revitalized inner-city commercial areas, including ethnic enclave businesses, reduce the outflow of city shoppers to suburban malls and smaller shopping centers.

As noted earlier, immigrants are overrepresented in low-wage industries such as apparel, shoes, and furniture, which have traditionally depended on alien labor. Immigrant workers in California and Texas cities have made these areas rich in such industries. Do cities actually benefit from the presence of these low-wage sectors? Would it not be better to locate such factories in a less-developed country with abundant cheap labor and retain for ourselves the higher-wage industrial jobs? The labor movement struggled for decades to rid the United States of sweatshops, and yet we now appear to applaud the proliferation of such enterprises in American cities.

In reality, older American cities in particular would have difficulty with the concentrated production of capital-intensive goods, which require high technology. Most of these cities are not considered by investors as potential sites for new industry. Shortages of undeveloped land, obsolete physical plants, excessive tax rates, and high transportation costs are among the drawbacks cited to explain the lack of private investment. Privately, foreign enterprises are fearful that a central-city facility would be exposed to the urban ills and dangers portrayed almost daily in the American and international media. For a stagnating urban economy, any productive economic activity is a plus. A Newark, New Jersey, is not likely to attract large research laboratories and certainly not a Japanese automaker. But with both commercial space and immigrant labor available at low cost, older cities can attract labor-intensive manufacturing and service industries. If the United States aimed to produce only high-tech goods, not only would its trade balance be distorted by the move, but the effort would exacerbate its difficulties in the competitive world market as a result of overspecialization.

Unfortunately, the list of products in which the United States is fully competitive is short. Many consumer and commercial electronic products (including most video equipment) are essentially no longer produced within our borders. As for other products, such as computers, the American competitive edge has been eroding. Sad to say, the biggest "exports" to Japan today are American office buildings, land, corporations, and natural resources. Should the United States abandon the manufacture of clothing, which can be produced more cheaply abroad, in order to concentrate on regaining a foothold in the market for electronic products, it may find only that these, too, can frequently be imported at a price lower than they can be produced domestically.

The benefits of relatively low-wage industries extend well beyond the employment they provide. First of all, these plants pay local taxes. They also generate business for local suppliers. The workers at manufacturing plants spend most of their paychecks locally, helping to stimulate retail sales. All in all, older cities that have difficulty attracting high-tech business enterprises can benefit mightily from industries that at first glance might seem less than glamorous.

Highly skilled immigrants also make a valuable contribution to urban economies. These craftsmen—stonemasons, jewelers, and others—help fill the gap left by the reluctance of our talented high school graduates to learn skilled trades, despite the relatively high wages they offer. Many immigrant workers are trained by their parents and grandparents; others receive more formal instruction in technical schools in their native lands prior to settling in this country. The city provides them the opportunity to earn a higher wage than they would in their country of origin.

Native workers with specialized skills may have once worked in the urban core, but they have increasingly been lured to more attractive positions in the suburbs. Immigrants help fill the gap. The availability of a skilled labor force can offset some of the disadvantages common to central-city locations, such as congestion and high taxes, that discourage industries from expanding their operations within the inner city. Generally speaking, the absence of a ready pool of both unskilled and skilled workers has contributed to the decision of companies to move from central cities.

Even more valuable than skilled immigrants are those who come to our shores with professional training, particularly in science and engineering. The ability of cities to attract these immigrants has allowed some small firms to maintain their operations within the urban core. The 1980 census enumerated 23,300 Asian-born engineers and natural scientists living in central cities. Upward of 95 percent of all such foreign-born professionals reside in urban areas. In the economically stagnating city of Detroit, 44 percent of all Asians are professionals. Many trained immigrants find jobs with ethnic entrepreneurs who, having some scientific training themselves, have established small companies. Asians have been particularly successful in combining technological and managerial skills to create companies that produce technologically advanced products.

Perhaps the best-known scientist-entrepreneur is the Chinese-born An Wang, who attended college in the United States and remained to form Wang Laboratories. At its peak, this corporation, specializing in office automation equipment, had sales in excess of $2 billion and more than thirty-one thousand employees. The company headquarters is located in the aging industrial city of Lowell, Massachusetts, which was revitalized by the growth of the corporation. Other Asians head small companies in Silicon Valley, Boston, and elsewhere. These high-tech firms, employing thousands of American-born workers, would simply not exist if our immigration laws had continued to restrict Asians. Since World War II America's serious shortage of trained scientific personnel has been mitigated by immigrants trained in our schools or overseas, and their presence has clearly enhanced the competitive position of white-collar urban industries.

The ability of cities to compete depends not only on the availability of labor but also on the willingness of residents to invest. Ethnic entrepreneurs have become a significant source of capital in gateway cities. Some obtain capital from their counterparts in Hong Kong, Japan, Korea, or Taiwan; others generate it internally through individual savings or by pooling resources. The internal savings are facilitated by the presence of low-wage ethnic enclaves and the propensity of both the very young and old to work in family enterprises.

Surrogate banking institutions, such as the Korean *keh*, or its Ethiopian equivalent, called the *ekub*, are an essential source of financing for ethnic groups not able to import capital.

In some instances large investment by foreigners in one place can lead to the formation of small ethnic communities outside large central cities. This is particularly noticeable in the manufacturing sector, where 1.4 million Americans in 1985 were employed in foreign-owned factories. The Toyota automobile plant that opened in 1988 in Georgetown, Kentucky, is a good example. Three years later, the plant had about 3,500 American workers earning relatively high wages. About thirty Japanese families and one hundred short-term Japanese workers without families have already moved to this small community and live in town houses owned by Toyota. Local grocery stores carry Japanese food. As part of the deal involved in Toyota's decision to locate in Georgetown, the state has built a school for the children of Japanese technicians. Kentucky spent over $200 million to entice Toyota to locate there—a high price, but also an indication of how valuable an asset the state considers Japanese manufacturing. The local response to the Japanese has been very positive—not only because of the jobs generated, but also because Toyota, although exempt from certain property taxes, contributed substantial sums to public schools and other institutions. Not accidentally, Toyota advertising in early 1992 featured smiling workers from this facility, an interesting twist to the "Buy American" campaign.

Additional Japanese companies—two of them controlled by Toyota—are planning facilities in the area, and the Japanese are also planning to invest in a golf course and residential development near Georgetown. The same phenomenon—small colonies of Japanese nationals reshaping the economic landscape—can be observed near Nashville, Tennessee, where a Nissan automobile plant has been operating since the mid-1980s. Several years after its opening, this facility rejected a United Automobile Workers (UAW) bid to unionize its employees, an indication that the American workers were satisfied with Japanese management, which may encourage further foreign investment.

Most foreign investment, though, large manufacturing plants excepted, is in cities. By the late 1970s, all major Japanese trading companies had established offices in New York City. The economic boom enjoyed by Manhattan during the 1980s can be attributed, in part, to foreign investment in real estate. Japanese investors have purchased some of the largest office structures in Manhattan, including the Exxon and Tower 49 buildings. According to the Port Authority of New York and New Jersey, Japan now ranks second to Canada as an investor in Manhattan real estate, providing funds for additional construction. These investments help stimulate the local economy. Although purchases of real estate by foreign banks and corporations frequently turned out to be poor investments by the standards of the 1990s, native sellers were able to convert their equity into cash. These funds, in turn, were often used to finance new development in New York.

International banking and commerce also encourage immigration. The number of foreign banks in New York grew by more than 50 percent between 1976 and 1987. In the late 1980s the city was home to 435 such institutions, employing more than thirty-one thousand workers. In 1987 Japanese investors held one-third of the total assets of all state-chartered California banks (mostly in Los Angeles and San Francisco).[30] Thirteen of the twenty-five largest banks in the state have majority foreign ownership. Los Angeles is second only to New York in the number of foreign banks based locally; next are Chicago and San Francisco. The management of these banks is frequently foreign-born, and their presence attracts additional investment and more foreign nationals to these cities.

The Japanese are not the only non-Europeans to invest. Korean banks are thriving in Los Angeles, while South American institutions proliferate in Miami and, to a lesser extent, New York. Investors from Hong Kong have poured billions of dollars into San Francisco real estate since the mid-1980s. The major contribution of foreign investment is not to expand immigration but to create jobs for natives in central cities. Although Japanese trading companies in the mid-1970s employed almost 11,000 Japanese nationals in New York City, the majority of their employees were Americans. A 1978 survey estimated 140,000 city residents worked for foreign firms.[31] This number appears to have risen substantially during the 1980s, but precise statistics are unavailable.

A 1987 Coldwell Banker survey found that 13 percent of the commercial real estate in large cities, but only 2 percent of all such property nationwide, is foreign owned.[32] The presence of ethnic enclaves in these cities strengthens investor confidence in their economic potential. Investors are also thereby assured that the bilingual services they may require for business or personal use will be available. In fact, the demand for bilingual personnel by foreign corporations has created jobs for immigrants in everything from stenography to travel services. Most foreign nationals located in the United States maintain schools for their children, creating a demand for foreign-born teachers. Although the presence of Asian and European business communities in American cities encourages permanent immigration, most persons hired by foreign firms are nonetheless local residents.

Immigrants, by their own activities, generate international trade. For instance, Chinese-American entrepreneurs in California are financing numerous projects, including hotels, shopping centers, and office buildings in China. Henry Y. Hwang, head of a small Los Angeles bank, fled the Communists in 1948. Despite ideological differences, Chinese officials welcome Hwang and other capitalist entrepreneurs and take great pride in their accomplishments on American soil. Cultural, linguistic, and family ties to China have enabled Hwang to finance a new $150 million shopping and office center in Beijing.[33] Wang Laboratories has negotiated the manufacture of computer products in several Chinese cities, using the influence of Chauncey Chu, a Chinese-American who is also a Wang vice president. Action Computer Corporation, a California-based company owned by a Chinese-American, has assembled a large staff of Chinese-speaking persons to penetrate the market, a difficult task for an American firm.

Immigration, Jobs, and Wages

Cities as a whole clearly derive many advantages from the presence of immigrants. But cities are made up of many groups—employers and workers, sellers and consumers, rich and poor, white and black, young and old, owners and renters—each with distinct interests. Which groups and classes benefit from immigration?

The effects on workers are considered first because the fear of job competition and lower wages has fueled the most bitter anti-immigrant sentiment. In the earlier discussion of how immigration laws evolved, "taking jobs from American workers" was found to be the most consistent theme voiced by opponents of liberal entry policies, whatever their actual motivation may have been. Although the claim that native workers as a group were harmed was never substantiated, the relationship between job opportunities for these workers and immigration is complex and not fully understood by economists.

The analysis presented in this chapter and observation of the labor market in gateway cities during the 1970s and 1980s suggest that the addition of immigrant workers to a local economy enhances the competitiveness of its industries. Concurrently, the demand for locally produced goods and services rises. This is especially apparent in New York and Los Angeles, where a large population base and a diversified economy mean that many of the goods consumed in the area are also produced there. Expanded payrolls thus have a large "employment multiplier effect" on the entire region.

Some of the jobs that immigrants help to create—notably in retail trade and personal services—are taken by other immigrants. But in many other areas—utilities, banking, finance, real estate, and communications—new jobs tend to be filled by natives. Similarly, added economic activity creates new demand for nontechnical professionals—lawyers, accountants, and bankers—primarily natives because language and licensing requirements make it difficult for immigrants to enter these fields. For example, the 1980 census found that only 320 recent male immigrants in New York were working as professionals in the legal field—a mere 0.5 percent of all male attorneys in the city.

Generally speaking, immigrants create substantially more jobs than they take in such fields as communications and utilities. By contrast, they take more jobs than they create in manufacturing, retail trade, and restaurants. Thus, in Los Angeles, New York, San Francisco, and other cities, the net effect of immigration has been to *redistribute* the jobs available for native workers away from manufacturing and lower-skill services toward the white-collar sector, particularly in management and the professions. This redistribution, which began in the 1970s, accelerated during the 1980s, with more and more native men and women shifting to white-collar jobs, while immigrants, particularly Hispanics, expanded their hold on manufacturing. By 1991, 23 percent of all blacks, but only 10 percent of all Hispanics, working in Los Angeles held professional or managerial positions. In the same year, nondurable goods manufacturing attracted fewer than 13,000 blacks compared to 194,000 Hispanics.[34]

The vast majority of jobs taken by immigrants are in the private sector. The proportion of recent immigrants holding nonprofessional public-sector jobs is extremely small. But the presence of immigrants expands the demand for public services and increases local tax revenue, leading to an expansion of public, particularly municipal, employment. The number of teachers, for example, rises in almost direct proportion to increased enrollment. The demand for other municipal services—police, utilities, social services—is also linked to population growth. About one in seven persons employed in the New York metropolitan area, and one in nine in Los Angeles County, works for the local, state, or federal government. Of course, population is not the only factor determining public employment levels. During the 1970s, New York City's fiscal crisis was primarily responsible for severe reductions in municipal employment. During the 1980s, however, as economic conditions improved and population grew modestly (owing exclusively to immigration), municipal employment expanded significantly again. The 1990–91 fiscal crisis forced New York City once more to curtail municipal jobs, but the employment level remained well above the low point that followed the earlier cutbacks.

Public-sector jobs are more important for blacks than for whites, Asians, or Hispanics. In New York City* almost one-fourth of all black men and one-third of all black women in 1980 worked for local, state, or federal government. All net gains in jobs experienced by native blacks during the 1970s were generated by the public sector. This pattern continued into the next decade. Between 1983 and 1989, blacks gained fifty-nine thousand jobs in government at all three levels, which accounted for about seven out of ten new jobs for blacks in the city. Among the 508,000 government jobs in 1991, almost two out of five were held by blacks, although blacks constitute only about one-fourth of the employed labor force. The gains accrue primarily to native blacks; aside from the health-care field, relatively few black immigrants obtain public-sector jobs. On a per capita basis, black women in New York are seven times more likely to hold jobs in the public sector than women who are recent immigrants.

Moreover, for blacks the public sector means not only more stable jobs than typically found in the private sector but also relatively high

---

* The importance of government employment for blacks extends well beyond New York. Almost three out of ten blacks employed in Los Angeles County and Miami/Dade County in 1991 worked for the government. In Chicago, Detroit, Houston, and nearly all other large cities, blacks' share of public-sector jobs is disproportionately high. About as many Hispanics as blacks work for the government in Los Angeles, although Hispanics outnumber blacks in the labor force by a ratio of more than three to one. Hispanics generally hold many fewer government jobs, except in San Antonio, which has a majority Hispanic population. In most other cities an expansion in the public sector means more jobs for blacks rather than Hispanics.

pay. The earnings of blacks in government exceed earnings in the private sector. Blacks employed by the police and fire departments in California earn one-third more than blacks in the private sector. Because wage gains in government have outpaced private industry and a disproportionately high number of blacks work in the public sector, this has contributed toward reducing wage disparities, particularly between black women and other women.

On the whole, native workers are benefiting (as have previous generations) from their transition to white-collar jobs, a process accelerated by the presence of immigrant workers. As older, urban-dwelling native workers in manufacturing retire or decide to take jobs in other sectors, immigrants emerge as the newest generation of industrial workers. In several large urban areas, the percentage of industrial workers that were immigrants in the early 1990s approached (and in Los Angeles and Miami exceeded) the historic peak of immigrants' share in the manufacturing work force nationwide attained during the early decades of the twentieth century. There were, nonetheless, notable differences from the earlier period. High-wage, unionized Pennsylvania steel mills and Michigan assembly plants, industries dominated by immigrants in 1910, saw few foreign-born workers eight decades later.

Job expansion nationally and in gateway cities that can be linked to immigrant consumers and entrepreneurs has probably equaled, and in some areas exceeded, jobs taken by immigrant workers. The most visible impact of their entry into the labor force is the overall growth in employment levels and the change in sectoral distribution of jobs among native workers. In this respect, the impact of immigration parallels the experience during earlier periods when foreign-born workers filled the nation's factories and small immigrant shops lined the ethnic neighborhoods of American cities.

The relationship between immigrant workers and wages has been a matter of controversy for a century or more. An increase in the number of workers, regardless of their origin, competing for the same job can be expected to result in wage depression. Fortunately, because not all immigrants are concentrated in one occupation or industry, substantial wage effects are rarely observed.

Since the late nineteenth century there have been numerous attempts to correlate wages with immigration, none of which demonstrated conclusively long-term effects. Following the economic downturn in

1894, Congress debated the cause of the general wage decline and appointed a commission to determine the linkage between immigration, wages, and the economic climate. The report, quoted in the House of Representatives, found no such relationship.[35] Recent research finds the effects of immigrants on native worker earnings to be temporary and minor. This conclusion is shared by Robert Topel, an economist at the University of Chicago, who found the impact of foreign-born workers on native wages in 1987 to be, in most instances, negligible.[36] Similarly, a study determined that wage effects associated with undocumented Mexican workers also appear to be small.[37]

Immigration had a more significant impact on low-skilled workers in Los Angeles, where wages in the metropolitan area during the 1970s declined in comparison to the nation as a whole. This trend was due in part to the presence of immigrants, particularly illegal entrants, during a period of slow growth.[38] Immigrants themselves, and to a lesser extent native Hispanics, absorbed a considerable share of the fall in wages in Los Angeles as natives left low-paying jobs for more lucrative positions. By the mid-1980s immigrants dominated the work force in several Los Angeles industries. Their presence encouraged the inflow of more undocumented workers as jobs expanded. Laborers to fill these low-paying jobs could be most readily obtained only a few hours away across the international border. Wages dropped as a result in the apparel industry, but because virtually all production workers were Hispanic immigrants, the native population was little affected. Among the beneficiaries of lower wages were those holding white-collar jobs in apparel factories and those supplying goods and services to the apparel industry.

The Los Angeles wage pattern was also observed in New York during the 1970s—relative declines in wages in manufacturing and retail trades. As in Los Angeles, immigrants were replacing natives in these sectors. The large immigrant flow to New York was one cause of the decade's modest wage depression, but more recent data shows how temporary this condition was. In a sharp reversal, wage growth in New York in the 1980s exceeded the national rate in nearly every sector, even though the rate of immigration accelerated.

How to explain this phenomenon? The most likely answer is that the New York City economy stagnated during the 1970s as a result of massive outmigration, a sharp decline in manufacturing jobs, and a fiscal crisis. This caused a temporary surplus of workers, which was exacerbated by immigration. Because these new immigrants were concentrated in the manufacturing sector, factory wages declined. The stimulative effect of immigration on the local economy was more than offset by the loss of the native population. As the economy strengthened in the 1980s—in response to the expanding national economy, growth in the financial sector, and the resurgence of newcomers from abroad—both the alien and native adult workers found employment. With the economy improving, native workers had the opportunity to seek high-wage employment. But because the rate of immigration was lower than the capacity of the economy to absorb new workers, wages rose faster in New York and unemployment declined more rapidly than elsewhere.

In 1987 unemployment in New York fell to 5.7 percent, the lowest rate since 1970; and in mid-1988, when the economy peaked, the rate declined further to 3.9 percent, a level that can be considered sufficiently low to create serious labor shortages in some industries. Unfortunately, the city's economy began to deteriorate toward the end of the decade. In the early 1990s, unemployment climbed, real estate prices crumbled, and relative wages in the private sector declined. New immigrants were not immune from the economic and fiscal woes that once again engulfed New York. Nonetheless, similar to the 1981–82 downturn, immigration to the city did not appear to slow.

In southern California, the need for additional workers was quickly met by an influx from Mexico, which led to a tempering of wages for less-skilled workers in the 1970s and early 1980s. Yet unemployment rates in the late 1980s in this region remained below the national average. Not until the early 1990s, when defense contractors' payrolls began to fall and the building boom collapsed, did the regional economy falter.

From these and related data, it becomes clear that a large influx of unskilled and semiskilled immigrant workers during periods of economic stagnation (as in the early 1980s and early 1990s) can temporarily depress wages and increase unemployment above the national level. When the economy rebounds, the opposite effect is observed. Growth in areas with substantial concentrations of new immigrant workers and entrepreneurs tends to accelerate, causing income and wages to rise more rapidly than elsewhere. This thesis is supported by an indirect but nonetheless significant indicator of economic activity in gateway cities: Three cities that absorbed a disproportionate share of immigrants—Los Angeles, New York, and San Francisco—all had per capita income gains close to or above the national average during the most recent period of economic expansion. Surprisingly, these cities were able to absorb the new population—many of whom arrived with few skills, limiting their earnings potential (illegal aliens comprise perhaps 7 percent of gateway city population, other low-income immigrants another 10 percent or more)—without reducing *average* per capita or household income. This suggests that either the majority of legal immigrants were earning substantially more than natives—an unlikely proposition—or that native earnings were rising disproportionately fast.

An examination of the income components that contributed to above-average per capita income growth in Los Angeles supports the hypothesis that there is a link between immigration and income growth. Total private earnings in Los Angeles County increased from 4.5 percent to 5.0 percent of the national total between 1977 and 1989, faster than the county's share of the U.S. population. Proprietor (entrepreneurial) income rose the most (from 3.5 to 4.4 percent of the national total), followed by income from services, nondurable manufacturing, and retail trade.[39] The growth in the nondurable manufacturing and services component would have been stimulated by immigrant workers. Income from manufacturing durable goods also spurted, primarily because Los Angeles was the recipient of large defense contracts during the 1980s.

The Middle Class as Beneficiaries

Several groups benefit from the immigrant presence. These include consumers, property owners, businesses dependent on low-wage labor, and families seeking domestic help.

Ethnic enclaves are popular destinations for shoppers, who frequently find goods that are either unavailable or for sale at substantially higher prices elsewhere. The popularity of restaurants that have proliferated in ethnic neighborhoods is a measure of both their affordability and of the variety sought by consumer palates. When immigrants own stores outside their ethnic enclaves, they are often in poorer neighborhoods, and these businesses are typically open fourteen or more hours a day, providing customers with virtually around-the-clock convenience. These enterprises are usually small and rely on free family labor, so overhead expenses tend to be modest, enabling neighborhood grocery stores, for example, to charge prices no higher than supermarkets.

Customers are usually known by name, and some are given credit, a practice supermarkets would not tolerate. Convenience, service, and price are ingredients for successful immigrant stores outside enclaves.

The ability of small Asian enterprises to remain in business is well illustrated by examining the operation of a local Chinese restaurant in a neighborhood shopping center in northern Virginia. The enterprise is typical of others sprouting in shopping centers across the land. The average hourly wage for its employees—all but one a member of an extended family, including two teenage boys—is well below the minimum wage. American teenagers would probably not tolerate going to school, working six to eight hours a day, and studying, with little sleep. But because immigrants will, consumers find meals prepared to order on the premises at a cost comparable to the fast-food outlets with which the ethnic restaurants compete.

Consumers of ethnic products are not limited to a particular segment of society in American cities. Nonetheless, it would be difficult to argue against the proposition that more affluent groups gain the most from the immigrant presence. This pattern is consistent with the distribution of benefits associated with earlier waves of aliens who came to American cities. As shoppers, middle-class families obtain some goods and numerous services at lower prices than would be the case in the absence of immigrants. Restaurant prices, housekeeping, and gardening services, in particular, are moderated by the availability of immigrant labor. Because families that dine in restaurants and hire help have above-average earnings, they stimulate much of the demand for undocumented workers in cities. Similarly, business clients and the more affluent families stay in hotels and utilize tourist services, which creates employment for immigrants.

Immigrant production workers, on the other hand, benefit people at all income levels because apparel, furniture, food products, shoes, and textiles are purchased—in differing quantities and qualities—by all income groups. Factory owners also gain from the use of immigrant labor. Interestingly, when California residents were asked whether consumers or owners benefited from the presence of illegal workers, more than four out of five believed all the benefits accrued to employers.[40] In their view (but contrary to economic theory for competitive sectors), savings from lower wages were not passed on to the consumer.

As property owners, natives profit from the increase in property values that immigrants induce. Within or on the periphery of immigrant enclaves—be it the Lower East Side of Manhattan; Flushing, New York; the Ironbound section of Newark, New Jersey; the mid-Olympic area of Los Angeles; or Westchester County, New York—property prices have uniformly soared. Native property owners have sold their real estate at prices far in excess of what they would have received if immigrants had not increased the demand for it. In some cases the original properties—boarded-up buildings—were almost valueless, with unpaid taxes exceeding the market price.

The immigrant presence could not prevent property values from sinking in a depressed market, as evidenced by the severe declines in the early 1990s. However, losses were the steepest at the upper end of the housing and commercial markets, segments that experienced the sharpest rise in the 1982–90 period. Prices of the more modest housing typically occupied by recent immigrants remained relatively stable.

Native landlords also benefit when immigrant businessmen lease space. In shopping centers located in areas of immigrant-led revival, rents are rising sharply. This revival also helps some native merchants who have businesses in older shopping areas because more active stores encourage additional consumers. Other native merchants, however, especially those who sell products similar to those available in immigrant shops, may face stiffer competition and higher rents.

The influx of illegal immigrants benefits not only the clients but also the owners of restaurants, hotels, and personal service establishments who would otherwise find it difficult to obtain labor. The manager of one large hotel chain in Washington, D.C., that does not hire immigrants without proper documentation expressed bitterness because he cannot find people to clean rooms or to work in the kitchen. His labor turnover has become so great that it has caused profits to plunge. His competitors, undeterred by the Immigration and Naturalization Service (INS), continued to hire undocumented workers and found sufficient help at bargain wage levels. The clients of the hotels and restaurants are generally unaware of the importance of these workers, but corporate earnings directly reflect the ability of these establishments to keep labor costs down, in part by hiring illegal aliens.

On the level of the individual family, immigrant housekeepers play a key (but not widely recognized) role in enabling both husband and wife to work. Without Mexicans and Central Americans (mostly illegal in this case) willing to work for low wages (the number of illegal housekeepers is unknown—the census enumerated only a small fraction of the total), thousands of California two-income families would simply not be able to afford a clean house and care for the children. Families in very afflu- ent as well as middle-class neighborhoods in large cities have discreetly managed to obtain alien domestic help. The phenomenon of house- keepers is most visible in Los Angeles, the Washington, D.C., suburbs, and other urban centers with a large Hispanic presence. To a lesser extent, Caribbean housekeepers have taken the place of native blacks in the New York region; within one generation, the native black housekeep- er all but disappeared from the domestic scene, too expensive a proposition for most families.

Neighborhoods and Schools

Debate on the impact of recent immigration frequently overlooks some of its most important side effects—the revitalization of neighborhoods and schools in both inner cities and aging suburbs. Ethnic enclaves in America's northern cities have generally arisen in the same neighbor- hoods once settled by blue-collar and lower-middle-class families who came to the country from abroad in the late nineteenth and early twentieth centuries. The flight of these families to the suburbs after World War II left whole blocks of houses empty. Some of these vacancies were filled by blacks moving from the South, by newly formed minor- ity households, and by black families relocating from substandard ghetto or public housing. Nonetheless, more than one million units remained abandoned nationwide; even occupied units deteriorated, as a result of poor maintenance by absentee slumlords and lack of incen- tives for improvements by tenants.

Throughout the North and in California, the arrival of fresh immigrants in central cities and the formation of ethnic enclaves slowed, and in some cases reversed, neighborhood decline. From Brooklyn's Brighton Beach to San Francisco's Tenderloin district, from Newark's Ironbound section to Chicago's North Side, immigrants are spurring neighborhood revital- ization. The pattern in Chicago is typical: During the 1920s the North Side neighborhood was home to the fashionable and upwardly mobile. By the 1960s the area had become so deserted that the *Chicago Tribune* called it "the urban jungle—a neighborhood of last resort for those unwanted castoffs the city had abandoned."[41] Now the area is making a comeback, thanks to five thousand or more Asians, mostly refugees from Southeast Asia, who call this neighborhood home. Rents have risen as much as 70 percent in recent years as a result of the immigrant presence.

In New York City immigrants are helping to upgrade many neighborhoods. One real success story is Brighton Beach, an area that began to deteriorate in the early 1970s, with vacant apartments and boarded-up stores. During a temporary thaw in Soviet emigration policy, as many as 60,000 mostly Jewish immigrants from the Soviet Union settled in the neighborhood, transforming it into a large Russian ethnic enclave. Today, Cyrillic alphabet signs identify *apotekas* (pharmacies), physician offices, and bookstores beneath the elevated trains along Brighton Beach Avenue, the busy thoroughfare that forms the commercial center of this revitalized neighborhood. Although the area's ethnic composition is similar to what it was in the early part of this century, contemporary non-European immigration is evident in Korean fruit and vegetable stands and in Chinese restaurants dotting the area. At a fish and meat market a hastily added, handwritten Cyrillic sign advertising Russian meat delicacies has been placed beneath a large red Chinese symbol.

Along Atlantic Avenue in the Brooklyn Heights section, Arabic signs point to the ethnic identity of restaurants, export-import businesses, and Middle Eastern groceries. Most of these enterprises are owned by Lebanese, including those that fled their war-torn land in recent years. But across the street from these shops is an Indian, and on the same block a Mexican, restaurant, as if to signify the third world presence in all of New York's ethnic neighborhoods. Redevelopment in these newly thriving areas is likely to shift the location of particular enterprises away from the major thoroughfares. Nonetheless, both the population and business ownership patterns will increasingly reflect the presence of new immigrant groups.

Not all of Brooklyn, Newark, or other inner cities are being revitalized. Not far from the upscale precincts of Brooklyn Heights, drug- and crime-infested Bedford-Stuyvesant remains a poverty-stricken neighborhood that seems to defy improvement. But there is little question that new immigrants, be they Koreans, Poles, or Armenians, represent a revival of numerous inner-city neighborhoods that had been facing a bleak future.

The New York immigrant revival can also be observed in the aging, industrial satellite cities of New Jersey, which were immigrant strongholds a half-century ago. Jersey City is home to an estimated fifteen thousand middle-class Asian Indians; Elizabeth is filled with Hispanics from Central and South America; and in Paterson, an old industrial city that has been home to waves of immigrants since the 1820s, a polyglot of languages once again fills the air.

The Portuguese community in Newark, located less than a dozen miles from midtown Manhattan, recalls the many European immigrants who crowded the area in the late nineteenth century. The recent arrivals, predominantly from the rural areas of northern Portugal, now live in the same housing that Irish railroad workers occupied a century earlier. Arriving by both legal and illegal means since the 1960s, most of Newark's Portuguese currently live in the Ironbound section, where some thirty thousand residents own well-maintained, small houses. Only a mile or two to the north, massive public housing projects have been vacated and await demolition. In the Ironbound, by contrast, the streets bustle with dozens of Portuguese-owned restaurants, bakeries, grocery stores, and travel agencies. The neighborhood is strikingly similar to formerly Italian and Jewish immigrant enclaves in the city that were virtually abandoned in the 1960s and 1970s.

Newark, long in the shadow of New York, is beginning to recover from the stigma associated with its name. The Portuguese and other groups of immigrants are among the pivotal contributors to the city's economic recovery.

Across the continent, the San Francisco Bay Area has become what the Census Bureau calls the most ethnically diverse area of the United States. San Francisco's crowded Chinatown boasts the nation's largest concentration of Chinese-Americans. Their growing numbers show up in school population statistics: in 1987 nearly one of every four students in elementary and secondary classes was Chinese, a higher percentage than whites, blacks, or Hispanics. The original Chinese enclave is growing in all directions. The North Beach area—center of the city's Italian population a generation ago—is now part of the vibrant Chinatown. In the Richmond district, north of Golden Gate Park, recent ethnic shifts are evident as Chinese, Japanese, and Filipino residents buy homes and open businesses.

Near the bulging Chinese community is the more sedate, orderly, and prosperous enclave known formally on city maps as Japantown. This

small area is not only the cultural center for the Bay Area Japanese population but also forms the core of restaurants and shops catering to the
many thousands of affluent Japanese tourists coming to San Francisco.

The city of Oakland, on the eastern shore of San Francisco Bay, lacks
the glamour of its neighbor but not its population diversity. In recent
years the large black population has been supplemented by Asians. Chinese
immigrants have revived the moribund nineteenth-century Chinatown
in the heart of the downtown commercial district. They have been
joined by Koreans and Vietnamese, and the three ethnic groups now
account for about one thousand Asian shops in the city. Other parts of
the area shelter different ethnic groups. Numerous Far Eastern banks—
always a sign of wealth—dot the Chinatown area. A massive urban
redevelopment project, aptly called the Pacific Renaissance Plaza, is under
construction there. Partially financed with Hong Kong capital, it
includes condominiums, apartments, offices, and small businesses. Within
a few hundred yards of this site a new high-rise condominium houses primarily Asians. Within a mile or two of downtown are the homes
of relatively low-income Hispanics and Filipinos. The affluent foothill
communities east of Oakland and Berkeley are attracting Asian professionals and entrepreneurs. It is ironic that Oakland, once the home of
Jack London, a strong believer in the superiority of white Anglo-Saxons,
is now part of the most ethnically diverse region in the United States.

Los Angeles' Koreatown is the largest Korean community in the
country. Twenty years ago the area was a stagnating commercial zone.
But during the late 1960s new immigrants (mostly Koreans) began to
arrive and to renovate the empty storefronts. Today Koreatown—the
economic and social heart of the estimated 200,000 Koreans living in the
greater Los Angeles area—is among the city's most thriving commercial
centers. Almost all the businesses in the district are owned by Koreans,
and a visitor to the area might think himself suddenly in Seoul. Actually,
only about one-fourth of Koreatown's residents are Korean; another
fourth are non-Korean Asians, and most of the others are Hispanics (a
fact reflected in the "Se habla espanol" signs that have sprouted in many
store windows). Until the May 1992 riots that devastated parts of the shopping area, real estate prices in the neighborhood had soared; in fact, one of
the major problems for local businessmen was to find affordable space.

In San Francisco, as in Los Angeles, Miami, Oakland, and parts of New
York City, one can no longer speak of ethnic "enclaves" surrounded by

a majority white population. The boundaries of ethnic- or minority-dominated areas are rapidly expanding in gateway cities, with the white population increasingly isolated in pockets of mostly expensive housing. Such isolation is by no means total. In gateway cities there is white—and to a lesser extent black—gentrification of some neighborhoods that remain racially mixed, and elderly whites can still be found in sections that have become predominantly Hispanic or Asian. Nonetheless, if present trends continue, in a few decades most of the non-Hispanic whites to be seen in cities such as Miami and San Francisco will be commuters and tourists.

The upgrading of neighborhoods, particularly those now inhabited by Asian and European immigrants, is partially attributable to comparatively high rates of homeownership. In Los Angeles one-fourth of recent Asian immigrant households own their residences—about the same rate as non-Hispanic whites. Among Asians who came to the city two decades ago homeownership rates are higher. Of all Chinese-Americans in San Francisco, 41 percent own their homes, a higher share than the 30 percent rate among other city residents. To the dismay of some, this has resulted in an increase in housing prices, feeding fears that the Los Angeles and San Francisco areas might follow the path of Oahu, where buyers from Japan have virtually excluded middle-income residents from the single-family housing market. The upsurge in prices has proved to be a bonanza for those selling their property to the Japanese.

The revitalization of the urban neighborhoods since the 1970s cannot, of course, be explained solely by immigration. In New York, San Francisco, Washington, D.C., and other cities, change has also been spurred by "yuppies"—young professionals without school-age children. In such cities as Richmond, Virginia, and Charleston, South Carolina, revitalization of formerly middle-class neighborhoods has been progressing despite the lack of any real immigrant presence.

There are, however, noticeable differences between the two groups in their approach to revitalization. Initially, immigrants tend to seek the cheapest housing, much of it once occupied by earlier immigrants. Even in their heyday, these structures were never the "quality housing" associated with New York's brownstones or Washington's town houses. Yuppies have shown little inclination to move into the Ironbound area of Newark or the Tenderloin section of San Francisco. Similarly, Boston's "combat zone," whose peep shows and strip joints cater to adult tastes, does not hold much appeal for upwardly mobile natives. Asians, however, are now building a China Trade Center in the area, and, spurred by this and other developments, the district is becoming part of Boston's growing Chinese and Vietnamese ethnic enclave.

Asian immigrants and yuppies do share certain characteristics. Both groups buy housing rather than rent; and both are eager to maintain their property, not only as a place to live but as a solid financial investment. The quality of neighborhood schools is a high-priority issue for both, but the more affluent whites have the option of sending their children to private academies. Immigrants, on the other hand, must rely on public education. The formation of an enclave frequently facilitates the process of improvement of public schools as the swelling immigrant enrollment changes their ethnic composition, filling classrooms with pupils eager to learn English and get ahead.

Asian children, driven by the high expectations of their parents, are remarkably hardworking, ambitious, and disciplined. One school administrator interviewed in New York maintains that the enrollment of Asians represented the most positive development for the city school system since the influx of Eastern European Jews earlier in the century. A Manhattan school principal calls the new Asian students the "backbone" of his school. A telling photograph ran on the front page of the *New York Times* on January 14, 1988, showing the eleven students from New York City high schools who qualified as semifinalists in the Westinghouse science competition. All were Asian.

The impact of Asians on school systems is also evident from studies in California showing that the expulsion and suspension rate for these students is only a fraction of the rate for other groups; the high school dropout rate is 40 percent lower for Asians than for native, non-Hispanic whites; and the proportion of Asians in gifted and talented classes in the state exceeds the rate for white students and is three times that for blacks and Hispanics. Thus, in Alhambra, a Los Angeles suburb with a majority Asian enrollment, the local high school is the only one in the nation in which the number of students taking the Advanced Placement calculus examination exceeds that of New York's two most prestigious—and selective—schools, Stuyvesant and Bronx Science.[42] Asian high school graduates are twice as likely as other students to be accepted by the University of California. This is not surprising, given their high scores nationwide on the Scholastic Aptitude Test in 1989—an average of 525 out of 800 on the math test, compared with 491 for non-Hispanic whites and 386 for blacks. (On verbal tests, whites outperform Asians, many of whom are not fluent in English.)

In the affluent suburbs of Washington, D.C., where Asians constitute only a small minority of students, they consistently win scholarships to outstanding universities. Their presence in area elementary and high schools tends to enhance the schools' already above-average test scores, particularly in mathematics. Not surprisingly, when area parents were asked whether immigrant students have helped or hurt the school their child is attending, 39 percent said that they helped, and only 5 percent that they hurt.[43] Three of every five of those polled expressed a preference for their children to attend a school with some immigrant children; only 4 percent said they would prefer a school with no immigrants. It is important to note that only about one-half of the new immigrants in the Washington area are Asian. These results suggest that immigrant children in general—not only Asians—are viewed as having a favorable impact on the schools.

In part, the strong performance of immigrant students, particularly Asians, can be traced to the schooling of their parents. An estimated 35 percent of all Asian adults have college degrees—the highest rate for any major ethnic group except Jews. But parental schooling is far from the whole answer. The performance of the children of recent Southeast Asian refugees, mostly poor farmers, fishermen, and laborers from Vietnam and Cambodia who have nothing like the educational background of the Koreans, Taiwanese, and Asian Indians in this country, is also impressive. Their children do almost as well as those of other, more established groups. The only precedent that comes to mind is that of the poor Jews who came here from the small towns of Eastern Europe at the turn of the century and whose children did spectacularly well in the public schools of New York. In both cases, parental pressure, combined with a centuries-old culturally ingrained stress on education, has driven children to study remarkably hard. In both the Asian and Jewish milieus, education has been the path to respectability. This is less evident in contemporary mainstream American society, with its emphasis on material well-being. Revealingly, Indochinese refugee students from homes where material possessions are given considerable weight in polls achieved lower grades than others from families attaching less importance to material goods.[44]

The near obsession of Asian students to do well in school, fueled by parental pressure to achieve, can have negative consequences. American students typically divide their days between school activities and recreation, but Asian-American students have little time for sports and play. Conflict can develop between parents and children who observe that a greater degree of freedom is allowed their peers of other backgrounds. There are other drawbacks as well. The awareness that immigrants perform well leads to the belief among some native parents that the opportunities for their children to attend prestigious colleges will be limited by the Asian presence. Their concerns need to be weighed against the knowledge that the school system, and ultimately the quality of the labor force, is enhanced by the capabilities and drive of the Asians. It is also important not to exaggerate this situation. Not all Asian students score high on their SAT math exams; not all behave as "model minority" teenagers. Some are juvenile delinquents; a few are even violent criminals.

Universities are caught in a dilemma. Restricting Asian enrollment is not only illegal but could weaken their academic standing; at the same time they are under pressure to admit underrepresented blacks and Hispanics in greater numbers. This means that middle-class whites—traditionally the dominant group attending elite universities—perceive themselves to be at a serious disadvantage when applying to these schools. Financial, educational, and prestige factors limit enrollment in most of the nation's elite schools, a problem that will become more acute with the expected sharp rise in the American-born Asian student population. Admissions criteria are bound to be more controversial.

A related concern is that foreign students are being subsidized by American taxpayers. For example, at the University of Michigan, one-half of the students in its engineering school are foreign-born. But the out-of-state tuition covers only one-half the cost—the balance is borne by Michigan residents. Were most of these students to return and work for Japanese, German, or Indian firms, low tuition would result in subsidies to foreign enterprises that are competitors of Michigan companies. Fortunately, many of these students plan to remain in the United States, benefiting our own industries.[45]

The presence of Asian students has enriched some of our most prestigious institutions of higher learning. At the University of California, Berkeley, about one-fourth of the students are Asian in origin. Since Asians make up only 5 percent of the state population, they are overrepresented by a ratio of five to one. Both blacks and Hispanics are underrepresented at the university. One researcher estimates that 55 percent of all Berkeley students in 1985 were foreign-born.[46] Asians comprise 10 percent of Harvard students and a similarly disproportionate share at the Massachusetts Institute of Technology and at Cal Tech. Their presence has been felt most strongly in the field of engineering, helping to boost the quality of university departments. The Asian emphasis on engineering and science not only reflects their mathematical competence but also demonstrates their desire to obtain degrees in marketable skills that do not require English-language proficiency.

Hispanic students, both foreign-born and the children of immigrants, perform notably less well than other recently arrived groups. Mexicans, in particular, are plagued by language problems and have a high dropout rate. In California only 34 percent of all Hispanic ninth-graders graduate from high school. In New York and across the nation, the dropout rate is considerably higher for Hispanics than for blacks, leading to concerns among educators and others that a permanent Hispanic "underclass" is developing.

Leaving aside the Hispanic dropout problem, immigrants collectively have helped upgrade the quality of the student body in central-city public schools, braking the steep decline brought about by the exodus of middle-class students to the suburbs and by the growing popularity of private and parochial schools. Immigrants are also attending public institutions of higher learning in large numbers. In New York City one of four foreign-born students attend such schools, and their academic accomplishments have been impressive.[47]

These observations and supporting data bolster the contention that the economic vitality of gateway cities has been strengthened by immigrants—Hispanic, Asian, and European. Population stability is the most obvious impact, but it is not the most important. Immigrants, ranging from young, unskilled entrants to highly trained scientists, make a major contribution to the nation's labor force. By spurring neighborhood revitalization, immigration has enhanced the ability of cities to retain middle-class residents.

Ethnic entrepreneurs are thriving in America's cities not only because of their own ambition but also because of the vitality and openness of our economic system. There are perhaps fewer impediments to starting a business in the United States than anywhere else in the world. We have no constraints on the amount of capital that can be brought into the country, no citizenship requirements, and no special rules and regulations that would prevent aliens from owning businesses. Most receptive of all are large cities, which lack the self-protective business elite common in smaller, tightly knit communities.

Despite all the structural changes that have occurred in our economy, cities continue to offer business opportunities to all those willing to work hard and take risks. Immigrants who are supported by an ethnic cohort network are particularly well situated to take advantage of these opportunities. In the process of bettering their own position, these entrepreneurs are also helping to revive commercial and residential activity in formerly deteriorating neighborhoods. Not that immigrants are immune from the economic downturns that periodically trouble the nation. But the ethnic enclave is more resilient and can better endure economic hardships than the more open economy.

Focusing unduly on aggregate measures of the economic benefits of immigration, however, can be misleading. First, impressive totals, such as changes in per capita income, can mask less benign redistributional effects upon the working class and native minorities in particular. Second, while immigration generally has a positive impact on private enterprise, its effects on the public sector may be less in evidence. Finally, an analysis concentrating on economic issues can easily overlook pressing social problems.

Earlier, the economic benefits of immigration were shown to date back many years, to a period before the Republic itself was founded. Congress mandated immigration constraints in the 1920s less out of economic than social concerns. Americans feared that a continuing influx of immigrants would dilute traditional values, undermine the nation's social stability, and alter its political balance. These potentially negative consequences of immigration, both economic and social, perceived and real, remain fixed in the minds of many people as we move into a decade in which the number of immigrants will probably exceed the record attained in the first decade of the twentieth century.

5

The Price of Immigration

There can be little hope for advantage [from immigration] unless the people have peace and contentment at home.

Sir John Holland, 1664[1]

Recent immigrants have delivered the same kinds of economic benefits to cities as did immigrants who arrived in earlier waves. If the overall economic health of cities were the only concern, there could be few objections to a policy of virtually unrestricted admission of immigrants with skills. But a realistic immigration policy must also take into account citizen perceptions of immigrant contributions as well as the way in which benefits are distributed.

In an ideal economic environment, all natives would either benefit or at least not be hurt by immigration. The alternative situation would be a zero-sum game—the benefits to some from immigration are offset by equal losses to others. For example, immigrants may raise business profits but concurrently reduce the wages of native workers. Similarly, while some immigrants could create new jobs, others would take a roughly equal number of jobs now held by native workers. In the zero sum examples, the effects are said to be distributional. Opponents of liberal immigration policy argue that the economic costs to native residents of such an approach far outweigh the benefits. Proponents of lax entry standards maintain that the gains associated with an inflow exceed any adverse effects. Most residents, according to public opinion polls, share the view of immigration opponents.

Because there appears to be widespread popular discomfort with the idea of an increasing alien presence, it is appropriate to turn the discussion toward the costs of immigration. Although most media accounts in recent years have focused on illegal immigrants, from an economic perspective, as noted earlier, they are barely distinguishable from legal entrants. Therefore, this chapter will deal with all recent entrants, including refugees, regardless of their formal legal status.

The contemporary arguments against large-scale immigration—particularly the inflow of undocumented workers—have been forcefully raised by former Colorado governor Richard D. Lamm and his associate Gary Imhoff. In their 1985 book, provocatively titled *The Immigration Time Bomb: The Fragmenting and Destruction of America by Immigration,* the authors attribute to recent entrants virtually all the economic and social ills charged to members of each earlier wave of immigration going back two centuries.[2] These include taking jobs from Americans, lowering wages, burdening welfare rolls, and raising crime levels. The country is going downhill today, argue the authors, because of the large inflow of immigrants, especially undocumented workers. The book received considerable media exposure, including book reviews by the *New York Times,* the *Washington Post,* and numerous periodicals.[3] Although some reviewers criticized the authors for carrying their arguments to an extreme, *The Immigration Time Bomb* was generally praised for raising important issues while the Simpson-Mazzoli bill was being debated by Congress.

Dan Stein, executive director of the Federation for American Immigration Reform (FAIR), the only national organization aiming to limit immigration, focuses on economic issues. Specific FAIR concerns cited by Stein are schools, housing, employment, living standards, and deteriorating infrastructure.[4] The organization also challenges the view that immigrants create more jobs than they take, or that our aging society needs more workers.

Another impassioned economic rationale in opposition to increased immigration is found in the writings of Vernon Briggs, a labor economist. His premise is that a substantial number of American workers face "employment and earnings disadvantages."[5] For instance, the argument goes, many dishwashers, laborers, and restaurant workers are underpaid because a large pool of workers is available to perform these functions. In labor markets such as Los Angeles, New York, and San Francisco, where immigrants are concentrated, Briggs believes native workers in such low-wage occupations are disadvantaged by the presence of illegal workers.

Writing in 1984, Briggs conceded that under conditions of full employment there would be economic benefits to society from immigrant workers. However, he dismissed that scenario as purely theoretical, asserting that unemployment cannot fall below 6 to 6.5 percent without triggering unacceptable inflation. Briggs apparently cannot conceive of lower levels of national unemployment, particularly in areas where immigrants are concentrated. (In fact, unemployment fell below these thresholds for several years in the late 1980s.) Therefore, he concludes that a benign attitude toward immigrant workers cannot be justified.

Does the American public share the views of Lamm and Briggs that American workers are disadvantaged by the presence of immigrants? Public opinion polls are one useful way to gauge perceptions; polls on the admission of immigrants at the national level were first taken in the late 1930s. Although it is not possible to precisely gauge changes in public attitudes from these surveys, responses provide "snapshots" of public sentiment on this issue across the years.

In May 1938, in the midst of the depression, when first asked if the United States should allow political refugees to enter, 68 percent of the respondents stated that "with [economic] conditions as they are, we should keep them out." Among professionals who responded, 43 percent would allow their entry, but only 15 percent of factory workers shared this view.[6] The strong anti-immigrant sentiment continued beyond World War II. Thus, when asked in 1947 if 100,000 refugees annually should be settled in the United States, 72 percent of those polled answered no.[7] Again, those with high income and education were the most kindly disposed toward allowing refugee entry. The strong link between socioeconomic status and willingness to admit more immigrants suggests that those with less education and few skills fear immigrant job competition. However, job issues cannot explain why 42 percent of the public in 1940 opposed permitting English and French women and children to come to these shores and remain until the war was over. It is therefore evident that both xenophobic and economic concerns motivate public opinion.[8]

Public opinion polls during the 1960s and 1970s focused on levels of immigration considered most desirable: was the nation admitting too many or too few immigrants? Respondents were not asked to identify the reasons for their response. Not until the 1980s, as illegal immigration became a national concern, did polls include questions to determine if the public believes that illegal and other immigrants contributed to American worker joblessness or lower wages. The fewest

Table 5-1

Public Attitudes on Employment Effects of Immigration

Proposition/Survey Area	Date	Unemployment Rate (%)	Percentage of Respondents Agreeing with Proposition			
			White	Black	Hispanic	All
Undocumented Aliens Take Jobs from Others:						
United States[a]	Jul 1983	9.4	0	81.0	58.0	—
California[b]	Jul 1982	10.7	—	—	—	52.0
Southern California[c]	Jul 1983	9.5	49.0	59.0	42.0	41.0
California[b]	Jul 1987	6.0	30.0	38.0	21.0	30.0
Houston Area[d]	Feb 1989	—	—	—	—	54.0
Immigrants Take Jobs from Americans:						
United States	Mar 1981[e]	8.3	—	—	—	40.0
United States	Jun 1984[f]	7.5	—	—	—	61.0
Washington, D.C., Area	Aug 1987[g]	3.1	—	—	—	22.0
Florida	Oct 1989[h]	—	36.0	58.0	24.0	35.0
California	Dec 1991[i]	7.7	—	—	—	39.0
Many Immigrants Take Jobs Others Don't Want:						
United States	Mar 1981[e]	8.3	—	—	—	48.0
United States	Jun 1984[f]	7.5	—	—	—	80.0
Washington, D.C., Area	Jul 1987[g]	3.1	—	—	—	67.0
Florida	Oct 1989[h]	—	64.0	42.0	—	—

[a] "Hispanic and Black Attitudes toward Immigration Policy," survey prepared by V. Lance Associates for the Federation for American Immigration Reform, June–July 1983.
[b] California Opinion Digest, "Immigration" (mimeo), Field Institute, San Francisco, October 1987.
[c] "A Survey of Public Attitudes toward Immigration" (mimeo), report prepared for the Urban Institute by Field Research Corp., Washington, D.C., June 1983.
[d] Rice Institute survey as reported in *American Public Opinion Poll Index* (microfilm), Opimion Research Service, Boston, 1989.
[e] *Los Angeles Times* poll 040, March 1981.
[f] Nathan Alter and Joseph Contreras, "Closing the Door?" *Newsweek*, June 25, 1984, p. 18.
[g] *Los Angeles Times* research department (mimeo), 1989.
[h] David Hancock, "Poll: Many Floridians Lukewarm to Immigrants," *Miami Herald*, October 22, 1989, p. 1B.
[i] *Los Angeles Times* poll 264, research department (mimeo), 1991.

respondents linked joblessness to immigration in areas where unemployment was the lowest. When workers are insecure in their jobs, they seek causes for their condition—immigrants, foreign competition, and Wall Street are among their targets.

As roughly one-half of all undocumented workers are California residents, one would expect that state's nonimmigrant work force to be most threatened by illegal workers. As shown in Table 5-1, in a poll taken in 1982 (when unemployment in the state exceeded 10 percent, the highest level since the depression), 52 percent agreed that undocumented workers were taking jobs from others. But five years later, as the economy improved and unemployment fell, only 30 percent agreed with the proposition. Contributing to the more benign public perception of immigration in California may have been the extensive media coverage given to two studies, the first by the Urban Institute in 1984, the second by the Rand Corporation in 1985, both concluding that there was no empirical evidence to suggest unemployment in California was linked to illegal aliens.[9]

Surveys suggest that public attitudes are also shaped by characteristics of the respondents, not only occupational status but race as well. Blacks are more likely to link unemployment to immigration than whites, Asians, or Hispanics. Part of the difference is probably attributable to high unemployment rates among blacks even during periods of economic expansion. Black unemployment in California, to take one case, was 10.8 percent during 1987, exactly twice the white rate. The public accepts the view that blacks are more vulnerable to immigrants than others. When Washington, D.C., area residents were asked whose jobs are the most affected by immigrants, 51 percent said blacks; only 4 percent said white jobs were more at stake.[10] However, the views of Hispanics are shaped less by their own economic conditions than by concerns about blanket discrimination. In California, despite a high joblessness rate, Latinos expressed less discomfort over the presence of illegal workers, mostly Mexicans, than did whites (see Table 5-1).

On the matter of wages, the 1983 southern California survey found that seven in ten residents believed undocumented workers lowered wages in occupations where they are concentrated.[11] About 29 percent of black respondents (but only 13 percent of whites) stated that these workers brought down wages in their own occupations. When

Washington, D.C., area residents in 1987 were asked whether the presence of immigrants reduced wages in their own occupations, more than eight of every ten said no. However, more than one-third held the view that immigrants depress wages in menial jobs.[12]

When asked, "Do immigrants (no distinction made as to their legal status) take jobs from Americans?" four out of five surveys identified in Table 5-1 show a majority of respondents disagreeing with this proposition. Notably, a California poll taken in late 1991, when statewide unemployment was above the U.S. average, found that only 39 percent believed that immigrants take jobs from natives, with 48 percent responding that they mostly take jobs others don't want. In Florida, the majority of nonblacks agreed that immigrants tend to take jobs most native-born workers shun. Some variation in poll results is attributable to differences in the wording of questions by the polling organizations. Taking this into account, the results indicate the public is ambivalent on the jobs issue, with a majority of nonblacks generally not concerned that immigrants will compete for their jobs.

Perceptions that immigrants contribute to unemployment have stimulated researchers to gauge the impact of recent immigration on the job opportunities and wages of American workers. Their findings, as already noted, show that immigrants have little, if any, detrimental impact on jobs for native workers.[13] This conclusion should be modified to cite explicitly "no long-term impact" because the presence of immigrants in large numbers can be expected to cause short-term dislocations.

Findings indicating the absence of a substantial adverse impact have been based primarily on studies at the national level. To relate these findings to the gateway cities, it is necessary to compare the economic situation of native workers in general, and minority workers in particular, in areas with and without large numbers of immigrants. To begin with, are unemployment rates higher than average in labor markets with many immigrants?

In the late 1980s, the four gateway cities—Los Angeles, Miami/Dade County, New York, and San Francisco—had unemployment levels below the national mean.[14] Unemployment rates were highest in Buffalo, Houston, New Orleans, and Pittsburgh—cities that (with the exception of Houston) have virtually no immigrants. This, of course, does not demonstrate cause and effect. It is only natural for immigrants to prefer booming locations and to shun stagnating areas.

However, immigrants during the 1970s did not flock to Miami, New York, and Newark because jobs were plentiful but because ethnic enclaves were already established in those cities.

Above-average unemployment rates in gateway cities during the early 1990s did not appear to alter immigration patterns. Entry levels in New York, for example, remained essentially stable between 1970 and 1990, insensitive to the economic roller coaster challenging its residents. By contrast, there are a few prosperous areas in the nation, such as Burlington, Vermont, where the immigrant population is small.

Immigration settlement patterns are determined first by the presence of earlier immigrants, who were typically concentrated near major commercial ports (Europeans in Boston and New York, Asians in San Francisco and Seattle) or in proximity to their place of origin (Mexicans in southern California, Cubans in southern Florida). Secondarily, settlement follows economic opportunities, with the more skilled and entrepreneurial immigrants relocating to areas some distance from their initial place of residence.

Have earnings stagnated in areas heavily populated by immigrants? In Los Angeles and San Francisco, total per capita income growth between 1970 and 1990 has not deviated substantially from the national average, even though the earnings of immigrants are lower than those of the native population. These and other economic statistics would seem to indicate that a large alien presence in a particular city does not translate into obvious economic problems for the local native population. It is impossible to control statistically for all the variables involved in unemployment and income growth, but an earlier book that made valiant attempts to do so pointed to the same conclusion— that the presence of immigrants at the metropolitan level does not adversely affect native workers taken as a whole.[15] High unemployment is caused not by the size of the immigrant labor force but by local economic conditions, such as the decline of basic industries in Buffalo and Pittsburgh.

Opportunities for Minorities

To say that immigrants do not aggravate unemployment for native workers in general is not to assert that particular segments of native populations, such as minorities, do not suffer. More than any other group, blacks have complained that immigrants, especially illegal ones, have adversely affected their economic standing. Polls in California and elsewhere found blacks to be considerably more concerned than Asians, Hispanics, or whites about the presence of undocumented workers.

To understand the nature of black anxieties, it helps to place them in historical context. Black leaders argued prior to the imposition of immigration restrictions during the 1920s that had there been no European inflow, labor shortages would have developed in the North, providing significant job opportunities for blacks. This position has considerable merit, as the black outflow from the South did in fact accelerate when immigration slowed. However, a comparison of the occupational distribution of blacks in northern cities with and without a large immigrant presence indicates that in both groups of cities they were limited to the least desirable jobs. This suggests that bias, combined with lower education levels, figured strongly in the inability of blacks to obtain nonmenial jobs. For many decades following emancipation, blacks in both the North and South faced greater hurdles than competition from immigrants. Limiting immigration in the 1870s or 1890s would not have softened the racial attitudes of white Americans. Further, there is no evidence to suggest that the immigrant's perceptions of blacks were more negative than the native's. Economic opportunities for blacks did not improve until white attitudes changed during and after World War II.

Traditionally, the fears of blacks about the economic effect of immigrants have been based on two premises. The first was that immigrants were willing to accept work conditions and wages that blacks themselves would not endure. The second was that employers, given their ingrained prejudices, would, if afforded the opportunity, always hire an immigrant over a black. Looking in retrospect, the first concern proved to be generally inaccurate. European immigrants typically joined unions and demanded, not always successfully, decent working conditions.

The second premise has merit; black workers were regarded by many industrialists as a last resort. The record shows that employers in the early decades of the twentieth century frequently hired blacks to break strikes or to handle menial jobs that others, including some immigrants, would find intolerable. Some employers may have accepted the arguments of geneticists that East Europeans and Italians were inferior to those who traced their ancestry to England or Germany. Nonetheless, these employers consistently gave preference to immigrant workers over blacks.

But this historical experience, while contributing to an understanding of black concerns, does not necessarily apply to recent conditions. It is impossible to conclude, in an era of civil rights progress and affirmative action, that the absence of the "fourth wave" immigration to cities, which began in the late 1960s, would have made a real difference in minority job opportunities in urban areas. The economic position of blacks has improved throughout the postwar period, particularly since the days of the Great Society. Black educational levels have risen, although black male college enrollment, after a steady rise, declined modestly in the late 1980s.

Notwithstanding rising educational achievement, Vernon Briggs shares the view that those who are most hurt by immigrant workers are the young and less skilled, especially minorities.[16] This seems to be a reasonable concern because minorities, particularly blacks and Hispanics, are typically less skilled and more likely to work in occupations and industries that also attract immigrants—for example, as operators in manufacturing plants or as retail or restaurant service workers. In part because they are concentrated in these occupations, minorities have higher unemployment rates than whites.

To assess the impact of immigration on minority employment opportunities, it is necessary to trace black migration to and from gateway cities. It is also necessary to examine unemployment rates, labor force participation rates, income growth, and job mobility for minorities in areas with a large immigrant presence. And finally, it is important to examine black business opportunities.

Among indicators that can shed light on immigration's effects is the pattern of internal migration. Were native minority job opportunities limited by the influx of immigrants to gateway cities, a net outflow of minority workers would be the most likely result. On the other hand, a continuation of or rise in economic opportunities would encourage migration of minority labor to these cities from other areas of the nation.

Despite the arrival of multitudes of Asians and Latin Americans and the departure of many non-Hispanic whites during the 1970s, blacks (most of them white-collar) steadily moved to Los Angeles from other parts of the country. The same pattern occurred in Miami/Dade County, where the number of immigrant workers nearly doubled during the 1970s; forty thousand more blacks entered the area during the 1970s than left, an amount equivalent to the net outflow of white "Anglos" from the area.

In the 1980s, the population of Los Angeles County rose by nearly 1.4 million, but the Hispanic and Asian population increased by about 1.7 million. Whites continued to leave, and there was a net outmigration of black households as well. Miami had substantial gains in the number of both Hispanic and black households, with the white population declining more than 20 percent. It is likely, however, that a substantial percentage of the black increase (and perhaps all) is the result of Caribbean immigration rather than an inflow of native blacks from other areas.

The pattern in San Francisco differed from Los Angeles and Miami. Both the non-Hispanic white and black population have declined in the city since the early 1970s, but there was considerable black in-migration to its suburbs from elsewhere in the nation. New York City's experience paralleled San Francisco's with a massive middle-class exodus. Between 1960 and 1990, the white population of New York City fell by about half. Blacks contributed to the exodus, with 200,000 more blacks estimated to have left New York than entered. The outmigration of native blacks was even larger than these statistics suggest, since in the three-year period 1988–90 alone, about 100,000 immigrant blacks (mostly from the Caribbean) immigrated legally to the city. Most of those leaving moved to nearby counties, swelling the suburban black population, but a considerable number relocated to other states, particularly California and Florida.

Blacks in New York appeared to be little affected by the recession years of the 1970s. In fact, the number of employed blacks in the city rose by more than 60,000 despite an overall loss of 330,000 jobs across the city in that period. During the decade the city absorbed several hundred thousand immigrants, who came undeterred by the economic slowdown, and unsurprisingly the local unemployment rate soared. Yet New York's black unemployment rate remained significantly lower than the figure nationwide for blacks. Perhaps the city's black workers were filling a gap left by massive white outmigration, which continued into the recovery of the 1980s, albeit at a much-reduced pace.

New York's recovery began shortly after its mid-1970s fiscal crisis was sorted out. Immigrants continued to arrive (about 90,000 legal entrants per year in the 1980s), and blacks continued to progress. Between 1983 and 1990, black job gains in New York were the second-highest in percentage terms of any gateway city, behind Miami. Citizens of Hispanic heritage did less well, bearing the brunt of increased unemployment in the lean years of the 1970s and coping with a higher than average jobless rate even throughout the economic boom of the 1980s.

When New York's economic revival began to lose steam in the late 1980s, the city's black population stopped its advance and even slid back in some respects. Black women held their own, with an unemployment rate steady at 7.7 percent in 1991. But for black males, the rate had reached 12.9 percent by 1990 and was still rising. Seeking explanations for the dramatic rise in joblessness, the head of the New York State NAACP claimed that non-English-speaking immigrants were taking hotel and restaurant jobs from blacks, a charge that was hotly denied by Hispanic leaders.[17] Contrary to the position taken by some prominent figures in the African-American community, there is little evidence to show that immigrants are displacing blacks in the course of gaining employment in hotels, restaurants, and other low-wage services.

Is minority unemployment higher in gateway cities? At a time when unemployment for white men and women exceeded the national rate in each of the four gateway cities, Hispanic unemployment during the recessionary year 1991 was also above average in Los Angeles and New York. By contrast, joblessness among black women was below the mean in three gateway cities, and below the nationwide rate for black men specifically in Los Angeles and Miami (1991 data for blacks in San Francisco are unavailable). Black jobless rates remained relatively modest in part because more than one out of four blacks worked for government.

The economic slowdown in the early 1990s was different from most previous recessions in that unemployment rates nationwide remained relatively low for all ethnic groups. This was in part a measure of the recession's shallow nature. Probably more important was that fewer young native-born men and women were entering the labor force. Because immigration rates to gateway cities once again showed no sign of declining despite a stagnating economy, the presence of additional alien workers likely contributed to unemployment rates in these cities. To the extent unemployment rates were higher, native Hispanics probably absorbed a disproportionate share of joblessness. Most new Asian aliens probably found work within ethnic enclaves. It is very doubtful, however, that the primary blame for the growth in the ranks of the jobless can be assigned to national policies toward the admission of foreigners. In New York, for example, the retrenchment of the sectors that expanded most rapidly in the 1980s—banking, financial markets, and real estate—was the primary culprit for the downturn. And in Los Angeles, defense procurement cutbacks and the collapse of the construction sector were to blame for much of the joblessness.

An earlier analysis by the author, applying 1980 data, found that black unemployment rates were not increased—in fact, they were marginally lowered—by a rise in the proportion of Mexican immigrants in metropolitan labor markets across the nation.[18] A similar analysis applying 1989 data was undertaken for this book. However, this time regional unemployment was computed separately for black men and black women. In addition, the research examined links, if any, between Korean immigration (a proxy for Asians) and black joblessness. It found a statistically significant *negative* correlation between the percentage of Mexican immigrants in a population and local unemployment rates for black men as well as black women, with gender having little effect.* As revealed in the earlier study, black

* **Effect of Mexican Immigration and Other Factors on Black Unemployment in Selected Metropolitan Areas, 1989[a]**

Independent Variable	Coefficient		T-statistic	
	Black Women	Black Men	Black Women	Black Men
Constant	24.5	20.4	4.7 [1]	2.98 [1]
Mexican Immigration, 1987–88	-0.0003	-0.0005	-2.12 [2]	-2.23 [2]
Manufacturing Employment, 1989	0.01185	0.01975	2.06 [2]	2.68 [2]
Per Capita Income, 1989	-0.0008	-0.0006	-3.15 [1]	-1.82

R^2 .46 (black women)   N = 19
R^2 .36 (black men)   N = 22

[1] Significant at 1 percent level of confidence
[2] Significant at 5 percent level of confidence

[a] Areas with substantial Mexican immigration during the 1980s.

unemployment in 1989 tended to be lower wherever there was large-scale Mexican immigration, although the magnitude of the impact was very small. Similarly, black joblessness was lower in areas experiencing large Korean immigration. These results can be interpreted to mean that Mexicans and Asians are attracted to urban areas, where employment opportunities for all groups, blacks as well as Hispanics and Asians, are favorable. A plausible, but less certain, interpretation of the data is that immigrants create economic growth, which, in turn, improves job prospects for blacks. In any case, these data provide a reasonable empirical basis for the proposition that the presence of immigrants is not a direct cause of increased joblessness for either black men or black women.

A similar analysis applying 1990 census data to 37 large Standard Metropolitan Statistical Areas (SMSAs) confirmed the other findings.* White income, the percentage of population that is black, percentage of blacks with college degrees, and manufacturing as a percentage of all jobs are statistically significant in explaining black unemployment. There were negative, but not statistically significant, relationships between the percentage of foreign-born in the population and black joblessness. All of these correlations combined explain about 60 percent of the variations in black unemployment among large metropolitan areas.

Black unemployment tends to be the highest in manufacturing centers such as Detroit and Flint, Michigan (with unemployment rates exceeding 20 percent in 1990), as industrial jobs in durable goods, a major source of employment for black males, are declining. Black unemployment also tends to be high in areas where per capita income is low.

---

* Factors Explaining Black Unemployment Differences in Large Metropolitan Areas, 1990

Independent Variable	Coefficient	T-statistic
Constant	15.5385	6.37 [1]
White Household Income	-0.0001	-2.03 [1]
Hispanic Household Income	-0.0001	-1.41
Percentage Black Population	0.1208	2.74 [1]
Percentage of Blacks with College Degrees	0.0296	-2.57 [2]
Percentage Foreign-born	0.0222	-0.58
Percentage Manufacturing of All Jobs	0.2566	4.50 [1]

R_2 (adjusted)   .60   N = 37
[1] Significant at 1 percent level of confidence
[2] Significant at 5 percent level of confidence

A related issue is to what extent, if any, immigration benefits or hurts black earnings in large metropolitan areas. The results of statistical analyses applying preliminary 1990 census data to the 51 largest SMSAs are consistent with other findings. First, there is a strong positive correlation between the percentage of foreign-born and black household incomes (holding other factors constant). Second, there is a highly significant negative correlation between the percentage of blacks in the population and black earnings. That is, black income is higher in areas where there are fewer blacks. Finally, black income, as one would expect, rises with black educational levels as well as with white (and Hispanic) area incomes. These five variables explain about 85 percent of the variation in black metropolitan area income.* These data can be interpreted to mean that blacks with college degrees migrate to urban areas with a relatively small black presence but large foreign-born population. Nonetheless, black income rises even when the analysis controls for education and size of the black population.

Among the nation's 334 metropolitan areas, 22 have few (less than 1 percent) residents who are foreign-born. In 21 metropolitan areas, 15 percent or more of the population is foreign-born. As shown in Table 5-2, income for several groups varies substantially with the size of the immigrant population.

Blacks do poorly in areas with few immigrants (which are concentrated in southern states), but Asians earn considerably more than other groups. The white/black income differential narrows in urban centers where immigrants make up a substantial (one out of every six) share of all residents, and the white/Asian income gap is also

* Effect of Immigration and Other Factors on Black Household Income in Large Metropolitan Areas, 1990

Independent Variable	Coefficient	T-statistic
Constant	-7053.70	3.15 [1]
Percentage Foreign-born	117.60	2.76
White Household Income	0.68	8.54 [1]
Hispanic Household Income	0.21	2.42 [2]
Percentage Black Population	-158.90	3.84 [1]
Percentage of Blacks with College Degrees	34.40	2.64 [2]

R2 (adjusted)   .85   N = 51
1 Significant at 1 percent level of confidence
2 Significant at 5 percent level of confidence

Table 5-2

Metropolitan Area Household Median Income in 1989

	White	Black	Hispanic	Asian	Ratio Black/White
Few Immigrants	$25,273	$15,132	$22,110	$33,785	.60
Numerous Immigrants[a]	35,704	25,697	25,979	35,219	.72
Metropolitan Average[b]	34,197	21,147	23,552	37,258	.62

Source: U.S. Department of Commerce, Bureau of the Census, *1990 Census of Population*, special computer runs by the Population Division, August 1992

[a] Includes metropolitan areas along Mexican border with earnings considerably below average for whites and Hispanics.

[b] All metropolitan areas.

decreased in metropolitan areas with a large immigrant component. The proportion of blacks with relatively high income is also higher in gateway cities compared to other cities. In Los Angeles, the proportion of black households earning over $75,000 was 77 percent above the average of all metropolitan areas, and the proportion earning less than $10,000 was 20 percent below this average in 1989. The same pattern is also evident in New York City (where 45,000 households earned over $75,000) and San Francisco, but in Miami fewer blacks than average were in the high-income category.

The table also shows that Asians fare better relative to other groups in urban areas with few foreign-born than in areas with large immigrant populations. This is explained by the high concentration of employed Asians outside gateway cities in professional occupations. New York and San Francisco have their share of professionals but are also home to many low-wage Asian workers employed in Asian-owned industries.

Does immigration affect youth joblessness rates? Certainly, teenage unemployment is one of the most serious problems confronting our large cities. Although black youth unemployment in 1954 across the nation was the same as for whites, the percentage of young black males employed has fallen sharply in recent decades. Again, though, immigration seems to bear little relation to black youth unemployment. The highest proportion of black youth unemployed is found in the states of Illinois, Michigan, and Florida; the lowest in New Jersey and South Carolina. The highest urban black youth jobless rates during 1991 were in the Chicago and Detroit metropolitan areas.[19] Local economic conditions, not the level of immigration, best explain the situation.

Unquestionably, immigrants are found in jobs—fast-food operations, parking lot attendants, and the like—that unskilled teenage blacks could hold. But many of these jobs go unfilled when immigrants are not present. Whether it is because they have other sources of income or because they find such jobs economically unrewarding, many black teenagers are simply not motivated to take marginal, low-paying positions, even when available.[20] This situation is recognized by some black community leaders, including George Givens, the key organizer of an advocacy group representing black families in Los Angeles. As he notes, "Young blacks today don't want to start at the bottom. After the Civil Rights movement there was a false message that you didn't have to work yourself up."[21] In contrast, immigrant youths typically have few options; many must work to support their families and are therefore more willing to accept menial jobs.

Such differences in attitude may be due to varying perspectives on future success between black and immigrant youth. Discussions with foreign-born Asian youths at their fast-food workplaces, particularly in the Washington, D.C., area, indicate that the majority work to supplement their family income. Many are attending college part time and work an eight-hour shift to pay their way. These immigrants tend to view such jobs as a way station on the road to bigger and better things; black youths are more likely to see this work as dead-end in nature. Generally, immigrants are more optimistic than blacks about the future, especially where their children are concerned. Immigrants who become frustrated with their progress often return to their place of origin—an option unavailable to blacks.

Interestingly, for New York City residents between the ages of twenty-five and forty-four, both foreign-born blacks and Hispanics—men and women—had much higher labor force participation rates in 1980 than their native counterparts. While 80 percent of native black men took part in the labor force, for foreign-born black men the figure was 90 percent. Given that one-fourth of all immigrants to New York during the 1970s were black, immigration has served to raise the city's overall black labor force participation rates.

The pattern holds for 1980 unemployment rates, which measure the joblessness only of those actively seeking work. The level of joblessness for foreign-born blacks, Hispanics, and Asians (men and women) was considerably lower than the corresponding native rates. The unemployment rates for all foreign-born black men in New York in 1980 were one-fourth less than the level for black men born in the United States. How best to explain the disparities?

Differences in education levels can be ruled out, for the average recent arrival from Jamaica, Haiti, or Central America has less schooling and fewer skills than the native black worker in the New York area. Only one of five native blacks has a grade school education or less. Nor do differences in the occupational nature of employment structure suggest a cause for unemployment disparities. About 15 percent of all native black males, but only 10 percent of all Jamaicans, hold professional or managerial jobs. Jamaicans are much more likely than native blacks to hold jobs in the blue-collar sector, which has traditionally high levels of joblessness. Yet, fewer Jamaican-Americans are without work.

Among Hispanics, about 40 percent of Puerto Rican natives in 1980 had eight or fewer years of schooling, compared with only 9 percent of those born in the continental United States. Yet unemployment among those born in Puerto Rico was 10 percent, well below the 15 percent for Puerto Ricans born in the United States.

Competition may be fierce between immigrants and domestic minorities in occupations where both groups are well represented. In 1980, recently arrived male immigrants to the New York metropolitan area outnumbered native black men in several job categories, including managers and health professionals. Among the nonprofessional white-collar occupations, immigrant sales workers and technicians outnumbered native blacks as well. Immigrants were also more prevalent in food services and construction. Native black men outnumbered immigrants in teaching, administrative support staff, cleaning and building maintenance services, nonprofessional health services, protective services, and transportation. Blue-collar male immigrants compete head-on with native blacks and Puerto Ricans, especially as the number of manufacturing and construction jobs declines. Direct job competition between native black and immigrant women, at least for the present, appears more limited. In part, this can be explained by the high proportion of black women in the public sector and administrative support positions for which few recent immigrant women qualify.

Competition has arisen where enterprises now hire immigrants for contractual services that previously employed mostly native workers. For instance, unionized workers in California who had negotiated above-average wages in the office-cleaning industry have been displaced by companies employing immigrant workers at considerably lower rates. A similar pattern has occurred in Washington, D.C., where Southeast Asians undercut contracts held by blacks to clean airports. With limited marketable skills, blacks who work in the unionized service sectors have few prospects of finding other jobs at or near their union wage levels. The streets of the nation's capital have also become focal points of tension between native blacks and African immigrants. As the number of taxicab drivers from Gambia, Ethiopia, and Nigeria grows, native drivers come to resent the newcomers moving in on their turf. And on city sidewalks, American-born blacks complain that vending stands owned by Asians are taking over. Some blacks believe Asians came with "boatloads of cash" and are therefore competing unfairly, although, in fact, most started out with only sufficient money to pay for the $500 vendor's license.[22]

More generally, blacks are adversely affected by the weakening of trade unions, especially in manufacturing and construction. Although the underlying problems of the unions have little to do with immigration, newcomers do happen to be concentrated in industries where unions have lost some strength. In New York City, blacks have a strong presence in unionized construction, but the nonunion sector of the industry has been growing, largely because of immigrants. Carmenza Gallo finds that immigrants in New York have a much better chance than blacks to work in or form their own small contractor firms.[23] She offers two reasons. First, she argues that the cohesive immigrant community provides clients, obtains workers, and helps contractors gain expertise. Second, blacks are less able than immigrants to develop personal contacts outside their neighborhoods. This highlights a general problem for black entrepreneurs: they are less able than other ethnic groups to count on their own kind for support, and they face more obstacles than others to acceptance from the white community. However, there is no direct evidence that in New York, immigrants actually displaced blacks in construction; other factors, such as discriminatory practices by union locals, are more likely to be the cause of black underrepresentation.[24]

Another possible explanation for jobless rate differentials between immigrant and native minorities is that employers prefer to hire immigrants who are more often willing to accept disagreeable work conditions, lower pay, and fewer fringe benefits. During the 1980s, many California employers listed Hispanic immigrants (usually undocumented workers) as their first choice among workers. Managers of several industrial plants in California have expressed a preference for Mexicans because they are considered to be quiet and passive. Employers may also perceive immigrants to be more productive than native workers. A survey of employers in San Diego found immigrants high on the list of preferred workers and blacks at the bottom. Employers in the electronics industry, asked to judge workers on a scale of 1 to 9, rated Asians at 7.3, Hispanics and non-Hispanic whites at 6.3, and blacks at 4.8. According to Joseph Nalven and Craig Frederickson, among employers of kitchen crews in San Diego restaurants, undocumented workers ranked very high in terms of performance; next were Asians; and last, again, were blacks.[25]

Furthermore, businesses in ethnic enclaves are more reluctant to lay off workers in the event of an economic downturn than are enterprises owned by native employers. Some employers fear that once they hire blacks dismissal will be difficult because discrimination charges may be filed, making termination costly even if justified. Undocumented workers have better attendance records and stay on the job longer than blacks or whites, as they have fewer alternatives. Finally, illegal workers are unlikely to seek legal recourse over such issues as overtime pay and benefits.

Although there are differences in the labor market characteristics of black and Hispanic foreign-born versus native-born workers in New York, education levels and the proportion of both groups with jobs in higher-wage occupations are below those of the white and Asian populations. This would suggest that minority immigrants compete with native blacks and Hispanics rather than with white workers. Similarly in Los Angeles, Mexican immigrants tend to hold jobs similar to those of natives of Mexican heritage.

Gender differences figure starkly in the examination of high native black unemployment rates. The employment pattern for native black women in New York differs from that for both native black men and immigrant black women. In fact, native black women in 1980 out-numbered in absolute terms recent women immigrants in almost all white-collar and personal service occupations. Only in blue-collar occupations, which black women left in droves during the 1970s, are female immigrants dominant. For example, in 1980 more than thirty thousand black female immigrants were machine operators—more than double the number for native black women. Evidently, immi-grant women were replacing black women in lower-paying blue-collar and service jobs. Native black women experienced upward occupa-tional mobility, gaining about twenty-six thousand professional and managerial jobs and considerably more in other white-collar fields between 1970 and 1980.

Although total black employment in New York rose by about sixty thousand during the 1970s, this growth was limited to women, as employment of black men overall fell modestly. Black male immi-grants gained over sixty thousand jobs, however, implying a substan-tial decline in native black male employment. Despite the overall employment decline in New York, black men gained white-collar jobs. But black women still are advancing faster than their male counter-parts in cities across the nation: in 1992, 19 percent of the women, but only 15 percent of the men, held professional and managerial jobs.[26]

Blacks hold a share of better-paying jobs out of all proportion to

Table 5-3

High-Wage Jobs as a Percentage of Total Employment, 1991

	Percentage of Jobs Managerial			Percentage of Jobs Professional		
	Total	Black	Hispanic	Total	Black	Hispanic
New York City	14.0	9.3	7.6	16.5	10.0	7.5
Los Angeles County	13.9	10.9	5.3	14.4	12.3	4.4
Miami/Dade County	11.0	4.4	11.2	12.9	9.1	9.1
San Francisco (city)	14.2	N/A	3.0	19.2	N/A	5.6
Chicago (city)	11.6	8.9	3.2	14.5	10.7	6.0
United States	12.9	8.0	6.7	13.2	9.8	7.6

Source: U.S. Department of Labor, Bureau of Labor Statistics, *Geographic Profile of Employment and Unemployment, 1991*, BLS Bulletin no. 2410, August 1992

Table 5-4

Gains in Private and Public Employment by Race and Ethnicity, 1983–89
(in thousands)

	Number of Jobs Gained				
	Total	White	Black	Other	Hispanic[a]
New York City	402	218	85	99	(178)
Los Angeles County	751	572	88	91	(617)
Miami/Dade County	88	38	35	15	(127)
Chicago (city)[b]	239	150	65	24	(109)
Total, Four Cities	1,480	978	273	229	(1,031)
Total, United States	16,508	12,691	2,578	1,239	(3,270)
	Percentage of All Jobs Gained that Were Professional/Managerial				
New York City	53	68	56	18	(13)
Los Angeles County	39	36	42	58	(26)
Miami/Dade County	35	58	11	27	(32)
Chicago (city)[b]	35	35	37	25	(13)
Total, Four Cities	40	49	36	32	(21)
Total, United States	41	44	21	31	(13)

Source : U.S. Department of Labor, Bureau of Labor Statistics, *Geographic Profile of Employment and Unemployment, 1983* and *1989,* BLS Bulletin no. 2216 (1983 Report) and no. 2361 (1989 Report), October 1984 and May 1990

[a] Can be of any race.

[b] Chicago replaces San Francisco in the table because data on black employment is unavailable for the latter for years prior to 1987.

their nationwide presence in the upper echelons not only in New York but in other gateway cities as well, with the notable exception of Miami, as shown in Table 5-3. San Francisco and Los Angeles rate especially high in providing white-collar jobs for blacks. Hispanics, however, are not as well represented. In fact, with the exception of Cubans in Miami, the proportion of Hispanic professional workers in gateway cities and across the nation remains low. This seems primarily a result of the constant supply of illegal unskilled workers coming from Mexico and Central America.

Upward job mobility for blacks in four of the large urban areas with a large immigrant presence was evident during the 1983–89 period of economic expansion. Blacks netted 273,000 jobs, or about 18 percent of all jobs added in these cities over the seven-year period (see Table 5-4). More significant than the numerical gains in employment is that in three cities (excluding Miami) on average 45 percent of new black jobs were in higher-wage managerial and professional occupations.[27] By comparison, only 21 percent of black employment gains across the United States fell into the high-wage categories. There was, concurrently, a decline in low-wage, blue-collar jobs held by blacks, a pattern observed in large cities for two decades. Progress was most evident in Chicago, Los Angeles, and New York, with Miami lagging the nation. Black employment opportunities have risen in the San Francisco area as well; during the 1970s, the number of jobs held by blacks rose by one-third. More than three of five blacks in 1980 held white-collar and skilled blue-collar jobs in San Francisco, a higher percentage than in most large urban centers. This is not to suggest that all blacks are improving their economic lot. Those with limited skills have not fared well in many urban centers compared to others. But those working in gateway cities are more likely to secure professional positions or other high-paying jobs than elsewhere.

The proportion of Asians—most of them foreign-born—who are employed as professionals is the highest of any group, including non-Hispanic whites. In some metropolitan areas—Philadelphia, Dallas, and St. Louis—more than one in three working Asians are professionals. The fact that the concentration of professionals in these cities is higher than in gateway cities illustrates that Asians who are professionals are the most mobile. Still, about a third of all job gains among Asians in the four cities were in high-wage categories.

Notwithstanding impressive gains by blacks and Asians, Hispanics have been capturing most—two-thirds—of the jobs added during the 1980s in gateway cities. Unlike blacks, however, most Hispanics (with the exception of Cubans in Miami) have been taking lower-paying jobs in industry and services. Hispanic workers now form the backbone of the new labor force in gateway cities. Their job growth has been unprecedented. Despite reductions attributable to the recession, Hispanics increased their employment levels by 87 percent in Los Angeles, to 1.5 million workers, between 1983 and 1991. With Hispanic, Asian, and, to a lesser extent, black employment swelling, the number of non-Hispanic white jobholders fell.

While native minorities improved their economic positions in other gateway cities, the conflict over job opportunities between blacks and immigrants simmered in Miami, and the city has been rocked by several disturbances linked to ethnic tensions. Statistically, at least, blacks have been progressing: the presence of Cubans did not prevent blacks from experiencing 50 percent growth in employment within Miami/Dade County during the 1970s. The rate of unemployment for black men in Miami in the mid-1980s was less than the national average; it was even lower than the rate for black women. Moreover, about three out of ten blacks (but less than 8 percent of all Hispanic workers) work for government—on a par with Los Angeles and New York.[28] Yet black unemployment rates increased between 1981 and 1987—a period during which white and Hispanic jobless rates fell sharply—and reached almost 12 percent in 1990.

To what extent black immigration from the Caribbean during the 1980s is contributing to black unemployment is not known. During the 1970s, about one-third of black migrants to Miami came from abroad. In 1989 and 1990 alone, about 10,000 legal immigrants from Haiti and Jamaica (and no doubt many more illegal aliens) came to Miami. Because the vast majority of Haitians have few skills, opportunities for natives in professional and managerial positions should not have lessened. However, competition for unskilled jobs no doubt intensified.

The extent of black joblessness also may be linked to the relatively small black middle class in Miami/Dade County. In 1990, the percentage of blacks with four or more years of college was lower there than across the nation. Some argue that this is because most blacks came to the area from the rural South in the 1920s to work in local hotels and restaurants. As a result of narrow specialization in low-skill, low-wage occupations, the conditions for the formation of a middle class were not present. The data do not fully support this position, since nearly 10 percent are classified as professional workers. The percentage of blacks employed in managerial positions does in fact remain very low, as it has been for two decades. Among forty-two metropolitan areas with a large black labor force, only one (St. Louis) had a lower percentage of black managerial personnel during 1990 than Miami. This may be partly due to the Cuban presence; Hispanics control a substantial share of all business enterprises. Because few native blacks speak Spanish, and possibly because of racial attitudes, management positions for blacks remain limited not only in Miami, but in Fort Lauderdale, Tampa, and other southern Florida urban areas as well.

The data considered thus far combine public- and private-sector jobs. Because more than one out of every four employed blacks in gateway cities work for government, it is instructive to separate them from workers in private organizations. The results, shown in Table 5-5, confirm the employment patterns shown in the previous table. In three gateway areas—Los Angeles County, New York, and San Francisco—the proportion of blacks in 1981 holding high-paying jobs in the private sector was 52 percent above the national average.[29] In Miami/Dade County, where Hispanics are concentrated in higher-paying jobs, the black occupational profile in the private sector showed weakness, but still it closely approximated the national average. Blacks were least likely to hold high-paying, private-sector jobs (both in absolute terms and relative to whites) in urban areas with few immigrants, such as Baltimore, Cleveland, New Orleans, and Philadelphia.

The inroads that blacks have made into the professional and managerial sectors in gateway cities far exceed their gains on a national basis. In the Northeast and South, the proportion of such jobs held by blacks in the 1980s remained essentially stable, but gains have been recorded in the West, particularly California. Black family income is also highest in the West. These findings suggest that, at least for these occupations, economic growth among diversified populations has benefited the black middle class.

Table 5-5

High-Paying Occupations as a Percentage of Private Employment, by Occupation and Race, 1981

	Management			Professional		
	White	*Black*	*Asian*	*White*	*Black*	*Asian*
Gateway SMSAs[a]	17.9	5.7	8.6	15.2	6.3	23.6
Other SMSAs[b]	14.4	4.2	7.8	12.2	3.5	29.2
United States	13.3	4.3	7.4	10.7	3.6	22.4

Source : Job Patterns for Minorities and Women in Private Industry (Washington, D.C.: Equal Employment Opportunity Commission, February 1984)

[a] Standard Metropolitan Statistical Area.

[b] Baltimore, Cleveland, Dallas, New Orleans, Philadelphia, St. Louis. These SMSAs have a large black labor force.

Perhaps the most significant phenomenon in gateway cities is that educated blacks, like their white counterparts, have moved into higher-status jobs at a rapid rate, while non-Asian immigrants have taken a larger share of the unskilled and semiskilled jobs. This shift has come about through educational gains and, to a lesser extent, fair employment legislation.

Overall gains in higher-paying private and government jobs by gateway city blacks are evident in income statistics. During the 1970s, mean family income rose more rapidly for blacks than other groups in each of these cities. This pattern continued in the 1980s, with black income gains in Los Angeles, Miami, and New York City exceeding those of other groups, thus reducing income disparities. However, black poverty rates still showed little change, suggesting that rising income was attributable primarily to gains by middle-class blacks. The black-white income gap for two-parent, middle-class urban families is being reduced but has by no means been eliminated.

Black and Immigrant Entrepreneurs

The data uncovered no evidence that the presence of immigrants reduced job opportunities for middle-class blacks. But the effects of immigration on another route to economic progress for both foreign-born and native minorities—self-employment—needs exploration. Are native minorities disadvantaged by increased competition for government contracts attributable to minority immigrant business enterprises? As already noted, some immigrant enterprises succeed by employing family members without pay, by using illegal aliens, or by working hours most Americans would find intolerable. Do these practices limit the ability of blacks and others to compete fairly?

In recognition of the many problems that black businessmen face, the federal government, since the 1970s, has set aside a fixed percentage of its contracts for minorities. The amounts awarded are substantial—$3.6 billion in prime contracts for minority-owned firms in 1985. Blacks, Hispanics, Asians, American Indians, and, increasingly, women are considered eligible to participate. Questions have been raised as to whether Asian men—who earn more on average than their white counterparts—should qualify. But because all minority groups, including those with a large immigrant component, are currently eligible to bid for a fixed level of contracts, the pool of potential bidders is growing. One way or another, recent immigration will clearly make it harder for blacks to take advantage of the set-aside programs.

In January 1989, the U.S. Supreme Court, by a vote of 6 to 3, struck down a set-aside program in Richmond, Virginia. One reason cited was that various minority groups that had not experienced discrimination would be eligible for preference. For example, Eskimos and Aleuts (there are only five in Richmond) would receive such preference. Whatever the long-term implication of the Supreme Court ruling, there is evidence that black businesses have benefited from government procurement directed toward minority-owned enterprises. Reduced access to such procurement, as evidenced by fewer contracts to black firms in the early 1990s, has therefore limited their opportunities to progress.

In a related, controversial issue, blacks frequently contend that immigrants "squeeze out" black small businessmen and exploit ghetto consumers. "Militants Aim to Seize Stores," declared the headline over an article appearing January 28, 1985, in *City Business*, a weekly New York tabloid.[30] It told of how a group calling itself "The Concerned People of Harlem" threatened to use violence against the Korean greengrocers in the area. These militants charged that, as long as aliens kept coming to Harlem, local blacks would never succeed in operating their own businesses. Several years later, a boycott of two Korean grocery stores in Brooklyn that followed accusations of mistreatment of a black customer by a Korean store employee received national attention. Despite several efforts by David Dinkins, the mayor of New York, to diffuse tensions, the boycott continued for months, at one point leading to the arrest of numerous protesters.

Such ethnic tensions are not unique to New York. Conflict between Koreans and blacks seems to plague virtually all large cities in which the two groups come into contact. In the predominantly black Anacostia area of Washington, D.C., a group of blacks, led by a local pastor, spent several months in 1986 picketing a Korean carryout food shop because a black customer was insulted. In Atlanta, Koreans, who operate hundreds of convenience stores in black neighborhoods, have been subject to periodic outbreaks of violence, including several murders in 1986. In Newark, two Koreans were brutally assaulted by blacks a year later. Although the attacks were not laid directly to race,

Newark's mayor said through a spokeswoman that he was concerned about the "building resentment in black neighborhoods over the increasing presence of Korean business."[31] In Chicago, Philadelphia, and Baltimore, picket lines have been formed, and the black news media have issued harsh attacks on Korean merchants.

Perhaps the ugliest situation now exists in Los Angeles. As noted earlier, Los Angeles has the largest Korean community in the nation, but it also contains a black population that outnumbers Koreans three to one. Koreans first moved into black neighborhoods in the early 1970s, purchasing shops previously owned by whites (in many instances Jews) or abandoned. Black opposition to the Korean businesses centered on several complaints. First, unlike previous owners, Koreans hired only other Koreans rather than blacks as employees. Second, Korean stores were competing unfairly with blacks because they had greater access to capital. Third, Koreans were charged with reinvesting their profits outside the ghetto. Finally, Koreans were seen as unfriendly shopowners who considered blacks inferior.

The validity of these charges is in dispute. It seems evident that Koreans prefer fellow ethnics because of cultural and social ties and would only hire others under pressure. The Korean response is that the pay they can afford to give and the long hours they require would not entice outsiders. The question of unfair competition is difficult to resolve. Black entrepreneurs, in most instances, did not seek to purchase stores in the ghetto when they became available. Either Koreans invested to keep them going or they were lost. And when these stores closed, shopping opportunities were curtailed. In theory, residents dissatisfied with high prices, or the lack of large chain stores, or poor service, could shop outside the ghetto. But the inconvenience of shopping many miles from one's residence, particularly in sprawling Los Angeles, is what allows small businesses to survive. As for the charge that Koreans take black customers' money and invest it elsewhere, it would be difficult to ask merchants—be they Asian, white, or black—to reinvest their profits in the ghetto if doing so made little sense from an economic standpoint, that is, if opportunities were limited. Nonetheless, such investment could help reduce tensions between merchants and consumers.

The black response to the rise of Korean enterprises in the vast Los Angeles ghetto was to declare a boycott, but it was not successful, in part, because the black leadership (including the mayor) preferred to negotiate with the Korean community. In the late 1980s, signs were posted in major thoroughfares within ghetto neighborhoods urging residents to patronize black-owned stores, but the continuing growth of Asian-owned businesses suggests that the campaign did not divert substantial numbers of shoppers. Violence against shopowners, however, has accelerated, with nineteen Koreans killed in their stores during a four-year period. Racial tensions worsened in 1991 following the shooting death of a black teenager accused of stealing. To the dismay of the black community, a court sentenced the Korean-born shopkeeper to probation rather than a jail term. This led to a renewal of boycotts and the forced closure of two Korean-owned businesses.

These tensions reached a violent climax during the 1992 Los Angeles riots, precipitated by a jury verdict in another case. Several thousand businesses were either burned or looted and more than fifty deaths were attributed to the upheaval. Images of the riots, particularly scenes of tearful Koreans gazing at their destroyed property and of other Koreans firing at looters, received front-page coverage across the world. Although numerous Hispanic and some black stores were also ransacked (and at least as many Hispanic as black looters were arrested along with some whites), the Korean community businessmen considered themselves the prime targets and victims of black anger. Small Cambodian shops were the victims of rioting that erupted in Long Beach on a lesser scale a day after the Los Angeles explosion. Fortunately, Asian businesses were not looted in other cities. In Los Angeles the tension remains.

During the 1980 Miami riots, many of the stores looted were owned by Cubans. Although some Cuban-owned stores moved, others remained. In an attempt to uncover the causes of the 1980 riots, one book cited the belief by the black community that government favored Hispanics.[32] Particularly galling to blacks, it noted, was that most federal business loans to minorities were given to Hispanics. Blacks received only 6 percent of Small Business Administration loans in Miami between 1968 and 1980, although their share of the population was three times as large. It may well be that the disparity was linked to a lesser number of loan applications from blacks, but the perception within the black community is that the Washington bureaucracy favors Cubans.

It is difficult to ascertain the role of Cuban stores in the ghetto in fueling black resentment. Several Hispanic-owned stores were operating in the Liberty City neighborhood during 1988. Merchants were armed with licensed shotguns, and the tension was palpable. Little wonder that the situation exploded again in January 1989 as a result of the killing of a black by a Hispanic police officer. Six people were shot and twenty-seven buildings were set afire during the rioting that followed. Press reports indicated that, as during earlier disturbances, the frustration of blacks and their belief that Miami is giving special treatment to Hispanic immigrants fanned the violence.[33] The arguments against Cubans in many ways paralleled charges levied against Koreans elsewhere. However, blacks are even more resentful in Miami than elsewhere because many believe that Cuban immigrants dominate Miami commerce and are less appreciative of the black historical experience with discrimination than other groups.

In Detroit, blacks have come into conflict with Arabs, who own an estimated four hundred liquor stores in the predominately black city. But no doubt there exists a special frustration over the fact that immigrants are profiting from the drinking habits of the local population—and that black businesses are unable to compete with them. Arabs (as well as Koreans) have also come under attack in black Chicago neighborhoods.

Conflict between blacks and immigrant entrepreneurs is by no means new. In 1935 Mussolini's invasion of Ethiopia sparked a black boycott of Italian butchers and grocers in Harlem, thereby bringing into the open long-simmering tension between those two groups. In Los Angeles during the 1930s, blacks owned only thirty-two grocery stores, accounting for less than 2 percent of grocery sales to blacks. Most of the food stores in black neighborhoods were owned by Chinese or Japanese, a situation that continued until the mid-1960s, when the Watts riots prompted many of these store owners to leave the area.

The lack of black entrepreneurs is apparent from nationwide statistics. Although sales and employment in black-owned enterprises expanded substantially in recent years (the number of workers in these businesses almost doubled between 1982 and 1987), sales only represent 1 percent of the national total. Blacks own only two-thirds as many businesses per capita as Hispanics, and only one-sixth as many as Asians. There were substantially more Asian- than black-owned enterprises with employees in the country in 1987, and the differential continues to widen. Business sales in Asian ventures in 1987 totaled $33.1 billion, compared to $19.8 billion in black enterprises (and $24.7 billion in Hispanic-owned businesses).

In New York metropolitan area, there were more Asian- than black-owned firms in 1987, although blacks outnumbered Asians four to one. In 1982, there were 1.2 Asian-owned retail stores in the area for every black-owned store. Five years later, the ratio had changed to 2.3 to 1. Nor is this pattern limited to New York. In nearly every city and region, black self-employment, despite progress during the 1980s, remains low.

What explains the lack of native black enterprise relative to other ethnic groups? Racial prejudice would not seem to figure greatly in large cities, given the relative success of blacks from the Caribbean and Senegal. More important are cultural traits and a historical lack of experience. Unlike Italians, Greeks, and Jews, many of whom come from commercially oriented backgrounds, blacks have little tradition of entrepreneurship.

The black historian Robert A. Hill traces the lack of business tradition to both Africa and slavery in America.[34] Hill argues that the notion of private property was not part of the black heritage. Others argue that blacks are envious of black entrepreneurs, saying that "what it means for blacks trying to make it in a ghetto business is that they are resented if they do make it, and broke if they don't."[35] More generally, the economist Thomas Bailey concludes, based on his examination of this issue in New York, that "conditions that promote self-employment among immigrants either do not exist or are much weaker for blacks."[36] For whatever reason, highly qualified blacks seem more inclined to work for public agencies or large corporations than to undertake the risks associated with starting their own enterprises.

Blacks also face a problem in obtaining investment and have never developed the loan clubs typical of other ethnic groups. Residents of the ghetto often have no access to the sources of capital that are commonly available to other groups, such as family loans and inherited wealth. Bank lending may also be a problem. In the Miami area, blacks own only one bank, while Hispanics control thirty banks, providing a major source of capital to their own community. A survey of minority-owned businesses found that blacks obtained only 8 percent of their debt capital from friends and relatives, whereas Asians obtained 29 percent. In terms of total capitalization levels—critical to business success—black businesses suffered by comparison to Asian enterprises.[37] This restricted access to funds is reflected in the physical condition of black-owned stores. In southern Los Angeles, for instance, Korean-owned stores tend to be bright and well stocked; black stores are often poorly maintained. Differences in capitalization are also reflected in sales volume. The average Asian-owned enterprise chalks up twice as much in sales as the average black-owned one—about the same ratio as the difference in capital investment. This sales gap is particularly wide in Los Angeles, with its concentration of immigrant businesses. Yet, disparities in sales, particularly in retail businesses, are also seen in cities like Indianapolis, where immigrants are relatively scarce.

One would assume that in areas with a smaller immigrant presence, blacks, facing less competition on their own turf, would have greater success in opening small businesses. But the statistics, summarized in Table 5-6, tell a different story.

Table 5-6
Black-Owned and Asian-Owned Business Enterprises in Selected Cities, 1987[a]

	Black Firms per 1,000 Black Population	Ratio of Asian to Black Businesses	Percentage of Population Black	Population Growth in Percentage Terms, 1980–90
Ten Cities with Highest Rates of Black Businesses[b]	23.2	1.63	20.2	14.7
Ten Cities with Lowest Rates of Black Businesses[c]	9.7	0.25	54.0	-10.6
Four Gateway Cities	20.4	2.18	19.5	11.7
United States	13.3	0.84	12.1	9.8

Sources: U.S. Department of Commerce, Bureau of the Census, *Minority-Owned Businesses— Asian American, American Indians and Other Minorities*, MB 87-3, and *Survey of Minority-Owned Business Enterprises—Black*, MB 87-1, July 1990

[a] Cities with 100,000 or more residents.

[b] Austin, Inglewood, San Jose, Houston, Los Angeles, Oakland, Pasadena, Seattle, San Francisco, San Antonio.

[c] Philadelphia, Chicago, Cleveland, Detroit, Birmingham, Newark, Memphis, St. Louis, Baltimore, Mobile.

In the ten cities with the highest proportion of black enterprises to black population, there were substantially more Asian than black businesses. However, those with the fewest black-owned enterprises also had few Asians. Indeed, research for this book found a statistically significant relationship between black ownership and Koreans. Black enterprises were concentrated in urban areas with a large Korean population. This suggests that low black entrepreneurial activity in Chicago, Cleveland, Detroit, Newark, Philadelphia, and several southern cities was unrelated to immigrant competition, but had more to do with poor local economic conditions implied by outmigration trends. Gateway cities, however, exhibit above-average black self-employment. Notably, a majority black population, which characterizes many of the cities with few black enterprises, does not enhance the likelihood of black self-employment. Many areas with rapid population growth, particularly cities in California and Texas, are attracting the most minority enterprises, both native- and foreign- born. Incidentally, these cities also have a large Hispanic presence. The same pattern is also observed in large metropolitan areas where the number of black enterprises per 1,000 black residents rises as the percentage of all foreign-born and blacks with college degrees rises.*

These results imply that, at the very least, the presence of immigrants does not discourage blacks from starting their own businesses. One

* **Factors Explaining Differences in Black-Owned
Enterprises in Large Metropolitan Areas[a]**

Independent Variable	Coefficient	T-statistic
Constant	18.0898	3.82 [1]
Percentage Foreign-born	0.1579	2.71 [1]
Percentage Black Population	0.1569	-2.14 [2]
Percentage of Blacks with College Degrees	0.0492	2.49 [2]
White Household Income	0.0001	1.36
Percentage Black Unemployment	-0.3775	-1.61
Percentage Manufacturing of All Jobs	-0.1081	-1.06

R^2 (adjusted)   .55   N = 40
[1] Significant at 1 percent level of confidence
[2] Significant at 5 percent level of confidence

[a] Black-owned enterprise data for 1987; independent variables data from Department of Labor, Bureau of Labor Statistics, *1990 Census of Population*. Metropolitan areas in the sample have a population in excess of 1 million.

might even be tempted to conclude that a large immigrant population encourages black enterprise, but this would be going too far. The relative success of black entrepreneurs in western cities is more likely due to local economic vitality stimulated by immigrants, which has attracted blacks with above-average levels of education and access to capital. Blacks in Los Angeles and San Francisco are considerably more educated than in other regions, suggesting a link between business formation and education. Sales per black enterprise in these cities also exceed the national average, but they remain substantially below sales in Hispanic- and Asian-owned enterprises.

Although black entrepreneurs seem unconstrained by immigrant enterprises, the situation may change as the latter's share of retail activity grows. In particular, the ability of blacks to compete with a closely knit ethnic business structure will come into question. But the strength of Asian enterprises raises potential concern beyond the minority community. Could not one group gain dominance over a particular industry and restrain trade through informal ethnic channels? Once in control, the group, by eliminating competition, could increase prices freely. While it is certainly possible to imagine such conditions arising, a monopoly of this sort, involving thousands of individuals, would be very hard to sustain. In the area of small motels, for example, Indian immigrants might one day gain enough control to be able in theory to collectively raise prices. But national motel chains, some of which aim for the same moderate-priced market, and which enjoy such assets as central reservation systems, would no doubt seek to undercut artificially high prices. Fortunately, the American economy is too large and diversified for any one group to exercise long-term monopoly power at the retail level.

A more serious concern is the insular nature of immigrant hiring practices. These enterprises tend to employ only a handful of people, most of them members of the same family or ethnic group. The majority of Asian-owned stores have no paid employees. As a result, the job openings for native workers, particularly minorities, in these businesses are very limited. Retail wages in any case, regardless of ownership, are lower than in other sectors, and opportunities for advancement are virtually nonexistent. But the presence of immigrant eating establishments also reduces the number of fast-food outlets that hire young persons. In this respect, job opportunities for native teenagers, particularly inner-city youth, may be dampened.

Immigrant businessmen have also sparked resentment by creating exclusive, ethnic-based business federations. These associations exercise more power and control over their members than was the case with earlier generations of immigrants, who formed only loose networks among their fellow ethnics. The absence of just about any non-Asian business establishments from several shopping centers built by Chinese investors in the Los Angeles area may be accidental. More probably, there is a conscious intent to informally exclude non-Asians in order to increase the leverage owners have on all aspects of operations. Native businessmen (and their workers) would be more likely to complain about violations of labor laws or sanitary codes, or to protest rent hikes, than immigrants.

Disparities and Disturbances

Gateway cities typically afford blacks opportunities for economic self-advancement through white-collar work and entrepreneurship. In Los Angeles and San Francisco, for example, the proportion of black professional and technical workers is close to the area average for all groups and is considerably higher than in most other urban areas in the nation. The most prosperous black families in the nation live within Consolidated Metropolitan Statistical Areas (CMSAs) with gateway cities at their core. In these areas, which include Nassau and Suffolk counties (near New York City), Ventura County (near Los Angeles), and Santa Clara County (near San Francisco), black household income is 85 percent of the white household level.

These areas offer fewer opportunities to unskilled black men, forcing them to compete with a large pool of undocumented workers. The presence of immigrants thus appears to be increasing the gap between the black middle class—with economic characteristics more typical of the white middle class—and less well-off black households. This widening gap is particularly evident in Miami. It would be unfair, however, to hold immigration responsible in any major way for the emergence of an underclass. Numerous inner cities with few immigrants are faced with rising ghetto poverty. Immigration is but one of many contributors to the widening class differences among urban blacks.

This conclusion sheds no light on why immigrants, *regardless of race*, seem to be progressing faster than native minorities. Are the native black and immigrant experiences so different as to rule out any insights on the issue of economic progress? The diverging economic paths of immigrants, native white Americans, and blacks have been examined by sociologist Stanley Lieberson in his book *A Piece of the Pie*.[38] He found similarities between new immigrants in the early decades of the twentieth century and blacks. Both labored under incredible hardships, including poverty, and were viewed by the dominant white population as inferior. But Lieberson found that new Europeans were not considered as inferior as Orientals, who, in turn, were relatively more acceptable to native-born whites than blacks.

In some respects, conditions facing blacks then were no worse than those facing immigrants. For example, unemployment for blacks in 1930 was considerably lower than for foreign-born workers, and only slightly higher than for native-born whites. Education appears to be a key difference in the rates of progress between the two groups. In 1960 the children of European immigrants, except those from Mediterranean nations, were three to four times as likely as black children (and more likely than white children of native parents) to attend college. Although in recent decades the educational gap between blacks and immigrants has narrowed, it has not closed.

Lieberson found Chinese and Japanese residents in the first half of the twentieth century most closely resembling blacks in terms of discrimination because of skin color. But despite intensive bias, both immigrant minorities forged ahead economically. Lieberson attributes their economic success to their small numbers caused by the early cutoff of Asian immigration. Unfortunately, he does not discuss the validity of his thesis for explaining Asian success since the 1970s, as renewed immigration swelled their ranks to several million.

The future of inner-city blacks and new immigrant groups is also a subject examined by sociologist William Julius Wilson. In his widely praised book *The Truly Disadvantaged*, he cites the earlier work of Lieberson as one basis for his conclusion that recently arrived Hispanic and Asian populations will become increasingly subject to the urban poverty and other problems facing inner-city black neighborhoods. Whereas, Wilson writes, "urban blacks could [over the next several decades] record a decrease in their rate of joblessness, crime, teenage pregnancy, female-headed homes, and welfare dependency, Hispanics could show a steady increase in each."[39] As for Asians, he suggests they will face difficulties not unlike those observed in the black ghetto; as their numbers increase, they will no longer find special occupational niches that enable them to improve their economic status. Wilson further implies that, as the numbers of Asians and Hispanics grow, they will be seen as a threat to the white majority. Therefore, ethnic hostility could be redirected from blacks to these new minorities.

The transformation of the urban economy and the loss of jobs requiring relatively little education are seen by Wilson as the major culprits of growing inner-city poverty. He also attributes the sharp fall in labor force participation rates among blacks to structural changes in the economy. Wilson lists other economic, social, and demographic causes as well, but he considers loss of urban employment opportunities as the fundamental cause of inner-city poverty.

His view that the loss of manufacturing jobs hurts black city dwellers more than other groups seems valid, but it is risky to call economic changes the major reason for the rise of an underclass. Economic woes in New York City, including the loss of several hundred thousand jobs, did not prevent about half a million immigrants from finding employment. The economic-transformation argument does not explain why recent inner-city black immigrants appear to be moving forward faster than native-born blacks. In New York, for example, since the 1920s black Caribbean immigrants appear to have exercised economic and political influence disproportionate to their numbers.[40]

Ethnic enclaves such as Manhattan's Chinatown confront many of the same problems facing the black ghetto, including overcrowding and youth gangs. Yet, the despair and frustration observed in black ghettos only a few miles to the north and east are not in evidence among the well over 150,000 persons estimated to reside in this teeming area. The contrasts in life-style between Bedford-Stuyvesant and Chinatown are too extreme to suggest, as does Wilson, that these differences will substantially lessen in the foreseeable future. Nor is there evidence, so far, that ethnic hostility of whites has shifted from blacks to nonblack immigrants.

Asians are advancing in virtually all endeavors and occupations. Their across-the-board progress lends little credence to Lieberson's theory of occupational niches as the explanation for their achievements. On the contrary, larger numbers appear to encourage rather than retard economic advancement.

Perhaps part of the ghetto problem was identified by James Fallows when he interviewed both immigrant and American blacks in Miami in the early 1980s. He found that American blacks had lost faith in the system, but young Haitians and Jamaicans believed that their hard work would be rewarded.[41] Alex Stepick, an anthropologist studying race relations in Miami, confirmed Fallows's observations: Young Haitian immigrants in Miami schools tend to have a positive outlook. They feel superior to and typically outperform American blacks.[42] The optimism Fallows and Stepick found in the immigrant slums of Miami can also be observed among immigrants in New York, San Francisco, and Washington, D.C. They, too, have faith that there are opportunities for ambitious youth, even those born in other nations.

Although considerable work remains before we have a full understanding of black—and other—immigrant progress, noneconomic characteristics such as attitudes and expectations of success appear to be dominant. One potentially serious consequence of black immigration may be that the widening gap between American and foreign-born blacks will dishearten both groups, with immigrants more likely to join the black middle class in abandoning the inner city. Such migration from the urban core would leave behind an increasingly frustrated native black underclass.

Because Los Angeles has few black immigrants, the tensions observed in other cities between foreign-born and native blacks are not apparent there. But the well-publicized conflicts between blacks and the expanding Asian and Hispanic communities have led to speculation that the April–May 1992 Los Angeles riots were at least partially attributable to the belief that these mostly immigrant groups were taking jobs at the expense of the resident native minority community. The trigger for the eruption was unrelated, but some commentators were nonetheless prompted to link the root causes of the riot directly to immigration. Before the rubble was even cleared from city streets, several of the nation's most prestigious newspapers carried "instant analysis" editorial page articles by social scientists that cited too many immigrants as the explanation for the disturbances.

On May 15, 1992, a *New York Times* column titled "The Riots: Underclass vs. Immigrants" argued that the upheaval was caused by the loss of traditional underclass jobs, such as day laborers and maids, to immigrants.[43] A few days later, a blistering column in the *Los Angeles Times* stated that "we should not have to rediscover that massive immigration widens the divide between wealth and poverty, storing up social dynamite, especially diminishing life for African-Americans."[44] The writer also claimed that the 700,000 immigrants who came to Los

Angeles in the 1980s moved into already strapped black job markets. The lead article by Joel Kotkin in the "Outlook" section of the Sunday *Washington Post* at the end of May 1992 discussed "the lessons from California for the nation." Flanked by a cartoon showing a despondent Statue of Liberty collapsing of its own weight, the article Kotkin wrote stated that "the working class and the poor in many major cities find themselves assaulted by competition from refugees from Third World poverty."[45] The writer acknowledged some benefits to Los Angeles from immigration but saw the nation as facing a fundamental choice between "cosmopolitan multiracialism or a descent into tribalism."

The three articles are probably not representative of the views held by the editors of these newspapers. But the prominence given these commentaries (without concurrent opposing opinions) gives credence to a revival of the questionable anti-alien sentiment disseminated by the American press during the early decades of this century.

Would ghetto discontent in Los Angeles (and elsewhere) be erased by additional day laborer, waiter, and maid jobs? Youths in the ghetto understandably perceive such work as a throwback to the Jim Crow era. To argue that immigrants compete for jobs already held by blacks ignores the new employment opportunities created by their presence, such as in the public sector and in sales, which are frequently assumed by native blacks. Besides, disturbances may be set off for any number of reasons; there were relatively few aliens in Chicago, Detroit, or Newark during the 1960s, when these and other cities erupted. Contrary to the inference drawn by press commentaries, curtailing immigration would not have prevented the Los Angeles riot, nor will it prevent urban disturbances in the future. Faulting immigrants for inner-city problems is the path to more interethnic conflict.

The Public Sector

For centuries, opponents of immigration have held out the specter of immigrants becoming public wards. In the 1830s and 1840s, propagandists for restrictions evoked images of ships sent across the ocean to dump their human cargo of beggars and paupers, the lame and the blind, on America's shores. At that time, however, the government had few responsibilities for public welfare, and most of the care of the needy was carried out by private charities. But as the role of the public sector expanded during and after the Great Depression, immigrant demand for public services became a serious issue.

The American public feels that immigrants receive more in services than they contribute. Sixty-five percent of respondents to a national poll taken in 1988 agreed with the proposition that "immigrants get more from the United States economy through social services and unemployment than they contribute to the economy through taxes and productivity." Only 19 percent believed immigrants contribute more than they receive.[46]

In considering the effects of immigration on government services, it is necessary to classify legal entrants, refugees, and illegal immigrants as distinct groups. Persons who enter as permanent immigrants are typically eligible for the same services as native residents. Refugees can receive specific federal assistance, including welfare, but illegal entrants are ineligible for most aid.

Illegal aliens have borne the brunt of charges that immigrants are abusing welfare aid at the expense of American taxpayers. Contrary to public opinion, studies of undocumented aliens during the 1970s failed to show that these immigrants utilized welfare services extensively. However, critics of immigration policy charge that these studies were flawed, and that the actual use of public services by illegal entrants is extensive.[47] The public, ever conscious of "welfare chiselers," continues to express concern that illegals are taking advantage of welfare programs. A 1983 survey in California found that one-half of all respondents shared the view that illegal aliens, although ineligible for welfare assistance, nonetheless manage to receive such aid.[48] A review of Los Angeles welfare applicants found that a substantial number withdrew their applications—presumably because of their illegal status—when asked to document their eligibility, lending credence to these concerns.[49]

That some ineligible immigrants attempt to receive assistance to which they are not entitled should not be a surprise; after all, native-born Americans have been known to do the same. But in southern California, strict enforcement makes it unlikely that many ineligible applicants actually receive assistance.

The extent to which undocumented aliens have a right to receive government services other than welfare has been debated in the courts. In 1982, the Supreme Court ruled that the state of Texas had no right to deny an elementary education to children who were in the

United States illegally. The close (5 to 4) decision was based in part on the notion that public education of the young plays a pivotal role in maintaining the fabric of our society. In the words of the Court, "By denying these children a basic education, we deny them the ability to live within the structure of our civic institutions, and foreclose any realistic possibility that they will contribute even in the smallest way to the progress of our nation."[50] Further, the Court held that "there is no evidence that illegal entrants impose any significant burden on the state's economy. To the contrary, the available evidence suggests that illegal aliens underutilize public services, while contributing their labor to the local economy and tax money to the state." Congress has limited the access of aliens to services other than education, such as unemployment compensation. Given the close decision on education, it is unlikely that federal courts will overturn such restrictive legislation.

How has the tide of immigration affected the fiscal well-being of gateway cities? Because Los Angeles and New York have absorbed the largest numbers of immigrants in the nation, if the absorption of newcomers is creating an excessive burden on cities, it should be evident from the financial records of our two biggest municipalities.

Illegal immigrants are considered a serious fiscal problem by local officials in Los Angeles. In addition, the presence of a large Southeast Asian refugee population in the area has created demand for the various services this population is eligible to receive. In response to this drain on its resources, Los Angeles County maintains the most comprehensive data in the nation on social services requested and received by immigrants and refugees.

Southeast Asian households in Los Angeles (and elsewhere) tend to have very large families, which means, because children require extensive educational and health services, they are a greater burden than other immigrants. The number of refugees receiving cash benefits in Los Angeles County increased from 49,000 in 1982 to more than 60,000 three years later. In the late 1980s, more than 70 percent of all refugees receiving assistance in Los Angeles County were classified as "time expired"— that is, they had been in the United States for more than three years and were no longer eligible for federal reimbursement. Hence, some of the cost was shifted from the national to the state and local levels.

The largest cash outlays for refugees in Los Angeles come in the Aid to Families with Dependent Children—Unemployed Fathers (AFDC-UF) program, which provides assistance to two-parent families with children. In 1986, more than 30,000 "time-expired" refugees were receiving this aid, representing more than one-third of all county recipients. However, this high percentage reflects not only the poverty level of refugees but the fact that most native black and white households receiving assistance are headed by women and thus do not qualify for this particular program.

The social service most widely used by nonrefugee immigrants is Aid to Families with Dependent Children (AFDC). To qualify, applicants must verify U.S. citizenship or refugee status, but data from Los Angeles County indicate that these requirements are easily circumvented because children born in the United States are eligible for assistance. In late 1986, the county's Department of Public Social Services, using a special tracking system, found that about 66,000 children born in the United States of undocumented parents were supported by AFDC funds.[51] This represents one of every seven children supported by AFDC—a sharp increase from the early 1980s. Another 36,000 children of legal immigrants also received aid.

That a substantial number of AFDC recipients are children of immigrants should not be surprising, given the low earnings of undocumented aliens and legal immigrants from Latin America in particular. The number of undocumented aliens in Los Angeles County in the late 1980s was probably about 1.2 million, given that more than 800,000 persons applied for legalization. These aliens constituted 13 to 14 percent of the population, but 16 percent of all AFDC cases were attributable to their presence. These percentages suggest that children of illegal aliens are somewhat more likely to receive assistance than the general population. But the proportion of *legal* entrants receiving AFDC payments is not only lower than among the undocumented population but also below the countywide average.

Transfer payments to needy immigrant families are sizable, but Los Angeles residents actually experienced a relative decline in the aggregate of these payments. In 1976, 13.5 percent of all area personal income was in the form of transfer payments. By 1986 this fell to 12.9 percent (compared to a higher share, 13.8 percent, in other metropolitan areas).[52] Los Angeles County, housing the largest illegal immigrant and refugee populations in the nation, was not being crushed in the 1980s by welfare and other transfer payments to meet their needs.

Immigrants in Los Angeles make a significant demand on public education. This is due in part to the tendency of aliens, especially

Hispanics and Southeast Asians, to have large families. Most of them send their children to public rather than private schools. In all gateway cities, but particularly in California, immigrant enrollment is rising and overcrowding is becoming a serious problem. One manifestation of the immigration surge is bilingual-program enrollment. During 1986, 19 percent of all students in Los Angeles were in such programs; in Orange County the figure was 13 percent, and in San Francisco, 30 percent. The consequent need for bilingual teachers has created large additional costs for local school districts. Asian enrollment in New York City schools more than doubled between 1976 and 1985. By the late 1980s, 7 percent of all public school students in the city were Asians. Not only are operating costs increased by immigrant students, but their numbers require that additional schools and classrooms be constructed. This means local school districts find their debt service soaring, while their revenue base may not be expanding at a corresponding rate.

Immigrants make extensive use of public medical services because they lack access to private health care and medical insurance. An estimated 62 percent of all women giving birth in Los Angeles county hospitals were born in Mexico. The vast majority of maternity patients had been in the United States for more than one year, indicating that only a few came to California for the express purpose of giving birth. Interestingly, almost no women from Asian countries were found to deliver in county hospitals.

A New York survey of health care indicates that immigrants require somewhat higher municipal outlays per household for medical services than other groups, placing a burden on city hospitals and other public health facilities. Health care is also an issue in other cities. Washington, D.C., health officials claim that Hispanic immigrants from the suburbs are straining city clinics. The District of Columbia attracts these immigrants because services are usually free, for both adults and children. The city has no information on the legal status of those seeking care, but the suspicion is that they are mostly illegal aliens.[53]

The provision of health services to illegal aliens has been a thorny issue, legally, morally, and financially. Until 1986, undocumented aliens were considered ineligible for Medicaid, and local governments absorbed the cost of unreimbursed Medicaid payments. In that year, however, a federal district judge in New York City ruled that illegal aliens were in fact entitled to benefits. Aside from the legal issue, many believe that setting limits on basic health care to illegal aliens is shortsighted because the public may be faced with higher medical bills down the road if proper care is not provided in a timely fashion. In consequence of the sharp escalation in medical service costs, health care may well constitute the largest public cost associated with immigration. The situation is aggravated by the unique medical needs of arrivals from third world countries. Diseases not seen for decades—if ever—in this nation are now commonly diagnosed in county hospitals.

In contrast to Los Angeles, interviews with New York City officials did not reveal serious anxieties that immigrants are overtaxing local services.[54] The attitude in New York, as expressed by former mayor Edward Koch in 1985, was that the municipality provides services to all its needy residents, whatever their legal status.[55] Unlike in Los Angeles and San Francisco, the Southeast Asian refugee population in New York is small. Most refugees are from Eastern Europe and are quickly absorbed into the large ethnic communities that have made New York City their home for a century or more.

Tabulations based on Census Bureau data indicate that, on average, native women in New York City in 1980 received $306 in public assistance, compared with only $187 for female immigrants.[56] Among recent arrivals, only those from one country, the Dominican Republic, exceed the native average in welfare payments. Moreover, Asian immigrants (other than Southeast Asian refugees) are unlikely to receive public assistance at all. Only about 1 in 8 Asian families in New York, most of whom are immigrants, has an income below the poverty level, compared with 1 in 6 non-Asian families. Furthermore, very few of those with low income receive public assistance. Asians account for only 1 of every 160 New Yorkers receiving such payments, although 1 of every 30 city residents is Asian in origin.

Overall, the 1980 Census indicates that 8 percent of foreign-born households in New York City received public assistance, compared with 13 percent of native households. Among households headed by females, the public assistance rate for immigrants was 38 percent, and for natives, 53 percent. Notwithstanding the comparatively high rates of assistance among such recent arrivals as Colombians and Dominicans, immigrants can claim below-average public assistance levels.

There are several reasons why immigrants make less of a claim on public resources than might be expected. First, many immigrants in New York lack documentation and are thus ineligible for welfare payments. Even some of those who do qualify are inhibited by cultural attitudes from seeking such aid. Among some ethnic groups, including most Asians and Europeans, welfare is considered to be degrading. Those immigrants in need of financial assistance tend to rely on their families and fellow ethnics. Finally, the responses to the "source of income" question on census returns, which are the basis for the statistics used here, may understate actual receipts. But there is no reason to believe that immigrants have a greater tendency to understate public assistance than natives do.

New York City has also examined the demand for services by immigrants and their tax contributions. City statistics support the conclusion that foreign-headed households used public assistance at just half the rate of native-headed households. The explanation given by Elizabeth Bogen, who ran the New York City Office of Immigration, is that "many immigrants are willing to find work at low-paying, low-status jobs if the only alternative is welfare. The stereotype of the hard-working, 'we-help-our-own' immigrant is rooted in reality."[57] In New York only 13 percent of Asian families—but 52 percent of non-Asian families—with incomes below the poverty level received public assistance, substantiating Bogen's perception.

Miami and San Francisco do not maintain detailed records on the demand for public services by immigrants. However, Miami has been greatly concerned that the flood of Central American and Caribbean refugees in the late 1980s has overwhelmed its ability to cope. Dade County officials argue that the federal government has not met its obligation to provide care for these refugees, and their presence has aroused racial tensions in incidents like the Liberty City riots. One of the problems facing Miami health officials has been the high incidence of both AIDS and tuberculosis among Haitians, and the high cost of treating patients with these diseases. San Francisco has been able to absorb Southeast Asian refugees without excessive rancor. Because most of these refugees are gainfully employed, local officials do not appear concerned that their presence is causing an undue burden on local taxpayers.

From the government's perspective, examining demand for services is only half the fiscal equation. These costs must be balanced against the revenue contributions immigrants make.

As a group, recent Hispanic immigrant households in Los Angeles pay less in taxes than they receive in services. The main reasons for the fiscal imbalance are low income and large families.[58] Although no analysis was conducted for this book to examine the fiscal implications of the Asian presence, available income and social service statistics suggest that Asians (other than Vietnamese) contribute more revenue to local and state government than they receive back. High earnings and low demand for social services distinguish these immigrants from the Hispanic population.

The average income of recent immigrants in Los Angeles and New York is below the native average, meaning that property tax and sales tax receipts from this group would also fall short of the mean. There are differences among ethnic groups, however. Recent Asian immigrants, for example, pay considerably more in monthly mortgage payments and rents than natives do. Therefore, these immigrants may contribute as much as or more in property taxes than other residents. Hispanic immigrants typically live in rental housing, frequently sharing quarters with other families. Therefore, property tax contributions from these families tend to be low.

Calculations are complicated in that many immigrants, especially owners of small businesses, belong to the nontaxpaying urban "underground economy." Small businesses of all types are less likely than larger enterprises to collect sales and Social Security taxes, but this is especially true of immigrants. Their use of family members as workers, their lack of accounting records, and their problems with language all interfere with the proper collection of taxes from these enterprises.

In Los Angeles, several thousand Southeast Asian refugee women work in the apparel industry for below-minimum wages; because their earnings are unreported, their families are simultaneously eligible to collect federal welfare checks. These workers do not pay any taxes and thus are not eligible for unemployment benefits, but as long as their welfare checks are received they do not give much thought to the absence of unemployment compensation. Likewise, thousands of illegal Mexican immigrants who work in the factories of California and Texas receive earnings that go unrecorded, with neither the employer nor the worker paying taxes on such wages. This problem is not unique to immigrant workers. Americans, both skilled and unskilled—from teenagers cutting lawns to electricians and plumbers—prefer to be paid in cash in order to avoid liability for taxes. The proportion of full-time working immigrants who are "off the books" is no doubt higher because more are willing to accept the lack of benefits and protection that cash wages imply. Nonetheless, most immigrants do not belong to the underground economy and must pay taxes to all levels of government.

An analysis of the situation in New York indicates that the new immigrants, while having a modestly negative net effect on the city's finances, do not represent a drain when viewed in the context of the overall budget. Some groups, such as nonrefugee Asians, earn a lot and make low demands on services, producing a fiscal surplus; others, including many from the Caribbean, create a deficit. In San Francisco, probably only Southeast Asians and Central Americans represent net losses for local government. In Miami the influx of Central Americans and Haitians has imposed burdens on others.

How do these financial considerations balance out for the rest of the country? Several researchers have attempted to estimate the fiscal impact of immigrants at the national level. Julian Simon has concluded that, on average, recent immigrants across the nation use fewer social services than do natives.[59] Other researchers reviewing fiscal impact studies found that the demand by immigrants for public assistance varies by race and ethnicity.[60] A survey undertaken for the Department of Labor in 1984 shows that, as a group, immigrants are less likely to receive government benefits than the native-born.[61] Recently arrived aliens do receive more services than other residents, but immigrants that settled in our urban centers prior to 1970 create a surplus, for their demands on public assistance are generally low while their revenue contributions are close to average. Thus, intergenerational transfers take place between earlier arrivals and more recent ones.

A comprehensive study of census tabulations by George Borjas and Stephen Trejo confirms these conclusions.[62] The authors, who limited their analysis to national data, found that male-headed immigrant households are more likely to require assistance than native households. Tabulations of the data presented by the two authors indicate that 12.9 percent of all households coming from the Western Hemisphere (excluding Canada) received welfare payments in 1980. The rate for Asians (excluding Vietnamese, who are eligible for payments other immigrants are not entitled to) was only 6.8 percent, considerably below the average for the native-born population.[63] The highest percentage of welfare recipients other than the Vietnamese was found among immigrants from the Dominican Republic and Cuba. The least likely to receive welfare were households from Denmark, India, Iran, Israel, the Netherlands, Switzerland, and West Germany. The list has no surprises, other than the relatively high welfare load for Cubans.

The data collected from Los Angeles and New York are consistent with findings that at the national and city levels recent immigrants contribute somewhat less in taxes than the balance of the population. Below-average revenue collections are mostly attributable to low earnings, particularly among immigrants from the Western Hemisphere, and, to a lesser degree, to their legal status. Illegal aliens are less likely to pay Social Security and income taxes than legal immigrants or citizens because many are paid in cash. Passage of the 1986 Immigration Reform and Control Act may have exacerbated this problem because penalties discourage employers from acknowledging their presence. Social service costs for aliens may also be below average because transfer payments, including welfare aid, are lower for most immigrant groups than for native households. Among exceptions to this pattern are refugees heavily dependent on public services and possibly Hispanic families of undocumented aliens with children born in the United States.

The ledgerlike approach undertaken here has not taken into consideration the longer-term, and typically positive, financial effects of the immigrant presence on America's cities. Their rehabilitation of housing has returned thousands of buildings to local tax rolls. The economic activity they spur increases the amount of money collected in local taxes. In most large cities, about one-third of total revenues are generated by taxes on business enterprises. (In New York, the proportion is nearly one-half.) Were these revenues to be counted in, the deficits incurred by recent immigrants might disappear altogether.

In some situations, the movement of people across borders can pose serious difficulties, at least in the short term. In the late 1980s, several southern Texas communities and Miami found their services swamped by a sudden inflow of Central Americans admitted as refugees. Unlike most legal immigrants, these families had no relatives or jobs waiting for them. Refugees required extensive public outlays for resettlement, and impacted communities demanded more federal assistance to cope with the problem. The federal government has responded by assuming at least some of the responsibility for the care of refugees.

On the other side of the coin are poor cities where immigrants are heavily concentrated and become a productive force in the local economy. The Portuguese community in Newark contributes considerably more in local taxes than it receives in services. Few Portuguese families receive social services, and many of their children attend parochial schools, but nearly all pay property taxes. The surplus this ethnic enclave creates accrues mainly to the other, predominantly minority, city residents. Taking both short- and long-term effects into account, financial burdens on government should not be a pivotal issue in immigration policy decisions. Admitting more legal immigrants because they possess needed skills will not impose undue burdens on localities or states.

Regional and Environmental Consequences

Prior to the Civil War, waves of immigrants tilted the economic balance between North and South away from Dixie. Subsequently, they contributed to the heavier concentration of wealth and income in the urban north. Has the current wave of immigrants also affected regional disparities and the distribution of income? New immigrants have flocked to a number of large cities in a handful of states—California, New York, Florida, Texas, and Illinois. The ten states (excluding Texas) that form the nation's midsection, the West Central region (as defined by the Bureau of the Census), are home to one of every eight Americans but only one of every twenty-five recent immigrants.

It is no coincidence that the coastal areas are growing more rapidly than the rest of the nation, and that the economic disparities between the two coasts and the central spine of the nation widened in the 1970s and 1980s. California, facing the Pacific, has been among the most economically vibrant of states for generations, and the northeastern states along the Atlantic coastline were economically revitalized during the 1980s. Although California and the New England states, both heavily dependent on defense contracts, absorbed the brunt of the lengthy early 1990s recession, the longer-term prospects are for the coastal area economies to continue to outpace other regions well into the next century. Current immigration patterns have helped boost the economies of these states; meanwhile, the poorest—such as West Virginia—continue to be hurt by the lack of newcomers. These and other states in the central regions of the United States lack the foreign investment, immigrant entrepreneurs, and the formation of new ethnic enclaves that could promote economic activity. One exception to the pattern is the location of Japanese automobile plants in Kentucky and Tennessee. These facilities were built in southern, semirural settings, primarily to avoid the threat of unionization and secondarily to take advantage of generous financial inducements offered by states eager to attract high-wage jobs. But the level of activity added by these plants represents only a fraction of the growth induced by immigration in coastal states.

During the 1980s, states with a large immigrant presence, including Florida, New Jersey, and New York, experienced the highest per capita income growth rates. Concurrently, only 2 percent of recent immigrants were attracted to the ten states with the lowest income (and 9 percent of the nation's population). The dearth of immigrants is only a secondary reason for their poor performance; reductions in federal domestic program assistance, the lack of lucrative defense contracts and other federal largess that was spread around elsewhere in the 1980s, and high poverty levels battered their economies, discouraging both immigrants and native Americans from settling in those states.[64]

The gateway cities of Los Angeles, New York, and San Francisco had Asian enclaves long before revised immigration laws allowed increased entry from Asia. Similarly, Latin Americans are drawn to the Miami area by the well-established Latin population and close commercial and cultural ties to Central and South America. The existence of ethnic enclaves attracted three out of four legal entrants during the 1980s who were admitted on the basis of family preference; these were naturally drawn to cities where family members live. The new immigrants, once financially secure, invite other close relatives to join them, initiating a chain that keeps immigration concentrated in gateway cities.

Among inland cities, only Chicago has an immigrant population sufficiently large to affect the local economy. In this urban center, the Hispanic population has remained somewhat stable in recent years, probably because the industrial jobs that employ two out of five Mexicans in the city have been declining.

Immigration has not been a powerful enough force to cause a regional realignment with serious economic implications at the national level; nonetheless economic disparities can create social problems and raise concerns about equity. The large-scale presence of immigrants and foreign investment in coastal urban areas creates additional job opportunities, pulling in talented native-born Americans from other regions.

Blacks are among the groups that may be hurt by regional shifts, as many lose unionized jobs in the industrial Midwest. Their economic progress, both in absolute terms and relative to whites, is most evident in the Pacific states, where the percentage of blacks holding managerial and professional jobs in 1990 was 85 percent of the equivalent for whites and twice as high as for Hispanics. In certain regions of middle America (West North Central and East South Central states), the proportion of blacks holding higher-paying jobs falls to 58 percent of the white average.

Politically, these inner regions tend to be opposed to increased immigration, in part because their residents cannot perceive any economic benefits from such a policy. To the contrary, they (correctly) envision an erosion of their economic and political strength as population and resources shift to the coastal states.

Immigration has affected not only regional vitality and development but also patterns of growth and deterioration within cities.[65] The earlier part of this chapter dealt extensively with the income and wealth effects on cities of large-scale immigration, but the social and psychological implications of changing fortunes among enclaves and neighborhoods needs further consideration. It has already been said that, although third world migration to our shores increases the number of those living below the poverty line in the short run, typically within a generation immigrants from many parts of the world can be expected to outperform economically people who have lived in the United States from birth.

There are exceptions, though, and these may be a cause for growing concern. Like blacks who have been left behind in the inner cities of the North or Southeast, Mexican-Americans and refugees from Central America may be creating a permanent underclass, especially in southern California and along the Texas border. Although the economic misfortune of this group may be insufficient in magnitude to drag communities in recession down into depression, it could produce social problems that, over time, do portend adverse economic consequences. The concern is not with the immigrants themselves, but with their children. Weaned on American television and socialized in American schools, these youngsters, as do black youth, have much higher expectations than their parents. Their frustration could accelerate problems that are increasingly prevalent in the ghetto, such as the disintegration of family units, alcoholism, and drug abuse. Looting by some Hispanic youth, including illegal aliens in Los Angeles during the 1992 riots, may be a warning that discontent among this group is mounting.

There is a great, unstated fear that new immigrant groups whose economic advancement is slow will threaten social cohesion in the nation's cities. The once stable West Indian population that immigrated to New York City in the early decades of the twentieth century may be disintegrating under the weight of its environment. At the same time, youth gangs are thriving among the Vietnamese and other Asian groups, and the school dropout rate among Hispanics is soaring. Clearly, some of the sons and daughters of the newest immigrants will become burdens to society.

Yet, one should not underestimate the ability of most poor newcomers to transplant their strong family structure and culture onto American soil. Only half a century ago, it was generally thought that Greeks and Italians would never succeed. Only a fool would have suggested in the 1930s that the son of a Greek immigrant half a century later would have a reasonable chance to become president of the United States. So, while the danger remains that the urban ghetto will swallow new immigrants, it is more likely that the newcomers will eventually leave the ghetto, helping to shrink it—with the important caveat that illegal entry does not accelerate to higher levels than observed in the 1980s.

Concerns about immigration extend far beyond what some consider esoteric issues of income and wealth concentration. A more immediate fear is that the population increase caused in some cities by immigration is fueling excessive development and overrunning public facilities. Apprehension is most evident in California, where numerous referenda in Los Angeles and Orange counties have restricted the rate of development. Resistence to growth in California eased in the early 1990s as the economic downturn and other woes left the state treasury barren and the immediate outlook for many bleak. Residents quickly became less concerned with more abstract, quality-of-life issues that could threaten their economic well-being. Nonetheless, as California continues to add new faces (primarily as a result of immigration), political pressure to restrain development will never be far from the surface. In San Francisco, permission for more intensive development in Chinatown has been denied on the premise that new construction will encourage more people to reside in the area. Chinese contractors have charged bias in these regulations, citing the need to house growing families.[66] However, San Francisco, like numerous other cities, is attempting to restrict the level of development, worried that its infrastructure will be unable to cope with more people. In the New York area, population and economic growth in the late 1980s pushed public transportation to its physical limits, and local officials were concerned that, in the absence of massive infrastructure investment, the future economic development of the region would be hampered.

Americans as a people—with those living in crowded Manhattan a possible exception—are less tolerant of high-density living than Asians or Europeans. Perhaps this is a vestige of our frontier, open-space mentality. A more likely explanation is that most of our population can afford to live in suburban housing because land has always been relatively inexpensive.

Though they continue to prefer the detached suburban house as a life-style, Americans are increasingly eager to preserve the environment, but population growth and explosive development clash with ecological concerns. Immigrants, the majority coming from areas of the world where population density is much higher than in the United States, seem less sensitive to these issues than natives. Their first priority is to improve their economic status.

As immigration induces an acceleration of suburban growth, more open space is swallowed by development and the quantity of agricultural land is diminished. This is not essentially an economic issue because our nation enjoys a surplus of farmland, but a food shortage at some future date is possible. Fragile, environmentally sensitive land could be bulldozed in the building process, causing soil erosion and other damage.

Environmental problems appear to be most serious in the metropolitan areas where new immigrants are concentrated. In the most densely populated megalopolises—New York, Los Angeles, and San Francisco—population-control groups have seized environmental issues to argue against increased immigration. They note that without immigration the population would stabilize or increase very slowly after the year 2020. Their position is valid; a report issued by the

Census Bureau in 1989 suggested the population would peak in the year 2038 and steadily decline thereafter.[67] The census report assumes (very conservatively) annual net immigration of 500,000 persons after 1997 to derive its projections. In the absence of net immigration, the population would stabilize earlier—in the year 2030.

Advocates of "zero population growth" maintain that any additional population, such as projected by the census over the next five decades, will destabilize the physical as well as human environments. The "no-growth" movement contends that a slowly decreasing population would cause incomes to rise, maintain open spaces, and allow more leisure time.

However utopian this view may be, the image of an overcrowded society taps a deep reservoir of anxiety in many Americans who treasure their mountains, lakes, and leafy suburban streets. Unquestionably, an expansion in population and the consequent increase in land prices would make it harder for the middle class to maintain its customary standard of privacy and space. In the 1980s, inflated housing costs in New York and San Francisco forced moderate-income families not "locked in" by rent controls to tolerate substandard, overcrowded housing in the city or to relocate to outlying districts.

About one-third of our population growth in the 1980s was due to immigration. But this proportion (the highest since the early 1900s) reflects the falling birthrate, particularly among native, non-Hispanic white women, as much as rising immigration levels. The overall fertility rate in the late 1980s translates as only 1.8 children per mother, which is below the replacement rate. Were American birthrates today equal to those of the early 1900s, the immigrant share of population gains would be small.

Despite the influx, our population density remains very low compared with that of most other nations. Still, even the most vocal proponents of liberal immigration cannot deny that population growth, coupled with economic expansion, can have adverse repercussions on the quality of life.

The most immediate worry for many city dwellers is crime, which is both an economic and social issue. Immigrants have been popularly associated with criminal activity since the early nineteenth century, when nativists charged that European countries were emptying their prisons and loading thieves and murderers aboard ships headed for our ports. Widely circulated following the first great Irish surge, these charges resurfaced during the wave of immigration from Eastern and Southern Europe during the early twentieth century. Various studies were sponsored to demonstrate the criminality of these new arrivals. The most exhaustive was by the Dillingham Commission, which, in an effort to link crimes to a person's place of birth, examined the records of New York City's magistrate courts. Despite the commission's generally anti-immigrant sentiments, its report—"Immigration and Crime"—failed to demonstrate that the foreign-born—particularly those from Italy and Russia—committed more crimes than others.[68] These two groups accounted for only about 16 percent of all offenses in the city; if "violation of corporation ordinances" (misdemeanors) had been excluded from the offenses tabulated, the percentage of crime committed by them would have been lower than their share of the population. Nonetheless, New York police officials continued to blame most of the crime in the city on Italians and Jews.

Records maintained in Los Angeles in the early decades of the twentieth century also failed to demonstrate that immigrants were more likely to be engaged in criminal activities than native residents. The incidence of alcoholism among immigrants in large cities was found to be considerably lower than among the native population. Despite these findings, many Americans, their views shaped by the tabloid press, continued to believe that immigrants had criminal behavior "in their blood."

During the 1980s, the immigrant crime issue reemerged, thanks largely to the arrival in Miami of several thousand Cuban criminals (estimates range from 2,700 to 40,000) as part of the Mariel flotilla. The murder rate in Miami, already high, climbed further when the so-called Mariellos, whom Castro gladly released from prison, returned to their chosen trade after arriving on our shores. From Miami, the Mariel criminal element spread outward, and the repercussions continue to be felt across the country. In Elizabeth, New Jersey, six hundred of the several thousand Mariel refugees who settled in the city were arrested for felonies; in Union City, a Cuban stronghold in New Jersey, one-third of all felonies in the mid-1980s were committed by Mariellos. According to the sheriff of Las Vegas, one-fourth of all the Cuban refugees who settled in the city were career criminals. In retrospect, the acceptance of these criminals ranks as one of the most ill-conceived decisions of the Carter administration.

The drug trade, too, has been a significant source of immigrant crime. Illegal Colombian aliens and other Latin Americans have played key roles in bringing drugs to Miami, New York, and Los Angeles. More recently, Jamaicans and Chinese have sought a share of the lucrative drug trade. In New York, in fact, the Chinese have taken over the heroin trade from the Mafia. In cities with large concentrations of Chinese, Koreans, and Vietnamese, organized gangs terrorize local residents.

Can high crime rates in gateway cities be linked to recent immigration? It is true that Los Angeles, New York, and, in particular, Miami have crime rates well above the level of most American cities, but it is essential to examine the relationship between immigrant groups and crime to establish a pattern. The Department of Justice compiles arrest rates by race and ethnicity. These national data show the highest arrest rates for blacks, followed by Hispanics.[69] Asians' rates, despite media accounts of gang activity, are less than one-third of the national average, accounting for only 0.8 percent of all arrests in the country. These calculations are of limited relevance because they do not distinguish foreign- from native-born residents. Thus, it is necessary to examine local statistics to draw inferences about recent immigration and crime.

In some California communities, there is evidence that immigrants have contributed to high crime rates. Police officials declare that organized groups cross the border from Tijuana and commit robberies in middle-income neighborhoods. Criminal activity in towns near the Mexican border led San Diego County to undertake the nation's most comprehensive analysis of arrest rates according to legal status. These data suggest that illegal aliens were involved in a high proportion of crimes relative to their estimated numbers. In the city of San Diego, 26 percent of all burglary arrests and 12 percent of all felony arrests involved undocumented workers, who are thought to comprise less than 4 percent of the population.[70] Similarly, fragmentary data from Los Angeles indicate that illegal aliens are involved in a disproportionate share of narcotics arrests.

The sheriff in Los Angeles County estimates that 10 percent of all inmates are illegal aliens. This figure seems high, but if, as estimated, aliens who entered illegally account for 1.2 million of the 8.8 million people in Los Angeles County, then this arrest rate would actually be proportionally somewhat low. Moreover, many illegals may be arrested without cause; according to one study conducted by the Center for U.S.-Mexican Studies in San Diego, aliens are sometimes arrested solely because of their appearance and limited language skills.[71] Still, this is small comfort for law-abiding residents of the border towns where aliens have committed numerous crimes. In the New York area, officials in Tarrytown (Westchester County) charge that illegal aliens are causing crime and drug problems to increase. They also cite incidents between Hispanics and blacks that have flared into violence as disruptive to the community.[72] But no statistics are available to document that the incidence of crime attributable to immigrants exceeds the area average.

Such developments have led some observers to implicate the new tide of immigrants in the national rise in crime that took place during the mid- and late 1980s. The presence of a large population from South America and other drug-producing regions has facilitated the narcotics trade, and inevitably leads to incidents among drug dealers and addicts. Most of the crimes committed by aliens are perpetrated against other aliens, as in Santa Ana, California, where the police found that 70 percent of all recent homicide victims were illegal aliens and the majority of their assailants were also undocumented.

However, a closer look at crime statistics does not reinforce such claims. For example, rising crime in Texas in the past few years has been blamed by local politicians on the influx of undocumented Mexicans as well as on deteriorating economic conditions. But an examination of crime statistics in the state does not support the illegal-entrant thesis. El Paso, with its predominantly Hispanic population, did not experience any greater rise than the rest of the state. San Antonio, with the highest concentration of Mexicans in the nation, experienced a less than average increase in crime. The sharpest hikes in criminal activity were found in Fort Worth, Amarillo, and Austin, all of which have relatively low immigrant populations.

On a national basis, there is no evidence that immigrants as a group are more likely to commit crimes than the native-born. In fact, the available records suggest the opposite. In Los Angeles there are no statistics to support the contention that Hispanic neighborhoods have higher crime rates than the city as a whole. Arrest data for southern California, adjusted for age—most crimes are committed by young males—indicate that the rate of arrest for violent crimes is lowest among Asians (they make up 6 percent of the population but commit only 3 percent of the crimes), and that Hispanic arrests are close to the regional average. Taken together, Asians and Hispanics (native-born and immigrant) make up 38 percent of the region's population between the ages of fifteen and twenty nine and commit 34 percent of all violent crimes.[73] In Newark, meanwhile, few arrests are made in the Portuguese districts—islands of relative security in a city with much violent crime.

Whatever their numbers, the immigrants' language and cultural barriers limit the ability of police agencies to apprehend criminals within their communities. Links between drug cartels and ethnic enterprises in several cities point to this problem. However, it should be noted that among Colombians, Central Americans, and Jamaicans arrested for drug-related offenses, virtually all are illegal aliens, not legal entrants.

One problem directly linked to immigration is overcrowding in our cities. In Los Angeles, for example, low earnings and large families have caused more than one-half of all newly arrived Hispanics to live in overcrowded conditions (defined as more than one person per room—admittedly a high standard). Immigrants from other ethnic groups must endure similar conditions. Such an environment can lead to social and health problems—but not always. In the nineteenth and early twentieth centuries, New York's Lower East Side was among the most densely populated slums on earth. However intolerable, those conditions did not produce symptoms of social disintegration. In New York and San Francisco, conditions in Chinese enclaves are not much better than were found in the worst city slums a century ago. There appears to be no imminent threat to public health or safety, but crowding and poor sanitation invariably raises the risk of an epidemic striking at the most vulnerable. In any case, immigrants tend to upgrade their housing rapidly as their income rises. Hispanics who arrived a generation ago are now leaving crowded East Los Angeles, and Asians are scattering throughout the Los Angeles and San Francisco basins.

Related to the issue of overcrowding is the increased demand for low- and moderate-income housing, particularly rental units. The number of newly built federally subsidized units in this sector is wholly inadequate to meet the rise in demand, and federal policies during the 1980s exacerbated the shortage. The result is an increase in rents, affecting natives and immigrants alike.

Minority advocates argue that immigration has escalated housing costs. It is difficult to assess this claim, given the spotty nature of the data on immigration and public housing. In particular, blacks fear being displaced by immigrants who move into ghettos in search of moderately priced housing. Such a process does seem to be taking place in many cities. In San Francisco, Chinese, Japanese, and Filipinos have been buying homes in the predominantly black neighborhoods of Bayview-Hunters and Richmond Point. In Watts and nearby Los Angeles ghettos, blacks are increasingly resentful that Hispanics are moving in, competing for scarce housing. Feeling threatened, some blacks believe the government should curb immigration to relieve the housing shortage.[74] At Compton Community College in Los Angeles, a virtually all-black institute a decade ago, the student body now includes many Hispanics and Asians. Spanish and Korean can now be overheard in Watts elementary schools that had been mostly black since World War II.

Cultural differences toward housing may provide insight into one source of tension in these neighborhoods. Blacks appear less likely to own housing than do immigrants with similar income whose cultural heritage places a premium on ownership of land and property. Immigrants search to buy rather than rent affordable housing in deteriorating neighborhoods, and these are typically inhabited by native minorities.

Not only blacks resent intrusions by immigrants. In both New York and San Francisco, middle-income white families have also been forced to relocate under the pressure of rising rents. In Boston, Southeast Asian immigrants moving into white working-class neighborhoods have been assaulted, and several Cambodians in racially mixed neighborhoods have been murdered. Generally, however, there is little resistance to Asians moving into middle- or high-income neighborhoods (although middle-class blacks continue to find some resentment of their presence in similar neighborhoods).

A litany of distributional, environmental, and housing problems have been associated with immigration. Some are only perceived, containing little substance; others are both perceived and real. Public intervention could mitigate some problems, and none appears to be particularly severe. For example, the Cuban criminal presence was the result of poor judgment, not broader immigration policy.

Reducing immigration would have only a marginal, if any, impact on the flow of drugs from the Western Hemisphere, Asia, or the Middle East. Immigration is only one of numerous developments contributing to urban congestion and pollution. These problems cannot be resolved by changes in immigration policy, although the continuance of immigration increases the cost of remedying them. Perhaps the strongest argument—more social than economic—against immigration is that its benefits are by no means equally distributed. Beneficiaries of liberal immigration policies tend to be the more privileged segments of our society.

In spite of the evidence presented in this chapter, public opinion polls indicate the majority of the American population remains unconvinced that the benefits associated with immigration outweigh the costs. We therefore need to search for noneconomic concerns that mold public attitudes toward immigration.

6

Social and Political Stability

They [the Germans] will soon so outnumber us that [despite] all the advantages we have, we will, in my opinion, not be able to preserve our language, and even our Government will become precarious.

Benjamin Franklin, 1753[1]

The last chapter assessed the costs of immigration and came to the conclusion that, on balance, the inflow of up to fifteen million persons from abroad during the 1970s and 1980s was an economic plus. Virtually all studies by economists indicate that adverse effects on native-born workers have been minor and offset by positive contributions to the American standard of living. The majority of the public, however, sees immigration, particularly illegal immigration, as a serious concern. Do other social scientists perceive the effects of immigrants as do economists, or do their views more closely reflect general public attitudes? As shown in Table 6-1, there are substantial differences between economists and others—anthropologists, historians, political scientists, psychologists, and sociologists.

Noneconomists responding to the survey are less certain, and only a minority believe that lower immigration could raise living standards. As to the effect of illegal immigration, there is a sharp cleavage between economics and other disciplines. About half of all social scientists, but only 11 percent of economists, stated that illegal aliens had a *negative* effect on the economy.

Table 6-1

Survey of Views on Economic Impacts of Immigration

What level of legal immigration would have the most favorable impact on American living standards?

	More	Same	Less	Don't Know
Economists	56%	33%	0%	11%
Other Social Scientists	31	49	17	3

What impact does illegal immigration have on the U.S. economy?

	Positive	Neutral	Negative	Don't Know
Economists	74%	11%	11%	4%
Other Social Scientists	18	24	51	7

Source: Stephen Moore, "Social Scientists' Views on Immigrants and U.S. Immigration Policy: A Postscript," *Annals of the American Academy of Political Science* 487 (September 1986), pp. 15–16.

Social scientists share the public's doubts that immigration is necessarily positive from an economic perspective. But the populace has other, perhaps more serious, concerns that transcend economic issues. As noted in an earlier chapter, only 30 percent of California residents in 1987 believed that illegal immigrants take jobs from Americans; yet 69 percent of those surveyed stated that the *overall* effect of the alien inflow was unfavorable.[2] Five years later, only a minority of Californians believed that immigrants take jobs from Americans, but 63 percent, as shown in Table 6-2, stated that too many immigrants were being admitted. Respondents to another California survey agreed that Asian and Hispanic immigrants were also making important economic contributions to the state. But 55 percent of the respondents were "somewhat worried" or "very worried" about the changing racial and ethnic makeup of the state.[3] The extent of anxiety did not differ by income. Those with high earnings, for the most part having little reason for concern that their jobs may be threatened by immigrants, were as worried as anyone that the composition of the population was being altered.

Views on immigration levels have been reasonably consistent over three decades, but the percentage of the population favoring reduced immigration appears to be on the rise, with a solid majority sharing this view in the early 1990s. There is virtually no support for increasing immigration at the national or state levels, although economists have

Table 6-2

Public Opinion on the Appropriate Level
of Immigration to the United States

Survey Year and Scope	Should Immigration Levels Be:			
	Increased	Kept the Same	Reduced	No Opinion
1965 (U.S.)[a]	8 %	39 %	33 %	20 %
1977 (U.S.)[b]	7	37	42	14
1982 (Calif.)[c]	5	31	62	2
1984 (U.S.)[d]	8	38	40	14
1987 (Calif.)[e]	8	38	40	14
1988 (Fla.)[f]	6	24	67	3
1990 (U.S.)[g]	9	29	48	14
1992 (U.S.)[h]	5	28	59	8
1992 (Calif.)[h]	8	18	63	11

[a] George H. Gallup, *The Gallup Poll: Public Opinion, 1935–1971*, vol. 3 (New York: Random House, 1972), p. 1953.
[b] George H. Gallup, *The Gallup Poll: Public Opinion, 1972–1977*, vol.2 (Wilmington, Del.: Scholarly Resources, Inc., 1979), p. 1050.
[c] California Opinion Index, "Immigration" (mimeo), Field Institute, San Francisco, June 1982.
[d] Jonathan Alter and Joseph Contreras, "Closing the Door?" *Newsweek*, June 25, 1984, p. 18. Average of responses to immigration level.
[e] California Opinion Index, "Immigration" (mimeo), Field Institute, San Francisco, October 1987.
[f] *Atlanta Journal*, January 31, 1988.
[g] *Los Angeles Times*, June 5, 1990, p. A23 (Roper Organization poll).
[h] *American Attitudes toward Immigration* (New York: The Roper Organization, April 1992).

shown that this would increase the standard of living. A substantial majority of the public, particularly in Florida (and, more recently, California), would prefer a reduced level of legal immigration. In these surveys, blacks (but not Hispanics) are considerably more inclined to favor reduced immigration than whites.

Clearly, Americans' attitudes toward immigration are not always based on economic self-interest. Many—perhaps a majority—of Americans would continue to oppose more liberal immigration guidelines on social and political grounds. Such a position has a long history. Benjamin Franklin was impressed by the economic contributions that

German immigrants made to colonial life, but he nonetheless worried that their growing numbers would irrevocably alter the traditional way of life in his home state of Pennsylvania.

Today, immigration is causing some undeniable changes in American society. Our cities, already polarized between black and white, have had to accommodate many new ethnic groups, further developing tensions. In addition to black ghettos, there are now large Spanish-speaking barrios and "Asiatowns" of many varieties—Chinese, Korean, Indian, and Vietnamese. As these ethnic enclaves expand into suburbs on the periphery of the city, whites are departing for the outer suburbs. Of the nation's largest cities, only two, San Diego and Phoenix, retained a solid, non-Hispanic white majority in 1990—a development that, thirty or forty years ago, no demographer could have imagined. In all but Detroit and Philadelphia, Hispanics comprise a fifth or more of the population. Non-Hispanic whites are expected to become a minority in the nation's most populous state, California, by the year 2003.[4]

The California public school system reflects the ethnic changes. In the 1988–89 school year, for the first time in the state's history, the majority of its 4.6 million students were Hispanic or nonwhite. Hispanics constituted 30.7 percent, blacks 9.0 percent, and others (mostly Asian) 11.1 percent of the state enrollment.[5] Only 17 percent of the elementary and secondary student body in the city of Los Angeles in 1990 was non-Hispanic white. The low white enrollment is not due to higher private school attendance (that has remained unchanged) but to a fall in the white birthrate.

According to the Census Bureau's demographic projections, the non-Hispanic population nationwide will drop to 52 percent by the year 2080.[6] This projection considerably underestimates nonwhite growth, as it is based on two assumptions that appear unrealistic. The first is that total immigration (legal and illegal) to the United States will fall in the 1990s and beyond. The second is that minority birthrates will fall to the levels of the non-Hispanic white population—that is, to only 1.8 children per woman. A continuation of the current high birthrate for Hispanics would imply a fall in the proportion of non-Hispanic whites to only 41 percent of the population by 2080. Regardless of changes in nonwhite birthrates, the Census Bureau expects the white population to begin declining by the year 2040. High birthrates for minorities and a rise in immigration would mean that the majority of the U.S. population could be nonwhite by the middle of the next century.

The movement toward multiracial societies is an irreversible and worldwide phenomenon. Prior to the 1960s, it was rare to catch sight of a nonwhite person in the cities of Europe. Today, Turks and Algerians, hungry for jobs, crowd the centers of nearly every Western European metropolis. In the port city of Marseilles, France, one of every four residents is foreign-born (primarily from Muslim North Africa). Their presence has transformed Jean-Marie Le Pen and his National Front party into a political force. The party platform, which demands a crackdown on North African immigration, has gained support not only in Marseilles but also in other cities in southern France, where much of the rundown housing in the urban core is occupied by Arab workers and their families. Le Pen's xenophobic, racist stand—he promised to expel Arab workers—gained him the vote of 15 percent of the national electorate in the late 1980s. The majority of French citizens do not support the policies of neofascist parties but nonetheless believe the presence of foreigners has increased crime and social costs. Concurrently, they fear it has diluted national identity.

Nor is the French experience unique. Extremist parties throughout Western Europe are rallying to the anti-immigrant cause. The right-wing Republicans, who play on hostility to foreigners, received almost 8 percent of Berlin's vote in 1989, an omen of forthcoming violence. By late 1991, physical attacks on immigrants and refugees were on the rise, spreading from the eastern to western regions of Germany. Two black Africans were killed and numerous foreigners beaten by mobs, forcing the removal of others to military bases for their safety. Anti-immigrant activities accelerated a year later as German legislators pondered revising the constitution to restrict the growing inflow of refugees. As in France, the majority of citizens appear to agree that the large number of refugees—Germany has admitted more than any other European nation—poses a threat. In Denmark, the Progress party promised "war" on illegal immigrants. Fear that Muslims, mainly Iranian and Lebanese refugees, were "invading" the small nation enabled the party to score impressive gains in 1988 parliamentary elections. In nearby Norway, a rightist party with an antiforeigner platform received 20 percent of the national vote. Anti-immigrant, xenophobic parties scored impressive gains in Switzerland, and did even better in Austria, by portraying their nations as under siege from hordes of foreigners. In such far-ranging locales as Australia and Canada, growing racial diversity has raised fears of social instability. Of all the industrially advanced nations, perhaps only Japan, which has adamantly sought to remain racially homogeneous, has been relatively free of internal conflict.[7] When Japan was faced with several thousand Chinese and Vietnamese boat people, authorities totally isolated those refugees from the public. Life for the refugees was made miserable, no doubt to discourage others with thoughts of approaching the Japanese islands.

The former Eastern bloc, too, has avoided problems by keeping its doors closed. Traveling east from Berlin, one sees few minorities, except for a diminishing number of (generally disliked) foreign students and a handful of tourists. Short of labor in the days when the Soviet Union was their primary market, these nations could have used more Asian and African workers, but, their pro-third-world rhetoric notwithstanding, the former Soviet-bloc nations were never willing to accept nonwhites in large numbers. One rarely sees third world faces on the streets of Budapest, Prague, or Moscow. The large and rapidly growing indigenous nonwhite and Muslim population may be one reason the USSR was historically reluctant to admit nonwhites. No doubt the new republics emerging from the Soviet Union will adopt strong policies to discourage nonwhite immigration. African and other third world students are among the casualties of the central government's collapse.

That the rising European extremism of the early 1990s has not found fertile ground in the United States has astonished foreign observers. Perhaps the long history of successfully absorbing immigrants has prevented a backlash. Cynics may argue that blacks, part of the American experience since its inception, have absorbed the enmity directed at ethnic groups elsewhere.

The first discernable voices echoing the European extreme right on the American political scene came with the candidacies of Pat Buchanan and David Duke for the 1992 Republican presidential nomination. Buchanan's anti-immigrant "America First" platform was not seen as a serious challenge to the political establishment. Nonetheless, his views mirror fears in the United States—to a lesser extent about jobs than about language, assimilation, and cultural fragmentation. Such anxieties cannot be rejected as mere manifestations of racism. Too many urban residents, black or white, exhibit such concerns for them to be a matter of simple intolerance.

Nor should the political consequences of immigration be discounted. Are the new immigrants likely to tilt the national political balance or cause change in our foreign policy? Certainly, immigration is having an important impact on the political life of American gateway cities. Minority set-aside contracts, municipal employment, bilingual education, and the distribution of neighborhood services—all are affected by the changing ethnic composition of the nation's cities.

Two Languages, One Nation

The Great Seal of the United States on the dollar bill, the symbol of America's economic might, shows a shield with thirteen stripes. The proud motto "e pluribus unum" above the shield is thought to signify the collective strength of the original states that joined the Union. But historians found that Benjamin Franklin and Thomas Jefferson recommended the shield bear an ethnic emblem of each nation that peopled the United States. They intended that the motto represent major immigrant groups, not states.

The past two centuries vindicated the early leaders, who had faith that immigrants from many lands would quickly assimilate, forging a unified nation. America has derived much of its vigor from the interplay of its many diverse races and nationalities. Nonetheless, the dramatic racial, religious, and ethnic changes projected for the next century above all raise a troublesome question. Will the nation continue to gain strength from increased diversity?

As a direct result of massive, predominantly white immigration, the black share of the population dropped from 20 percent in 1830 to 10 percent in 1930. Without this influx of Europeans, the black population—boosted by higher birthrates—would have accounted for 30 percent or more of the total by the 1990s. Unconstrained immigration thus had the significant, if unintended, effect of diluting the political and economic importance of America's black population.

Following the introduction of immigration quotas, the black percentage of the population began to rise slowly. By 1980, nonwhites—blacks, Asians, American Indians, Hispanics, and others—made up 17 percent of the population. Ten years later, nonwhites constituted more than one-fifth of all U.S. residents, about the same share represented by the black population when the first census was taken exactly two hundred years earlier.

While the proportion of whites in the total population has not changed drastically over the decades, their share of urban population is at its lowest point ever and is continuing to decline, with no reversal in sight.[8] Asians, who until 1965 were essentially prohibited from entering the country, now constitute the third-largest and most rapidly growing racial group in cities. In California, as well as eight other western and New England states, Asians now outnumber blacks.

To what extent do racial considerations affect implementation of current immigration policies? It is difficult to say. Black groups have charged that Haitians trying to flee repression are victims of discrimination by the U.S. government, which is detaining them and sending them back, because of their race. However, the proportion of all immigrants who are black—only 4 percent prior to 1970—doubled during the 1970s and is continuing to rise. The Census Bureau estimates that 12 percent of immigrants in the twenty-first century will be black. The 1965 Immigration Act allowed legal black immigration to substantially increase. Nonetheless, black immigrants lack a powerful domestic constituency to lobby on their behalf, in the manner that the politically influential Cubans in South Florida were able to pressure the Carter administration to accept the Mariel boatlift.

Gauging public attitudes on matters of race and immigration is difficult, for those approached by pollsters are often reluctant to disclose their true feelings on such sensitive issues. Nonetheless, polls provide insight on how various groups are perceived. In a national poll reported in *Newsweek* in June 1984, when asked if too many immigrants were coming from Latin America, 53 percent responded yes. Forty-nine percent felt that the number of those entering from Asia was excessive. However, only 26 percent thought European immigration was too high. Most respondents in California, requested to state a regional preference for immigrants, cited Europe. When asked from which regions immigration should be curtailed, more than half named Asia, followed by the Caribbean and Mexico.[9] But a later (1988) California survey revealed that a slightly larger percentage of its population considered the growth in the number of Asians to be positive than looked favorably upon greater numbers of Hispanics.[10] A majority of respondents indicated they were not affected significantly by the presence of either Asians or Hispanics.

Although some persons prefer not to express their racial views openly, surveys and other indicators point to a substantial and continuing diminution of racial prejudice in the United States since World War II. Our nation, in fact, has abandoned its policy of giving preference to immigrants from certain nations. This is borne out by the diminishing number of Europeans admitted each year.[11] Although the British government apparently pursued in recent years what the *New Statesman* calls a "Fortress White" immigration policy, no one can reasonably argue that American policy favors whites.[12]

Whatever role race plays in popular perceptions of immigrants, the current social environment rules out any policy explicitly based on the consideration of color. In recent years, the public has become somewhat less uneasy about race and ethnicity than during earlier periods of mass immigration, though many Americans today wonder if our sense of national identity can survive the prospect of Spanish challenging English as the dominant language in some areas.

The current widespread opposition to bilingual education and the pressure to declare English the official national language should not be dismissed as a vestige of the nativist sentiment that swept this nation in earlier decades. Our common language does, in fact, provide the cement that binds our multiethnic nation together. Had the North and South spoken different languages prior to the Civil War, the nation's ultimate survival as a federal republic would have been in jeopardy. Would Canada have survived a civil war such as engulfed the United States? The sense of single-minded purpose that sustained this nation through two world wars may well have been weakened had we been divided by language.

The language issue is far from new. As noted earlier, Benjamin Franklin was among the first Americans to worry that the English language was under siege by immigrants. Germans in Pennsylvania, and later in Missouri, assiduously sought to preserve their language. Their attitude was based on a deeply ingrained belief that German "high" culture, as expressed in music, literature, and art, was superior to anything England or America had to offer. This sense of cultural superiority lasted into the twentieth century, when Germany's role in the two world wars created a serious backlash. During World War I, school systems in New Jersey, Massachusetts, and New York City dropped German from the curriculum, offering, in many cases, Spanish as a replacement. Although many immigrants continued to speak German at home, its usage waned. Because the number of German-speaking persons entering the United States since the 1930s has been relatively small, no new German-language enclaves have developed.

Spanish usage raised little controversy throughout most of our history. Thomas Jefferson, more tolerant of foreign language inroads than Franklin, presciently recognized the importance of Spanish. In a letter to his nephew, he advised him to "bestow great attention on this [Spanish] and endeavor to acquire an accurate knowledge of it. Our future connection with Spain and Spanish America will render that language a valuable contribution."[13] Jefferson's advice notwithstanding, Spanish was rarely taught in American schools until introduced as a replacement for German. Only recently has Spanish gained due recognition, now that it is about to become the world's third most widely spoken language, behind Chinese and English. The number of Spanish-speaking persons in the United States already exceeds that in all but four other nations.

In 1980, 23 million persons over the age of five reported to the census that they spoke a language other than English at home. Almost one-half (11 million) spoke Spanish; three other leading languages together— Italian, French, and German—were spoken by fewer than 5 million people. By 1990, the Spanish-speaking population had grown by 50 percent to 17.3 million. Its use, however, is concentrated in a few metropolitan centers and in the Southwest, particularly near the Mexican border. One of three, or 5.6 million, speaking Spanish at home live in Miami/Dade County, Los Angeles County, New York City, and the Chicago metropolitan area. In 1990, only 8 percent of the residents in the Laredo, 12 percent in the McAllen, and 22 percent in the Brownsville metropolitan areas near the Mexican border spoke English at home, although the majority of the population was born in the United States.

In the cities of Miami and San Antonio, Spanish is spoken more frequently than English; in Los Angeles and much of southern California, it is a de facto second language. Its importance to business is illustrated by the numerous Korean and Vietnamese merchants in East Los Angeles that speak reasonable Spanish but minimal English. In the subways of New York, one of every four advertisements is in Spanish.

The language debate has centered on bilingual teaching in the schools, which became a political and legal issue with the passage of the 1964 Civil Rights Act. This landmark legislation included a provision that prohibited "discrimination and denial of access to education on the basis of a student's limited English proficiency." In 1968, Congress passed the Bilingual Education Act, and the Department of Health, Education, and Welfare (HEW), in response to the legislation, promulgated regulations. Local districts, in order to receive federal aid, were required to provide appropriate services to limited-English-proficient (LEP) students. At the time, no one expected that within two decades 1.3 million students would be enrolled in programs involving more than one hundred languages.

The U.S. Supreme Court, in its 1974 *Lau v. Nichols* decision, upheld the HEW requirements when it ruled, without dissent, that a Chinese student in San Francisco, unable to obtain instruction in his native tongue, was being deprived of equal educational opportunity. Interestingly, the Supreme Court did not specify *how* a local school district should assist English-deficient students. The best means to serve these students has become the subject of frequently acrimonious debate that extends well beyond pedagogical issues.

The arguments for bilingual education are stated at two levels. From an educational perspective, it is said to enhance learning. Essentially, the position of proponents is that English and the student's native tongue interact in the learning process, each reinforcing the other. Proponents cite numerous studies showing that students enrolled in "well-implemented" programs do well in both English and Spanish. Their views are buttressed by a report of the General Accounting Office (GAO), which said that seven of the ten experts it contacted believe current research supports bilingual programs.[14] Some proponents state flatly that "educational research proves that the use of primary language in the educational programs of students with limited English accelerates their acquisition of English".[15] The National Education Association (NEA) is a supporter of bilingual programs because, in its view, they offer students the opportunity to learn English without embarrassment.

The broader (and more controversial) case for bilingual education is that it helps students retain their self-esteem and cultural links. This view is shared by the NEA, whose president states that such programs "allow immigrant children to maintain ties with family customs and traditions."[16]

Bilingual education opponents challenge its value and point out that studies are essentially inconclusive. This was the finding of a *New York Times* writer who reviewed the existing research.[17] Although the majority of studies show that bilingual education, if properly implemented, can help students, so can other education programs with good teachers, financial resources, and motivated students.

Were the bilingual program controversy limited to narrow pedagogical disputes, each school district would adopt an approach that appeared suitable for its needs. However, the issue has become politically charged. Some opponents of bilingualism claim that "the political forces behind bilingual education are those which promote cultural separatism."[18]

A less extreme view of the bilingualism controversy is presented by a political moderate, Nathan Glazer, an articulate writer and arguably the nation's leading authority on ethnic issues. His position is that the language component of education should be considered important by the majority only if it provides a base for academic achievement. Glazer questions the educational value of bilingual programs on the ground that such programs fail to enhance student achievement or improve their future economic performance. Available data buttress his skepticism. But Glazer's real concern is the impact of bilingual education on assimilation:

> American culture assimilates because it sets its face against the maintenance of a foreign language and culture and makes this difficult, and it assimilates because it is itself a new culture adapted to new immigrants.[19]

Maintenance of non-English languages, he argues, particularly as a matter of public policy, will slow the assimilation of immigrants. Others, such as the Mexican-American author Richard Rodriguez, also question its value. He writes that the appeal of bilingualism is essentially a form of latent romanticism left over from the civil rights and ethnic revival movements of the 1960s.[20] Hispanics, particularly Mexicans, favor the concept because Spanish is associated with pride, culture, and celebration of their diversity. Rodriguez believes that

Mexican students will suffer psychologically from the bilingual approach—just as proponents argue the child is helped psychologically when he is taught in a language spoken at home.

Whether or not children benefit educationally from bilingual programs is not at the core of the controversy. The more fundamental issue is to what extent bilingual education promotes a two-language society. Were Swahili, Laotian, and Mandarin the languages taught to the majority of immigrant children, few would become anxious that the dominance of the English language could be threatened.

Spanish, however, is perceived to be a threat, if only because it is spoken by more persons in the Western Hemisphere than English (Latin America, less Brazil, has an estimated 1990 population of about 300 million, compared to 275 million living in North America). A hybrid language, "Spanglish," has emerged from the barrios and is now spoken by millions of Hispanics. This has created some concern that the English language will become diluted, as the French fear English is usurping their tongue. The relative ease of learning Latin-based Spanish (as distinct from, say, Chinese or Korean) may actually heighten anxiety over its widespread use.

How has the public responded to bilingual programs? A 1986 national poll shows that almost half of all adult Americans oppose bilingual education, while 36 percent support these programs. Across the nation and in California specifically, a higher percentage of Hispanics than whites or blacks approve of bilingual education; but the gap, contrary to expectation, is not substantial.

As on other immigration-related topics, gateway cities (and their respective states) differ in their outlook on bilingual education. California's governor in 1987 vetoed a bill that would have required districts to follow state guidelines in bilingual programs. In effect, the state now allows local school districts to experiment with alternative approaches aimed at educating immigrant children. In the same year, the Los Angeles Teachers Union voted to urge a policy shift from bilingual education to one favoring an English-immersion approach to teaching non-English-speaking students. In part, the vote was a reaction to a plan that would require teachers in bilingual classrooms to learn a second language.

In Dade County (which includes the city of Miami), Florida voters in the early 1980s approved a measure that declared English the official language. An interesting sidelight on the language issue in Miami is the report by the Civil Rights Commission that considered the causes for the 1980 riots. The report concluded that one problem contributing to ethnic tensions was the failure of the educational system to teach black youngsters Spanish. An editorial in the *Miami Times* suggested that "young black people who want to work should be insisting on the opportunity to not only learn Spanish but to become fluent in the language."[21]

However well intended the commission's advice may have been, it is naive to believe that a few years of high school Spanish would open the doors of Hispanic enterprise to young blacks. Although blacks agree that their lack of Spanish disqualifies them from good jobs, they argue that the language should not be a barrier to obtaining jobs in an English-speaking nation. Most Miami non-Hispanic whites, particularly the elderly, also understandably resent the need to learn Spanish to find work or to even communicate in their own country.

In New York City, where about 90,000 students in 1987 were receiving bilingual instruction, the program has not aroused passions. This tolerance may be attributable to a century of experience in instructing non-English-speaking students, including Spanish-speaking Puerto Ricans after World War II. But in 1987, across the Hudson, New Jersey officials decided to use an English-language proficiency test to transfer students from bilingual to English-only classes. The test is designed to reduce the length of time students are in bilingual programs. Unlike New York City, where teachers and parents can recommend that students remain in bilingual programs even if they pass an English proficiency test, New Jersey allows no exceptions.

San Francisco has a substantial percentage of its students, mostly Chinese and other Asians, in bilingual classes. As in New York, there appears to be little opposition to the concept in a city to which immigrants have flocked for well over a century.

Differing attitudes on bilingual education are mainly attributable to each individual's perception of its aim. Such education, if it eases an immigrant's adjustment and is a temporary measure to promote English, should be not only acceptable but encouraged. But such publicly funded programs should be rejected if they cause immigrant youngsters to sustain their native language at the price of relegating English to a secondary status.

The school bilingual controversy is part of a larger issue—the importance of the English language in maintaining national cohesion. The fact is that many Americans feel threatened by bilingualism—not only in Los Angeles and Miami but across the nation. The public does not oppose immigrants preserving their own language; 55 percent of whites and 50 percent of blacks polled in California believe it is good to preserve one's tongue. However, the same poll revealed that 66 percent would not allow citizens who cannot fluently read English the right to vote.[22]

The U.S. English movement was spawned in California in 1983 as a response to growing immigration and the resulting increase in the usage of Spanish. The 400,000-member organization, originally spearheaded by the late U.S. senator from California and linguist S. I. Hayakawa, has formed an advisory board with such diverse personalities as Walter Annenberg, Saul Bellow, Alistair Cooke, Arnold Schwarzenegger, and former senator Eugene J. McCarthy. Its objective is "to preserve English as a unifying force in the United States." As stated by Hayakawa, "We are concerned about the future unity of our nation. We are convinced Americans must share a common language. And that language must be English."[23] The most significant success of U.S. English since its inception was the 1986 passage of Proposition 63, which designates English as the official language of the state. The proposition, which instructs the legislature to "take all steps necessary to insure that the role of English as the common language of the State of California is preserved and enhanced," received 73 percent of the vote. Although several states, including Nebraska and Virginia, designated English as their official language before 1952, California was the first with a large Hispanic population to pass such a measure. In November 1988, two other states with substantial Spanish-speaking minorities, Arizona and Florida, amended their constitutions following bitter campaigns with amendment opponents charging U.S. English with racism. Nonetheless, Florida voters gave the amendment overwhelming approval. In Arizona, the amendment barely passed with 51 percent in favor. A bill to designate English as the official language of the U.S. government gained 101 congressional cosponsors in 1991 but did not become law. The failure of Congress to pass such legislation has no practical importance, as it would have no impact on the usage of other languages. A law promoting the legal status of English would be comparable in effect to the constitutional amendment adopted by the French parliament in 1992 proclaiming the language of the republic to be French. Ironically, this action was intended to guard the Gallic language against the infusion (or, as the French would no doubt argue, intrusion) of English.

No matter its practical limitations, support in California and Florida for an amendment is a measure of concern among their residents that Spanish has become the de facto second language. The sensitivity to non-English usage can be illustrated by the seemingly trivial language-related disputes involving the use of Chinese, Korean, and Vietnamese signs. Both "Anglo" and Hispanic residents in several southern California communities strongly oppose storefront and billboard signs in unfamiliar script, usually without English subtitles. Non-Asian residents feel intimidated by the proliferation of shopping centers where the signs are indistinguishable from those in Hong Kong, Saigon, or Seoul. Nor is this anxiety limited to California. During the 1980s, numerous older shopping centers a few miles south of the U.S. Capitol were taken over by Koreans and other Asians. Southern accents, to the consternation of older residents, have been replaced by, to their ears, less melodic sounds.

Several conservative writers have also expressed the same anxieties observed among the populace at large. George Will, in his brief essay "In Defense of the Mother Tongue," lays forth his support for an amendment to the Constitution declaring English the nation's official language. The "idea of citizenship has became attenuated and now is defined almost exclusively in terms of entitlements, not responsibilities. Bilingualism, by suggesting that there is no duty to acquire the primary instrument of public discourse, further dilutes the idea of citizenship."[24] Citing the Canadian experience, William F. Buckley writes, "The availability of Spanish alternatives to English laws, instructions, communications and other forms of public assistance should be in the nature of transitional courtesies: not an invitation to bilingualism."[25] The conservative view is shared by some who are accustomed to taking more liberal stands on most issues. Former Minnesota senator Eugene McCarthy's opposition to bilingual education has a more novel basis: He maintains that this challenge to the dominance of English is one manifestation (illegal immigration and foreign investment are others) of neocolonialism in an unfamiliar guise. By weakening the position of English and failing to control our borders, McCarthy argues, we are becoming controlled, if subtly, by other nations.[26] In some respects, these assertions are similar to those of another liberal ex-politician, former governor Richard Lamm from Colorado.

Notwithstanding the opposition to bilingualism, there is no movement afoot to "Americanize" immigrants by discouraging the use of their native tongue, such as took place during the 1920s. The democratic ethos bars the sort of repressive measures that were imposed in the Soviet Union to eradicate non-Russian languages, a policy that failed in any case. Opponents are motivated not by fear that the language itself will suffer from the presence of competing tongues—English will be in the twenty-first century the world's first truly international language—but by a desire to reduce any risk, no matter how remote, that national unity will suffer. As remarked by the *Economist,* "Language symbolizes the United States' fear that the foreign body within its borders is growing too big ever to be digested."[27] Perhaps this is an overly pessimistic assessment. But Hispanic and other advocates of programs that promote bilingualism need to understand that opponents to liberal entry feed on the fears of the seemingly incessant ethnic strife witnessed on almost every continent. On a less dramatic plane, the two-language model of Canada is in serious trouble at this time and can offer little inspiration. The public responds favorably to encouraging American students to study Spanish on a voluntary basis. Nonetheless, it can be expected to vigorously resist liberal immigration policies if it perceives that bilingual programs in schools and elsewhere will foster a dual-language society.

Public sentiment aside, the nation's Spanish-speaking population has reached a level that will assure rising usage of Spanish not only for decades but for generations to come. Restrictive immigration policies or language-status legislation cannot reverse this trend. The long-term implications of an essentially bilingual society in much of urban America cannot be gauged now, as they ultimately depend on how well the nation amalgamates economically, as well as socially, its Hispanic immigrants and their American-born children.

Integration or Fragmentation?

Language forms only one component of broader social fears—loss of national identity and culture are among others—cited by opponents of liberal entry policies. How quickly are new immigrants absorbed into the American mainstream? In contrast to earlier entrants, who hungered to dress and speak like native Americans, many members of ethnic groups today look with disfavor on the notion of assimilation. The term now conjures images of a minority consumed by the dominant culture without retaining a sense of its own identity. America in recent years has experienced a flowering of ethnic pride. Every year, our cities play host to nation-day parades, sponsored by Italians, Puerto Ricans, or Portuguese. Immigrants are increasingly reluctant to relinquish their difficult-to-pronounce foreign names in favor of Anglo adaptations, which was a common practice in the first four decades of the twentieth century. But despite these symbolic manifestations of ethnicity, Italian-Americans, once thought to be unassimilable, are now almost indistinguishable from other Americans of European ancestry.[28] This leads to speculation that perhaps skin color, rather than nationality, may explain differences in assimilation rates.

An examination of non-European immigrant behavior calls this conjecture into question. Entrants from Asia (other than the Indochinese) attain in their own countries the highest educational and economic levels of any immigrant group before arriving here, and, not coincidentally, they adapt most quickly to American society. They appear to be assimilating more rapidly than did immigrants who came from Eastern and Southern Europe at the turn of the century. The speed of absorption is linked to class; those who had middle-class status in their native lands learned English in school and received large doses of American culture. Adults read *Time* magazine and watched "Dallas" on the television screen; their children wore jeans and danced at discos to American records. For these families, culture shock was nothing like the one experienced by Italian or Polish peasants in the 1900s.

One manifestation of rapid adaptation is the high and rising rate of intermarriage between Asian-Americans and non-Asians. In the 1980s, more than one-half of all Japanese-Americans, and 40 percent of Chinese-Americans, married outside their ethnic group. This contrasts sharply with the rate of marriages between blacks and whites in 1990: 4 out of every 1,000. The high rate of intermarriage is perhaps the strongest indication that the larger white society accepts Asians into the American mainstream on an equal footing.

The prevalence of American mass culture abroad facilitates the integration of immigrants in the United States. It seems particularly strong in several nations, including Korea and the Philippines, that generate large numbers of emigrants to the United States. American culture has also penetrated the Spanish-speaking world, but most Hispanic immigrants are not middle class. This may explain, at least in part, why Spanish-speaking immigrants are absorbed more slowly into the national mainstream than others. The political scientist Fernando Torres-Gil commented that, unlike other groups, Hispanics (particularly Mexicans) "appear unlikely candidates for either full assimilation or full acculturation, at least in our lifetime."[29]

This conclusion is shared by Glazer, who believes that, in addition to bilingual education, other forces are slowing assimilation, particularly among Hispanics. These include changes in public schools and laws passed during the 1960s and 1970s designed to eliminate discrimination.[30]

Not everyone agrees with this assessment. The respected sociolinguist Joshua Fishman, for one, believes that reliance on Spanish is in fact weakening, although at a somewhat slower rate than among other ethnolinguistic minorities.[31] To back his position, Fishman cites several studies, including one that shows the Spanish language to be employed to a lesser extent in the third generation in the United States than French is among third-generation French Canadians in Ottawa. This, of course, would be expected, as French and English are the officially sanctioned languages in Canada, although the Francophone community constitutes only a small minority in Ottawa. Fishman's overall assessment is that any fear that Mexican-Americans are not learning English is unjustified.

Viewed historically, Fishman's findings are no doubt correct; the vast majority of children whose parents are Spanish-speaking immigrants have learned English. However, it seems premature to reach any conclusions as to future absorption rates based on current language-retention studies, since many were undertaken prior to the bulge in illegal and legal immigration from Mexico and, increasingly, Central America.

The Hispanic population has become so large and concentrated in recent years that in some communities in California and Texas only Spanish is spoken. Even in larger cities like Los Angeles and San Antonio, Mexican immigrants can go about their daily business without knowing English. Having little contact with the Anglophone world, these newcomers have few incentives to give up their language or culture. Given the high degree of stability of their neighborhoods, Spanish seems likely to retain its hold for generations to come. The increasing use of Spanish by the advertising media and the prevalence of Spanish-language television and radio further lessen immigrants' exposure to English.

In the past, immigrant groups became integrated within one or two generations, but there are differences that call for caution in applying this experience to Latin Americans. Spanish-speaking settlers preceded Anglo-Americans in the Southwest, and their culture left a permanent mark on the region. Although their numbers were small, the Spanish language has remained in use for centuries. Mexicans have been pouring into the Southwest since the early 1900s, interrupted only by the Great Depression. At no previous time has a non-English-speaking group in the United States been continuously replenished over the course of several generations. Sizable German immigration lasted no more than five decades, and large-scale entry from Eastern and Southern Europe extended over forty years. The reality is that the Spanish-American influence, particularly the extent of the language, has no precedent. The high proportion of nonimmigrant Hispanics speaking Spanish at home revealed in the 1990 Census demonstrates this point.

Should varying rates of integration into American society really matter? Should the public be distressed that some groups retain their language and are slow to assimilate? Anxiety would seem appropriate were our sense of national identity or culture weakened by linguistic and cultural diversity. This issue has been explored by law professor Peter Schuck, who asks, "At what point does diversity erode the moral sense of national community?"[32] His concerns are centered on illegal immigrants and their American-born offspring, who are automatically entitled to citizenship despite the parents' status. Schuck notes that the willingness to confer citizenship as a birthright on the American-born children of illegal aliens (though about half of the respondents to a 1992 poll opposed the practice) is unique among nations, and, according to him, this illustrates that Americans place little value on citizenship. Schuck is worried that illegal entrants may encourage social and cultural fragmentation, intergroup hostility, and political conflict. For American democracy to endure and flourish, we "must maintain a core of common values, public symbols and social commitments." In the face of sustained illegal immigration, these values may not be sustainable. Schuck perceives no such problems with legal entrants and states that the nation could, and probably should, absorb larger numbers of these immigrants than are currently admitted.

The distinction made between legal and illegal settlers is that the first group is invited to enter; the second crosses the border in violation of our laws, leading to resentment among the populace. From a legal and moral (as distinct from an economic) perspective, the difference is critical. It is, however, less certain that the difference means much with respect to social and cultural fragmentation, given the ethnic composition of immigrants since the passage of the 1965 Immigration Act. The motivation for integration and assimilation is no doubt lower for the many illegals who intend to return to their country of origin. As for aliens who became legalized under provisions of the 1986 Immigration Reform and Control Act, surveys find that they are satisfied with conditions and share an optimism about the future often missing among natives. As such, these immigrants are unlikely to create social tensions. Unfortunately, most are constrained by their inability to speak English, which can be expected to slow their absorption. Legal entrants do not differ appreciably from illegal aliens in their cultural makeup and the diversity they bring, but there may be behavioral differences. During the 1992 Los Angeles riots, about 1,200 illegal aliens (8 percent of all persons arrested) were detained by police. UCLA demographer Leo Estrada observes that equally poor but established Mexican neighborhoods in East Los Angeles remained quiet.[33]

Schuck appears unsure whether or not illegal immigration will damage the nation's social fiber, but former governor Lamm and Gary Imhoff, whose book was cited in the previous chapter, have no such qualms. They are convinced that American culture and identity are threatened by both legal and illegal entrants. To buttress their argument, the authors point to cultural changes taking place in Washington, D.C.[34] Such potential harm, however, presupposes an identifiable urban culture unconnected to recent immigration; something many long-term Washington, D.C., area residents do not perceive (leaving aside the political establishment).

One problem with imagined or real threats to national identity and culture is that these terms are not adequately explained or defined by those who believe they are being eroded. It is impossible to assess the risks that immigrants pose to the social fabric without a workable definition of nation identity. The concept has a much different sense in the United States than in most other nations. Nationhood traditionally includes a government derived from the same ethnic stock as the majority of the population and a common culture. In older countries, nationalism, and hence national identity, is usually based on biological or historical determinism. For the English and French, it is primarily historical; for Koreans and Japanese, it is both biological and historical. These Asian nations, having absorbed their aboriginal populations, are not only ethnically homogeneous, but also share a common, centuries-old cultural heritage. Virtually all ethnic disputes plaguing the European continent, such as within the confines of the former Soviet Union or former Yugoslavia, have roots reaching back hundreds of years—conflicts so deep that border realignments cannot overcome them.

During its formative years, the United States could not (nor did its leaders wish to) claim descent or "ethnic purity" as its unifying force. In the biological sense, the United States was never a nation. There were no mythical or real historical roots in the land—only the American Indian could even suggest such links to the past. Further, the country lacked a common religion or unique cultural traditions that could lay the foundation for national identity. Bertrand Russell was among those who remarked upon these differences when discussing American and British patriotism. What Americans lacked, he stated, is the cozy safety afforded by what is familiar, the comfort of known traditions and prejudices that bind the British. The antebellum deep South (excluding a substantial share of the area's population—its mostly black slaves) was the only region that even approached the traditional characteristics of national identity, including a shared Anglo-Saxon ethnic descent, a common religion, and a dominantly agrarian, plantation-oriented culture.

The United States established a new form of identity based on free self-determination of the individual. The American Constitution and the Bill of Rights gave political and legal expression to this philosophical concept. What the United States shared in the late eighteenth century with most nations was a common language. Throughout American history there have been non-English-speaking pockets, but they usually included only a small percentage of the national population.

Because the United States lacked ethnic and cultural homogeneity, as the historian Hans Kohn, a prolific writer and expert on nationalism, observed, the nation became the first in human history to be formed on the concept of individual freedom. But this abstract idea would have been a difficult, if not impossible, platform from which to launch and sustain a nation without a more perceptible bond—the English language—to facilitate integration and assimilation.

Skin color and culture are other common denominators. About four-fifths of all Americans are of European descent, and the American political and economic leadership has always been predominantly Caucasian. Needless to say, blacks and other nonwhite groups have made major contributions to American life; nonetheless, most components of what is seen as "American culture," including its institutions and art, are European in origin. The evolving Hispanic culture also derives its language and religion from Europe, enriched by the adaptation of elements from cultures that thrived on the American continent in the pre-Columbian era. The preeminence of European-derived culture has lately come under challenge from persons championing multiculturalism and asserting to represent minority-group interests. In response, others have expressed concern that an emphasis on a multicultural society would be detrimental. The eminent liberal historian Arthur Schlesinger, Jr., takes a dim view of those advocating such a direction:

> Instead of a transformative nation with an identity all its own, America increasingly sees itself as a preservative of old identities.... The national ideal had once been a pluribus unum. Are we now to belittle unum and glorify pluribus? Will the center hold? or will the melting pot yield to the Tower of Babel?[35]

These provocative words are aimed principally at those responsible for the rewriting of public school and university curricula to downplay Western traditions and culture while introducing alternative approaches, including Afrocentrism.

A common culture is a critical component of national identity, yet the pluralism of American society inherent in the democratic ideals of its founding has been a fact from the start. Germans and later Scandinavians in the Midwest succeeded in creating and maintaining, for several generations, strong ethnic communities in the mid-nineteenth century. Yet a century and a half later, most of these communities have lost their ethnic character, retaining only vestiges of German, Danish, and Swedish influence. Nonetheless, the fears expressed by Schlesinger should not be viewed lightly. Perhaps no nation has ever attempted to digest the cultural, ethnic, and religious diversity observed in American cities today.

Since the 1960s, inner cities and their suburbs have seen a renewal of ethnic enclaves on an even larger scale than in the early decades of the twentieth century. These enclaves, like their Italian or Polish predecessors, encourage the maintenance of the homeland culture, once again raising fears that those who remain in that environment will not absorb the values of the mainstream population. Public schools were important in promoting national values within these enclaves during earlier periods of immigration. Now, pressure from minority groups and, to a lesser extent, bilingual programs and other changes in the public school system have made it difficult, perhaps impossible, for them to continue playing this role.

Concern that immigrant values may clash with the dominant culture is more pervasive outside the United States, where "dominant culture" is more strictly defined. For example, the relationship between cultural pluralism and national identity has become an issue in Great Britain, which accepted a large immigrant population from its Commonwealth following World War II. In the 1960s, the government established a policy on minorities that did not call for a "flattening process of assimilation" but rather equal opportunity accompanied by cultural diversity. This policy, called by the British "multiculturalism," was challenged in the late 1980s by conservatives and some liberals who believe it has weakened the national fiber. They cite bookburning incidents by Muslims in British cities in response to the Salman Rushdie affair as evidence that the 1960s approach has not worked.

Most American academics and the public appear less apprehensive than their British counterparts, at least in part because the specter of Muslim fundamentalism has not reached the United States. The cultural impact of immigration, particularly from Spanish-speaking nations, has received considerable, mostly favorable, attention in the American media. One manifestation of the Hispanic cultural impact was displayed in a special issue of *Time* (July 11, 1988) devoted to the subject, its cover page emblazoned with the word MAGNIFICO!

Numerous articles described how Latinos were "exploding" into the cultural mainstream. As this culture is continually replenished from its Latin American fountainhead, the Hispanic influence will continue to grow for generations to come.

No one doubts that Hispanics (and, to a lesser degree, other groups) will remold our "mainstream" culture. The question is whether our culture is improved thereby, or does it degenerate with large-scale immigration? Individual answers are necessarily highly subjective. When social scientists were asked if twentieth-century immigration had a positive or negative impact on American culture, 85 percent declared that the impact was favorable, and only 9 percent said it was unfavorable.[36] A nationwide Gallup survey taken in 1984 found that 61 percent of the public agreed that immigrants improve our culture. Other polls indicate that a majority of Americans believe that immigrants actually strengthen the society. This perception was confirmed in California, where 78 percent of all respondents believed one positive outcome of Asian growth has been to enrich the culture by providing new ideas and customs; 72 percent believed Hispanics also enrich our culture.[37] Most respondents also supported the notion that immigrants should preserve their own customs.

Has cultural pluralism eroded our national identity and social fiber? No polls were found that inquired directly whether immigrants had an adverse impact on national identity (probably because the term would be difficult to explain or define for respondents), but several questions California residents were asked do allude to this topic. In middle-class, conservative Orange County, 62 percent of whites believe Hispanics are patriotic, and 63 percent believe they want to assimilate.[38] When asked to compare U.S.-born to foreign-born citizens, a 1982 statewide survey found that 9 percent believed immigrants become better citizens; 22 percent shared the opposite opinion. In 1987, 13 percent believed immigrants were better citizens, and only 9 percent supported the contrary belief (the majority made no distinction between immigrant and native-born citizenship. The positive shift in public perception is notable, given the continuing high rate of immigration to California during the five-year interval.[39]

There is an implicit appreciation that immigrants share the basic values of the nation, particularly freedom of the individual. Most immigrants not only adhere to the Protestant ethic of hard work, thrift, and an entrepreneurial spirit, but they hew far more closely to it than the majority of native-born Americans. The public appears to recognize these traits among newcomers. A willingness to work hard ranks the highest among positive characteristics attributed to Asian immigrants.

The contributions immigrants have made to American society are not perceived to be less significant today than they were in earlier periods. The continuing addition of new ethnic groups helps to broaden and enrich the national culture. Nonetheless, Americans continue to feel a nagging unease about immigration. It is discernible in private conversations, letters to legislators, media talk shows, and public forums. This sense of anxiety extends beyond such specific matters as fear of unemployment, bilingualism, culture, and national identity. Only by pinpointing its sources can the phenomenon of the current opposition to immigration be understood.

As to why Americans respond favorably when polled on the contributions of nonnatives and concurrently tend to regard present immigration levels as too high, there is no single answer. On the one hand, the public believes that immigrants work hard and provide needed labor for expanding sectors of the economy. On the other hand, it expresses worry that taxes will rise because immigrants will require more services, and that unemployment could worsen. Although natives recognize the benefits, they also fear changes in their environment brought about by persons whose habits and language differ from their own. In the abstract, Americans believe in cultural diversity, but most become less than enthusiastic when confronted with change in their own neighborhood, as when store signs with Asian symbols appear in local shopping centers. The stability and intimacy that come with familiar language, faces, and streetscapes appear threatened as strange sights, sounds, and smells crowd the surroundings.

Examples of such personal response can be seen in communities where rapid, immigrant-related transformation has taken place. Monterey Park, California, a pleasant, low-density community a few miles from downtown Los Angeles, was two-thirds white in 1970 but one-third white by the mid-1980s. Elderly white locals criticize the new Asians as being "pushy," "impolite," and "bad drivers," but had Hispanics, Italians, or Poles come in large numbers, similar (or other) complaints would be heard in private conversations. In Lowell, Massachusetts, an influx of Southeast Asian refugees—one of every seven residents is a recent immigrant—has aroused ethnic fears. Residents complain of overcrowded housing and "strange behavior," but the irritation with these newcomers stems from rapid changes perceived in the social environment.

At a more detached level, overpopulation worries some Americans, although the link between immigration and overpopulation is not always perceived. According to a nationwide poll taken in 1983, Americans ranked overpopulation as the second most serious problem that the United States will face in the year 2000.[40] About 40 percent of all respondents listed this as a serious future problem, with only the threat of nuclear war ranking higher. But immigration ranked sixteenth, roughly on a par with inadequate housing and a "decline in morals."

In some areas, Americans make a more direct connection between immigration and quality-of-life concerns. In crowded southern California, for example, the endemic problem of congestion elicits strong emotions, especially among non-Hispanic whites. Over the next quarter of a century, the region's population is expected to increase by well over three million, and many fear that the local infrastructure will be overwhelmed. This has prompted numerous so-called quality-of-life citizen initiatives aimed at curbing growth rates. Developers, however, charge that reducing the stock of new housing simply raises the prices and creates overcrowding without reducing congestion.

Many Californians relate excessive growth to immigration. They fear being overrun by an invasion from the overpopulated reaches of the third world—China, India, and, especially, Mexico. With millions of poor massed just across the border, Mexico seems to many a population bomb waiting to explode in their midst. These apprehensions are rarely expressed in public but nonetheless are ingrained in the minds of many. Four out of five California residents believe steps, including immigration controls, should be taken to curtail the state's population growth.[41] In the absence of immigration, it is doubtful that an equally high percentage of residents would respond as negatively to the prospect of additional population gain.

Consider the case of Orange County, south of Los Angeles. The area—once nearly all native-born white and middle-class—was notorious in earlier times as the home of the John Birch Society. By the early 1990s, however, the county had grown at a dizzying rate, inflating its population to almost two and a half million (from 700,000 in the early 1960s)—and many of the newcomers were from Asia and Mexico. Clogged freeways have caused growing dissatisfaction among "Anglos." In contrast to attitudes nationwide, Orange County residents now rank immigration and congestion as the nation's two most serious problems. In reality, the immigrant inflow is only partly responsible for the changes that have overtaken Orange County; many of its new residents have moved from Los Angeles and elsewhere. Nonetheless, the alien presence has become a convenient scapegoat for those frustrated with overpopulation and overdevelopment.

In general, wherever an influx of immigrants coincides with rapid growth, local residents are prey to feelings of insecurity and disorientation. For many native-born Americans, the pagoda-style facades that have sprouted in the shopping centers of Los Angles make a jarring, alien impression. In Miami, people who do not know Spanish may find themselves unable to read the signs in neighborhood stores. More generally, white, middle-class Americans living in regions thick with immigrants often feel like strangers in their own land. Whatever economic benefits they bring, immigrants in large numbers induce strong feelings of discomfort.

That discomfort is often heightened by the success of recent immigrants. The rising proportion of Asians admitted to prestigious universities has caused anxiety among native-born white students about their own chances of acceptance. Because these schools are not expanding their enrollment, admission is a zero-sum game. In addition, the apparent ease with which Cubans, Lebanese, and Koreans have "made it" has created envy among lower-class Americans, black and white. Some natives, particularly among minorities, accuse these newcomers of succeeding only because they receive government assistance for which the American-born do not qualify. Such charges are generally false. That they are made, however, reflects the resentment that many Americans feel at being outperformed by people who arrive here with precious few resources.

Discontent is also fueled by what can be described as the "transfer phenomenon." A young, unemployed steelworker in a Pennsylvania town dislikes Asians because he associates them with cheaper Japanese and Korean products that have flooded American markets and cost American jobs. Some Vietnam veterans also resent refugees from Southeast Asia because they are a reminder of a costly, terrible war.

In addition to those immigration opponents who find the pace of change in the environment and the form it takes undesirable, the antagonism of others stems from a sense of insecurity. As noted in an earlier chapter, the most virulent anti-alien sentiment frequently originated in regions and communities whose residents never set their eyes on a foreigner. These insular communities suspected any "outsiders" whose race, religion, or nationality differed from their own. Although mass communication has probably reduced their ranks, a considerable number of Americans continue to view immigrants (and ethnic groups generally) negatively.

It is important to bear in mind that resentment of immigrants is not universal. Americans are certainly aware of the positive contributions that immigrants have made to culture. Food is a good example. Exotic cuisine, which not long ago was limited to a few cosmopolitan centers, has now come to Main Street. Like bagels and pizza from an earlier generation of immigrants, sushi and tacos have become staples on American menus.

In addition, although the discipline and academic achievements of Asian students may cause envy, Americans across the country are eager to enroll their children in schools with such students. In El Paso, where the Japanese have established their own schools for math and science, parents are pleading to have their children admitted. A positive effect of the Japanese presence has been a new willingness to reexamine the American educational system.

The acceptance of traits and ideas from other cultures is bidirectional. As American palates gain appreciation of foods and arts from across the borders and oceans, Coca-Cola, McDonald's, and popcorn have been accepted in Japan and Mexico. Satellite communication has enormous power to link nations and cultures. A switch on the television set gives a viewer in faraway La Paz, Bolivia, access to every major American channel. Even in the days when Prague was tightly controlled, one could see American television programs, if only in its international hotels. Cheap transportation, an integrated international economy, and mass communications inevitably lead to cultural cross-fertilization, but there are still limits.

There remain clashes between the Western concept of individual freedom and some cultures driven by fundamentalist movements that communication cannot bridge. These clashes raise fears among some that immigrants influenced by these movements will attempt to impose their views or create internal dissension; but to most of the American public this hardly seems an imminent threat. Americans' acceptance of aliens and refugees is premised on the belief that basic values that form national identity are not weakened by their presence. Much of the opposition to immigration today is driven more by fear of rapid change to the social fabric than by anxiety that the nation will lose its unique identity or hybrid culture.

Immigration and Political Change

Ethnic politics has characterized the American political landscape since the Republic was formed. Liberal naturalization laws allowed aliens to quickly gain citizenship and become part of the electorate. Thomas Jefferson, in his bid for the presidency, was the first to seek immigrant votes, but both he and George Washington expressed fear that immigrants from nations lacking our democratic traditions would have problems in our open political environment. Jefferson was successful in his bid for immigrant support. A century later, Woodrow Wilson's party was less fortunate. Opposition to his European policy following World War I by some ethnic groups, including Germans, more than offset support he had garnished among those East Europeans who favored his position on self-determination. Defections to the Republican party, particularly among Italians (over the disposition of Trieste) and the Irish (over his position on home rule for Ireland), contributed to the Democrats' 1920 loss to Warren Harding.[42] Temporary defections to Harding notwithstanding, Democrats generally cornered the immigrant vote during the first six decades of the twentieth century. In 1928, immigrant support for the Democratic (and Irish Catholic) candidate, Al Smith, was overwhelming. Eight years later, 81 percent of the electorate in Chicago's immigrant wards voted for Franklin Roosevelt. These ethnic voters and their children backed Harry Truman, John F. Kennedy, and Lyndon Johnson. But passage of the 1965 Immigration Act and the admission of refugees from Communist nations had a discernible impact on the voting patterns of the newest immigrants.

Leaving aside Cubans, who tend to be vehemently anti-Castro and conservative, the Democratic party receives the support of Hispanics, particularly Mexicans. In 1980, Ronald Reagan received only 30 percent of the Texas Hispanic vote, but exit polls of Hispanics in California in November 1988 found that 35 percent backed the Bush/Quayle ticket, implying some erosion of their support for Democrats.

While Hispanics (who form a potentially formidable block—twelve million were of voting age in the late 1980s) lean Democratic, Asian-Americans tend to vote Republican. They are attracted to the Republicans' probusiness orientation and, in the case of Chinese, Koreans, and Vietnamese, anticommunism. In 1984 President Reagan received two-thirds of the Asian-American vote across the nation. The large Asian community in California also favored George Bush over Michael Dukakis by a considerable margin. (It is interesting to note, however, that five of the six Asian-American members of Congress in 1991 were Democrats.) The 1992 Republican party platform, which states that "our nation of immigrants continues to welcome those seeking a better life. . . . Today, we are stronger for our diversity," is an indication of the importance attached to the immigrant electorate.[43]

All in all, Asian-American and Cuban-American support for the Republicans tends to offset the (non-Cuban) Hispanic tilt toward moderate Democrats. As such, recent entrants may have a lesser effect on the relative strength of the two national parties than those who came earlier. There is a larger issue here: Has the historical tilt in our immigration policy that favored refugees from Communist societies had the effect of making America more conservative? Today, for instance, it is much easier for Nicaraguans to gain entry to the United States than it is for Salvadorans and Guatemalans. Will this have a long-term effect? Or will the Mexican presence overwhelm it?

Post–World War II refugees from Hungary, Czechoslovakia, and other Eastern European nations, and, more recently, those fleeing Cuba, Nicaragua, and Poland, are typically conservative, particularly on foreign policy and defense issues. The 1965 Immigration Act opened the door to Asians, most of whom either left Communist nations in Southeast Asia or came from countries that confront Communist neighbors—South Korea, Taiwan, Hong Kong. Because many Asians (as well as Cubans and Nicaraguans) are professionals or self-employed, they favor probusiness legislative initiatives. The more numerous Mexicans negate any swing to the right, but in spite of economic deprivation they display a strong conservative streak on some issues. They tend to vote Democratic but are closer in their attitudes to the American center. When asked in 1987, "Do you consider yourself a Democrat, Republican, or Independent?" 32 percent of whites, 25 percent of Hispanics, but only 8 percent of blacks answered Republican. In the same year, 52 percent of whites, 55 percent of Hispanics, and 22 percent of blacks approved of the way Ronald Reagan was handling his job as president.[44] In summary, immigrants and their children will probably lean toward more conservative approaches to national issues.

Have recent immigrants affected U.S. foreign policy? For the most part, they have been less active than their predecessors during the Wilson presidency, when the map of Europe was being redrawn. Their involvement has been limited to specific issues of interest to only a few ethnic groups. Among these groups, Cubans have been most influential. Their anti-Castro stand ensures that the United States will continue its economic boycott of Cuba. The influx of middle-class Nicaraguans is also likely to affect U.S. policy in Central America, if these immigrants follow the path of the Cubans and become involved in conservative politics.

Asian-Americans are perhaps the least active politically of any ethnic group. To an extent, this reflects the generally friendly state of relations between Washington and the nations of the Far East; except on a few controversial issues (such as human rights in China), Asians are not likely to be galvanized into action. More generally, Asian immigrants tend to be politically cautious, intent on avoiding any appearance of meddling in American foreign policy.

The one issue on which there exists a broad consensus among the alien population is a domestic one—immigration reform. A rare instance in which various ethnic groups came together to lobby Congress was the Simpson-Mazzoli bill. After Latino groups complained that earlier versions of the bill discriminated against them, they succeeded in getting the legislation changed. A lengthy section aimed at prohibiting unfair employment practices was added to the bill originally proposed. As a result, the act requires that a special counsel be appointed with the responsibility for investigating charges of discrimination arising from the legislation. If violations are found, penalties are to be assessed against employers. This protection was added to supplement existing safeguards in the 1964 Civil Rights Act. In tribute to the political weight of immigrants on this issue, all six senators from California, Florida, and Texas took consistently pro-immigration stands on Simpson-Mazzoli and supported additional protection against discrimination. It is doubtful that any measure perceived to be anti-immigrant could be passed into law in the current environment.

To what extent have immigrants cooperated with native-born minorities? Blacks and Hispanics have similar interests on a wide range of issues—employment, job training, subsidized housing, affordable medical care, and affirmative-action programs. The most determined effort to bring these two groups together was undertaken by Jesse Jackson and his "rainbow coalition," an amalgam of blacks, Hispanics, Asians, and liberal whites. Jackson voiced opposition to the English-only movement, to cuts in government programs for the needy, and to the loss of unionized jobs to low-wage foreign nations.[45] His themes of fighting drugs and of improving day care strike a sympathetic chord among Hispanics, and he joined with their 1984 opposition to changes in the immigration laws. But how successful has this coalition been? If Hispanic votes for black candidates are a guide, there is little evidence that the nation's two largest minorities support each other. In the 1988 Democratic primary, Jesse Jackson received only 21 percent of the Hispanic vote in Texas. With most Hispanic elected officials in California supporting Dukakis, Jackson could only harness one-third of the Spanish-speaking vote there, a result criticized by his Hispanic supporters as an indication of racism within the Latino community.[46] And in the racially polarized Chicago Democratic primary in March 1988, the black incumbent mayor, for whom Jackson vigorously campaigned, received little support from Hispanics: exit polls showed that 73 percent voted for the winner, Richard M. Daley, the son of the legendary Irish mayor.[47] In 1991, Hispanics assured the election of a white mayor in Houston over the black candidate.

Immigrants and blacks part ways on several significant issues. Blacks are much more likely than immigrants to support federal intervention in economic matters. Surveys show that two-thirds of all blacks believe that the federal government should make every effort to improve the social and economic position of the black population. Immigrants—most of whom have left countries with unsavory regimes—tend to be much more skeptical about government intentions.

A 1988 California survey of attitudes toward affirmative action in the workplace and in college admissions illustrates differences among blacks, Hispanics, and Asians. Race-based preference, as indicated in Table 6-3, is favored only by a majority of blacks, with around one of five nonblacks agreeing that it should be granted. The majority of Hispanics and an overwhelming majority of Asians do not believe affirmative action is appropriate for any group. The position of Hispanics comes as a surprise since they earn less than blacks in similar occupations, and fewer (on a per capita basis) are admitted to state universities.

Differences observed among ethnic groups may be, at least in part, attributable to their experiences. When asked if they had personally suffered economic discrimination, 42 percent of blacks, but only 19 percent of Hispanics and 15 percent of Asians, responded affirmatively.[48] But beyond this, Asians and Hispanics simply tend to be more conservative than blacks. An examination of responses to five issues, shown in Table 6-4, suggests that California Hispanics are as conservative as whites on three, while more liberal on two (the death penalty and welfare funding). Asians are more conservative on defense spending, but take a liberal position on additional outlays for welfare. With the exception of prayer in school and funding for abortion, blacks take more liberal stands than whites or Hispanics. They generally support a reduction in military spending in favor of expenditures for education, housing, health care, and welfare. By contrast, Hispanics favor a strong military; so do many Asians, a reflection of their earnest anti-

Table 6-3
Preference in Hiring and College Admission for Minorities

Preference Should Be Given to	Hiring and Promotion For	Against	College Admissions For	Against
Blacks:				
Black respondents	56 %	44 %	55 %	43 %
Nonblack respondents	19	77	24	73
Hispanics:				
Hispanic respondents	36	58	37	58
Non-Hispanic respondents	18	79	23	73
Asians:				
Asian respondents	15	81	20	80
Non-Asian respondents	13	82	20	76

Source: California Opinion Index, "California's Expanding Minority Population" (mimeo), Field Institute, San Francisco, July 1988

Table 6-4
Views of Minorities in California on Political Issues

Conservative Position:	White	Black	Hispanic	Asian
For increased military expenditure	32%	18%	28%	38%
For prayer in public schools	50	62	53	46
For death penalty for murder	75	47	57	73
Against increased spending for welfare	30	6	16	24
For ban on federal funds for abortion	35	36	32	31

Source: Bruce E. Cain and D. Roderick Kiewiet, "The Political Impact of California's Minorities," paper prepared for a major public symposium entitled "Minorities in California," Division of Humanities and Social Sciences, California Institute of Technology, Pasadena, March 5, 1986

communism. Their stated positions appear consistent with the voting preferences of these groups.

Recent immigration can be expected to alter the ethnic composition and, to a lesser degree, the agenda of local government in numerous cities. In a time-honored tradition that started with the Irish, the most numerous group among the "first-wave" immigrants, ethnic constituencies have discovered that their political power at the local level is considerable. Beginning in 1873, when "Honest Jim" Kelly became mayor of New York, the Irish—with their gift for language, patronage, and organization—began to dominate big-city Democratic political machines. By the mid-1880s they controlled not only the two largest centers of Irish population—Boston and New York—but also Buffalo, New Orleans, Pittsburgh, St. Louis, and San Francisco. The Irish were almost never a majority (except in Boston) but gained political dominance by attracting the votes of immigrants.

As urban demographics changed with the rise in the black city vote and white outmigration to the suburbs, Irish power began to wane. The descendants of ethnic groups that arrived during the second wave from Eastern and Southern Europe came into their own politically during the 1960s, almost concurrently with a rise in the black urban population.

The political clout of the descendants of "second-wave" European immigrants and non-European minorities was evident at both the state and local levels in the late 1980s. The mayor of Los Angeles was black, the mayor of San Francisco was of Greek extraction, and the governor of California was of Armenian descent. In New York City, the mayor was Jewish (subsequently replaced by an African-American). The governor of New York State was an Italian-American. Both the mayor of Miami and the governor of Florida were Hispanic. Thus, all the gateway cities and their respective states were headed by ethnics. On the extended list of gateway cities, which includes Washington, D.C., Chicago, Houston, and Atlanta, only one—Houston—had a non-ethnic, "Anglo" mayor. In 1990, a black governor was inaugurated at the seat of the Confederacy, at Richmond's historic capitol designed by Thomas Jefferson. The message is clear: at the city and state levels, blacks and members of newer ethnic groups have done very well in winning elective office.

The changing of the guard is evident in other large cities where blacks have made considerable inroads. There is a black mayor in practically every city with over 100,000 residents that had a black majority in the 1980 Census—Atlanta, Birmingham, Detroit, Gary, New Orleans, Newark, Richmond, and Washington, D.C. The Irish have also maintained a hold on Boston, where they remain the largest voting block. Outside Florida, Hispanics have been less successful than blacks in translating their numbers into political power at the local level. Many are not citizens and thus cannot vote; those who can vote are often apathetic. Los Angeles County, with the largest Hispanic population in the nation, had no Hispanics (nor other minorities) as recently as 1989 on its Board of Supervisors; this changed only as a result of court intervention. As more and more Hispanics gain citizenship, though, their representation will rise. Also, they are showing greater interest in the political process, as demonstrated by a sharp rise in the number of elected Hispanics on city councils, school boards, and county commissions. The two large cities with majority Hispanic populations, Miami and San Antonio, have Hispanic mayors. But a Hispanic mayor was also elected in 1983 in Denver, where most of the electorate is white. As more members of the young Hispanic community reach voting age, their political might is sure to increase.

Hispanics are now coming into conflict with the established power structure. They are demanding representation in elected bodies in communities where they make up a large minority. As blacks did during the 1960s and 1970s, Hispanics have successfully challenged in federal court at-large municipal elections—common in California—as discriminatory. Because Hispanics are increasingly concentrated in cities with large black minorities—Dallas, Denver, Hartford, Jersey City, Pasadena, Paterson, Tampa, and Washington, D.C., to name a few—increased Hispanic representation can only mean fewer black officials.

Blacks have reacted unenthusiastically to the rise in the Hispanic (and Asian) vote, which is not surprising in light of how little time they have had thus far to enjoy the fruits of the civil rights struggle. Some blacks privately complain that Latinos, facing less discrimination than they did, are reaping the most fruit from the civil rights movement. Hispanics, in turn, charge that they are victims of a new form of discrimination, in that neither the white establishment nor black elected officials appoint them to important positions.

Tensions are particularly evident in the nation's capital, where Hispanics make up 10 percent or more of the population but less than 2 percent of the municipal workers (the vast majority of whom are black). Only 1 percent of the police force is estimated to be Latino. Hispanics are shortchanged on city jobs in part because they make up less than 2 percent of the electorate. But they believe they receive fewer jobs and fewer public services than the majority population because those in power are not willing to share the pie. The riots that erupted twice in Central American neighborhoods of Washington, D.C., during the early 1990s were the outcome of growing frustration with the local government and residents' inability to progress, economically or politically. Similar charges have been aired by Puerto Ricans in Newark, New Jersey, who claim they are "invisible" and receive insufficient support from the city leadership.

In several gateway cities, Hispanics have improved their political standing during the 1980s. The Los Angeles City Council had no Hispanics for two decades, until 1985, when Richard Alatorre was elected from a district that was 75 percent Latino. Two years later, a second Hispanic, Gloria Molina, was seated on the council following a lengthy struggle between Latin candidates. The first Asian to be elected to the city council, Michael Woo, was also seated in 1985. Two years later, Woo found that his colleagues proposed a redistricting plan that would have placed him in a district that was two-thirds Hispanic. The local Asian community protested loudly. Ethnic harmony was maintained only by the chance death of an "Anglo" council member. This enabled the council to carve out a new, predominantly Hispanic district, thereby making it possible to preserve the Asian seat while maintaining two Hispanic seats. The mayor (who in Los Angeles has little political power) remains the affable Tom Bradley. First elected in 1973, he will probably be replaced by a Hispanic after his current term expires. None of the five Los Angeles County supervisors were Hispanic for decades, until lawsuits persuaded the courts that this was the result of district boundaries drawn to maintain "Anglo" control. Such legal actions are disturbing to others, particularly blacks, who believe that housing patterns dictate that it is not possible to create majority Hispanic districts without diluting the black voting strength.

Immigrant groups have done less well in New York. Hispanics account for about 24 percent of the population but hold only 8 percent of the city council seats. Given their numbers, a coalition of blacks and Hispanics would have enormous political clout in the city, but the prospects for such a joint venture appear dim; witness the failure of the two groups to agree on a candidate to oppose Mayor Koch in 1985. The choice of a black politician by minority Democratic party leaders disillusioned with Koch caused resentment among the Hispanics, who supported the candidacy of fellow ethnic city comptroller Herman Badillo instead. Their split ensured the nomination of the incumbent. Four years later, David Dinkins captured the Democratic primary in a race against three white opponents. Dinkins received over 60 percent of the Hispanic vote, a higher percentage than his support among the non-Hispanic white community. In the November 1989 election, Dinkins became the city's first black mayor, receiving 65 percent of the Hispanic vote. Since his election, however, Hispanics have complained of inadequate representation in the new city administration.

In contrast to New York, Miami's political life is dominated by immigrants. Hispanics (mostly Cubans) accounted for 63 percent of the 1990 city population, and that proportion is continuing to grow. In 1983, Maurice Ferre, a Democrat from a patrician Puerto Rican family who had won five successive two-year terms for mayor, was challenged in his bid for reelection by Xavier Suarez, a Cuban-born conservative Republican. Blacks, 25 percent of Miami's population, viewed Ferre as a counterweight to the Cubans. Traditionally Democrats, they helped him to overcome strong Republican support from the Hispanic community and win a sixth term. In 1985, however, the growing Cuban vote and dissatisfaction among blacks over what they viewed as indifference by city hall to their needs produced a Republican victory by Suarez. Then, in 1987, the black community, trying to avoid having to choose between Hispanics, placed one of its own, Arthur Teele, on the Republican primary ballot. But Teele failed to gain the nomination, and Suarez, with the black vote split, was reelected by a huge majority.

The Cubans are not likely to relinquish control of city hall, to the consternation of blacks who, despite their growing numbers (thanks to Caribbean immigration), have been unable to slow what they bitterly refer to as the "Cubanization" of Miami. Their substantial population notwithstanding, blacks exert little political power in the city. That there are other racial fault lines in the area was evident in the fall of 1989 when the city elected the first Cuban-American, Ileana Ros-Lehtinen, to Congress. The race was marred by a divisive campaign that reflected ethnic tensions between the city's original white inhabitants and Cubans. Ros-Lehtinen, the successful Republican candidate won 90 percent of the Cuban-American vote, while 96 percent of blacks and 88 percent of "Anglos" supported her Democratic opponent for the seat vacated by the late congressman Claude Pepper.

In San Francisco, the black population is too small (under 11 percent) to exert much political influence. During the 1980s, Hispanics surpassed blacks as the second-largest minority, following Asians. But neither Hispanics nor Asians are well represented in city government. Both immigrant minorities appear to have backed a white moderate, Frank Jordan, for mayor in 1991 following two decades of liberal control over city hall.

Increased Hispanic participation in local politics in gateway cities and elsewhere has several important policy implications, particularly for the black community, on issues such as busing and jobs for minorities in positions of influence. Hispanics, who generally prefer to send their children to neighborhood schools, oppose busing children to distant locations as a means of achieving racial balance. Their children might, as a result, have less interaction with English-speaking children, but Mexican-American families, at least, do not appear to consider this a problem. Furthermore, because Mexican wives mostly do not work outside the home, having their children nearby is considered more important than integration. By contrast, many blacks are convinced that their children receive an inferior education in predominantly black schools and so accept the need to bus them to schools with white students. As Hispanic political strength increases, busing is likely to become a less acceptable means of correcting problems with inner-city schools.[49]

The prospect of growing immigrant political power also unsettles blacks because of its possible impact on black municipal employment. Researchers have shown that the single most important determinant of black public administrative and professional employment levels is the percentage of blacks elected to city councils; the size of the black population is secondary. The same pattern is true for Hispanics; in cities where they are elected to public office, the number of Hispanics in government management positions generally rises—often at the expense of blacks. The municipal jobs struggle is already evident in Los Angeles, where Hispanics are now close to two-fifths of the population but hold less than one-fifth of the sixty-five thousand county jobs. An analysis by the Los Angeles County Chicano Employees Association shows that 30 percent of all county jobs and 22 percent of management positions are held by blacks; Hispanics hold only 8 percent of the management jobs.

The high rate of black public employment is probably due to earlier discrimination in the private sector. Nonetheless, Latinos are pressing for more management positions, claiming that the large number of blacks in these jobs is linked to their political clout.[50] Because the stakes in the battle for political power in Los Angeles and elsewhere are high, the drawing of new electoral lines in districts with heavy concentrations of blacks and Hispanics following the 1990 Census was accompanied by considerable tension and heated exchanges. The conflict over boundaries is symptomatic of a broader struggle for dominance in cities with both large black and large Hispanic populations. As seen by a Los Angeles black commentator, recent clashes between blacks and Hispanics should "shatter, perhaps for good, one of the most enduring myths of our time: The myth of black-brown solidarity." The writer describes the growing ethnic insensitivity on both sides, with each claiming that gains made by the other in jobs or politics results in losses for their group.[51] Discord surfaced during the rebuilding of Los Angeles neighborhoods damaged by the 1992 riots; blacks complained that Hispanics were given most of the construction jobs.

Asians, like Hispanics, can also be expected to flex their muscles in coming years. To date, most Asians have not been active politically, earning them the nickname the "Silent Americans." However, as they attain greater economic success and as more and more of them become citizens, they are likely to show an increased interest in politics. Michael Woo, the Asian member on the Los Angeles City Council, may run for mayor.

In San Francisco, where Asians now make up one-fourth of the population, none were elected to the Board of Supervisors in 1986, although a Hong Kong-born candidate lost by only a few thousand votes. Local politicians, however, expect an Asian to win a seat in the early 1990s. Asian-American leaders are already demanding that the city institute a strong affirmative-action program in hiring and in city contracting in order to secure their share of jobs and contracts. Although not many have been elected to public office, they are heavy contributors to political parties. In California, one of five Asians made a campaign contribution in the 1980s—higher than the proportion for whites.

Many native-born residents seem to find the idea of Asian political power more palatable than power in the hands of other minorities. In California, for example, two-thirds of Asian officeholders represent areas that are less than 10 percent Asian.[52] The opposite is true for blacks and Hispanics, who are more likely to be elected in areas where they form either a substantial minority or a majority of the population. The growing power of Asians has drawn the ire of some commentators, though. In a May 1986 article in *Washington Monthly,* a federal civil rights official, writing under a pseudonym, discussed the political muscle of Asians. He complained that "an ethnic group's clout tends to grow in inverse proportion to the hardship it endures."[53] Asians are typically affluent and suffer little discrimination, yet they reap the benefits of civil rights legislation aimed at helping blacks and other less fortunate minorities.

As with Hispanics, the growing influence of the Asian community could bring it into conflict with established political groups. Consider the San Gabriel Valley outside Los Angeles. It is estimated that the Asian population there doubled between 1980 and 1987, reaching one-fifth of the total. The highest concentration is found in Monterey Park,where Asians (mostly Chinese) in 1990 made up 57 percent of the total population of 61,000, Hispanics accounted for 31 percent, and non-Hispanic whites, the remainder. In the mid-1980s, an Asian and two Hispanics were elected to the city council. In the following election, these officials were challenged by three non-Hispanic white candidates who wanted to limit development and to declare English the official language. Whites, turning out in numbers sufficient to off-set their less-than-majority status, succeeded in defeating the three minority members. The new council proceeded to proclaim English the official language and to set strict controls on development—a measure aimed at limiting Asian commercial activity. But the political reversal in Monterey Park represented only a "holding action." As white families left and sold their homes, the political balance shifted to Asians. The Monterey Park experience will be repeated in other communities during the next two decades, although Asians are more dispersed and less numerous than Hispanics and therefore require the support of other groups to gain public office in large cities.

Growing Asian economic and political influence could intensify interethnic tensions. The perceptive black columnist William Raspberry deals with one potentially divisive issue in an insightful article entitled "When White Guilt Won't Matter."[54] Raspberry notes that, given their drive, Asian-Americans in the future could dominate universities and have a strong voice in both industry and government, a development that might have adverse effects on the black community. Affirmative action, contract set-asides, and special school admissions policies are tolerated by the white majority, he believes, because blacks have been victims of white racism. Since Asian-Americans do not share the guilt for the history of slavery and racism, they may, Raspberry argues, have less empathy for programs to assist blacks.

Raspberry's fears of a weakening black voice are justified because the conditions in gateway cities are likely to be representative of the nation in the coming decades. Native minorities face a long struggle as new immigrants press their claims for equal political representation and job opportunities, particularly in the public sector. As immigrant populations (and their American-born children) continue to increase, the political power of Asians and Hispanics in cities will inevitably rise at the expense of native-born blacks and whites.

7

More Immigration:
An Economic Windfall?

Recent research suggests that the projected major decline in new labor
force entrants could raise the issue of encouraging immigration.

National Commission on
Employment Policy, 1982[1]

Overpopulation, ethnic tension, rapid social and cultural change—
all clearly limit the nation's tolerance for increased immigration. But
there has never been a time in American history when immigrants
were welcomed on the grounds that their presence would promote cultural pluralism or social diversity. Immigration policy has always been
based on other criteria—at times humanitarian and political concerns,
but mostly economic considerations. With entry laws and rules now subject to constant congressional scrutiny and buffeted by political pressures, it is ever more essential for the United States to define clearly how
its interests are served by immigration. At this point in time, one of America's most pressing economic needs is ensuring an adequate long-
term supply of productive workers. In considering possible changes in
current immigration policy, U.S. policymakers should focus on anticipated labor shortages and the contribution immigrants can make in
meeting the projected demand for both skilled and, to a lesser extent,
unskilled workers.

The nation's increasing reliance on immigrant labor can be deduced by
examining the slowdown in the growth of the overall labor force. During
the 1970s, total employment grew at a rate of 2 million jobs a year. During

the first seven years of the 1980s, a period of stronger economic expansion than seen at any time in the previous decade (and of higher immigration compared to the 1970s), the annual gain was less than 1.7 million. The labor force is projected to grow by only 1.2 percent between 1988 and the year 2000, down from a 2.2 percent rise between 1972 and 1986. The projection incorporates immigration levels prevalent during the 1980s. Were immigration to be halted altogether, the slowdown in the growth of the labor force would be even more pronounced.

The data from gateway cities are even more striking. (The statistics used here are based on ethnicity rather than country of origin, for they are the best available.) As shown in Table 7-1, Asians and Hispanics (mostly immigrants) held 88 percent of the 1.4 million net minority jobs added between 1983 and 1990, a time of economic expansion in gateway cities. Non-Hispanic whites incurred an overall net loss as many moved to outer suburbs.[2] By 1990, non-Hispanic whites held only two out of five jobs in gateway cities. Nationally, fewer than three out of five net jobs added during this period were taken by non-Hispanic whites—a proportion likely to fall in the coming decades.

Table 7-1

Distribution of Employment Added between 1983 and 1990 by Race/Ethnicity (in thousands)

Race/Ethnic Group[a]	Los Angeles County	Miami/ Dade County	New York City	Chicago (city)	Four-city Total
Non-Hispanic White	-81	-66	28	32	-87
Non-Hispanic Black	10	35	76	52	173
Non-Hispanic Asian and Other	99	9	102	25	235
Hispanic	718	123	173	83	1,097
TOTAL	746	101	379	192	1,418
Non-Hispanic White as Percentage of All Workers in 1990	*46.2*	*26.2*	*47.8*	*46.7*	*41.7*

Source: U.S. Department of Labor, Bureau of Labor Statistics, *Geographic Profile of Employment and Unemployment, 1983* and *1990*, BLS Bulletin no. 2216 (1983 Report) and 2381 (1990 Report), October 1984 and June 1991

[a] Estimates of allocation between Hispanics and non-Hispanics by author, based on *1990 Census of Population* and Bureau of Labor Statistics employment data for whites, blacks, Hispanics, and others in 1983 and 1990.

By contrast, the share of new jobs going to immigrants during the 1980s, one of the longest periods of uninterrupted growth in recent memory, reached the highest level since the first decade of the twentieth century. An estimated 26 percent of the rise in the number of jobholders was attributable to immigration.[3] Will immigration prove as important and economically beneficial in the future as it was in the 1980s?

Articles in major newspapers, leading business publications, and trade journals indicated during the second half of the 1980s that the country was experiencing a serious shortfall in the supply of workers. When the Department of Labor stated in 1987 that the nation would soon begin to face labor shortages in numerous skilled occupations, the forecast had already been overtaken by events. The problem had surfaced in many metropolitan areas, as illustrated by a sampling of media reports that highlighted these concerns. The February 1988 cover story of *Nation's Business,* titled "Desperately Seeking Workers," detailed the plight of numerous industries and suggested long-term measures to deal with the problem, particularly improvements in the educational system.[4] The article quoted Secretary of Labor William E. Brock to the effect that the nations' schools were unprepared to meet the demand for new workers. A lead article in the *Wall Street Journal* in early 1989 reported that the labor supply was shrinking and businesses across the country were increasing wages to attract new workers and to keep those already employed.[5] A 1988 front-page article in the *Washington Post,* titled "Area Hit by Labor Shortage," detailed the scarcity of young workers.[6] This came as no surprise to Washington-area residents, who could hardly pass a store—particularly in the suburbs—without seeing a "Help Wanted" sign in the window. The same newspaper featured another front-page article, "Illegal-Worker Ban Leaves Firms Hurting," a few days later.[7] The story recounted how local hotels and restaurants faced labor shortages as the supply of immigrant workers dwindled, a theme echoed by service industries in other cities dependent on illegal aliens to fill low-wage jobs.

The severity of the shortage in the greater Washington, D.C., area in the late 1980s was described in a report issued by a local research institute that noted causes for the worker shortfall and suggested several steps, including the employment of welfare mothers, to cope with the problem.[8] The report concluded that the labor shortage was threatening the area's continued economic progress. A survey of Washington business executives echoed this concern, with 20 percent of the respondents listing labor shortages as their major problem. Elsewhere, a *Christian Science Monitor* lead story, "Help Wanted in U.S. Factories," described how a Philadelphia metal-parts factory could not obtain workers at $10.00 per hour.[9] Jewelry manufacturers were among those scrambling to find entry-level and semiskilled workers. In Providence, firms in several industries were offering cash bonuses to their employees for referring prospects to their personnel offices. The California-based swimsuit industry was particularly hard hit, with orders delayed or canceled as a result of the labor shortage.[10] The industry blamed much of its troubles on the 1986 Immigration Reform and Control Act, which restricted the flow of illegal workers. Discount department stores, particularly in New England, redesigned their interiors to minimize the need for employees. Owners realized that they would pay a price because consumers would receive less personalized service.

Among the beneficiaries of the favorable job environment were teenagers. Whereas youngsters in the 1970s and early 1980s had to search several weeks to find summer jobs at the minimum wage, recently teens have had a larger selection, often at a dollar or two above the minimum. There was even a backlash from some teachers and parents, as high school students' grades appeared to suffer if they spent too much time at after-school jobs. Desperate to find workers, some employers were willing to violate labor laws and take on underage teenagers. Across the nation, trade organizations lobbied state legislators for looser child labor statutes because few adults were willing to accept jobs in fast-food outlets or gasoline stations. Even with higher wages, summer resorts were unable to find sufficient seasonal help. Cape Cod resorts in 1988 and 1989 found the answer—recruit temporary workers from Ireland and Jamaica. This process involved extensive paperwork, but, to serve tourists adequately, it appeared to be the most practical solution.

To those persons seeking a job during the steep economic decline of the early 1990s, these labor shortages seemed but a faded memory. Nonetheless, unemployment levels did not descend to the levels of earlier downturns, even though other economic indicators were bleaker. This paradox is attributable to demographic changes—particularly to the relatively small number of youths entering the labor force.

The economic problems facing the nation in the early 1990s were due primarily to the excesses of the previous decade: huge deficits in an era of prosperity, financial resources allocated for speculation rather than for productive capital investment or research, and a myriad of other causes, none of which were linked, even indirectly, to immigration. Even the severe labor scarcity itself contributed, notably in New England, where the shortage of workers propelled wages upward without any commensurate improvement in productivity, causing the booming region to become uncompetitive. New England's economic slowdown preceded that of other regions and was by far more severe. By 1991 the country's longest peacetime expansion had been succeeded by a slump unparalleled in duration, if not depth, since the Great Depression.

Despite the rapid growth in jobs during the 1980s, some observers believe that a group of "new poor" emerged during the decade. These are formerly working-class people who, due to changes in the composition of the job market, have fallen on bad times. No one has suggested a direct link between this phenomenon and the rise in immigration, but the fact that they took place concurrently implies a need for a closer look. Do statistics support the thesis that the middle class is eroding? It is true that the nation's median income in constant dollars fell somewhat between 1978 and 1985 and rose but modestly in the latter part of the 1980s, only to fall again as the decade ended. Average wages, adjusted for inflation, grew by 2 percent annually during the 1950s and 1960s but were stagnant in the following two decades. Further, average cash income for the bottom one-fifth of the nation's households fell between 1973 and 1991. It is difficult, however, to deduce from these data anything about the emergence of a class of "new poor." According to the Bureau of Labor Statistics, the middle class has shrunk primarily because many have moved to the upper class.[11] Income became more concentrated as the number of both high-income and low-wage jobs rose.

Immigration, as suggested in Chapter 5, probably contributed to income concentration. The majority of Hispanic immigrants are found at the low end of the income spectrum, while a disproportionate number of non-Indochinese Asians have incomes that place them in the top two-fifths of all American households. Still, it would be imprudent to suggest that allowing more immigrants into the country would hurt the middle class. To the contrary, their entry could, in many instances, strengthen the position of the native-born middle class.

The Unemployment-Labor Shortage Paradox

Although the nation faced a labor shortage in the late 1980s and many jobs went unfilled, several million Americans remained out of work and the size of the minority underclass appeared to be growing. In early 1989, 5.8 million Americans were seeking work, an impressive figure, but as a percentage of those working, it was the lowest in well over a decade. Among the white adult population, the majority of those listed as jobless were in the midst of changing employers. However, the aggregate number also included 1.3 million teenagers, many in city ghettos, and black adults in search of full- or part-time work.

High youth unemployment among minorities has been blamed on excessive school dropout rates, although enrollment data do not support this contention. Hispanics, 10 percent of total enrollment, account for 23 percent of all dropouts. African-Americans, by contrast, drop out in proportion to their share of the student body. But the jobless rate among black dropouts was more than twice the rate of white and Hispanic dropouts. In part, high black joblessness is due to the slow growth of jobs in inner cities; most employment opportunities are happening in the suburbs, difficult to reach without a car. To what extent race itself is a factor is hard to measure. However, comparing the jobless rate for young blacks with college degrees with others of similar educational attainment suggests that it may not be a major cause. Among the college-educated, blacks are less frequently unemployed than Hispanics and are only moderately more likely to be jobless than whites.

In the black urban ghettos of Newark and East Orange in northern New Jersey, the severe labor shortages of recent years enabled ambitious minority youth to find work. But job-training specialists found that the boom bypassed the hard-core unemployed—those with inadequate schooling and poor social attitudes—and that the breakdown of the family structure in ghetto areas was contributing to the creation of a new class that appears unemployable.

Not only are the numbers of new nonimmigrant job entrants declining, but so are their skill levels, regardless of their racial background. American Express and AT&T are among the large American corporations spending millions each year to train their employees in the basic skills expected of an average fifth-grader. The quality of the labor force, business argues, is declining—a position backed by both major political parties, which list improving the educational system as a priority in their platforms.

Although the nation must recognize and deal with the special problem of minority youth unemployment, there is a critical need to focus more attention on the long-term supply, and particularly the quality, of workers. The problems that labor shortages can create have not received much attention in this country. There is a dearth of articles in professional journals on the subject. Labor economists have been absorbed for decades in studies of unemployment, and debate has centered on the creation of jobs, not on how to fill those that go unwanted. Nonetheless, in the United States—and in much of Western Europe and Japan as well—demographic changes are expected to bring about a crisis in the availability of labor. Sources of new workers include young persons leaving or completing school, adults first entering or rejoining the labor force, and immigrants. The future size of the American labor force (excluding immigrants) can be estimated with relative accuracy by subtracting the number of people expected to retire or die from the number born over a given period. Calculated in this way, America will experience only a small net gain in workers during the next two decades. In fact, the non-Hispanic white labor force will grow less than 1 percent annually in the 1990s and beyond.

The reason for this very modest increase is clear: American women are having fewer children. The birthrate fell during the 1960s and 1970s and did not stabilize until the late 1980s; as a result, the number of new workers as a percentage of the overall population is steadily declining. In the 1970s, the annual growth rate of new workers was 7.8 per 1,000 residents; by 1985, the rate had fallen to 5.7—a decline of just over one-quarter. This ratio is expected to fall further in the 1990s. The Bureau of Labor Statistics projects that the number of young men and women (eighteen- to twenty-four-year-olds) in the labor force will decline by 2.8 million from 1986 to the year 2000.[12] This dramatic dropoff—one that is especially marked among whites—explains why businesses that traditionally depend on young workers—fast-food restaurants, retail stores, and others—faced a dearth of applicants during the late-1980s expansion.

Besides youth, another possible source of new workers consists of adults who have voluntarily remained outside of, or have temporarily left, the labor force—primarily women who stay home to raise children. Since World War II, an increasing number of women of childbearing age have been taking jobs. With women's share of the labor force fast approaching that of men, their participation rates, though expected to rise further, cannot climb substantially above current levels. Two possible exceptions are women over the age of forty-five and those with small children, especially if better child-care facilities and affordable domestic workers (mostly immigrants) become more available. But neither group seems a promising source of new labor.

Offsetting the modest addition of women to the work force, men's labor participation rates are expected to decline in coming years for nearly all age groups. They are retiring earlier; during the 1980s, one of every three men aged fifty-five to sixty-four was not working. The loss of high-paying manufacturing jobs is one reason. Another is the early retirement encouraged or forced on white-collar workers following corporate consolidations. These "golden handshakes" (for the more fortunate employees) may help debt-fueled mergers but can hurt an economy pinched for skilled and experienced workers. In most instances, however, elderly men have chosen not to work—an avenue made possible by a combination of Social Security, private pension plans, and savings. The number of working men age fifty-five and over is expected to decline by more than one million by the mid-1990s—at the same time as the number of young persons in the labor force is decreasing. Indeed, we may be facing a "gray brain drain" as more Americans elect to retire earlier. There are now fifteen million people below the "normal" retirement age of sixty-five collecting Social Security benefits, in addition to several million military and civil service workers drawing pensions. Although some of these individuals continue to hold full-time or part-time jobs, most are not working and represent a drain on the economy. There is little prospect that any change in economic conditions can induce these former workers to reenter the labor pool in significant numbers.

Another traditional source of urban labor has been the migration of families from agricultural areas—a phenomenon that has continued almost without interruption for nearly two centuries. But the countryside has been essentially depleted of young workers at this stage of post-industrial development.

There is no consensus among economists as to what actually constitutes a labor shortage. The nation's experience immediately after World War II suggests that, when unemployment falls below 5 percent, wages tend to rise faster than productivity, thereby fanning inflation. This condition could be defined as a labor shortage. Presumably, a surplus of workers would have the opposite effect and depress wages. Yet inflation accelerated in the late 1970s and early 1980s, despite high levels of unemployment. And, notwithstanding a decline in unemployment between the mid- and late 1980s, inflationary wage pressures were confined to New England and other rapid-growth areas.

The current slowdown in the growth of the native labor force is nationwide. However, as a result of different economic growth rates, some areas have been more affected than others—witness the large (but narrowing) differences in regional unemployment rates, the most common measure of labor surplus and shortage. The presence of such disparities is somewhat surprising. Compared to earlier periods, one would have expected the 1980s to have been a time of great labor mobility as a consequence of higher education levels, lower transportation costs, and more readily available information about the job market. There have in fact been some cases of large-scale movement in response to economic change. When the automobile industry slumped beginning in 1979, many jobless auto workers headed for booming Texas. Likewise, workers leaving depressed farm states were moving to metropolitan areas on both coasts. Nonetheless, the availability of unemployment benefits, pensions, and other transfer payments has mitigated the need for breadwinners to uproot their families and seek work far from home, as occurred during the depression. The high cost of living in labor-starved areas exacerbates the problem of limited mobility. Southern Connecticut, like most of New England, was desperate for unskilled workers in the late 1980s, but few were induced to come from other parts of the nation. Costly housing discourages the migration of workers with few skills, whose earning potential remains low even when labor is scarce.

Statewide unemployment in Maine, Massachusetts, New Hampshire, and Vermont reached levels below 3 percent in early 1989, with the 1.7 percent rate in Burlington, Vermont, among the lowest in the nation. At the same time, joblessness persisted in a few areas, including Mobile, Alabama (8.4 percent); Flint, Michigan (10.7 percent); and Decatur, Illinois (9.0 percent). In West Virginia and Mississippi, the two poorest states in the nation, 8 percent of the labor force could find no work. In these cities and states, structural unemployment was caused by such circumstances as aging industries and increased imports of manufactured products. The nation's midsection itself began to experience labor shortages in the late 1980s, as these regions bounced back from the slump in manufacturing. The recovery in Dallas and Houston, hardest hit by the oil price bust, led to a sharp decline in joblessness.

When labor shortages became evident in much of the nation during the late 1980s, overall unemployment among professionals was below 2 percent. Above-average joblessness nonetheless continued in sectors requiring little specialization—food services, janitorial services, and especially unskilled labor. The inability of many with limited skills to find work for which they are qualified, even when the economy is expanding, is disquieting.

By 1991, with the recession, labor shortages eased in nearly every occupation across the United States, but wide disparities in unemployment rates continued. Joblessness among professionals remained below 3 percent, but the percentage of machine operators and day laborers (jobs frequently held by immigrants) out of work soared. But unlike earlier economic downturns, most of middle America was less adversely affected than the coasts. Unemployment in the New England states nearly doubled between 1989 and mid-1992. In contrast, joblessness in Decatur, Flint, and Mobile remained essentially unchanged.

The poor quality of the work force and unmet labor needs may have contributed to the early 1990s downturn, although root causes were more directly responsible. Following the delayed economic recovery, labor shortages are expected to resume in specific occupations. No one contemplates too few lawyers, surgeons, or history professors. Instead, there are expected to be insufficient nurses and blue-collar workers with specialized skills in such areas as computer-assisted design and manufacturing. In addition to shortages of certain skilled workers, there may be too few among the unskilled native-born willing to work for near-minimum wages in jobs that offer little prospect of advancement.

Immigration during the 1980s essentially offset the lower rate at which native workers entered the labor force. As in earlier declines, the cause for the stagnant ecomony in the early 1990s was not surplus labor but insufficient capital investment and the inability of American business, with some notable exceptions, to remain globally competitive.

Labor shortages do mop up a certain portion of those whose skills or experience are so slight that their hiring constitutes a last resort. Thus, the cost to the economy of paying unemployment and other benefits to those out of work is reduced. Moreover there is no question but that teenagers and adult workers holding entry-level positions gain access to better jobs or profit from higher wages when workers are in short supply.

Yet the reality is that a dearth of workers creates several short- and long-term adverse conditions that more than offset these benefits. High inflation rates are the most serious outcome, as wages are pushed up with no associated productivity gains. Labor shortages in 1989 caused wages to rise twice as rapidly as in the previous year, with wage inflation in services particularly steep. Initially, higher prices for goods and services were most damaging to those on fixed incomes, particularly the elderly. But rising costs, as the New England experience demonstrated, ultimately hurt all sectors. Price increases for manufactured goods mean that American products are less competitive in the international market; the trade deficit widens and causes an outflow of dollars. The downturn that began in the early 1990s acted as a corrective, preventing wages from rising further, but at a high cost to workers who lost their jobs as consumer confidence plummeted.

The Impact of Immigration on Labor Needs

The prospect of a labor shortage in the mid- or late 1990s is disquieting, but at least economists and demographers have given fair warning, and there is time to fashion a response. Jobs that require relatively little skill are less problematic than high-skilled jobs. The demand for dishwashers, waiters, and store clerks can be lowered by introducing labor-saving machinery or by skimping on customer service. For example, a cafeteria requires considerably fewer workers than a typical restaurant, and central checkout counters in department stores reduce the need for cashiers. These alternatives have drawbacks as well. Reducing the number of employees in a retail business can be frustrating as customers frantically attempt to find merchandise and then must wait in long lines to pay for their purchases. Not all jobs can be automated, or the cost of doing so may be prohibitive. On balance, allowing a modest increase in immigration would seem a more feasible approach to the problem, at least over the next decade.

Not that immigration is a panacea—immigrants not only take jobs but also create them. Each job taken by a new immigrant in a labor-short economy lowers the aggregate demand for workers by less than one.

Assume that a labor shortage in the apparel industry attracts one thousand immigrants to New York, and they take relatively low-wage jobs that, at prevailing pay levels, would otherwise go unfilled. The new workers spend their earnings on food, shelter, health care, and other necessities. These outlays represent new demand for goods and services, requiring additional workers in turn. Because the immigrants' earnings in this instance are relatively low, the employment multiplier (the number of secondary jobs created per new worker) will be small. The influx of one thousand immigrant workers to take such jobs would probably result in the creation of 300 to 400 new jobs, mostly in New York but a few elsewhere as well.[13] Employment opportunities would be generated in nearly every sector of the local economy—professional services, retail stores, and local government.

Alternatively, let us suppose that one thousand foreign engineers are brought in to meet the demand in the United States. Because engineers generally earn high salaries, at least one secondary job will be created for each immigrant engineer. Thus, the arrival of these workers, while satisfying the demand for engineers, would not reduce the overall demand for labor.

If immigrants not only fill job requirements but also create new ones, are there advantages for the labor supply from immigration? The answer is affirmative. The low-skilled jobs typically held by illegal aliens induce relatively few secondary jobs. Moreover, since many illegals have no families in the United States, their savings rate is high and their consumption rate is low. As for professionals, their presence does create numerous other jobs, but even this process can be beneficial if it results in a more efficient redeployment of American workers.

The redistribution of jobs available to Americans may be a more important consequence of increased immigration than the alleviation of entry-level labor shortages. When immigrants accept the least desirable jobs, they create opportunities for American workers to move up in pay or job quality. This, of course, is not a new phenomenon. In the early part of the century, when immigrant women were recruited to work in apparel sweatshops, the factory workers they replaced—or displaced—moved into better-paying occupations. New York City industries employed former garment factory workers who had gained experience they could apply in other sectors. The same process takes place in service industries today, when unskilled fast-food jobs are taken by immigrants with limited language skills, native-born youths have a better opportunity to become assistant managers.

Americans should not be concerned that immigration will limit advancement opportunities for native workers. More lenient immigration policies can provide native-born Americans, if properly prepared, with a greater array of new possibilities But too often, black and Hispanic young people lack the training, schooling, and good work habits essential for advancement. For young Americans not up to the challenge, the importation of low-skilled workers could amount to a major setback.

The experience of other nations is instructive. In much of Western Europe, native youths tend to take jobs requiring skills and language proficiency, leaving more menial work to Turks, North Africans, and other foreigners. In the Middle East, West Bank Arabs have replaced Israelis in most construction jobs, freeing the Israelis for white-collar work. In oil-rich countries, few natives work with their hands; they have become dependent on Indian, Pakistani, Filipino, and Korean labor. A young Saudi, even one with limited skills, is likely to obtain a responsible, well-paid job because hordes of foreigners are performing the least desirable tasks. The near total reliance on foreign labor can become politically and socially explosive, as Kuwait discovered. Nonetheless, if there were no foreign workers in the Middle East, the standard of living would fall sharply.

Yet, as in the Middle East, dependence on immigrant labor to perform menial jobs can unquestionably have adverse social consequences in the United States. The association of toil and sweat with nonwhite minorities can create harmful stereotypes. Some Americans already avoid hospitals where a high percentage of the nursing and physician staffs are foreign-born.

If the United States is to maintain its position of leadership in the world, it will need a growing supply of highly skilled foreign-born workers. America's economic performance has unquestionably lagged since the 1960s, and a key reason has been the slow pace of its technological progress relative to other advanced nations, particularly Japan. Corporate management and the absence of government incentives have to share the blame, but contributing to this predicament has been a shortage of workers with innovative ideas and technical know-how. Since the early nineteenth century, the nation has always relied on immigrants who brought with them skills that could be applied in an environment conducive to new ideas. Together with entrepreneurs willing to risk capital on inventiveness, the nation's technology progressed, a fact not lost on other nations.

Mikhail Gorbachev astutely recognized the advantages the U.S. economy derives from foreign-born talent. The brain drain from the Soviet Union prompted him to support continued restrictions on emigration during the early years of glasnost.[14] Although Gorbachev exaggerated when he asserted that U.S. dependence on Soviet emigres—be they mathematicians or other professionals—he understood their historic role in America's achievement of economic preeminence.

The quality of American universities cannot be faulted for the shortfall in technological talent, for the United States continues to boast a disproportionately high share of the world's leading scientific and engineering faculties. The problem is that the nation's most talented students often choose to enter other fields. The proportion of college freshmen choosing engineering careers fell from 12 percent in 1982 to only 8.5 percent in 1987.[15] The number of doctoral degrees in the sciences earned by Americans has actually declined in recent years; at the same time, enrollment of foreign students in doctorate-granting institutions in the United States increased by 6 percent a year during the 1980s.[16] Fully half of the eleven hundred doctorates in physics awarded annually by American universities go to foreign nationals. As a result, the best technology institutes have been forced to hire foreign students as graduate assistants and junior faculty.

The problems actually begin at lower levels. According to the National Science Board, a severe shortage of science and mathematics instructors at the precollege level is keeping American students from learning the basic skills needed for modern manufacturing. The supply of new science and mathematics teachers fell by nearly one-half during the 1970s. As a consequence, the quality of high school-level instruction is likely to decline, with larger classes and fewer course offerings. Equally worrisome, and perhaps related to the teacher shortage, is the steady decline in achievement scores in science among high-school students since the late 1960s. American eighth-graders, meanwhile, score lower in mathematics and science than students in fourteen other nations.[17] The consequences of the lack of a solid educational foundation in the lower grades show up in the results of a massive survey taken by the American Council on Education in 1987, which found that interest among college freshmen in computing, engineering, technological, and nursing careers declined sharply during the 1980s. Young men as well as young women expressed little desire to enter these fields. Although most freshmen cite financial well-being as their primary goal, they shun fields such as engineering, which can offer high salaries after four years of college. Given this lack of interest among American students, it should come as no surprise that the country's most technologically innovative area, California's Silicon Valley, has become dependent on foreign talent.

In a survey of electronics firms in the Silicon Valley area, the *San Jose Mercury News* found that several firms would have difficulty continuing in business without foreign engineers. "Tapping foreign talent is a tradition in the Silicon Valley—part of the formula that made the area an industrial hothouse."[18] These skilled workers come mainly from India, Hong Kong, and Taiwan. In the laboratories of one of the nation's leading computer-chip makers, three-fourths of the research and development engineers were found to be foreign-born, and 40 percent of all engineers hired recently by another major chip producer were of Indian or other Asian descent. Corporate officials believe that at least one-third of all electronics engineers employed in the area are foreign born, and the percentage is rising.

The Department of Labor projects that between 1990 and 2005, the need for computer, mathematical, and operations research analysts will increase by 416,000, or 73 percent. The demand for engineers is expected to grow by 400,000, or 26 percent, over the next fifteen years. These numbers incorporate the reduced demand for engineers in the defense industry after the cold war ended (the study was undertaken in 1991). Earlier projections had indicated more opportunities for aeronautical and other engineering speciality occupations.

Large American corporations have been utilizing the "temporary worker" provisions in the immigration laws to meet their needs. Because insufficient numbers of engineers have entered the country as immigrants, corporations have taken advantage of the H-1 program, which allows the entry of nonimmigrants who qualify as "workers of distinguished merit or ability" as temporary employees. Under this program, professionals can be admitted for periods of up to three years if an employer obtains certification that no Americans can be found for the positions. Numerous engineers also enter the country as intracompany transfers. Further, engineering students remain illegally beyond the expiration of their visas.

The growing use of programs such as H-1 is a matter of public record. In 1984, about 1,500 engineers and scientists entered the United States under the H-1 program. Another 2,200 were admitted as L-1 entrants, the category for intracompany transfers. Three years later, more than 5,300 came under the H-1 provisions, and 4,300 arrived to work for foreign corporations with facilities in the United States. This rise is in response to the growing gap between the internal supply and demand for workers with technical skills. Overall, the number of temporary employees working in this country who were admitted for having "distinguished merit or ability" rose from 42,000 in 1984 to 90,000 five years later.

Some might oppose the importation of foreign scientists as a disincentive to Americans thinking about enrolling in science programs. The real problem, though, is internal—the lack of interest among our brightest students in technical fields. Financial considerations are not a major factor. The typical engineering graduate earns considerably more than graduates in most other fields of study; in fact, the high starting salaries for U.S. citizens with B.S. degrees discourage many from going on to graduate studies. Engineering and science require hard work and self-discipline, whereas law and business seem both less rigorous and more glamorous. One of every four college freshmen plans to major in business.

Although the engineering shortfall is well established, a small minority of American engineers have argued that U.S. firms hire foreign engineers at less than prevailing wages. But most professional associations see little danger to American engineers from the presence of foreigners.[19]

The shortages of engineers and computer programmers that would arise in the absence of foreign-born job seekers would cause wages to rise. But even doubling wages in a particular profession will not increase the supply of qualified people in the short run. Nor is it certain that some of the proposed ideas, such as offering American students large stipends to encourage enrollment in rigorous scientific and engineering programs, will be implemented. Only a thorough revamping of our educational system and changing the value society assigns to the sciences would cause school enrollment in these fields to rise—a task that could take two decades to complete.

In 1988, a committee was formed under the auspices of the National Research Council (NRC) to examine issues arising from the overwhelming presence of foreign engineers.[20] The report found that the influence of these engineers has become profound in industrial research and development. Surveys by the NRC indicate that the dependence on foreign engineers is growing. The chairman of the committee acknowledged that "U.S. engineering schools would be unable to continue current educational and research programs without foreign engineers."[21] Although somewhat concerned that the United States may become overly dependent on foreign engineers, the Council's report concluded that very significant benefits are derived from the unusually gifted foreign-born individuals working in American industry and universities.

The insufficient quantity and, to a lesser extent, quality of American engineers and scientists is not the only cause of the country's technological woes. Many of America's best technical personnel were involved in defense-related projects during the 1980s. Although technology developed for the military can have important civilian applications, in many cases it is simply too expensive or esoteric for direct use by the private sector. During the 1990s, however, a larger proportion of engineers will be available for nondefense work. The need for foreign-born engineers may diminish as a result of this industrial realignment.

Corporations themselves are often unwilling to invest sufficiently in research and development to spur technological progress. In this context, an increase in the pool of enterprising engineers and scientists—native- or foreign-born—could only enhance the nation's ability to compete in the international market. From a narrow, self-interested perspective, it would certainly seem to America's advantage to continue attracting talented people from Great Britain, Japan, Russia, Sweden, and elsewhere. The United States is fortunate that, for a variety of reasons—its relatively unencumbered social structure, emphasis on individual achievement, and, not least, high wages—highly trained people around the world have been eager to come.

In recent years, other nations, particularly Korea, Singapore, and Taiwan, have strengthened their technological base and are now inducing a growing number of their engineers trained in the United States to return home. As these Asian economies progress further, more will return, and the United States will therefore need an ever-larger inflow of foreign talent to maintain its industries. Immigration laws should be modified to encourage a greater number of talented individuals to settle permanently in the United States.

In addition to foreign-born scientists and engineers, the United States is increasingly reliant on foreign registered nurses. Over the next two decades, America's aging population will require 700,000 more RNs. Nursing homes are projecting a 44 percent increase in staff needs by the late 1990s. Already, the nationwide shortage of nurses has reached crisis proportions. There is a 14 to 20 percent vacancy rate for RNs in hospitals, leaving some acutely ill patients without adequate care. With nursing school enrollments down by 23 percent between 1983 and 1987, this problem will become more acute in the years ahead. A sizable increase in salaries could entice more young men and women into the field, but that would not help in the short term. Besides, a rapid rise in nurses' earnings would cause already bloated health-care costs to swell even more.

There has been a steady flow of nurses from the Philippines (where many people speak English) to the United States. American hospital administrators are also scouring Ireland, England, and the Caribbean for professional nurses. As the pool of registered nurses from these nations has dried up, hospitals have begun to recruit new graduates in Korea. Most of these nurses enter under the H-1 program and can only remain in the United States for a limited period of time. An indication of the rising demand is that the number of nurses entering the United States under the H-1 program rose from about 300 in 1984 to 5,220 only three years later.

The shortage is causing hospital costs to rise. Employment agencies are asking large commissions for each nurse hired, and large hospitals have been forced to close wards for lack of staffing, thereby forfeiting revenue. With the trend toward ever-growing demands for health care, additional foreign-trained nurses will be needed during the 1990s. Otherwise, the health establishment's ability to care for the sick and the aged will be seriously impaired.[22]

The Problems of Unskilled Immigrants

The benefits of attracting engineers, scientists, computer systems analysts, and nurses from other nations seem fairly obvious. Only the most xenophobic advocates of immigration controls would object to the entry of British academics, Russian scientists, Swedish medical researchers, or Hong Kong entrepreneurs. But the benefits of admitting lesser-skilled aliens are not as readily apparent. In an era when students are constantly being advised to stay in school in order to keep pace with technological advances, it might seem nonsensical to talk of a shortage of unskilled labor. The expansion of high-tech industries and the growth of automation create the impression that America's most pressing needs will be for skilled technical personnel such as computer programmers and electronics engineers. This impression is partially correct—demand in these occupations is outpacing others, and there will be a need for more skilled workers than the economy is likely to produce. Unquestionably, those with computer and other technical skills will have an advantage in the marketplace. Nonetheless, a substantial share of the new jobs created in the years to come will be in relatively low-wage, low-skill categories. It is estimated that by the year 2005 the nation will need about 5.3 million additional workers with limited skills.[23] As shown in Table 7-2, among the ten occupations expected to record the largest gains, only two—registered nurses and general managers—require a college degree, although some in other occupations also have four years of college. Two other categories—salespersons and

Table 7-2
Ten Occupations Projected to Record the Largest Job Growth
1990–2005

Occupation	Employment 1990 (thousands)	Employment 2005[a] (thousands)	Percentage of Total Job Growth 1990–2005	Education Requirement	Language Skills Needed	Illegal Immigrant Concentration
Salespersons, Retail	3,619	4,506	3.5	Basic	Good	Low
Registered Nurses	1,727	2,494	3.1	College	Good	Very Low
Cashiers	2,633	3,318	2.8	Secondary	Minimal	Low
General Office Clerks	2,737	3,407	2.5	Secondary	Good	Low
Truck Drivers	2,362	2,979	2.5	Basic	Minimal	Low
General Managers	3,086	3,664	2.4	College	Excellent	Very Low
Janitors and Cleaners	3,007	3,562	2.3	Basic	Minimal	High
Nursing Aides	1,274	1,826	2.2	Secondary	Moderate	Medium
Food Counter Workers	1,607	2,158	2.1	Basic	Minimal	High
Waiters and Waitresses	1,747	2,196	1.8	Basic	Moderate	Medium
TOTAL	23,799	30,110	25.2	—	—	—

Source : U.S. Department of Labor, Bureau of Labor Statistics, BLS Bulletin no. 2402, May 1992

[a] These projections assume a moderate economic growth scenario.

office clerks—require proficiency in English. Most of the occupations on this future "help wanted" list—cashiers, janitors and cleaners, fast-food counter workers, truck drivers, waiters and waitresses, and nursing aides—require few skills. Occupations on this list not requiring a college degree make up almost 20 percent of all expected new jobs between 1990 and 2005.

In several of these fields, immigrants already have a strong presence. Many Hispanics in New York and Los Angeles are janitors or work in restaurants as waiters, busboys, counter workers, and cooks. Most New York hospitals have practical nurses (those without college degrees) from the Caribbean. These positions are difficult to fill with American workers. The problem is twofold. First, the shrinking pool of American workers will open up opportunities for some less-skilled natives to obtain and hold jobs that pay better and command more respect than janitors or servers at McDonald's. Second, many natives who lack the skills needed for more desirable jobs—those requiring either technical or language proficiency—will not be motivated to take entry-level, low-wage jobs as long as they have the basic necessities of life, such as food and shelter. Immigrants are willing to hold these jobs because they have fewer alternatives. The presence of such workers promotes a higher standard of living for the middle class, providing it with services at an affordable price. The trend toward self-service is a prime, if seemingly minor, example of how quality of life is adversely affected by shortages of workers in low-paying occupations. No longer does a service-station attendant fill the gas tank and wipe the windshield—unless, of course, the customer is willing to pay a premium. In some fast-food outlets, customers must now dispense their own soft drinks.

To some extent, such changes, by transferring labor-intensive tasks to the consumer, save businesses money—but only within limits. At some point, a reduction in staff causes a reduction in sales because stores cannot stay open as long and because customers are unwilling to wait in long lines or tolerate rude or uncomprehending clerks. In many areas of the Northeast, a scarcity of clerks in the late 1980s caused a noticeable deterioration in service, which hampered retail growth. This is not an argument that long lines or flip behavior by salespeople will fundamentally affect America's well-being, but they do constitute an irritant that can diminish the quality of our life.

A lack of immigrants can also create problems for those who desire household help. As the number of working mothers increases, such help,once considered a luxury, is becoming more and more a necessity. Were it not for recent immigrants, nannies, maids, and gardeners would be a vanishing breed. Outside the home, there is an even greater call for this kind of labor. By the year 2005, America will need three million more workers in cleaning services, food preparation, and food-service occupations, and there is no ready pool of Americans eager to accept these jobs.

The United States needs a vigorous manufacturing sector across the board, including production of such low-technology products as apparel and furniture. Otherwise, it will have a predominantly service economy where most consumer goods are imported. Too much reliance on imports would create a staggering balance of payments deficit and, eventually, result in a lower living standard. Although the number of manufacturing jobs is expected to grow only modestly over the next two decades, immigrants will be needed to fill the void because fewer and fewer young Americans seem willing to take low-paying manufacturing jobs. In theory, higher wages could help, but not if the quality of the workers recruited is inadequate; with productivity weakened, marginal labor-intensive factories would be forced to close and the country's competitive standing internationally would be harmed. Comprehensive classroom and on-the-job training programs for American workers can help to improve the quality of the labor force and should be expanded. Nonetheless, evaluations of these programs, which receive substantial federal funding, have shown the results to be often less than salutary.

Some, no doubt, will argue that, as long as many Americans remain unemployed, there is no need to admit more unskilled aliens. The fallacy in this reasoning is that the United States will have some level of unemployment no matter what immigration policy is adopted because immigration is not a direct cause of joblessness. In addition, the nation needs to recognize the importance of keeping the immigrant labor force balanced. To accept only holders of doctorates would be preferable to accepting no one; but allowing in only those with advanced degrees could foster the creation of a foreign elite that, from a social standpoint, would hardly seem desirable. The economic growth fostered by immigrants in cities has depended as much on low-skill as high-skill labor, for the two complement each other.

Effects of Worker Shortages in Gateway Cities

Turning from broad national and regional trends to the four gateway cities, it is worth exploring whether the influx of immigrants has been sufficient to offset the reduced ranks of young American workers. Unemployment levels in three of the four gateway urban labor markets fell below the national average in late 1988. Low rates were observed in San Francisco (3.2 percent), Los Angeles (4.5 percent), and New York (4.9 percent) at a time when the national rate was above 5 percent.[24] In suburban areas near gateway cities, jobless rates were even lower. Orange County, south of Los Angeles, experienced a jobless rate of only 3 percent, and Stamford, Connecticut, part of the greater New York metropolitan area, had less than 3 percent. These data imply that labor shortages were present in gateway labor markets during the boom of the 1980s, although they were most pressing in the outer suburbs.

The foreign-born population in the New York metropolitan area increased by 754,000 in the 1970s. Between 1981 and 1987, another 700,000 came to the area legally, and the influx shows no sign of abating. The area attracted 93,000 aliens in 1988 alone, and in the following year, 116,000, numbers not seen since the early decades of the century.[25] One indicator was the steady increase in wages being paid to young people working in fast-food restaurants, convenience stores, and other retail establishments. "Help Wanted" signs, once limited to the suburbs, have recently sprouted at Burger Kings in lower Manhattan, where most employees observed recently spoke little English (and some also seemed younger than the state minimum working age).

A 1986 study by the Port Authority of New York and New Jersey concluded that reduced immigration would substantially widen the gap between the supply of and demand for labor.[26] Even assuming a sizable inflow of immigrant workers, the study predicted that job growth would exceed the labor supply. The most severe labor shortages were projected for the manufacturing sector, leading to a drop in the production of goods in the region. In the event of lower-than-projected immigration rates, the report asserted, the region would suffer a disproportionate rise in inflation, reducing its ability to compete with other areas. The Port Authority projections assumed no net in-migration of workers to New York and northern New Jersey from elsewhere in the country. This was certainly a realistic assumption, given the high cost of living in the region.

New York could conceivably gain workers by attracting a larger share of the legal immigrants entering the country. In the 1980s, however, the region attracted a slightly lower proportion of all legal immigrants than it had two decades earlier. This reflects a decline in entrants from Europe—a group that historically has settled in New York in large numbers.

The continuing need of the New York region to attract immigrant workers in the aftermath of the early 1990s downturn will not be shared by all sectors of its economy. Due to changes in the regional economy (the continuing hemorrhage of manufacturing jobs to lower-cost areas and the diminished necessity for certain kinds of service industries to cluster in New York), the metropolitan area may not experience any substantial employment rise. Immigrants may not be needed because native-born workers entering the labor force could easily fill any meager job gains. Between early 1989 and late 1991 the New York region lost nearly half a million jobs, offsetting 40 percent of the gains it made during the 1980s. A likely outcome for the mid-1990s is only slow economic expansion until the regional economy regains its competitive position. Thus, the demand for immigrant workers will be tempered for several years. Most new immigrants will be replacing native-born workers, who will continue to migrate away from the urban core rather than take newly created jobs in the city.

The economies of gateway cities appear to grow more rapidly than others in periods of expansion, but their decline also seems deeper when the national economy falters. Unemployment in New York and elsewhere, nonetheless, remained lower than during earlier downturns because fewer young persons were entering the labor force and outmigration from the city and inner suburbs continued.

The severe downturn in the New York region, by reducing bloated housing prices and the excessive cost of doing business, is creating the base for a more economically competitive region. The need for unskilled labor in the 1990s will be lower than was projected during the 1980s. But the conclusion of the Port Authority that the region is unlikely to have enough workers to fill all the jobs predicted to open up during the next decade remains valid.

Other cities close to New York also anticipated a tight labor market. A 1987 analysis of Philadelphia, for example, indicated that the supply of labor would grow much more slowly than projected needs. Due to an aging population, little internal migration, and meager immigration, unemployment rates in the Philadelphia region during 1990 were well below 5 percent. If employment were to grow at a modest 1 percent a year, the city was projected to have 100,000 more jobs than workers within a decade. Only with a sharp and unexpected rise in the size of the labor force could the city succeed in meeting the projected demand.[27]

Things were not much different in the Los Angeles area. Although Los Angeles is anticipating more job growth than New York or the nation as a whole, no net internal migration was projected by a study published in 1986. From 1984 to 2010, southern California (excluding metropolitan San Diego) was expected to generate 3.1 million new jobs, a net increase of more than 50 percent.[28] This forecast assumed that illegal immigration would continue at the rate prevailing from 1970 to 1980, with between 40,000 and 50,000 undocumented aliens appearing every year. Undocumented workers could in this manner fill more than one million jobs, a third of the expected total increase, over a twenty-year period. Only with these illegal immigrants could the region sustain the rapid economic growth it enjoyed in the 1980s. As in New York, however, the number of jobs also fell in Los Angeles during the early 1990s. The accelerated drop in defense-related jobs and the favorable prospects for a free trade agreement with Mexico—events were unforeseen at the time these projections were calculated—will probably dampen the demand for unskilled workers.

For the San Francisco area, a similar report predicted in 1987 that the number of jobs in the next two decades would increase by more than one-third, to 1.1 million. The demand for labor was expected to exceed the supply by more than 237,000 workers.[29]

All these forecasts warn that, the large intake of legal immigrants notwithstanding, the numbers coming to gateway cities may not be sufficient to meet rising demand over a decades-long time horizon. Part of the explanation lies in the observation that immigrants themselves create new jobs. The presence of immigrants may also discourage native-born Americans from seeking work in Los Angeles, Miami, or New York. An earlier study, for example, found that internal migration to southern California ceased during the 1970s when immigration surged.[30] The same phenomenonhas also been evident in Miami. The outmigration of native-born New Yorkers that began in the 1960s is continuing, reducing the supply of workers in that city. To what extent the American-born have also been discouraged by high housing costs and congestion in gateway cities is not known, but the result was that immigrants, as numerous as they were, did not saturate the local labor market during the 1980s.

Do Industrially Advanced Nations Need Immigrant Labor?

Do these data suggest that the United States should encourage immigration in its effort to maintain its living standards? There seems to be no question that, in order to maintain its technological position, more skilled immigrants will be needed. If the nation falls substantially behind others in technology and productivity enhancement, income is likely to fall. As for less-skilled jobs, the expected dearth of workers may reduce the quality of services and redistribute income, with middle-class household purchasing power marginally reduced. Structural changes in the American and world economy during the 1990s could lessen, but not eliminate, the need for immigration.

It may well be that, as a consequence of economic adjustments that will follow the economic slump of the early 1990s, regional labor demand patterns will change. The less-skilled immigrants coming to gateway cities would then follow the path of foreign-born professionals and seek job opportunities in smaller metropolitan areas with few immigrants. There are numerous urban centers where more than 99 percent of the population is native-born and unemployment (in 1992) was below the national average, including Evansville, Indiana; Owensboro, Kentucky; and St. Cloud, Minnesota.

A reasonable question to ponder at this juncture is how some nations manage to maintain high living standards without immigrants to perform menial jobs. Japan is the prime example of a technologically advanced nation that depends on its own population for nearly all its workers. The only non-Japanese in the work force are a small Korean minority (700,000 out of a total population of 123 million and several hundred thousand illegal workers, mostly Asians). The bulk of the menial jobs are filled by Japanese themselves, at relatively high wages. One effect of this wage structure has been an equalization of income distribution. A Japanese worker with a junior high school degree earns on average about 75 percent of what a college graduate earns.[31] By contrast, in the United States, where income has become more concentrated since the early 1970s, a person with one to three years of high school receives less than half the earnings of a college graduate. Had Japan allowed Koreans, Chinese, and other workers to enter during its sustained post–World War II boom, the country's distribution of income would no doubt be more skewed. Based on the experience of the Koreans in Japan (and its small number of illegal aliens), it is likely that those foreign workers would be paid less than their Japanese counterparts and relegated to the least desirable jobs. Strikingly, Japan is also less reliant on women for its labor than the United States. While the labor force participation rate among American women rose from 38 percent in 1960 to 56 percent in 1987, it fell in Japan, from 53 to 48 percent during the same time interval. The low proportion of women employed in Japan places additional upward pressure on wages for low-skilled workers, as society expects a married man's earnings to support his family.

Japan's ability to maintain a high living standard with virtually no dependence on immigrant labor reflects some distinctive aspects of Japanese culture, religious philosophy, and nationalism. All work in Japanese culture is regarded as an end in itself, not as a means to achieve other ends. Self-esteem and pride are attached to labor, whether this involves nuclear research, arranging flowers, or wrapping a box. Even low-skill, menial jobs are well rewarded. This leads not only to high prices for personal services compared to Western countries, but also to quality service that Americans envy.

At the upper end of the occupational scale, Japan does not seek to attract scientific and engineering talent from other nations. Rather, for over a century, the brightest Japanese students have been sent overseas to study the latest technological advances and bring them back to the homeland. The roots of Japanese labor policy are essentially nationalistic. Employing immigrants is contrary to the country's deep sense of identity. Its strong desire to remain a homogeneous society springs from a belief that this has enabled the country to become the world's number-two economic power. The Japanese have overcome what would otherwise be a handicap—lack of immigrants—by paying high wages for unskilled work and, more important, developing a rigorous educational system with disciplined students that reliably produces workers for all skill levels and abilities.

The Japanese are not unique in their approach. Norway and Iceland are among the handful of other nations with high living standards whose policy is to severely limit immigration. The distribution of income in these countries is more equitable than in the United States, in part because all workers are provided generous benefits (even though it takes high personal income tax rates to finance these benefits).

Yet, these nations have not been able to completely escape labor shortages. Japan has insufficient workers at both the upper and lower ends of its occupational range, which parallels the problems facing the United States. High-technology positions remain unfilled; so do service and retail sector jobs, particularly in fast-food restaurants.[32] During the economic slowdown in the early 1990s, there were still 125 jobs available for every 100 job seekers—a fundamental constraint on Japan's recovery.[33]

The Japanese may be forced to modify their immigration policies in order to sustain their economic growth and high living standards. Nonetheless, their experience in the 1980s suggests that it is possible, except during periods of very rapid expansion, to fill even undesirable menial jobs as long as wages are kept at sufficiently high levels. Achieving this in the United States, however, would require a significant redistribution of income from the middle class downward, not to mention a radical change in the societal value attached to menial work. Even were such a wholesale transformation to occur (and economic history shows that such an event takes place only when the country seems to have no alternative, as in the crisis period of World War II, when demand for labor was extraordinarily high and overseas immigration was cut off), it is unlikely that all such positions could be filled; as in Japan, the hamburger emporiums could still go begging for counter help. Employers traditionally have exerted considerable pressure to maintain a stable supply of alien lower-skilled workers. In 1990, pro-immigrant groups (with the tacit support of some in the business community) successfully lobbied for higher admission levels to meet existing and projected labor shortages. The passage of this legislation implied that many lawmakers would rather respond to labor needs by continuing immigration than by sharply increasing minimum wages and taking other measures that could relieve shortages but would redistribute income as well.

8

Immigrants and America's Future

Immigration has played a critical role in shaping America, particularly its cities, and will continue to do so in the future. What that role will be, however, depends on the laws we adopt and whether we are willing to rigorously enforce them. Should current policies be maintained? Care must be taken in implementing changes because any sudden shift in course—any drastic opening or closing of the door—would be disruptive and could stir unrest.

Following the passage of what some consider a landmark immigration law in 1990, Congress appeared unlikely to contemplate curtailment of immigration levels. Although the struggle to pass the 1986 Immigration Act had left many legislators weary of tampering with the issue, Congress acted in 1990 to change the immigration statutes in order to increase the number of skilled workers and so-called "independent" immigrants allowed into the country. This resulted in a new annual ceiling of 700,000, which will decline to 675,000 after 1995, and reserved about 140,000 visas for individuals (and their dependents) with special job skills and talent. Remarkably, organized opposition to this considerable increase in legal entry levels was virtually nonexistent. Even the most vocal opponents of immigration did not at the time advocate radical changes in current (pre-1990) policy. For instance, former Colorado governor Richard Lamm, who has warned that a splintering of American society may result from continued large-scale legal and illegal immigration, proposed an annual aggregate limit of 400,000—only 25 percent below the actual level of the late 1980s. The Federation of American Immigration Reform (FAIR) too favored modest reductions but did not actively oppose the 1988 Kennedy-Simpson Senate bill that also sought to raise immigration levels. Seemingly exhausted by its earlier failures, FAIR was unable to mount a serious challenge to the more broadly based groups favoring higher ceilings. Opponents recognized that any proposal for reducing entry levels during the booming 1980s would lack political support. This very much reflected America's history of tolerance. Even during the Great Depression, when nativism reached its peak and the economy its nadir, Congress was reluctant to eliminate the admission of newcomers.

Since the 1990 legislation represented the sentiment of both parties in Congress and the executive branch, it is surprising that strong opposition to immigration would arise shortly after its passage. Yet just days before the Los Angeles riot, the conservative *National Review* published, an article with the provocative title "Our Disappearing Common Culture: The Forbidden Topic."[1] In a sweeping indictment of American immigration policy, the author argued that, contrary to the position of some leading neoconservatives, the pressure for multiculturalism in schools and elsewhere should be ascribed directly to America's criteria for the admission of aliens. The preponderance of immigrants from the third world was depicted as representing a direct threat to the preservation of Western culture.

In May 1992, shortly after the riot, FAIR suddenly called (for the first time since its formation) for a temporary moratorium on nearly all immigration (only spouses and minor children of U.S. citizens would be exempted). The rationale cited by FAIR for its request was a poll sponsored by the organization showing that more than half (55 percent) of the public supported such a step.[2] The timing of the poll's release, less than three weeks following the Los Angeles riots, gave FAIR considerable media exposure.[2] On the day of the FAIR announcement, an op-ed article written jointly by a historian and a journal editor in the *Los Angeles Times* supported an immigration "respite" (moratorium) on the premise that halting the inflow would help inner-city minorities.[4] At about the same time, Lawrence Harrison, writing in the neoconservative journal *National Interest,* also concluded that "while we study, articulate and legislate such [immigration] reforms and work toward better integration of recent immigrants, we should call for a moratorium on immigration."[5]

Finally, the prestigious *New York Times* added to the clamor two months later by featuring an op-ed piece calling for a five-year freeze on immigration.[6] The rationale given by the writer was to "reduce unfair competition for scarce jobs, give our economy a chance to recover, . . . and, above all, give the millions of immigrants here the opportunity to assimilate." Otherwise, the writer asserts, the United States will create a foreign underclass, thus weakening the nation's ability to compete globally.

Do these media-promoted challenges to the core of post-1965 American immigration policy—not to discriminate in admissions on the basis of geography, race, or ethnicity—represent a change in direction, among both liberals and conservatives? A profusion of negative images of immigrants from Eastern and Southern Europe in leading periodicals and newspapers preceded the immigration restrictions of the 1920s. However, the widespread political support that existed during the 1920s for limits based on ethnicity and national origin is not apparent today in Congress. Consider that the number of Hispanics in the House of Representatives reached a new high of seventeen after elections in November 1992, and it becomes clear that any move to substantially alter immigration policy will face an uphill battle. The sudden appearance in the media of so much skepticism regarding immigration, rather than signaling a popular groundswell or the beginnings of legislative momentum to clamp down on admissions, more likely reflects two frustrations: one over the nation's continuing inability to deal with delicate racial issues, the other over the ever-shrinking presence of non-Hispanic whites in large urban areas.

In direct opposition to those calling for a halt to foreigners settling in the United States, several publications still express pro-immigration attitudes, though perhaps with less gusto in the wake of the economic stagnation that engulfed the nation in the early 1990s. Their editors seek to open American borders to anyone that can meet certain health and moral standards and show a willingness to work. This position has been embraced by several business publications and some libertarian newspapers, such as California's *Orange County Register*. Their attitudes are based on a philosophical commitment to an open economy unencumbered by labor or regulatory constraints.

The position of business-oriented *Forbes* is that the nation should admit at least 1.5 million to 1.8 million legal immigrants annually as a means of enriching the United States.[7] This open view is endorsed by other conservative business media. A persistent and very influential voice urging more liberal entry policies has been the *Wall Street Journal.*

During the debate on the Immigration Reform and Control Act (IRCA) in 1986, a lead editorial concluded that "if Washington still wants to 'do something' about immigration we propose a five-word constitutional amendment: There shall be open borders."[8] The editorial drew an analogy between the 1986 immigration act and the Prohibition (Volstead Act) Amendment to the Constitution. Prohibition could not be enforced, and the amendment was eventually repealed, although 300,000 persons were convicted for drinking. Just as people continued to consume alcohol, the editorial argued, illegal aliens will continue to come and find jobs. When Senator Alan K. Simpson proposed that stronger measures to thwart crossings from Mexico be incorporated into the 1990 immigration bill, the *Wall Street Journal* challenged the move, with editorials charging Simpson with bias toward Mexicans and intent to wreck the bill appearing twice in a span of a few weeks.[9] The *Journal* not only reported the news, but its views became part of the congressional debate. Conservative opposition to liberal American immigration policies was virtually absent until Pat Buchanan challenged President George Bush for the Republican party nomination in 1991. But Buchanan's anti-immigration stance was immediately contested by another well-known conservative, columnist George Will.

The liberal *New Republic* also favors an essentially open-door policy, subject only to such criteria as proficiency in English (within a few years of entry to the United States) and a willingness to work rather than request welfare.[10] Its position is not based on a commitment to free enterprise but on a desire to overcome the problem of dealing with illegal entrants. The editors believe that such an approach would resolve this issue by eliminating the category of illegal aliens altogether. Concern for the welfare of aliens, seen as scapegoats for economic problems, explains the opposition of the *Nation*, a liberal periodical, to employer sanctions. Following passage of the 1990 Immigration Act, the *Public Interest*, a neoconservative quarterly, included an article by Julian Simon urging substantially greater immigration levels.[11] Virtually unrestricted immigration thus finds support at both ends of the political spectrum.

How many people would enter under an essentially open-door policy? During the peak immigration period—1910 to 1915—more than a million arrived every year. (Because many of these eventually returned to their native lands, net population transfers were actually much lower.) Immigration during this five-year period turned out to be somewhat less than 6 percent of the national population at the time. If a similar percentage of today's population were immigrants, the total would be about 15 million. Converted to an annual rate of 3 million a year, this would be about three times greater than the current level of combined legal and estimated illegal entry. No doubt, this crude calculation understates the numbers that would come. For one thing, more of today's would-be arrivals have the financial means to pay for the trip. Mass communication disseminates information about the United States unavailable at the turn of the century and encourages immigration, although an open entry policy would also increase the number that would return to their homeland, particularly during periods of slow economic growth. An annual net immigration flow of 4 to 5 million might be a reasonable estimate.

From a narrow economic standpoint, a return to the open immigration laws in effect before 1922 does not seem out of the question. The nation could absorb several million more immigrants a year than are currently admitted and maintain growth; in fact, economic expansion would probably accelerate were new entrants predominantly young and skilled workers. However, such an increase would displace some American workers and have long-term adverse social, distributional, as well as environmental consequences. It seems safe to say that the vast majority of Americans would be unwilling to accept the many millions who would come in the event that most restrictions were lifted. Global economic competition and domestic needs, however, justify raising legal immigration levels for some groups above what is allowed under the 1990 law.

Reflections from the Past and Present

The congressional debates on immigration will continue into the mid-1990s and beyond as the nation searches for policies that will respond not only to changing domestic labor needs but also to events beyond its borders. These debates need to be viewed against the backdrop of American immigration policy as it has evolved over the last three centuries. An understanding of how these policies have emerged and how they have affected the national well-being can serve to guide those responsible for formulating new approaches.

The roots of American immigration doctrines can be traced to the sixteenth century, when Queen Elizabeth chided her subjects for their intolerance toward Protestants who came from the Continent. Her argument, repeated by Cromwell a hundred years later, was that immigrants were an economic asset. The same theme was echoed in the American colonies and subsequently by the leaders of the new Republic. Not until the 1920s did an American president support limiting immigration from the European continent.

In opposition to the pro-immigrant attitude of the executive branch were legislators whose constituents favored entry restrictions for a variety of reasons—some economic but most social in nature. They felt that the social discontent caused by admitting persons who differed from themselves in language or customs more than offset the economic benefits brought by their presence. This same sentiment was accepted in London by the Parliament, which restricted entry to Britain for centuries.

High birthrates and falling death rates in the United States during the eighteenth and nineteenth centuries caused the domestic labor force to multiply, but these gains were insufficient to meet rising demand. The agricultural labor needs of the South were met by the importation of slaves. Their use not only caused untold anguish and internal strife but carried with it a legacy that continues to haunt both blacks and whites well over a century after the Civil War. By contrast, the demand for labor by northern industries was satisfied without coercion by allowing Europeans unhindered entry. For this reason, business and industry usually sided with those favoring no barriers to immigration, recognizing that the promotion of such a policy served their interests. Some workers did not share these perceptions but believed that employers' attitudes were based on a desire to gain cheap, docile workers. No doubt this was true, as far as it went. But industry also recognized that more workers earning decent wages translated into additional consumers, and that higher sales generated greater profits.

If business interests had a stronger voice in Congress than labor, how did legislation to severely limit immigration pass during the 1920s? The explanation is that since the colonial period, American attitudes toward aliens have followed distinct generational cycles. These cycles are related less to economic circumstances than to changing perceptions of the nation's direction and its role in the world. When the populace is self-confident and looks outward, attitudes toward immigration are benign. Such attitudes prevailed in the eighteenth century, when the Republic came into being, during the period of expansion following recovery from the Civil War, and in the decades between John F. Kennedy's ascent and the early years of the Bush presidency. At other times—as in the decades prior to the Civil War and between the two world wars—the nation has turned inward and immigrants have been viewed with suspicion and even hostility.

Notwithstanding periodic pressure to limit immigration, business interests overcame resistance to sweeping measures by agreeing to certain constraints, such as excluding Asians and contract labor. But in the 1920s, public opinion, aroused by the Eugenicists, the Klan, and much of the press, turned against immigrants from Eastern and Southern Europe. Opposition to immigration found support across the nation but was strongest in the South, a politically potent region where industry had little influence. In the face of Southern opposition and rising anti-immigrant sentiment among the middle class in other regions, industry (but not southwestern agricultural interests) decided it could manage without additional immigrant labor.

The economic cost of restricting the inflow of workers became an irrelevant concern with the onset of the Great Depression, a few years after the National Origins legislation came into effect. The myopic public perception of immigrants during the 1930s was that they were taking the few existing jobs from Americans rather than creating new opportunities. In fact, the periodic but steep downturns that were part of the economic landscape, including the trough of the 1930s, developed not in response to an excess of workers but were attributable to imperfections in monetary, fiscal, and trade policy.

James Madison's astute observations in the late eighteenth century on the positive effects of immigration remain valid over the course of two centuries—the standard of living grows more rapidly in areas where immigrants settle. The prime beneficiaries of the immigrant presence continue to be the established middle class and business in regions where newcomers settle. As such, immigrants tend to widen the economic gap between regions, urban and rural areas, rich and poor. Ironically, the antebellum South, while caring little for immigration, could not escape the consequences. Had no aliens entered the country in the three decades prior to the Civil War—later swelling the Union army and supplying the North with hands for its factories—the outcome of the conflict might well have been different. The Confederacy did not need to win outright; it needed only to prevent a Union victory. Following the war, the virtual absence of aliens (except as merchants) in the South served to broaden the economic chasm between that region and the North. Regional disparities, in turn, further fueled a latent anti-immigrant sentiment that ultimately doomed open immigration.

Because they were poor and concentrated in the rural South, blacks (even more than nonurban whites) were practically unaffected by the economic expansion that immigrants stimulated. Contrary to the views of contemporary black newspapers, there was no validity to the contention that black progress was impeded directly by mass immigration. The most significant economic and social effect of alien workers was that they slowed the inevitable black exodus from the rural South to northern cities.

Although the economic impact of reduced immigration flows since the 1920s is difficult (and perhaps impossible) to quantify, secondary data strongly suggest that economic activity in urban areas has been slowed by the paucity of new immigrants to replace the middle class moving from the core. Together with technological change, this shift in settlement patterns has weakened the economic foundations of inner cities.

In comparison to earlier immigrants, how did the "Fourth Wave," those who came in the 1970s and 1980s, affect the urban economies? Our examination of four "gateway" cities found that the passage of time has not lessened the favorable economic role played by immigrants. In many respects, their impact in recent years has been even more immediate. Because many Asians came with or had access to capital, they rehabilitated hundreds of older commercial areas within a decade. It is also indisputable that Asians and other immigrants who moved into areas abandoned by working- and middle-class whites revived many residential districts as well. The resurgence observed in numerous neighborhoods of Los Angeles, Miami, New York, and San Francisco would not have taken place had immigrants not settled there.

Yet, many observers believe that racial strife is rising across the nation, including in large urban areas where the economic contributions of immigrants are most visible. The statistical data presented in this book establishes that, as a group, blacks are somewhat better off economically in gateway cities than in most urban areas. The data show that the economic conditions of blacks on average improved more rapidly in the gateway cities compared to the nation as a whole.

With the exception of Miami, blacks in these urban areas are also likely to earn more, be better educated, suffer lower unemployment, hold managerial or professional jobs, and own their own businesses than African-Americans in other parts of the country. Further, the analysis suggests that the presence of immigrants may be contributing to their advantageous position.

How can one reconcile these findings with the recent violent upheaval—one that caused more death and destruction than any riot within memory—in Los Angeles, the nation's premier destination for new immigrants? A definitive response has not emerged from the dozens of commentaries on the violence, but there seems to be no direct link between the eruptions and immigration. Aliens crowded into substandard housing on the periphery of the Los Angeles ghetto are even more deprived than the seething black underclass.

Korean stores were looted, but it would have made little difference had native whites owned the same businesses. A more fundamental cause of the violence, leaving aside antagonism toward the police, was that the black and Hispanic middle class had essentially abandoned these neighborhoods. Disparities in wealth are also more visible in the glitter of southern California than in other regions. This tends to feed resentment among the "have-nots," regardless of race, since materialism encourages rising (but usually unmet) expectations. While such sociological explanations seem plausible, a quick glance at the almost ominous cover of a recent issue of the *Atlantic* (October 1992), depicting male profiles—one black, the other brown—confronting each other, underscores that they have not convinced all.[12] The cover caption, "Black vs. Brown: Immigration and the New American Dilemma," refers to a lengthy feature story by Jack Miles on the Los Angeles riot and its causes. Miles, an editorial writer for the *Los Angeles Times,* subscribes to the view that blacks in Los Angeles (and elsewhere in California) are losing jobs and educational opportunities to Hispanics, fueling discontent and contributing to the magnitude of the violence. The article, however, fails to acknowledge minority economic progress during the period of massive immigration. Data showing a substantial and growing black middle class that is scattered throughout Los Angeles and Orange counties need to be considered in order to assess the full effects of immigration on Southern California.

Unfortunately, conditions in the inner-city ghettos—not only in Los Angeles but in Washington, D.C., as well as in other urban centers with few immigrants—deteriorated during the 1980s. Violence has reached unprecedented levels, and ghetto streets in several cities are now a virtual battlefield. Although the economic and social disintegration of the inner cities is not tied to the stress of immigration, immigrants have absorbed much of the low-cost housing vacated by both blacks and whites who could afford to seek homes in safer neighborhoods. This has reduced the supply of cheap housing in many areas, particularly Los Angeles, Miami, and New York. Tensions have risen as immigrants have moved into or established small businesses in predominantly black neighborhoods. Similar ethnic conflicts erupted in the early decades of the twentieth century in Chicago and Detroit. Disputes between alien and native "have-nots" are virtually unavoidable.

But the economic growth that immigrants facilitate can have two positive effects for native residents. First, additional local tax revenues generated by expanded commercial activity can be focused on programs to help the needy, particularly where native minorities have gained political control. Second, there may be a limited "filtering down" effect, as expansion creates some jobs for urban ghetto residents. These benefits are limited in scope and are insufficient to deal with the underlying causes of the problem, however. The South Bronx, Watts, and other inner-city ghettos have not been invigorated in spite of the presence of new minorities. Immigrant businesses locating in these neighborhoods, unless pressured to hire blacks, tend to employ coethnics, and their owners usually live elsewhere. A large tax base is more likely to benefit middle-class blacks on city payrolls than those searching for work. Nonetheless, the urban underclass needs to gain awareness that when immigrants become targets of those seeking an outlet for their rage, the resulting violence is typically devastating to both groups.

Immigrants Wanted—An Economic Rationale

Higher entry quotas for skilled workers than currently allowed (when need can be demonstrated) and other modifications of immigration laws can strengthen the nation's geopolitical status, raise its living standards, and improve the economies of its inner cities, thereby sharpening its competitive position in the world. America's rise to international dominance at the turn of the century was fueled by political stability, entrepreneurial ingenuity, abundant natural resources—

and mass immigration. The resources and stability were there, but immigrants enabled the country to exploit them fully.

That dominance is no longer what it once was, even though the United States is now frequently called the "world's only superpower." An issue debated among academics that has also been the subject of considerable media exposure is the apparent decline of the nation's prestige and economic standing. There is consensus that American economic and military dominance extended from the 1940s into the early 1960s, when the economies of other industrial nations, having fully recovered from World War II, gained momentum. Since then, our share of global production has continued to slide. The full economic weight of two populous nations with enormous resources—China and the former Soviet Union—is curtailed, at least for now, by a totalitarian system and a populace consisting mostly of impoverished peasants in the first, and by political as well as economic disintegration in the second. But Japan and other Pacific Rim nations, as well as the unified European economic market, pose an unprecedented challenge to American industry. No one questions these facts, but the causes of the relative decline, its extent, and the remedies necessary to halt the slide are in dispute.

Perhaps the most controversial theory on the causes of the decay of nations is espoused by the historian Paul Kennedy. His studies of major powers since the Middle Ages, including Spain and Britain, lead him to the thesis that these empires waned because the military obligations necessitated by their role outstripped their economic resources. In *The Rise and Fall of the Great Powers,* Kennedy associates the conditions that led to the downfall of these nations with the situation facing the United States today. He argues that America's far-reaching military commitments exceed its economic capabilities.[13]

The reality is that America's economy thrived and living standards reached unprecedented heights during the post–World War II decades when military outlays (as a share of the gross national product) were twice their current level. The United States is, of course, in a more competitive environment today, but reducing defense expenditures will have little long-term impact on its economy.[14] America's most costly military conflict since Vietnam, the Persian Gulf War, was essentially paid for by the big importers of Mideast petroleum, Japan and Germany, as well as the oil-rich nations of the Arabian peninsula. Another fault with the declining-power analogy, one particularly germane to the substance of this book, is this: the Kennedy thesis fails to distinguish the unique willingness and ability of the United States to absorb large numbers of immigrants, continually replenishing itself.

In contrast, Spain became a third-rate power by the early seventeenth century, its decline caused in part by the forced emigration of its minority populations. The expulsion of Jewish entrepreneurs and Moorish artisans weakened its commercial base and financial links to other nations. Its principal adversary, the Netherlands, was strengthened by accepting Jews fleeing Spain. Population decline, resulting from disease as well as religious intolerance—human losses that the massive influx of riches from the Americas could not overcome—helped bring about the fall of the Spanish empire.[15]

The United Kingdom, too, has paid an economic price for encouraging emigration and discouraging immigration. Between 1820 and 1870, when Britain was at the zenith of its economic and political influence, more than 4.5 million persons, one-fifth of its population, emigrated. Millions more left subsequently, and net outmigration continues to this day. Although nineteenth-century emigration relieved population pressures, the cumulative impact was that a weaker nation faced the more populous Germany at the onset of World Wars I and II.

In the 1930s, many of Germany's most gifted scientific minds found refuge across the Atlantic, and their talents aided the Allies in World War II. A half-century later, thousands of talented Chinese students were allowed to remain in America in protest against oppression in their native land.

Religious and ethnic intolerance forced millions to flee Czarist Russia in the decades immediately preceding the October Revolution. Once in control, the Communist regime virtually prohibited further emigration, which would have served as an outlet for discontented minorities. Not until the late 1980s did the Soviet Union lower the exit gates. Unlike the United States, which absorbed over fifty million aliens who came of their own free will, both pre- and post-revolutionary Russia forced the amalgamation of ethnic groups into an empire by means of aggressive geographic expansion and repression. A major cause for the collapse of the Soviet Union was the inability of its disparate population to achieve cohesion. As for immigrants, few could have been attracted even if the leadership had encouraged their entry.

Kennedy tends to ignore immigration's role in the ability of nations to maintain economic growth and military power. The only reference to recent immigrants in his chapter on America's future is his view that because the number of immigrants, native blacks, and native Hispanics is growing rapidly "it may be unwise to assume that the prevailing norms of the American political economy (low government expenditures, low taxes on the rich) would be maintained if the nation entered a period of sustained economic difficulty caused by a plunging dollar and slow growth."[16] Kennedy's suggestion that immigrant votes will become a vehicle for political change and greater government involvement in helping the needy has no basis in fact. The majority of newcomers, particularly Asians but also Europeans and to a lesser extent Hispanics, tend to be conservative and are less likely to support higher taxes aimed at income redistribution than native-born Americans.

These comments are not intended to detract from Kennedy's well-researched thesis that a strong economy is a prerequisite for maintaining international commitments, but to stress that enlightened immigration policies can help nations sustain their strength. Increasing the flow of immigrants, particularly those with technical skills, is one means of assuring that the United States has the capacity to retain its role as the guarantor of peace and leader of the industrialized world.

Although geopolitics should rightfully be considered, there are persuasive domestic economic reasons as well for maintaining sizable immigration. Additional immigrants would not only expand America's GNP but, as in the past, would modestly increase the per capita household income of the native-born. The principal causes of this rise in income rise would be the more rapid rate of technological innovation and the higher productivity that accompanied the addition of skilled immigrants to the labor force. However, even in the absence of any rise in per capita income, expanding the pool of young workers would ease the financial pressure on Social Security and healthcare programs that must take in a steadily growing number of older Americans. At a minimum, improving the quality of the work force through immigration (combined with other measures aimed at the native population) would confound the prognosis of doomsayers concerning the American economy.

Los Angeles riots awakened the public conscience, at least temporarily, to the plight of the inner cities. As noted earlier, one cause for the depopulation and economic decline of the urban core during the 1960s and 1970s was a dearth of immigrants to replace middle-income households moving to the suburbs. Urban decay had become serious enough by the 1970s to prompt the federal government, particularly during the Carter administration, to initiate numerous programs intended to revitalize neighborhood housing and provide financial assistance to inner-city businesses. It seems safe to say, however, that immigration by itself has sparked more neighborhood revitalization and commercial activity than even the most successful cases of government intervention. In a sense, immigration can be considered an economic development tool that comes complete with its own human resources and capital. The investment in small immigrant businesses within the urban core alone exceeded several billion dollars by the early 1990s. Had immigration to central cities been a federal urban aid program, it would be rated among the most successful and cost-effective approaches for invigorating the urban core.

Although those who entered the United States in recent decades continue to boost the economies of gateway and other cities, they, like those who came in earlier waves, tend to leave the ethnic enclave as their income rises. The 1990 Census shows dispersion rates, particularly among Asians, to be greater than those found among the foreign-born in earlier periods. New immigrants are moving to the suburbs at much faster rates than earlier arrivals. Only continued immigration can assure a steady flow of new entrepreneurs and workers to maintain vigorous urban economies.

Finally, immigrants with particular skills are needed to meet present and future shortages in the United States. Whatever the causes for the nation's inability to train enough scientific, technical, and other specialized personnel, immigrants provide the most efficient means to fill the void. Even a "crash" program aimed at America's talented youth could not by itself fully alleviate shortages during the next decade. Sadly, no one is even proposing such a program, which all but assures continued dependence on highly skilled immigrants well into the next century.

The Welcomed

Although much public attention during the 1970s and 1980s was focused on illegal entrants, it is important to remember that the vast majority of the foreign-born who came to the United States with the intention of settling entered lawfully. The "welcomed," those immigrants who came when entry was essentially unconstrained, together with the 20 million or so legal arrivals under various quota systems in effect since the 1920s, have had a profound effect on the American economy and culture.

During the nineteenth century, the primary role of immigration was to supply large numbers of predominantly unskilled and semiskilled workers to develop the nation's infrastructure and to expand its industry. Numerous highly trained individuals also came, but their entry did not follow from a deliberate policy or even preference. Except during colonial times, the nation did not explicitly select such workers. American industry sought primarily unskilled labor, anticipating that those with specialized skills would emerge from the ranks of the native-born labor force.

In the 1800s, most persons employed in factories, transportation, or trade—both native and foreign-born—had only rudimentary skills. Immigrants who came in the twentieth century were generally better trained than their predecessors. This reflects both the overall rise in education levels throughout the world and the growth in demand for skilled workers in the United States. Although immigrants seeking work could usually find it regardless of their occupation, professionals and those with mechanical training earned more and had easier access to jobs. These immigrants and their second- and third-generation offspring have been the source of considerable scientific, technical, entrepreneurial, and cultural talent.

Immigrants who come as family members of those already in the United States also provide essential labor. Nonetheless, it is in the nation's best interest to attract a higher proportion of workers that are trained in those occupations most needed by commerce and industry. The business community is justifiably worried about the qualitative decline of the American work force. The strength of Japanese production—perhaps the most dynamic to be found anywhere—lies in the high literacy and educational level of its workers compared to their counterparts in the United States—not in massive capital investment.

Economic projections point to a rising demand in the United States for more professional workers. Nonetheless there is an ongoing need for those with limited skills to provide personal services that are difficult to mechanize. Part and parcel of the high standard of living in the United States are dining out, lodging at full-service hotels, having household help when adults are employed outside the home, and enjoying other amenities that cannot be automated. In the manufacturing sector, labor-intensive industries such as apparel, leather goods, and furniture may need immigrants willing to work for modest wages to replace those obtaining other jobs. But the anticipated Mexico-U.S.

free trade agreement will further curtail the production of these goods in the United States, sharply limiting the demand for immigrant factory workers. As such, the treaty, although beneficial to some sectors, would be detrimental to these workers, who tend to be Hispanic.

Many of the adjustments taking place today in the American economy are linked to the growing importance of international trade. For many years dating back to the post–Civil War era, the economy had been essentially self-sufficient. International competition was not a major concern, as the United States primarily consumed goods manufactured within its boundaries. Because internal demand for manufactured products was rising rapidly, little thought was given to exports other than cotton, which dominated American sales abroad until the final decade of the nineteenth century and formed the backbone of the Southern economy. Collectively, sales to other nations dwindled as a share of total American output, and the importance of European capital finance declined as well. The nation's native ingenuity and its ability to attract talented individuals from abroad, combined with a favorable political climate, encouraged internal investment; this, in turn, assured that U.S. economic and technical leadership would be unchallenged in the first half of the twentieth century. Little thought was given to the use of immigration laws to further the goals of national economic development. The curtailment of immigration during the 1920s stemmed primarily from social causes. However, confidence that the nation could continue its rapid economic progress without a large number of immigrants contributed to the passage of restrictive legislation.

Today's less favorable economic environment requires a reexamination of family reunification and refugee status as the dominant criteria for permanent entry into the United States. The American technological edge is being eroded by others, and to regain our standing, new approaches to improving the quality of our human resources must be considered. The United States retains the advantage over its two main economic rivals—an economically integrated Europe across the Atlantic, and Japan on the other side of the Pacific—of its tolerance and magnetic attraction for persons with talent and ambition from all over the globe.

Both political parties place considerable emphasis on the need for (but are only willing to provide limited resources toward) improving our schools and on-the-job training. Unfortunately, these steps, even if effective, would require a decade or more to have a significant impact on productivity. In the interim, immigration remains the most pragmatic way to supplement the American work force in occupations short of dependable help.

Placing greater emphasis on the economic qualifications of potential immigrants is supported by both proponents and opponents of a more liberal entry policy, as well as by a majority in Congress. The labor economist Vernon Briggs, a strong advocate of the position that native workers are hurt by unskilled aliens, supports admissions based on occupational preference categories. Briggs argues that 50 percent of all available visas should be issued on this basis as a means to mitigate the adverse impact of immigration on those in the native population with limited skills.[17] The economist Julian Simon, a supporter of generous entry quotas, also favors a policy to admit more aliens with needed skills. Nonetheless, the 1990 Immigration Act remains focused on family reunification.

Any discussion of revised admission criteria cannot ignore refugees, since they account for about one of six immigrants to the United States. The 1980 Refugee Act for the first time established admission guidelines and separated refugee entry from the normal quota system. The president, in consultation with Congress, sets the annual number of these admissions. The courts have also clarified the basis for claiming asylum—a "well-founded fear" of persecution. The act appears to have worked smoothly, despite criticism from some quarters that its application has been ideological and (in the case of Haitians) racial. But the reality is that immigration policy cannot be separated from foreign policy or domestic politics. Large and vocal constituencies such as Cubans and Eastern Europeans are bound to influence the implementation of the Refugee Act.

A more controversial issue is how to distinguish between economic and political refugees. One inadvertent outcome of the 1986 Immigration Reform and Control Act has been a rise in the number of Central Americans applying for political asylum. Many of these would have come before as illegal aliens, but now plead repression in their native land, thereby qualifying for a temporary work permit. Some applying for entry really do face discrimination or worse because of their political beliefs or ethnicity, but improving their economic well-being underlies the decision of most to leave for the United States.

Revisions to the immigration statutes promulgated in 1990 excluded refugee issues. No doubt legislators believed that other concerns were more pressing. But as conflicts around the world continue to displace more people, Congress will be forced once again to reconsider refugee admission guidelines.

The Legislative Response

During the 1980s, several economists (including the author) pressed Congress to revise the immigration statutes. Specifically, legislators were urged to increase the number of legal immigrants admitted annually on the basis of their occupational qualifications. As the decade ended, a consensus formed that the nation was likely to face a labor shortage and therefore should attract more skilled workers from elsewhere. Nonetheless, numerous barriers remained in place because business, organized labor, and groups representing immigrant and religious associations had conflicting views on what revisions were needed. But the coalition of disparate organizations pushing for change was well aware at the end of October 1990 that, unless compromises were reached quickly, ominous prospects of higher unemployment and war in the Middle East could derail legislative action for years. The fear of recession and war pressured conference committee members to quickly settle differences between the House and Senate bills. In the waning hours of the 101st Congress, a final agreement assured passage of the 1990 Immigration Act by a wide margin.

The new law incorporates several noteworthy provisions. The most gratifying change is an increase in employment-based visas from the previous ceiling of 54,000 to 140,000 annually. Applicants with the potential to get in under employment-based criteria are now grouped into five categories. Persons with "extraordinary ability," university professors, and managers of multinational corporations form the first group, eligible for 40,000 visas. These persons do not require labor certification, and their entry can be speeded by an American sponsor. The second group, defined as persons with "exceptional ability" and advanced degrees, also receives 40,000 visas, and the same number is issued to the third group, consisting of skilled and semiskilled workers.[18] Would-be immigrants in the last two categories must follow labor certification procedures and their sponsors must provide the Department of Labor with documentation demonstrating that similar workers are unavailable in the labor market. New requirements include notification of the bargaining agent's (union) representative of the employer's request. Further, notice that the employer is seeking permission to hire one or more aliens for specified work must be posted in a conspicuous location in the workplace.

Although it represents a sharp rise from previous levels, the number of occupation-related immigrants admitted may still be insufficient, particularly during periods of economic expansion. As the average eligible household has about 2.35 persons, the new law admits only about 60,000 workers (including 4,000 semiskilled workers) annually in direct response to our labor needs. The *maximum* number allowed to enter permanently ought to be somewhat less than twice the new level, or about 100,000 each year. Further, of this total, 10,000 jobs should be allocated for less-skilled workers, who are almost totally excluded from entry under the employment-based provisions of the new law.[19] This category would include live-in child-care providers, an occupation that American workers generally shun but two-worker families with young children need. The proposed numbers are modest compared to those of some other nations. For example, Australia—with only 7 percent of the American labor force—admits 54,000 professionals each year. Canada, with a population one-tenth of ours, is now admitting up to 250,000 immigrants a year, most of them possessing skills the nation is seeking.[20]

This proposal for higher occupation-based quotas would raise annual immigration by up to 94,000 persons, but only during periods of economic expansion would it be necessary to admit so many. These numbers should not raise undue concerns that American professionals and others would have difficulty finding jobs as a result. Native workers should not be displaced owing to the stipulation that (with the exception of those with extraordinary ability) an employer must be able to demonstrate, on a case-by-case basis, that a native worker cannot be found for the position. The 1990 act already provides exceptional protection by requiring a reduction in admissions whenever there is an increase in the supply of American workers or a decline in demand in particular occupations. In particular, less-skilled alien workers could not be certified in areas where unemployment rates are high. Entry levels for immigrants requiring certification would fluctuate with the economic tides.

An additional means to encourage the flow of skilled workers is to modify admission criteria for some refugees who possess skills and abilities likely to benefit the nation economically and culturally. Refugees given priority would not receive social benefits that other refugees are entitled to, on the premise that they will be able to find jobs quickly.

Thanks to recent immigration, the ratio of those working to those retired in the United States in coming decades will be higher than in Europe or Japan. But the number of persons over the age of sixty is growing all the same and is expected to climb further. Modest increases in immigration will maintain a reasonable balance between working and retired Americans.

The Uninvited

Any serious discussion of immigration inevitably requires treatment of its most perplexing aspect—the uninvited alien. The continuous and growing presence of illegal workers and their dependents creates a dilemma for legislators, employers, and the public. Contrary to the position of its sponsors, the 1990 Act may actually spur the demand for unskilled service workers, a classification that fits the majority of illegal aliens, during periods of economic expansion. The number of visas for less-skilled workers has been limited to about 4,000 (10,000 including dependents) even as the number of highly skilled professionals allowed in rises to about 44,000. Professionals with high earnings will stimulate retail sales and services dependent on the less-skilled work force. Some, but probably not all, of the ancillary jobs stimulated by these professionals could be met by native-born workers or legal immigrants, including those admitted as "independents" or as family members.

Congress had hoped that the 1986 Immigration Act would at least slow the flow of illegal aliens to the United States, but this was questionable from the outset. Although the number of illegal aliens who have entered the United States since the mid-1980s and remained is not known, the IRCA-initiated legalization process documents the scope of illegal entry during the previous decade. About 1.8 million persons filed applications for legalization on the basis that they were in the United States illegally prior to 1982. An additional 1.3 million seasonal workers also applied for legalization. In fact, the act has not succeeded in substantially curtailing illegal entry. In 1990, when the American economy began to slow, nearly 1.2 million aliens were apprehended, a rise of more than 23 percent over the previous year, and the rate continued to climb in 1991.[21] Smuggling has, by all accounts, become more sophisticated. Therefore, apprehension levels are not a reliable measure of changes in the size of the illegal population because only a small percentage of those entering illegally are caught at the borders. No statistics are available on the number of visa abusers who come legally and remain after their entry visas expire, but their number is probably growing.

Early anecdotal evidence from employers traditionally dependent on undocumented workers suggested that the illegal alien labor pool diminished in the late 1980s, which is consistent with the reduced rate of border apprehension. Interviews with restaurant and hotel management staff and commentaries in trade publications indicated that the supply of illegal workers during this period was insufficient, resulting in critical labor shortages. The perception in the Washington, D.C., area was that fewer undocumented aliens were available to work in 1988 than two years earlier. But as the decade ended, the shortage of unskilled workers eased, at least temporarily. Although the economy slowed, curtailing jobs in construction and restaurants, undocumented aliens continued to cross the border in increasing numbers. The Department of Labor believes that most of the 1.5 million to 2 million workers shown in employer records but not reflected in household surveys are illegal aliens that entered the United States between 1982 and 1989.[22]

Employers fearing penalties may be less anxious to hire illegal aliens today than they were before 1987, but for many employers reluctance to employ undocumented workers is offset by the prospect of higher profits. The continued willingness to hire aliens is also linked to the knowledge that few employers have been fined or prosecuted for violations such as knowingly accepting fraudulent identity cards.

Within ethnic enclaves, the brisk business in falsified or stolen Social Security cards, driver licenses, and other forms of identification demonstrates that many illegal workers are purchasing needed documents on the street. Undocumented workers who are not part of the amnesty program frequently find jobs with relatives and friends within ethnic enclaves, making them extremely difficult to apprehend. Those who speak some English typically encounter few challenges in using the various forms of documentation to verify their legal status, particularly since employers are not responsible for the authenticity of identity documents. This may explain why only a few thousand illegal aliens from Taiwan, Hong Kong, and Korea applied for legalization, yet apparently substantial numbers are smuggled in and continue to work in large cities.[23]

The Immigration Reform and Control Act's primary impact has been on those undocumented aliens who are working for or seeking jobs with employers outside the ethnic enclave. Unquestionably, these workers have some difficulty finding jobs with large organizations that carefully scrutinize identity documents. In a few places, such as the Washington, D.C., metropolitan area, employers have been fined for knowingly accepting fraudulent identity cards. But these actions do not seem to have significantly deterred employers. As of mid-1989, fewer than 1,600 fines had been imposed, and a year later there were only 14 criminal prosecutions across the nation. The Immigration and Naturalization Service (INS) does not have sufficient personnel to track the millions of small businesses, as evidenced by its 2.2 sanctions staff workers per 10,000 employers in the Los Angeles area. That works out to less than ten minutes of staff time per employer per year.[24]

The evidence thus far suggests that the 1986 measure is not achieving its primary objective of permanently reducing the number of undocumented workers. The economic self-interest of both employers and workers is often stronger than the bite of the immigration laws. When the European transatlantic migration was constrained in the 1920s, entry was controlled more readily because nearly all immigrants came by ship. Air travel and lengthy national borders that cannot be fully screened for clandestine passage have severely limited the ability to control Western Hemisphere immigration.

Illegal workers came in the 1980s mostly to perform tasks most Americans were unwilling to undertake. Employers gain advantages by hiring such workers, most of whom do not receive benefits enjoyed by others, such as vacation pay or health insurance. Aliens appear more than willing to accept these conditions, for their earnings usually represent a vast improvement over what they could obtain in their country of origin. As long as employers, many of them fellow ethnics, are willing to hire these aliens, the latter will find the means to penetrate the border.

Economic arguments notwithstanding, there is concern that illegal workers continue to challenge the American legal system. Failure to enforce laws could encourage the entry of undocumented workers in numbers that would be difficult to absorb. What legislative actions, if any, can be taken in response? Congress could impose stiffer fines or longer periods of imprisonment for employers convicted of multiple violations, but courts are likely to view long prison sentences as excessive—particularly if the government cannot demonstrate significant harm to the public. Judges in Western Europe, where the hiring of undocumented workers is subject to severe penalties, are lenient and rarely impose maximum sentences on convicted employers. It is reasonable to anticipate the same response from many American courts.

The universal difficulty of controlling the use of illegal workers can be shown by their presence in other industrialized nations. Despite Israel's small population and extensive security network, the *Jerusalem Post* reports that Israeli firms in the mid-1980s illegally employed some 15,000 or more Poles, Portuguese, and other foreigners. And in ethnically homogeneous Japan, with its strict entry laws, there are more than 100,000 illegal workers. In both nations, employers seek illegal aliens to fill the least desirable jobs. In Japan, as in the United States, they work primarily in small, labor-intensive factories and fast-food operations. Because the number of illegal workers (and Japan-born Koreans) is only a small fraction of the work force, most menial jobs continue to be held by ethnic Japanese. The very presence of aliens in countries like Israel and Japan, though, demonstrates the intractability of the problem that an open, heterogeneous society such as the United States faces in attempting to keep out illegal workers.

Mandatory jail terms for all illegal aliens apprehended after a given date could be imposed, but crammed American jails would become even more overcrowded were such legislation implemented. The public could not be expected to tolerate the premature release of hardened criminals in order to accommodate illegal aliens in prisons. Build more penitentiaries? Even an accelerated rate of construction is not likely to meet the expected growth in the convict population, and the cost of maintaining prisoners is taking a large bite from government budgets. A small army of agents and prosecutors would be required to supplement the 2,000 INS agents responsible for monitoring millions of businesses. The United States finds itself in a dilemma because, compared to serious crime, the menace of drugs, and other ills afflicting the nation, the presence of illegal workers appears only a minor irritant.

As noted by Peter Schuck, "It is only a slight exaggeration to say that all policy innovations that would be politically, fiscally and administratively practicable have already been tried."[25] Nonetheless, he has an innovative idea that could place pressure on employers that hire illegal aliens and thus deter, at least modestly, illegal immigration. Schuck's approach is to mobilize private enforcement of immigration laws. IRCA already relies on such enforcement by requiring employer verification of identity cards. But he suggests a different (although compatible) enforcement mechanism—private action against an employer who violates the IRCA provisions.[26] The class of plaintiffs could be limited to those suffering competitive damage because of the employment of illegals, or it could be broadened to include anyone who knows of a violation (on the theory that society as a whole suffers damage and the plaintiff serves as a proxy for the societal interest in enforcement). The relationship of such private actions to the conventional enforcement programs of the INS would need to be clarified.

What would be the incentive to sue? If plaintiffs were limited to competitors or injured customers (as in antitrust cases), damage for lost profits might be a sufficient incentive. Were the right to sue extended to all, additional incentives might be needed, perhaps some sort of bounty of the kind authorized in old environmental statutes such as the Refuse Act of 1899. The new statute could specify a minimum recovery, in essence a civil penalty.

Opposition to private actions in response to the continuing employment of illegal workers can be anticipated from civil rights groups. Foremost, they will argue that subjecting both illegal aliens and their employers to snooping, meddling, and mean-spirited intervention by private citizens seems more appropriate to Cuba, Iraq, or other totalitarian regimes than to the United States. The proposed scheme would also encourage extensive litigation that would further congest the courts and claim scarce public resources.

Nonetheless, Schuck's innovative concept deserves consideration as an additional means to curtail employment of illegal workers. The current system is ineffective because employers are not responsible for verifying documents shown by applicants. Furthermore, if they proceed to vigorously check credentials and question prospective workers who appear by language or other characteristics to be potentially undocumented, they may be formally charged with discrimination. In the absence of stronger enforcement measures, the flow of undocumented workers will not be stemmed.

A more benign but also controversial approach would be to grant illegal aliens work permits on the basis of documentation provided by their employers. These permits (limited to those already in the United States with jobs) would be valid for a limited period of time—perhaps two years—with the possibility of renewal. The immediate families of such workers would be covered by these permits but would not be entitled to any benefits other than those required by law, such as public education. To make this program even partially effective, penalties on employers who continue to hire unregistered workers would have to be more onerous than those under the 1986 act. Congress may be amenable to severe penalties and additional funding for enforcement if illegal aliens currently holding jobs have an opportunity to work freely.

This proposal may be challenged on the grounds that it would create a "guest worker" class of persons denied access to the full benefits to which everyone else is entitled. In effect, however, the United States has already created such a class—those who were not covered by the amnesty program. Since most of the jobs performed by these clandestine workers are useful, it seems right to find a means of letting them stay on to work, if not settle. To have a million or more individuals and thousands of employers continue to violate federal laws insults the judicial system. The proposal would establish a middle ground, reducing the number of violations without granting permanent amnesty. Further, during recessionary periods, permits would not be extended for most holders.

The objection may nonetheless be raised that this proposal amounts to a backdoor amnesty. In truth, though, most illegal jobholders continue to work regardless of IRCA. Registering these individuals, and requiring that they become subject to labor standards and pay taxes, is preferable to the current situation. The additional taxes and registration fees that would be collected could more than pay for the cost of program administration. Unfortunately, political support for a worker-registration program would be nil, in part because the approach fails to deal with aliens unwilling to register or with others sure to come in the future.

Are there other means of reducing the problem? Immigration proponents who object to employer sanctions and others suggest that, to stem the flow of illegal aliens, the United States should help improve economic conditions in Mexico and other major sender nations through trade and aid.[27] Although this proposal is well-intentioned, it is naive to believe that foreign aid or trade concessions could ever be sufficient to narrow significantly the mammoth gap between this country and the third world. In economically expanding nations such as Korea and Taiwan, rising standards of living appear to be a spur rather than a deterrent to emigration—except for some U.S.-trained engineers who find high-paying jobs upon returning to their native land. These Asians continue to believe that opportunities in the United States for economic advancement surpass those in their native lands. The *maquiladora* program on the Mexican side of the border, which provides more than 400,000 Mexicans with jobs and improved economic conditions, also illustrates the futility of this approach. New job opportunities are an incentive for more aliens to cross into the United States. Most of the *maquiladora* industries are American or Japanese, and the skills gained by workers improve their chances of finding a job in this country. Raising living standards in the third world, while in desirable its own right, is the most simplistic of the ideas put forth to stem the flow of illegal aliens.

To be frank, the outlook for controlling illegal entry, is bleak, yet during periods of economic expansion the public does not appear to be greatly upset by the lack of success. But the muted response could become belligerent in the face of a deep recession. Only when large numbers of American workers believe their jobs are directly threatened by illegal aliens will Congress, frustrated by its inability to control the border, feel pressure to allocate additional resources to enforce immigration statutes.

In some respects, maintaining the status quo for now may be the best of the unpleasant alternatives. The lengthy struggle that would probably accompany any effort to substantially rewrite the 1986 act may not be worth the anguish. Passage of the 1990 Immigration Act demonstrated that proponents of liberal entry have gained strength over the last two decades. Therefore, the chances of success for substantive modifications to IRCA—unless the nation is faced with a long period of economic stagnation—are negligible. No one has demonstrated sufficient harm to the general public from the presence of these aliens to justify the extreme measures necessary to sharply curtail their employment. The weak commitment to employer sanctions can be satisfied through limited and selective enforcement typical of symbolic laws; this is preferable to adoption of defective new statutes. An annual net inflow of 150,000 to 200,000 illegal workers, particularly those without families, is not only tolerable but probably beneficial, at least for the middle class, in all but the worst of times.

The current, unstated policy of "benign neglect" toward illegal aliens poses few serious problems if annual net entry can be held to the levels of the 1970s and 1980s and the economy expands. There are, however, several scenarios that would upset the current balance between the need for less-skilled workers and the rate of illegal entry. The first is the implementation of the Mexico-U.S. free trade agreement, which could well incorporate Chile and other South American nations within a decade. After ratification, the agreement can be expected to limit the need for low-skilled immigrant workers in the U.S. manufacturing sector. Another is political and economic upheaval in Central America, the Caribbean, or other areas of the Western Hemisphere, which could create desperate conditions. Witness the situation in Haiti, where young workers are willing to risk their lives to escape to the United States. The turmoil and shortages in the former Soviet Union and Yugoslavia are creating immigration pressures on European nations that may also affect the United States.

An argument can be made that the potential for a larger influx of aliens will not be realized because immigration flows are self-adjusting. Presumably, when economic conditions in the United States are poor and job opportunities limited, fewer immigrants arrive and more already here decide to leave. Prior to the imposition of numerical restrictions, entries and departures indeed followed, more or less, the business cycle and the domestic demand for labor. Self-adjustment as a control mechanism would have continued to be effective until the 1960s and perhaps the 1970s, but it cannot govern the movement of illegal immigrants in the 1990s. The pressures to leave some countries are likely to become so great that even a lack of jobs and poor living conditions in the United States would not be a disincentive. The rising political strength of immigrant constituencies further limits legislative action. Therefore, solutions to the illegal alien dilemma will undoubtedly become more difficult in the years ahead. Were illegal entry to expand beyond the levels of the 1980s, proposals to deal with the problem would become a dominant topic of debate in both the United States and other industrialized nations.

The Quest for Balance

The case for increasing immigration of skilled workers beyond the 1990 ceiling seems highly persuasive. Still, those opposing a more liberal policy could make some reasonable arguments of their own. The vast majority of Americans, as shown in opinion polls, oppose higher immigration levels. Would not legislation to raise these levels be contrary to the will of the electorate? The geopolitical rationale for economic expansion—a critical plank in the pro-immigration platform—appears less convincing in the post-cold-war era, when the need to maintain wide-ranging military commitments is being questioned. Attention has shifted to global concerns, such as the deteriorating environment, nuclear proliferation, and narcotics—arenas where growth may be perceived as aggravating rather than solving problems.

Were more immigrants allowed, the nation might become overly dependent on them for both the least desirable, lowest-paying jobs and the most highly skilled professional positions. The use of foreign nurses and scientists could eventually dissuade young native adults from entering those professions. There is some (small) risk that, were a particular ethnic group or groups to dominate a profession, others would be discouraged by their monopolistic practices. More worrisome for many people, particularly within native minority communities, is the policy of allowing the entry of skilled nonprofessionals. Rather than attract more immigrants with needed skills, why not harness our resources to improve inner-city schools and training programs? Few would question the need for better programs to improve the skills of minority youth, but immigration policies and assistance programs each have to be weighed on their own merit. Admitting fewer skilled immigrants will not lead to more funding for the inner cities, nor would higher immigration be a deterrent to urban aid.

Possibly the most substantial and persuasive argument to be made against expanded entry is that it would benefit primarily those already comfortable while conceivably making life more difficult for those less prosperous. An influx of unskilled and semiskilled workers could provide greater competition for those Americans lacking in skills and education. A disproportionate number of these workers are black, Puerto Rican, and Mexican-American. If more immigrants were allowed, these minorities could face lower wages and higher unemployment during periods of economic downturn, when the demand for labor falls. Blacks, in particular, believe that they will have to absorb the economic cost of additional immigration.

No one suggests that such impacts are inevitable, but neither can anyone be sure that immigrants will not be given priority over native minorities when jobs are scarce. Undeniably, opportunities for native minorities in the public sector and in white-collar jobs requiring English-language skills expand with a rise in the immigrant population. However, these gains could prove short-lived as second-generation Asians and Hispanics become proficient in English and compete for government jobs. Moreover, black access to various programs geared to helping the economically disadvantaged—including assistance to small businesses—could diminish further as the nonblack minority pool expands.

More likely than the adverse direct economic consequences some native minorities fear will be the political fallout caused by ethnic changes. Blacks have been America's largest and most visible minority since the 1700s. With almost 90 percent of new immigrants non-European and mostly nonblack, blacks by the end of this century will be but one of several large minority groups. The transformation into a multiethnic society could well mean the nation will be less willing to give blacks distinct status to overcome past discrimination. Furthermore, the change in the ethnic mosaic will inevitably erode the political power of native blacks. Already in western and southwestern cities, including the two largest (Houston and Los Angeles), Hispanics and Asians are gaining political control at the expense of blacks, and this trend is likely to accelerate during the 1990s. By the year 2010, there will be more young Hispanics than blacks in the United States. Hispanic political strength will be concentrated in the rapidly growing, conservative regions of the nation. Blacks will continue to dominate in older industrial cities such as Detroit and Baltimore, but the influence of these aging urban centers on national politics will continue to dissipate. For two decades, local black elected officials have helped other blacks gain municipal jobs at both the management and lower levels. Black access to government contracts and services to minority neighborhoods also improved with the election of black mayors and city council members. A transfer of power to new groups will jeopardize these gains. Thus, political shifts can have indirect but serious repercussions that should not be ignored.

What weight should be accorded these concerns in formulating immigration policy? The research presented here (and substantiated by others) indicates that urban blacks as a group have not been hit with higher unemployment or lower income as a result of immigration. Nonetheless, the risk remains that the black underclass could be damaged economically, and perhaps even more psychologically, as the pace of immigration rises. Clearly, these matters are important, but the concept of "linkage" between immigration policy and anxiety over America's established minority populations in cities is difficult to justify. Rather, the United States should take direct and decisive action to assist minorities, be they native- or foreign-born, to compete with other groups. An essential first step is improving the quality of education. Until the nation reduces the number of functionally illiterate students coming out of ghetto schools, nothing—certainly not immigration controls—will solve the problem of minority unemployment.

Laws aimed at encouraging trained and skilled workers to migrate to the United States will find some opponents in less-developed nations. The third world may fault these laws for promoting a "brain drain" from nations in dire need of such labor. To Marxist ideologists, U.S. policies that beckon with economic inducements to the highly educated in poor countries appear as a disguised form of capitalistic exploitation that only deepens the economic division between rich and poor countries.

In response to the "brain drain" argument, the United States can demonstrate that it has consistently opposed limiting the rights of individuals to leave their place of birth. To the political scientist Alan Dowty, "there can hardly be a better test of a society's fundamental respect for human dignity" than the right to unrestricted movement.[28] Although it may, in the short run, gain from not allowing its talented citizens to emigrate, such coercive policies are not in the best long-term interest of any nation, be it well endowed or poverty-stricken. The willingness of the Soviet Union, even prior to its collapse, to moderate its exit policies at the risk of losing many of its most talented professionals demonstrates this fact.

Another group likely to view increased immigration warily is the ecology movement, which sees new residents, regardless of their abilities, as contributing to overcrowding. These fears are linked to broader (and legitimate) concerns that, if present trends continue, the world's cities will face environmental calamity. Unfortunately, worry that the globe may surpass its carrying capacity cannot be remedied by American immigration laws. Even the most liberal immigration laws would allow only a minute fraction of the globe's annual population increment to enter the United States. Yet, there has to be acknowledgment that congestion and environmental degradation are part of the price exacted by economic growth that is spurred by immigration.

For many Americans—probably a majority—the most worrisome immigration issue is not environmental, political, or even economic. The soaring numbers of foreign-born are seen foremost as a harbinger of rapid change in the nation's ethnic composition. There is fear that the amalgam of nationalities and cultures, ever growing in complexity, could fundamentally alter our long-held sense of national identity. The degree of anxiety varies, however, according to an immigrant's class and country of origin. Asians, for instance, have a generally positive image because their attitudes and values—ambition, stress on education, commercial enterprise—fit in well with the mainstream. As a result, Asians (including some Indochinese) have been absorbed quickly into middle-class, white suburban communities with a minimum of disruption. Similarly, immigrants from Europe arouse little concern. Few Americans would object to the entry of more people from, say, Ireland, France, or even the Soviet Union.

Spanish-speaking newcomers are a different matter, at least for some. Hispanic immigrants raise fears about the fate of the English language and the spread of an unassimilable culture. For these reasons, any substantial increase in entry by Hispanics should be accompanied by an expansion of programs aimed at helping them learn English. In addition, some bilingual programs may need restructuring to alleviate concerns that they could be contributing to the maintenance of a parallel language and culture. It is a good bet that the opposition to higher immigration levels expressed in public opinion polls stems primarily from fears that national identity will be eroded by a large non-English-speaking population. The public at times also appears apprehensive about the number of immigrant Muslims, whose values are seen as quite different.

To what extent economic arguments that favor immigration will once again, as in the 1920s, be overwhelmed by cultural and social concerns is not known. The emerging isolationism promoted by Pat Buchanan and a few archconservatives is manifested in such implicitly anti-immigrant slogans as "America First," last seen during the waning years of the Great Depression. Their reemergence may only be the product of frustration driven by economic woes and racial tensions. But they could also represent suppressed grass roots attitudes, as suggested by public opinion polls. Anti-immigrant sentiment appears also to be rising among some liberals, concerned that black-white tensions will be exacerbated by Hispanics and Asians seeking a stronger political and economic voice. An added worry is that these ethnic groups, less intent on being absorbed into the American mainstream than those in earlier waves, will create separate cultures at odds with cherished notions of American identity. If these views gain wider endorsement and the economy remains sluggish, America will turn inward again, entering a new cycle of isolationism. Ironically, this cycle would begin at the very time when the economy of the United States is almost fully integrated with the world economy and its popular culture a more formidable global force than ever. American immigration policies would mirror political trends, and pressure for restrictive entry measures would rise. These restrictions would be advanced in the forlorn hope that the pre-1960s cultural and demographic patterns could be restored.

Whatever the motive for the apparent rise in sentiment against non-white immigrants, those concerned with the changing ethnic composition will have to acknowledge that the demographic changes set in motion by the 1965 and 1990 immigration laws and the penetrability of the common border with Mexico are *irreversible.* The attitudes, customs, and political accommodations formed over the course of two centuries by the presence of blacks and whites are already being reshaped to fit a multiracial society. Native and new groups will tend to coalesce, a phenomenon that can be seen in the emerging distinctive culture and language of the Southwest. The sharp growth in the number of Asians in every state during the 1980s is evidence that, unlike earlier times, no area of the nation, large or small, will remain immune to ethnic changes.

The search for a way of measuring economic benefits that accrue from immigration against the costs of liberal entry policies—potential harm to low-income workers, ethnic diversity that can lead to strife, overcrowding, and the fear of losing national identity—has engaged the United States in virtually every decade since its inception. Throughout most of American history, legislators have had to weigh the arguments on behalf of, and in opposition to, liberal immigration. Economic success in the 1980s tilted the scales in favor of admitting a larger number of aliens than the United States has been willing to accept since European entry was restricted.

The 1990 legislation, with its emphasis on the admission of needed workers, began to return immigration policy to the principles of the pre-1920s era, when open admission was primarily driven by economic self-interest. Although severe limits on legal entry remain in place, the continuing (and quasi-tolerated) illegal flow responds to employer demand for less-skilled but productive workers. At this juncture, a cautionary observation bears repeating: Additional immigration cannot fully resolve expected long-term labor shortages because an enlarged work force stimulates economic growth, creating further employment opportunities. An influx of professionals with high earnings generates demand for additional service workers. Nor can foreign-born workers ever be a substitute for improving the quality of the American work force, without which the already faltering standard of living will fall even further.

Congress's recent actions to modify immigration laws do not eliminate the worrisome issues facing America in the decades ahead. Global
overpopulation and widening income disparities are creating immense
pressures at the borders of "have" nations. More draconian measures
than anyone now contemplates will be required to stem the illegal
alien tide in the next century—a tide that will surely exceed our tolerance if not our capacity to absorb. Unless birthrates in the third world
can be tempered, all developed countries, but particularly the United
States, will stagger under the pressure of illegal entry by those from poor
regions of the globe desperately searching for a means of survival and
work. Responding to this anticipated avalanche at America's entry
points without corrupting traditional freedoms will be a challenge to
both conservatives and liberals.

The United States continues to be afflicted by countless internal woes—
huge budget deficits, rising violent crime, drug addiction, corruption
in both government and industry, and an apparent faltering of national purpose. At such times of self-doubt, Americans can take solace in
their past, remembering that the United States forged the first modern nation, one where power is not vested in the state but in individual
freedom. Over two centuries, as revolution and strife raced across the
globe, the United States not only thrived but saw its basic tenets
echoed across the seas. And at no time has the appeal of these principles been more universal than now. The American vision of freedom
and private enterprise, not the hollow doctrines of state power and
centralized economies, has raced across Eastern Europe and the
Russian heartland.

Much of America's economic and moral strength can be traced to its
visionary founders, who wisely encouraged immigration. The response
to open its borders was unprecedented, as millions eagerly sought entry. Today the clamor at the nation's gates is ever louder and, to some,
more ominous. But the clamor should be a cause of pride, not anxiety;
a sign of vigor, not an omen of decline.

The ongoing quest to balance the economic, political, and social
consequences of immigration has no end. The United States will certainly remain a magnet to those seeking new opportunities, advancement, or a place of refuge. Immigration laws that tap their youth and
ambition without creating internal dissension will harness the human
resources America needs to sustain its vitality into the third millennium.

Notes

Chapter 2

1. Samuel Smiles, *The Huguenots: Their Settlements, Churches and Industries in England and Ireland* (1868; reprint, Baltimore: Genealogical Publishing, 1972), pp. 102–3.

2. For a discussion of forces and events that shaped the economic growth of England and other Western nations, see Douglass C. North and Robert P. Thomas, *The Rise of the Western World: A New Economic History* (Cambridge: Cambridge University Press, 1973).

3. Caroline Robbins, "A Note on General Naturalization under the Later Stuarts and a Speech in the House of Commons on the Subject in 1664," *Journal of Modern History* 34, no. 2 (June 1962): 177.

4. *Cobbett's Parliamentary History of England,* vol. 6 (London: R. Bagshaw, 1810), p. 781.

5. Maldwyn A. Jones, *American Immigration* (Chicago: University of Chicago Press, 1961), p. 14. Early Irish immigration to the United States is discussed in Francis G. James, *Ireland in the Empire* (Cambridge, Mass.: Harvard University Press, 1973).

6. For a discussion of differences between statutes governing entry and citizenship in Britain and its American colonies, see James H. Kettner, *The Development of American Citizenship, 1608–1870* (Chapel Hill, N.C.: University of North Carolina Press, 1978).

7. In discussing the prosperity of new Western Hemisphere colonies, Smith notes that much of the development was attributable to groups forced to leave their homeland, including Puritans, Catholics, and Quakers. He also notes that Portuguese Jews who were banished to Brazil proceeded to establish order and industry in that colony, introducing the cultivation of sugarcane and other products. Adam Smith, *The Wealth of Nations,* Modern Library edition (New York: Random House, 1937), p. 555.

8. Early German immigration to the colonies is discussed in Walter A. Knittle, *Early Eighteenth Century Palatine Emigration* (Philadelphia: Dorrance and Co., 1937).

9. Ray Allen Billington, *The Protestant Crusade, 1800–1860* (New York: Macmillan, 1938).

10. Emerson Edward Proper, *Colonial Immigration Laws* (New York: AMS Press, 1967).

11. Adam Smith shows that the wage level for both skilled and unskilled workers in the American colonies exceeded those in England, while the prices of American goods were lower. Smith, *Wealth of Nations,* pp. 69–70.

12. George Washington, "To the Members of the Volunteer Association and Other Inhabitants of the Kingdom of Ireland Who Have Lately Arrived in the City of New York," in *The Writings of George Washington,* vol. 27, ed. John C. Fitzpatrick (Washington, D.C.: Government Printing Office, September 1938), pp. 253–54.

13. "Letter to Thomas Jefferson, January 1, 1788," in ibid., vol. 29 (January 1939), pp. 348–51.

14. Thomas Jefferson, "Notes on the State of Virginia, 1781," in *The Portable Thomas Jefferson,* ed. Merrill D. Peterson (New York: Penguin Books, 1980), pp. 122–28.

15. James Madison, speaking before the Constitutional Convention, 1787, quoted in *Economic Aspects of Immigration* (New York: National Committee on Immigration Policy, 1947), p. 22.

16. Alexis C. de Tocqueville, quoted in Adna Ferrin Weber, *The Growth of Cities in the Nineteenth Century: A Study in Statistics,* vol. 11 (New York: Macmillan, 1899), p. 431.

17. Henry Duhring, "Immigration," *North American Review* 40 (April 1835): 459.

18. Bert James Loewenberg, "Efforts of the South to Encourage Immigration, 1865–1900," *South Atlantic Quarterly* 33 (1934): 365–67. Activities to promote emigration to the United States are also documented in Charlotte Erickson, *American Industry and the European Immigrant, 1860–1885* (Cambridge, Mass.: Harvard University Press, 1957).

19. Henry George, as cited in Alexander Saxton, *The Indispensable Enemy* (Berkeley and Los Angeles: University of California Press, 1971), pp. 100–104. The book focuses on the role of California labor in arousing anti-Chinese passions. For a broader discussion of immigration from a prolabor perspective, see Kitty Calavita, *U.S. Immigration Law and the Control of Labor: 1820–1924* (London: Academic Press, Inc., 1984).

20. Among the numerous studies of the Chinese and Japanese during this period are a group of essays on the subject in *Anti-Chinese Violence in North America,* ed. Roger Daniels (New York: Arno Press, 1978). See also Roger Daniels, *The Politics of Prejudice* (Berkeley, Calif.: University of California Press, 1962), for an analysis of the anti-Japanese movement in California. The

views of labor, employers, and religious groups on the Chinese and Japanese issue in the broader context of racism are discussed in Roger Daniels and Harry H. Kitano, *American Racism: Exploration of the Nature of Prejudice* (Englewood Cliffs, N.J.: Prentice-Hall, 1970).

21. Barbara M. Solomon, *Ancestors and Immigrants: A Changing New England Tradition* (Cambridge, Mass.: Harvard University Press, 1956).

22. For an analysis of causes leading to the formation and decline of the American Protective Association, see Donald L. Kinzer, *An Episode in Anti-Catholicism* (Seattle: University of Washington Press, 1964).

23. President Grover Cleveland, message to Congress, U.S. House of Representatives, H.Rept. 3021, 55th Cong., 1st sess., March 2, 1887, part 2, p. 5.

24. Issues related to how immigration was perceived in the South have received less attention than in other regions. One of the best articles on the subject is by Rowland T. Berthoff, "Southern Attitudes toward Immigration, 1865–1914," *Journal of Southern History* 17, no. 3 (August 1951): 328–60.

25. John Higham, *Strangers in the Land* (Westport, Conn.: Greenwood Press, 1981). pp. 167–68.

26. Decades later, when eugenicists were asked to explain why these "genetically superior" settlers did not progress, they asserted that their lack of advancement was due to their background—the early settlers were descendants of criminals and servants ousted from Britain.

27. Robert DeCourcy Ward, "Immigration and the South," *Atlantic*, November 1905, p. 614.

28. The response of the black community to an increase in immigration to the South is described in Arnold Shankman, *Ambivalent Friends* (Westport, Conn.: Greenwood Press, 1982), pp. 158–60.

29. Florette Henri, *Black Migration: Movement North 1900–1920* (New York: Doubleday, 1975), p. 148.

30. Opposition to immigration restrictions by business and other groups in examined in Henry Beardsell Leonard, *The Open Gates* (New York: Arno Press, 1980).

31. Andrew Carnegie, "Gompers Cries for Less Immigration," *New York Times*, December 8, 1905.

32. Ibid.

33. Samuel Eliot Morison, *The Oxford History of the American People*, vol. 3 (New York: New American Library, 1971), pp. 234–37.

34. For a historical perspective on eugenics and its influence on American thought, see Mark H. Haller, *Eugenics: Hereditarian Attitudes in American Thought* (New Brunswick, N.J.: Rutgers University Press, 1963). A newer, more readable account of the movement is found in Daniel J. Kevles, *In the Name of Eugenics* (New York: Alfred A. Knopf, 1985).

35. Most Progressives in the East, Midwest, and West shared similar racial views. Middle-class Progressives in California believed that races could not mix, and therefore ardently supported anti-Japanese legislation. See Roger Daniels, *The Politics of Prejudice* (Berkeley, Calif.: University of California Press, 1962).

In the South, notes Higham (*Strangers in the Land*, p. 175), progressivism and nativism joined hands after 1905.

36. Edwin Grant Conklin, *Heredity and Environment in the Development of Men*, 5th ed. (Princeton, N.J.: Princeton University Press, 1923), p. 302.

37. John R. Commons, *Races and Immigrants in America* (New York: Macmillan, 1907), pp. 160–77.

38. William Z. Ripley, "Census Figures Disclose Grave Racial Problem," *New York Times*, June 22, 1913, p. 14.

39. Edward A. Ross, *The Old World in the New* (New York: Century Company, 1914), pp. 238–41.

40. Robert F, Foerster, *The Racial Problems Involved in Immigration from Latin America and the West Indies to the United States* (Washington, D.C.: Government Printing Office, 1925), p. 57. Foerster correctly observed that the increase in Mexican immigration during the 1920s was attributable to constraints imposed on the entry of European workers during the decade. He concluded that even the "best" Indian or Negro strains did not approach the white stock and were not fit for self-government, hence his recommendation to exclude entrants from south of the Rio Grande.

41. Haller, *Eugenics*, p. 84.

42. For a discussion of media views, see Rita J. Simon, *Public Opinion and the Immigrant: Print Media Coverage, 1880–1980* (Lexington, Mass.: Lexington Books, 1985).

43. Kevles, *In the Name of Eugenics*, p. 97.

44. Statement of J. H. Friedel, National Industrial Conference Board, in U.S. Congress, House, *Restriction of Immigration: Hearings before the Committee on Immigration and Naturalization*, 68th Cong., 1st sess., December 27, 1923.

45. Actual admissions from these countries were higher because some came to join their spouses or were exempt from the quota. Nontheless, the total of arrivals was only a fraction of the earlier flow. The House of Representatives debate on quotas was lengthy. See *Congressional Record*, April 1–14, 1924, part 6, pp. H5825–6257.

46. Statement of Senator Albert Johnson, in U.S. Congress, Senate, *Hearing before the Committee on Immigration to the United States*, 66th Cong., 3d sess., 1921. At these hearings, numerous organizations, such as the Texas Chamber of Commerce and the Texas Cotton Growers Association, testified that Mexican labor was essential, because Americans were not willing to perform agricultural work.

47. David M. Chalmers, *Hooded Americanism: The First Century of the Ku Klux Klan, 1865–1965* (New York: Doubleday, 1965).

48. Robert Divine, *American Immigration Policy, 1924–1952* (New Haven: Yale University Press, 1957).

49. David S. Wyman, *Paper Walls: America and the Refugee Crisis, 1938–1941* (Amherst, Mass.: University of Massachusetts Press, 1968). Wyman discusses efforts to counter antirefugee sentiment that failed to overcome the strong nativist and racial prejudice.

50. John F. Kennedy, *A Nation of Immigrants* (New York: Harper & Row, 1958).

51. Statement of Allen Ellender (D.-La.), *Congressional Record,* September 22, 1965, p. S24772.

52. The practice of Asians coming to American universities has a long history. The first Japanese to enter this country came as students, and in a few years their total exceeded all other Japanese in schools overseas.

53. For a discussion of the Bracero Program in the context of the Southwest's economic development, see Niles Hansen, *The Border Economy* (Austin: University of Texas Press, 1981).

54. Statement of Barney Frank (D.-Mass.), *Congressional Record,* June 13, 1984, p. H5726.

55. "People Protectionism," editorial, *Wall Street Journal,* June 11, 1984, p. 24; "In Praise of Huddled Masses," editorial, *Wall Street Journal,* July 3, 1984, p. 24; Ronald C. Nairn, "We Need Not Fear Refugees," *Wall Street Journal,* July 6, 1984, p. 14.

56. "Statement of the Chamber of Commerce of the United States," by Robert T. Thompson, (vice-chairman), in U.S. Congress, *Immigration Reform and Control Act of 1982: Joint Hearings,* 97th Cong., 2d sess., 1982, p. 502.

57. Lane Kirkland, testimony in ibid., p. 410.

58. Althea Simmons in ibid., pp. 286–91.

59. Statement of Stan Lundine (D.-N.Y.), *Congressional Record,* June 11, 1984, p. H5537.

60. Statement of Kent R. Hance (R.-Fla.), *Congressional Record,* June 19, 1984, p. H6052.

61. C. M. Goethe, "Immigration from Mexico," in *The Alien in Our Midst,* ed. Madison Grant and Charles Stewart Davison (New York: Galton Publishing, 1930), p. 137.

62. Statement of Jack F. Kemp (R.-N.Y.), *Congressional Record,* June 20, 1984, p. H6117.

63. Testimony of Thomas Muller, in U.S. Congress, House, Committee on the Judiciary, Subcommittee on Immigration, Refugees and International Law, "The Costs of Legalization," 99th Cong., 1st sess., September 11, 1985.

64. Statement of Edward Kennedy (D.-Mass.), *Congressional Record,* March 14, 1988, p. S2120.

65. Statement of Dale L. Bumpers (D.-Ark.), *Congressional Record,* March 14, 1988, p. S2128.

66. Thomas Muller, "Immigration Policy and Economic Growth," *Yale Law and Policy Review* 7, no.1 (1989): 101–36.

67. Statement of Allan Simpson (R.-Wyo.), *Congressional Record,* July 12, 1989, p. S7787.

68. For a detailed description of the bill, see U.S. Congress, House, Committee on the Judiciary, *Report on Family Unity and Employment Opportunity Act of 1990,* H.Rept. 101-723, 101st Cong., 2d sess., September 19, 1990. The number

188,000 includes dependents of skilled workers. A total of 75,000 such workers were to be admitted; the balance were spouses and children of these workers.

69. Statement of George Gekas (R.-Pa.), *Congressional Record*, October 2, 1990, p. H8643.

70. Statement of John Bryant (D.-Tex.), *Congressional Record*, October 3, 1990, p. H8717.

71. For a brief discussion of changes to House and Senate bills, see "Joint Explanatory Statement of the Committee Conference," *Congressional Record*, October 26, 1990, pp. H13235–40.

Chapter 3

1. James Madison, speaking before the Constitutional Convention, 1787, quoted in *Economic Aspects of Immigration* (New York: National Committee on Immigration Policy, 1947), p. 22.

2. Simon Kuznets, *Growth, Population, and Income Distribution: Selected Essays* (New York: W. W. Norton, 1979), pp. 1–15.

3. Douglass C. North, *The Economic Growth of the United States, 1790–1860* (Englewood Cliffs, N.J.: Prentice-Hall, 1961), pp. 206–7.

4. Oscar Handlin, *Boston's Immigrants, 1790–1865* (Cambridge, Mass.: Harvard University Press, 1959).

5. The strong links between industry and immigrant labor are shown in Charlotte Erickson, *American Industry and the European Immigrant, 1860–1885* (Cambridge, Mass.: Harvard University Press, 1957), p. 4.

6. Julius Isaac, *Economics of Migration* (New York: Oxford University Press, 1947).

7. Brinley Thomas, *Migration and Economic Growth*, 2d ed. (New York: Cambridge University Press, 1973), p. 174.

8. Arcadius Kahan, "Economic Opportunities and Some Pilgrims' Progress: Jewish Immigrants from Eastern Europe in the U.S., 1890–1914," *Journal of Economic History* 38, no. 1 (March 1978): 235–51.

9. Ethnic discrimination in smaller communities is explored in Joan U. Hannon, "City Size and Ethnic Discrimination: Michigan Agricultural Implements and Iron Work Industries," *Journal of Economic History* 42, no. 4 (December 1982): 825–45.

10. Maldwyn A. Jones, *American Immigration* (Chicago: University of Chicago Press, 1960), p. 14.

11. Emma Brace, *The Life of Charles Brace* (New York: Scribner's, 1894), p. 240.

12. Kuznets, *Growth, Population, and Income Distribution*, p. 6. More generally, Kuznets states that the American economy could operate with a wider range of choices in those parts of the nation to which immigration flowed freely and in significant numbers.

13. Robert L. Brandfon, "The End of Immigration to the Cotton Fields," *Mississippi Valley Historical Review* 50, no. 4 (March 1964): 591.

14. Blaine A. Brownell and David R. Goldfield, eds. *The City in Southern History: The Growth of Urban Civilization in the South* (New York: Kennikat Press, 1976).

15. Will J. French et al., *Mexicans in California: Report of the Mexican Fact Finding Committee of the Governor of California*, Sacramento, September 1930. The 1930 Census enumerated 1.6 million Mexicans in the United States. The history of immigration in the Southwest is documented in Lawrence A. Cardoso, *Mexican Emigration to the United States, 1897–1931* (Tucson: University of Arizona Press, 1980).

16. For an early work documenting the Japanese presence in western cities, see Yamato Ichihashi, *Japanese in the United States* (Stanford, Calif.: Stanford University Press, 1932), pp. 100–101. As noted by Ichihashi, despite the fears of a "yellow peril," the proportion of Japanese in California cities was always low. Only 1 percent of San Francisco's and 2 percent of Los Angeles's population were Japanese in 1930.

17. J. G. Williamson, "American Prices and Urban Inequality since 1820," *Journal of Economic History* 36, no. 2 (June 1976): 303.

18. Peter J. Hill, *The Economic Impact of Immigration into the United States* (New York: Arno Press, 1975), pp. 41–43.

19. U. S. Department of Commerce, Bureau of the Census, "Color and Nativity of Gainful Workers," *1930 Census of Population* (Washington, D. C.: Government Printing Office, 1932), Table 13, p. 25.

20. The entrepreneurial skills of the Japanese is evidenced by the 157 Japanese-owned enterprises and offices in the city of Stockton, California, in 1929. As the total number of Japanese in the city was only 1,386, two out three Japanese heads of household were self-employed. See Ichihashi, *Japanese in the United States*, pp. 126–27.

21. Larry Neal and Paul Uselding, "Immigration, a Neglected Source of American Economic Growth: 1790–1912," *Oxford Economic Papers* 24 (1972): 68–88. The range of ideas shown is attributable to differences in the rate of compounding capital formed in the previous decade; a 6 percent rate, considered by the authors to be the most realistic, results in the 42 percent contribution.

22. Jeffrey G. Williamson and Peter H. Lindert, *American Inequality: A Macroeconomic History* (New York: Academic Press, 1980), p. 52.

23. Jonathan H. Turner and Charles E. Starnes, *Inequality: Privilege and Poverty in America* (Pacific Palisades, Calif.: Goodyear, 1976).

24. Lee Soltow, *Men and Wealth in the United States, 1850–1870* (New Haven: Yale University Press, 1975), p. 149.

25. Paul McGouldrick and Michael B. Tannen, "Did American Manufacturers Discriminate against Immigrants before 1914?" *Journal of Economic History* 37, no. 3 (September, 1977): 723–47.

26. Robert Higgs, "Race, Skill and Earnings: American Immigrants in 1909," *Journal of Economic History* 31, no. 2 (June 1971): 420–28.

27. Frederick Douglass, 1853, quoted in B. Schrieke, *Alien Americans* (New York: Viking Press, 1936), p. 122. Douglass is quoted on the same page as saying

that "a few years ago a white barber would have been a curiosity. Now their poles stand on every street [in the North]."

28. James Dawson Burn, quoted in Robert Ernst, *Immigrant Life in New York City, 1825–1863* (New York: King's Crown Press, 1949), p. 104. Ernst observes that race prejudice gave the Irish an advantage over the blacks and enabled them to advance to better-paying jobs.

29. For a somewhat dour view of how the nation treated blacks and other minorities during this period, see Benjamin B. Ringer, *'We the People' and Others* (New York: Tavistock Publications, 1986).

30. Black attitudes toward immigration prior to the Civil War are the subject of Jay Rubin, "Black Nativism: The European Immigrant in Negro Thought, 1830–1860," *Phylon* 39, no. 3 (Fall 1978): 193–202.

31. Information about several reported attacks that first aroused the Polish community in 1893 came from the Polish press. The *Chicago Tribune* and the *New York Times* noted the violence but did not identify the ethnic background of the workers involved. For a discussion of Polish perspectives on animosity toward blacks, see Thaddeus Radzialowski, "The Competition for Jobs and Racial Stereotypes: Poles and Blacks in Chicago," *Polish American Studies* 33, no. 2 (Autumn 1976): 5–18.

32. Arnold Shankman, "This Menacing Influx: Afro-Americans on Italian Immigration to the South, 1880–1915," *Mississippi Quarterly* (Mississippi State University) 31, no. 1 (Winter 1977–78): 67–88. Booker T. Washington traveled to numerous European lands, including Sicily, in 1910 and observed that "the condition of the coloured farmer in the most backward parts of the Southern States in America . . . is incomparably better than the condition and opportunities of the agricultural population in Sicily." See *The Man Farthest Down: A Record of Observation and Study in Europe* (Garden City, N.Y.: Doubleday, Page and Company, 1912), pp. 262–64. For the perspective of southern whites on Italian immigration to the region, see Brandfon, "The End of Immigration to the Cotton Fields."

33. Bureau of the Census, "Color and Nativity of Gainful Workers." By 1930, 2.4 percent of all black, 4.5 percent of all foreign-born, and 7.7 percent of all native-born workers were classified by the census as professionals. Most black professionals in cities and elsewhere were clergymen and teachers.

34. Patrick Renshaw, "The Black Ghetto, 1890–1940," *American Studies* 8, no. 1 (1959): 41–59. Several reasons given by Renshaw for the failure of black businesses in the 1920s and 1930s are their small scale and limited selection of goods, the low purchasing power of black consumers, and white prejudice, which denied blacks good locations for their stores.

35. Oscar Handlin, *The Uprooted* (New York: Grosset and Dunlap, 1951), p. 293. In this moving account of the immigrant experience, Handlin argued that because immigrants were at the bottom, their presence allowed native-born groups upward mobility. Their absence, he believed, would therefore reduce opportunities for the nonimmigrant population. Handlin also anticipated

greater income inequality resulting from reduced economic mobility and lower economic growth in the absence of free immigration. Immigrants from the Western Hemisphere, he perceived correctly, would replace those from Europe. But Handlin did not anticipate the magnitude of the Hispanic flow.

36. The estimate of 2.9–3.0 million additional aliens is based on the total net immigration from Southern and Eastern Europe between 1900 and 1914, excluding the period after the Bolshevik Revolution, as few persons could emigrate from the USSR between 1920 and 1924, and practically none after 1925. The average net inflow between 1901 and 1914 is compared to the actual net inflow from 1925 to 1929. One study estimated a "surplus" (individuals with no job prospects, given their skills) of 35 million persons in the two European regions in 1920. The additional inflow would represent less than 10 percent of the surplus. See Wilbert E. Moore, *Economic Demography of Eastern and Southern Europe* (New York: Arno Press, 1962), p. 63.

37. For an analysis of construction cycles, see Moses Abramovitz, *Evidence of Long Savings in Aggregate Construction since the Civil War* (New York: Columbia University Press, 1964).

38. Thomas, *Migration and Economic Growth*, p. 201.

39. Cited in Edward C. Banfield, *The Unheavenly City* (Boston: Little, Brown, 1968), pp. 30–31.

40. Alan Dowty, *Closed Borders: The Contemporary Assault on Freedom of Movement* (New Haven: Yale University Press, 1987). This book was also sponsored by The Twentieth Century Fund.

41. Laura Fermi, *Illustrious Immigrants: The Intellectual Migration from Europe, 1930–41* (Chicago: University of Chicago Press, 1968). Fermi noted that the ranks of mathematicians, physicians, biologists, and economists in American universities and research centers were particularly enriched by their entry.

42. "The Dispossessed," *Fortune*, February 1940, pp. 94–126. Southern states insisted on wage differentials between the private sector and WPA workers to prevent wages from escalating. Some also believed that high WPA wages would discourage blacks from leaving for the northern states.

Chapter 4

1. *Report of the President's Commission on Immigration and Naturalization* (Washington, D.C.: Government Printing Office, January 1, 1953), p. 26.

2. Miami, with its heavy Latin orientation, tends to be less of an international, polyglot city than New York, Los Angeles, or San Francisco; nonetheless, given its status as the dominant entry point into the United States for Latin Americans, and its majority Hispanic population, the city qualifies as a full-fledged gateway.

3. John Friedmann, "The World City Hypothesis," *Development and Change* 17, no. 1 (January 1986): 69–83.

4. Sassen-Koob also identifies "global cities" and considers New York and Los Angeles to be the foremost of these cities. Her position is that such cities,

in particular, require large numbers of low-wage jobs and contribute to the expansion of an underclass. Sassen-Koob argues further that the "expulsion of middle-income jobs" is especially pronounced in global cities. See Saskia Sassen-Koob, "The New Labor Demand in Global Cities," in *Cities in Transformation: Class, Capital and the State*, ed. Michael P. Smith (Beverly Hills, Calif.: Sage Publications, 1984), pp. 139–69

5. The concentration of population in large urban centers does entail substantial social and environmental costs. However, it is unrelated to international activity or the creation of low-wage service jobs catering to this activity. Mexico City, Shanghai, and other populous cities that lack the level of commercial activity seen in New York or Hong Kong have more serious economic, social, and environmental problems.

6. This decline assumes that there is no relationship between the immigrant inflow to and the middle-class outmigration from cities. Although no data are available that indicate a linkage, there is anecdotal evidence that the movement of both middle-class whites and blacks from the three gateway inner cities has accelerated because of rising housing costs, crowding, and preference not to live in neighborhoods that have become predominantly immigrant.

7. Richard D. Alba and Michael J. Batusis, *The Impact of Migration on New York State*, a report for the Public Policy Institute and the Job Training Partnership Council by the Center for Social and Demographic Analysis, State University of New York, Albany, 1984.

8. Net outmigration from San Francisco accelerated from 19,100 in 1960–65 to 43,082 in 1970–75, slowing to 22,610 in the 1975–80 period. The slowdown and consequent change in direction in the 1980s can be attributed primarily to the Asian influx and the entry of nearly 30,000 Southeast Asian refugees. For discussion, see *Migration Patterns in the San Francisco Bay Area*, Association of Bay Area Governments, Oakland, November 1987.

9. John K. Hill and James E. Pearce, "Enforcing Sanctions against Employers of Illegal Aliens," *Economic Review*, Dallas Federal Reserve Bank, May 1987, pp. 1–15.

10. D. Runsten, "Mexican Immigrants and the California-Mexico Shoe Industry," draft report prepared for the Project on Mexican Immigrants in the California Economy, Center for U.S.-Mexican Studies, University of California, San Diego, La Jolla, January, 1986.

11. Hill and Pearce, "Enforcing Sanctions against Employers of Illegal Aliens."

12. Benjamin Mark Cole, "Abundance of Space, Cheap Labor Pool Boost Local Manufacturing Employment," *Los Angeles Business Journal*, December 1, 1986, p. 8.

13. Sheldon L. Maram, Stuart Long, and Dennis Berg, "Hispanic Workers in the Garment and Restaurant Industries in Los Angeles County," report no. 12, Center for U.S.-Mexican Studies, University of California, San Diego, La Jolla, October 1980.

14. Productivity gains in men's and boys' suits, the one sector of the apparel industry for which annual productivity data are collected, averaged 2.3

percent per annum between 1984 and 1989, a respectable rate of growth. Household furniture industry statistics indicated an annual productivity rise of 1.4 percent for the same five-year period. See U. S. Department of Labor, Bureau of Labor Statistics, *Productivity Measures for Selected Industries and Government Services*, BLS Bulletin 2379, May 1991.

15. Hill and Pearce, "Enforcing Sanctions against Employers of Illegal Aliens."

16. National Research Council, *Foreign and Foreign-Born Engineers in the United States* (Washington, D. C.: National Academy Press, 1988), p. 2.

17. National Science Board, *Science Indicators: The 1985 Report*, NSB 85-1 (Washington, D. C.: Government Printing Office, 1985).

18. Ellen Sehgal, "Foreign-Born Workers in the U.S. Labor Market: The Results of a Special Survey," *Monthly Labor Review* 108, no. 7 (July 1985): 18–24.

19. C. Wright Mills, *White Collar* (New York: Oxford University Press, 1951).

20. "Street Peddlers from Senegal Flock to New York," *New York Times*, November 10, 1985, p. 52.

21. *Wall Street Journal*, February 18, 1988.

22. Ivan Light, "Immigrant Entrepreneurs in America: Koreans in Los Angeles," in *Clamor at the Gates: The New American Immigration*, ed. Nathan Glazer (San Francisco: Institute for Contemporary Studies Press, 1985), pp. 161–80.

23. The current distribution of Cubans and other Hispanics is so extensive that it may be more meaningful to describe the "Anglo" enclave within the residential neighborhoods of Miami.

24. Jon Nordheimer, "Nicaraguan Exiles Find a Place in the Sun: Miami," *New York Times*, July 29, 1987.

25. Joel Garreau, "For Koreans, 'Keh' is Key to Success," *Washington Post*, November 3, 1991, p. B-1.

26. For a discussion of Asian entrepreneurs in New York City, see Illsoo Kim, "The Koreans: Small Business in an Urban Frontier," in *New Immigrants in New York*, ed. Nancy Foner (New York: Columbia University Press, 1987), pp. 219–42.

27. Pyong Gap Min and Charles Jaret, "Ethnic Business Success: The Case of Korean Small Business in Atlanta," *Sociology and Social Research* 69, no. 3 (1985): 412–35.

28. Suvarna Thaker, "The Quality of Life of Asian Indian Women in the Motel Industry," *South Asia Bulletin* 2, no. 1 (Spring 1982): 68.

29. U.S. Department of Commerce, Bureau of the Census, "Minority-Owned Businesses: Asian Americans, American Indians, and Other Minorities," MB 87-3, *1987 Survey of Minority-Owned Business Enterprises*, June 1991.

30. Charles Waller, "Union Bank Moves from British to Japanese," *American Banker*, February 22, 1988, pp. 11–14.

31. Carl Sears and Robert Hawkins, "Foreign Firms in New York: A Survey," Occasional Papers in Metropolitan Business and Finance, New York University Graduate School of Business Administration, New York, 1979.

32. James O'Brien, "Coldwell Banker National Survey of International Investment Ownership of Major Office Buildings in 19 Largest United States

Downtown Office Markets," *Coldwell Banker Commercial Real Estate Services Report,* Boston, 1987.

33. Joel Kotkin, "The New Yankee Traders," *Inc.,* March 1986, p. 25.

34. U. S. Department of Labor, Bureau of Labor Statistics, *Geographic Profile of Employment and Unemployment 1991,* BLS Bulletin 2410, August 1992. In 1989, blacks held about 20 percent of all professional jobs and Hispanics (who make up 62 percent of school enrollment) only 12 percent of these jobs in Los Angeles schools. See Los Angeles Unified School District, *Ethnic Survey Report: Fall 1989,* publication no. 111, Los Angeles, Janaury 1990

35. *Congressional Record,* May 19, 1896, p. H5423.

36. Robert H. Topel, "The Impact of Immigration on the Labor Market" (mimeo), University of Chicago and National Bureau of Economic Research, Cambridge, Mass., January 1988.

37. Testimony of Frank D. Bean, in U.S. Congress, Joint Economic Committee, Subcommittee on Economic Resources, Competitiveness, and Security Economics, "Impact of Undocumented Mexican Immigration on the Earnings of Other Groups in Metropolitan Labor Markets in the United States," 99th Cong., 2d sess., May 29, 1986. A more recent analysis concludes that an inflow of Asian immigrants raises the wages of Hispanics but lowers the wages of other Asians. An inflow of Mexican immigrants reduces the wages of Mexican-Americans but raises the wages of Asians as well as professional workers. See Francisco L. Rivera-Batiz and Selig L. Sechzer, "Substitution and Complementarity between Immigrant and Native Labor in the United States," in *U. S. Immigration Policy Reform in the 1980s: A Preliminary Assessment,* ed. Francisco L. Rivera-Batiz et al. (New York: Praeger Publishers, 1991).

38. Thomas Muller and Thomas J. Espenshade, *The Fourth Wave: California's Newest Immigrants* (Washington, D.C.: Urban Institute Press, 1985).

39. U.S. Department of Commerce, Bureau of Economic Analysis, *Local Area Personal Income, 1984–1989: Southern Region,* vol. 4, July 1991.

40. "A Telephone Survey of Public Attitudes toward Immigration and Related Issues among California Adults" (mimeo), survey prepared for the Urban Institute by Field Research Corporation, San Francisco, June 1983.

41. Ron Grossman, "Boat People Create Comeback for Realty on Argyle Street," *Chicago Tribune,* April 19, 1985.

42. Jay Matthews, "American Journal: West Coast School Riding High with Offspring of Recent Wave of Asian Immigrants," *Washington Post,* May 21, 1988, p. A-3.

43. Dana Priest, "Schools Bring New World Home to Foreigners," *Washington Post,* December 14, 1987, p. A-1.

44. Nathan Caplan, Marcella H. Choy, and John K. Whitmore, "Indochinese Refugee Families and Academic Achievement," *Scientific American,* February 1992, pp. 35–42.

45. National Research Council, *Foreign and Foreign-Born Engineers in the United States.*

46. *Washington Post,* November 14, 1985.

47. Elizabeth Bogen, *Immigration in New York* (New York: Praeger Publishers, 1987).

Chapter 5

1. Sir John Holland, May 4, 1664, quoted in Caroline Robbins, "A Note on General Naturalization under the Later Stuarts and a Speech in the House of Commons on the Subject in 1664," *Journal of Modern History* 34, no. 2 (June 1962): 177.

2. Richard D. Lamm and Gary Imhoff, *The Immigration Time Bomb: The Fragmenting of America* (New York: Truman Talley Books/E. P. Dutton, 1985).

3. Jack Rosenthal, "A Flood outside Our Door," *New York Times,* January 5, 1986; and Hendrik Hertzberg, "Lamm's Tales from Colorado," *Washington Post,* Book World section, January 5, 1986, p. 1.

4. In May 1992, the organization also cited global population growth as an argument for slowing immigration. See *Los Angeles Times,* "Most Favor U.S. Immigration Freeze, Poll Says," May 22, 1992.

5. Vernon M. Briggs, Jr., *Immigration Policy and the American Labor Force* (Baltimore: Johns Hopkins University Press, 1984), p. 164.

6. Rita J. Simon, *Public Opinion and the Immigrant: Print Media Coverage, 1880–1980* (Lexington, Mass.: D. C. Heath, 1985), p. 33.

7. Ibid., p. 36.

8. George H. Gallup, *The Gallup Poll: Public Opinion, 1935–1971,* vol. 1 (New York: Random House, 1972), pp. 229–30.

9. Thomas Muller and Thomas J. Espenshade, *The Fourth Wave: California's Newest Immigrants* (Washington, D.C.: Urban Institute Press, 1985); and Kevin F. McCarthy and R. Burciaga Valdez, "Current and Future Effects of Mexican Immigration in California: Executive Summary," report no. R-3365/1-CR, Rand Corporation, Santa Monica, Calif., November 1985.

10. Chris Spolar, "New Working Class in the Making," *Washington Post,* December 15, 1987, p. A-1.

11. "A Telephone Survey of Public Attitudes toward Immigration and Related Issues among California Adults" (mimeo), survey prepared for the Urban Institute by Field Research Corporation, San Francisco, June 1983.

12. Spolar, "New Working Class in the Making."

13. Thomas Muller, "Economic Effects of Immigration," in *Clamor at the Gates: The New American Immigration,* ed. Nathan Glazer (San Francisco: Institute for Contemporary Studies Press, 1985). Also, George J. Borjas, *Friends or Strangers: The Impact of Immigrants on the U.S. Economy* (New York: Basic Books, 1990); Richard B. Freeman, "Immigration, Trade, and the Labor Market" (mimeo), National Bureau of Economic Research summary report, Cambridge, Mass., January 1988; and Robert H. Topel, "The Impact of Immigration in the Labor Market" (mimeo), National Bureau of Economic Research, Cambridge, Mass., January 1988.

14. As noted later in the chapter, unemployment in these cities accelerated during the 1990–92 economic downturn.

15. Muller and Espenshade, *Fourth Wave.*

16. Briggs, *Immigration Policy and the American Labor Force.*

17. David Gonzales, "Criticism Aimed at Statements on Immigrants," *New York Times,* October 5, 1990.

18. Muller and Espenshade, *Fourth Wave.*

19. U.S. Department of Labor, Bureau of Labor Statistics, *Geographic Profile of Employment and Unemployment, 1991* (Washington, D.C.: Government Printing Office, August 1992).

20. For a discussion of other income sources for black youths, see Richard B. Freeman and Harry J. Holzer, eds. *The Black Youth Employment Crisis: Summary of Findings* (Chicago: University of Chicago Press, 1986).

21. Joel Kotkin, "Black Economic Base in L.A. Erodes as Demographics Change," *Washington Post,* October 1, 1989, p. H-2.

22. Courtland Milloy, "While You Slept . . .," *Washington Post,* October 6, 1987, p. B-3.

23. Carmenza Gallo, "The Construction Industry in New York City: Immigrants and Black Entrepreneurs," unpublished paper, Conservation of Human Resources, Research Program on Newcomers to New York City, Columbia University, New York, January 1983.

24. Thomas R. Bailey, *Immigrant and Native Workers* (Boulder, Colo.: Westview Press, 1987).

25. Joseph Nalven and Craig Frederickson, "The Employer's View: Is There a Need for a Guest-Worker Program?" Community Research Associates, San Diego, 1982.

26. U.S. Department of Labor, Bureau of Labor Statistics, *Employment and Earnings* 39, no. 7 (July 1992): 31.

27. Mean earnings for blacks working full time or part time in these occupations in 1990 were $28,486, compared to $16,253 for all black workers. Unpublished data from the March 1991 *Current Population Survey,* tabulated by the Income Statistics branch of the Housing, Household, and Economic Statistics Division, Bureau of the Census (communication with Robert Cleveland, September 1992).

28. However, the proportion of black doctors, lawyers, and dentists per capita is the lowest among seven cities with a black population similar in size to Miami's. See Bruce Porter and Marvin Dunn, *The Miami Riot of 1980* (Lexington, Mass.: Lexington Books, 1984).

29. *Dade County Characteristics,* Department of Human Resources, Metropolitan Dade County, Florida, January 1983, p. 9.

30. Bennett Minton, "Militants Aim to Seize Stores," *New York City Business,* January 28, 1985, p. 1.

31. Winston Williams, "Newark Intensifies Search in Assault on 2 Koreans," *New York Times,* August 30, 1987, p. 36.

32. Porter and Dunn, *Miami Riot of 1980.*

33. "Miami Mayor Apologizes to Police for Act at Shooting," *New York Times*, January 19, 1989, p. 1.

34. Robert A. Hill, quoted in Joel Kotkin, "Why Blacks Are Out of Business," *Washington Post*, September 7, 1986, p. C-1.

35. Porter and Dunn, *Miami Riot of 1980*, p. 144. The insightful columnist William Raspberry shares the view that blacks do not support black enterprises. He is critical of the Washington, D.C., black community because its lack of support has resulted in the failure of many black-owned businesses. William Raspberry "Save a Black Business," *Washington Post*, July 15, 1992, p. A-19.

36. Bailey, *Immigrant and Native Workers*, p. 119.

37. *The State of Small Business: A Report of the President*, transmitted to Congress, 1987 (Washington, D.C.: Government Printing Office, 1987).

38. Stanley Lieberson, *A Piece of the Pie: Blacks and White Immigrants since 1880* (Berkeley, Calif.: University of California Press, 1980).

39. William J. Wilson, *The Truly Disadvantaged: The Inner City, the Underclass, and Public Policy* (Chicago: University of Chicago Press, 1987), p. 35. In an interview five years after the book was published, Wilson appears to have modified his earlier insistence that changes in urban economies are the dominant cause of the plight of the black underclass. He now ascribes some of the problems to what can best be described as social and cultural factors. See Jason De Parle, "Responding to Urban Alarm Bells at Scholarship's Glacial Pace," *New York Times*, July 19, 1992, section 4, p. 7.

40. Jim Sleeper, "The Caribbean Black Challenge," *Washington Post*, August 24, 1986.

41. James Fallows, "Immigration: How It's Affecting Us," *Atlantic*, November 1983, pp. 45–106.

42. Alex Stepick, quoted in Marshall Ingwerson, "Banishing Poverty: An Uphill Fight," *Christian Science Monitor*, February 13, 1989.

43. Edward N. Luttwak, "The Riots: Underclass vs. Immigrants," *New York Times*, May 15, 1992, p. A-29.

44. Otis L. Graham, Jr., and Roy Beck, "To Help Inner City, Cut Flow of Immigrants," *Los Angeles Times*, May 19, 1992, p. B-7.

45. Joel Kotkin, "America on Hold: Can We Learn to Rebuild the Nation?" *Washington Post*, May 31, 1992, p. C-1.

46. California Opinion Index, "California's Expanding Minority Population" (mimeo), Field Institute, San Francisco, 1988.

47. See, for example, Roger Conner, "Breaking Down the Barriers: The Changing Relationship between Illegal Immigrants and Welfare," Federation for American Immigration Reform, Washington, D.C., September 1982.

48. "Telephone Survey of Public Attitudes toward Immigration and Related Issues."

49. David S. North, *Government Records: What They Tell Us about the Role of Illegal Immigrants in the Labor Market and in Income Transfer Programs* (Washington D.C.: New Transcentury Foundation, April 1981).

50. *James Plyler, Superintendent of the Tyler Independent School District, and its Board of Trustees, et al., Appellants v. J. and R. Doe et al.,* S.Ct. 80-1538, together with *Texas, et al., Appellants v. Certain Named and Unnamed Undocumented Alien Children, et al.,* S. Ct. 80-1934, on appeal from the United States Court of Appeals for the Fifth Circuit (June 15, 1982). Justice Brennan delivered the opinion of the Supreme Court, p. 20.

51. Attachment to memorandum from Eddy S. Tanaka, director of social services, to Michael Myonovich, Los Angeles County supervisor, December 10, 1986.

52. U.S. Department of Commerce, Bureau of Economic Analysis, *Local Area Personal Income 1976–1981,* vol. 1 summary, June 1983, and *Local Area Personal Income 1981–1986,* vol. 1 summary, July 1988.

53. Zita Arocha, "Influx from Suburbs Strains City Clinics," *Washington Post,* June 28, 1986, p. B-1.

54. Demetrious G. Papademetriou and Thomas Muller, "Recent Immigration to New York: Labor Market and Social Policy Issues," National Commission for Employment Policy, Washington, D.C., February 1987.

55. Peter Kerr, "Koch Memo Directs City Workers Not to Report Illegal Aliens to U.S.," *New York Times,* October 18, 1985, p. A-1.

56. These data are average annual payments to all residents. Average payments to recipients are substantially higher. U.S. Department of Commerce, *Local Area Personal Income 1976–1981* and *Local Area Personal Income 1981–1986.*

57. Elizabeth Bogen, *Immigration in New York* (New York: Praeger Publishers, 1987), p. 101.

58. Muller and Espenshade, *Fourth Wave.*

59. Julian Simon, "How Do Immigrants Affect Us Economically?" Georgetown University Center for Immigration Policy and Refugee Assistance, Washington, D.C., 1985.

60. George Borjas and M. Tienda, "The Economic Consequences of Immigration," *Science,* February 6, 1987, pp. 646–48.

61. Ellen Sehgal, "Foreign-Born Workers in the U.S. Labor Market: The Results of a Special Survey," *Monthly Labor Review* 108, no. 7 (July 1985): 18–24.

62. George J. Borjas and Stephen J. Trejo, "Immigrant Participation in the Welfare System," *Industrial and Labor Relations Review* 44, no. 2 (January 1991): 195–211.

63. By comparison, the 1990 utilization rates for welfare by ethnic groups were as follows: whites, 7.4 percent; blacks, 27.3 percent; Hispanics, 17.2 percent. See Department of Commerce, Bureau of the Census, *Poverty in the United States: 1990,* Current Population Reports series P-60, no. 175, August 1991.

64. Thomas Muller, "The Impact of Reagan Administration Policies on Regional Income and Employment," Urban Institute, Washington, D.C., May 1986.

65. The extent to which population growth, from whatever source, leads to higher income concentration has been the subject of debate among development economists. There is evidence that high population growth leads to income inequality, but it is not conclusive. See David Cam, "Distribution Issues in the Relationship between Population Growth and Economic Development," in *Population Growth and Economic Development: Issues and Evidence,* ed.

D. Gale Johnson and Ronald D. Lee (Madison, Wis.: University of Wisconsin Press, 1987).

66. "Task Force," *San Francisco Independent*, May 25, 1988, p. 1.

67. Gregory Spencer, *Projections of the Population of the United States, by Age, Sex, and Race: 1988 to 2080*, U.S. Department of Commerce, Bureau of the Census (Washington, D.C.: Government Printing Office, January 1989). The report assumes net immigration will decline between 1988 and 1998, an unreasonably conservative proposition.

68. U.S. Congress, Senate, *Immigration and Crime*, Reports of the Immigration Commission (Dillingham Commission), S.Rept. 750, 61st Cong., 3d sess., 1911.

69. U.S. Department of Justice, *Crime in the United States, 1987* (Washington, D.C.: Government Printing Office, 1988). Although records are maintained by arrest, not conviction, the correlation between arrests and conviction has been found to be very high.

70. Susan Pennell and Christine Curtis, "The Impact of Undocumented Aliens on the Criminal Justice System," draft paper, San Diego Association of Governments, October 1986.

71. Daniel Wolf, "Undocumented Aliens and Crime," Monograph Series 19, Center for U.S.-Mexican Studies, University of California, San Diego, La Jolla, 1988.

72. Lydia Chavez, "U.S. Answering Unusual Request, Seeks Illegal Aliens in Westchester," *New York Times*, September 3, 1986.

73. Among the groups for which data is tallied, blacks have the highest, and Asians the lowest, arrest rates in Los Angeles.

74. Leon Daniel, "Racial Tension Brews in L.A.'s Big Melting Pot," *Los Angeles Times*, January 1, 1984, p. A-1.

Chapter 6

1. *The Papers of Benjamin Franklin*, vol. 4, ed. Leonard W. Labaree et al. (New Haven: Yale University Press, 1961), p. 485.

2. California Opinion Index, "Immigration" (mimeo), Field Institute, San Francisco, October 1987.

3. California Opinion Index, "California's Expanding Minority Population" (mimeo), Field Institute, San Francisco, July 1988.

4. California State Department of Finance, Population Research Unit, *Projected Total Population for California by Race/Ethnicity*, Report 88 P-4, Sacramento, February 1988.

5. Douglas Shuit, "Minorities Now a Majority in State's Schools," *Los Angeles Times*, September 7, 1988, p. A-1. In the fall of 1989, only 14.6 percent of the more than 600,000 students in Los Angeles city schools were non-Hispanic whites.

6. Gregory Spencer, *Projections of the Population of the United States by Age, Sex and Race, 1988 to 2080*, Department of Commerce, Bureau of the Census (Washington, D.C.: Government Printing Office, January 1989). The estimates incorporate "Projections of the Hispanic Population: 1983 to 2080," Series P-25, no. 995, November 1986.

7. The approximately 700,000 Japan-born Koreans are treated as third-class aliens who have no rights unless they change their names and seek Japanese citizenship. For an account of how this minority is treated, see Juan Williams, "Race and Japan," *Washington Post Magazine,* January 5, 1992, pp. 12–28.

8. Nathan Alter and Joseph Contreras, "Closing the Door?" *Newsweek,* June 25, 1984, p. 18.

9. California Opinion Index, "Immigration" (mimeo), Field Institute, San Francisco, June 1982.

10. California Opinion Index, "California's Expanding Minority Population."

11. When adjusted to take into account refugees, IRCA legalization, and other factors, the number of Europeans (primarily Irish, Poles, and Russians) admitted in 1989 and 1990 exceeded that of previous years. However, the percentage of all immigrants that are European in origin has declined sharply, from 13.2 percent in 1979 to 7.6 percent in 1989.

12. Jolyon Jenkins, "'Fortress White' Mentality," *New Statesman,* October 10, 1986, p. 16.

13. Thomas Jefferson, "Letter to Peter Carr, August 10, 1787," in *The Portable Thomas Jefferson,* ed. Merrill D. Peterson (New York: Penguin Books, 1980), p. 424.

14. "GAO Supports Bilingual Education," *Publishers Weekly,* April 10, 1987.

15. Stella L. Marquez, "Bilingual Education Still Needed," *Los Angeles Times,* August 23, 1987, p. B-12. Marquez is a high school principal in Anaheim, where 60 percent of the students are limited-English-proficient.

16. Mary Hatwood Futrell, "An Educator's Opinion: An American Opportunity," *Washington Post,* February 26, 1989, p. C-3.

17. Sally Reed, "What the Research Shows," *New York Times,* November 10, 1985, section 12 (Education supplement), p. 48.

18. Gary Imhoff and Gerda Bikalis, "The Battle over Preserving the English Language," *USA Today,* February 13, 1987, p. 12. The newspaper on the same date also ran an editorial stating its opposition to any referendum on making English the official language of the United States.

19. Nathan Glazer, *Ethnic Dilemmas, 1964–1982* (Cambridge, Mass.: Harvard University Press, 1983), p. 149.

20. Richard Rodriguez, "Bilingualism, Con: Outdated and Unrealistic," *New York Times,* November 10, 1985, section 12 (Education supplement), p. 63.

21. "Spanish for Survival," editorial quoted from the *Miami Times,* in *Christian Science Monitor,* September 28, 1982, p. 24.

22. California Opinion Index, "Immigration" (mimeo), Field Institute, San Francisco, October 1989.

23. S. I. Hayakawa, "Why English Should Be Our Official Language," *Education Digest,* May 1987, pp. 36–37.

24. George F. Will, "In Defense of the Mother Tongue," *Newsweek,* July 8, 1985, p. 78.

25. William F. Buckley, "Avoiding Canada's Problem," *National Review,* October 18, 1985, p. 62.

26. Eugene J. McCarthy, "Washington: Colony to the World," *Atlantic,* November 1982, p. 27.

27. "The Difficulty of Digesting a Foreign Body," *Economist,* January 16, 1984, pp. 21–22.

28. The issue of fading ethnicity among this group is explored in Richard D. Alba, *Italian Americans: Into the Twilight of Ethnicity* (Englewood Cliffs, N.J.: Prentice-Hall, 1985).

29. Fernando Torres-Gil, "The Latinization of a Multigenerational Population: Hispanics in an Aging Society," *Daedalus* 115, no. 1 (Winter 1986): 325–48.

30. Nathan Glazer, *The New Immigration* (San Diego: San Diego State University Press, 1988), pp. 30–37. For a somewhat different perspective on multiculturalism by the same author, see Nathan Glazer, "In Defense of Multiculturalism," *New Republic,* September 2, 1991, pp. 18–21. In this lengthy article, Glazer supports the argument that the drive for multiculturalism stems from the native black, not the immigrant, community.

31. Joshua A. Fishman, *Language, Ethnic Identity and Political Loyalty: Mexican Americans in Sociolinguistic Perspective* (Washington, D.C.: Urban Institute Press, 1986).

32. Peter H. Schuck, "Immigration Law and the Problem of Community," in *Clamor at the Gates: The New American Immigration,* ed. Nathan Glazer (San Francisco: Institute for Contemporary Studies Press, 1985), pp. 285–307.

33. George Ramos and Tracy Wilkinson, "Unrest Widens Rifts in Diverse Latino Population," *Los Angeles Times,* May 8, 1992, p. A-4.

34. Richard D. Lamm and Gary Imhoff, *The Immigration Time Bomb: The Fragmenting of America* (New York: Truman Talley Books/E. P. Dutton, 1985).

35. Arthur M. Schlesinger, *The Disuniting of America: Reflections on a Multicultural Society* (Knoxville, Tenn.: Whittle Direct Books, 1991), p. 2.

36. Stephen Moore, "Social Scientists' Views on Immigrants and U.S. Immigration Policy: A Postscript," *Annals of the American Academy of Political and Social Science* 487 (September 1986): 215–16.

37. California Opinion Index, "California's Expanding Minority Population."

38. Shawn Hubler, "Race: How the Races Get Along—or Don't," *Orange County Register,* May 11, 1986, p. A-1.

39. California Opinion Index, "Immigration," October 1987.

40. George Gallup, Jr., *Forecast 2000* (New York: William Morrow and Co., 1984), p. 40.

41. *American Attitudes toward Immigration,* Roper Organization survey, New York, April 1992, p. 7.

42. Joseph P. O'Grady, ed., *The Immigrants' Influence on Wilson's Peace Policies* (Frankfort, Ky.: University Press of Kentucky, 1967). See also Joseph Edward Cuddy, *Irish-America and National Isolationism: 1914–1920* (New York: Arno Press, 1976).

43. *New York Times,* August 18, 1992, p. A-10. The platform also favored stronger border patrols to interdict illegal aliens.

44. George H. Gallup, *The Gallup Poll: Public Opinion, 1987,* (Wilmington, Del.: Scholarly Resources, 1988).

45. Larry Peterson, "Jesse Jackson Takes Plea for Unity West," *Orange County Register,* August 23, 1987, p. A-3.

46. Antonio H. Rodriguez and Gloria J. Romero, "Latinos Snub Jackson: Is It Racism?" *Los Angeles Times,* July 15, 1988, p. 7.

47. Eric Harrison, "Daley Defeats Sawyer in Mayor Race in Chicago," *Los Angeles Times,* March 1, 1989, section 1, p. 17.

48. Bruce E. Cain and D. Roderick Kiewiet, "The Political Impact of California's Minorities," report prepared for a major public symposium entitled "Minorities in California," California Institute of Technology, Division of Humanities and Social Sciences, Pasadena, March 5, 1986.

49. Black civil rights groups continue to oppose reducing the level of busing of schoolchildren for integration on the basis that segregated schools afford black students fewer opportunities. See, for example, Cathy Corman, "School Integration: New Calls for Action," *New York Times,* March 3, 1991, section 12 (Education supplement), p. 1.

50. Ruben Castaneda, "L. A. Job Fight: A Bitter Struggle or an Alliance?" *California Tomorrow,* Winter 1989, p. 7.

51. Earl O. Hutchison, "Obstacles for Unity Multiply for Blacks and Latinos," *Los Angeles Times,* September 10, 1991, p. B-7.

52. Cain and Kiewiet, "The Political Impact of California's Minorities."

53. Thomas Massey, "The Wrong Way to Court Ethnics," *Washington Monthly,* May 1986, p. 21.

54. William Raspberry, "When White Guilt Won't Matter," *Washington Post,* November 4, 1987, p. A-23.

Chapter 7

1. National Commission on Employment Policy, *Eighth Annual Report of the National Commission on Employment Policy to the President and the Congress* (Washington D.C.: Government Printing Office, 1983).

2. Although some new Asian and Hispanic workers are not foreign-born, the employment data for whites and blacks also include immigrants. For example, New York attracted aliens from Ireland, Poland, and the Soviet Union during the 1980s, and even larger numbers of non-Hispanic blacks from Jamaica, Guyana, and Haiti. Therefore, it is reasonable to assume that the immigrant share of jobs added in these cities was 80 percent or more.

3. This estimate is derived as follows: legal immigration (1980–1989), 6.3 million; nonagricultural worker illegal entrants (1982–1990), 1.6 million; illegal agricultural workers (SAW applicants); 1.3 million; temporary workers likely to remain in the United States, (including H-1 and H-2 workers, intracompany transfers,

and students employed part time) 0.3 million. It is assumed 49 percent of all persons in the above categories are employed, or a total of 4.65 million immigrant workers. This is 26 percent of the 18 million gain in employed workers between 1980 and 1989.

4. Harry Bacas, "Desperately Seeking Workers," *Nation's Business*, February 1988, pp. 16–23.

5. Ralph E. Winter, "U.S. Labor Supply Seems to Be Shrinking," *Wall Street Journal*, March 10, 1989, p. A-2.

6. David S. Hilzenrath and Nell Henderson, "Area Hit by Labor Shortage," *Washington Post*, June 4, 1988, p. A-1.

7. Zita Arocha, "Illegal-Worker Ban Leaves Firms Hurting," *Washington Post*, June 6, 1988, p. A-1.

8. George Grier, "Special Report: Greater Washington's Labor Shortage," Greater Washington Research Center, Washington, D.C., August 1988.

9. Ron Scherer, "Help Wanted in U.S. Factories," *Christian Science Monitor*, March 25, 1988, p. A-1.

10. Mary Lynn Richmond, "Labor Shortage Pinches Calif. Swimwear Firms," *Women's Wear Daily*, February 17, 1988, p. 1.

11. Michael W. Horrigan and Steven E. Haugen, "The Declining Middle-Class Thesis: A Sensitivity Analysis," *Monthly Labor Review* 111, no. 5 (May 1988): pp. 3–11.

12. Howard N. Fullerton, Jr., "Projections 2000—Labor Force Projections: 1986 to 2000," *Monthly Labor Review* 110, no. 9 (September 1987): 19.

13. For a discussion of employment multipliers associated with various direct jobs in the New York area, see Thomas Muller and William B. Moore, *Economic Impacts of the Stapleton Homeport*, President's Economic Adjustment Committee, Office of Economic Adjustment, Department of Defense, December 1988, p. 5-4.

14. Interview of Mikhail Gorbachev by Thomas Brokaw, *New York Times*, December 1, 1987, pp. A-1, A-12.

15. Barbara Vobejda, "Teaching Regains Favor as Career Goal," *Washington Post*, January 14, 1988, p. A-5.

16. National Science Board, *Science Indicators: The Nineteen Eighty-Five Report* (Washington, D.C.: Government Printing Office, 1985).

17. Ibid.

18. G. Pascal Zachary, "Foreign Dependency," *San Jose Mercury News*, May 15, 1988, p. A-1.

19. Seth Shulman, "Engineers and Immigration," *Technology Review*, January 1987, p. 15. See also Booz, Allen, and Hamilton, "Characteristics and Labor Market Impact of Persons Admitted under the H-1 Program," report prepared for the Immigration and Naturalization Service, U.S. Department of Justice, June 1988.

20. National Research Council, *Foreign and Foreign-Born Engineers in the United States* (Washington, D.C.: National Academy Press, 1988).

21. Stanford S. Penner, "Tapping the Wave of Talented Immigrants," *Issues in Science and Technology* (Spring 1988): 77.

22. In 1987, more than 18,000 nurses took the Commission on Graduates of Foreign Nursing Schools examination, which must be passed in order to gain temporary employment in the United States.

23. George T. Silvestri and John M. Lukasiewitz, "Outlook 1990–2005: Occupational Employment Projections," U.S. Department of Labor, Bureau of Labor Statistics, BLS Bulletin no. 2404, May 1992.

24. U.S. Department of Labor, Bureau of Labor Statistics, *Employment and Earnings* 36, no. 1 (January 1989). Unemployment statistics cited in the chapter are for November 1988.

25. There was a striking rise in legal admissions to the New York metropolitan area (primarily New York City) in 1990. This can be credited largely to IRCA legalization of formerly undocumented persons living in New York prior to 1982. Refer to U.S. Department of Justice, *1990 Statistical Yearbook of the Immigration and Naturalization Service* (Washington, D.C.: Government Printing Office, December 1991), Table 18, p. 82.

26. *A Forecast of Employment, Labor Force and Population in the NY-NJ Metropolitan Region to 1995,* Port Authority of New York and New Jersey, April 1986.

27. Joel L. Naroff, "Labor Shortage in Philadelphia," paper presented at the Regional Sciences Association meeting, Baltimore, November 1987.

28. Dennis Macheski and Gordon Palmer, "Draft Baseline Projection," Southern California Association of Governments, Los Angeles, August 1986.

29. *The San Francisco Bay Area: A View to the Year 2005,* Association of Bay Area Governments, Oakland, July 1987.

30. Thomas Muller and Thomas J. Espenshade, *The Fourth Wave: California's Newest Immigrants* (Washington, D.C.: Urban Institute Press, 1985).

31. Yasusuki Murakami, "Toward a Socioinstitutional Explanation of Japan's Economic Performance," in *Economic Policies and Trade Issues of Japan: American and Japanese Perspectives,* ed. Kozo Yamamura (Seattle: University of Washington Press, 1982).

32. Masayoshi Kanabayashi, "Some Japanese Industries Face Prospect of Labor Shortage amid Boom Times," *Wall Street Journal,* August 1, 1989, p. A-10.

33. The labor shortage in Japan will worsen in the late 1990s, when the number of working-age persons will actually decline. See Paul Blustein, "When this Recession Is Over, Japan May Never Be the Same," *Washington Post,* June 22, 1992, p. A-1.

Chapter 8

1. *American Attitudes toward Immigration,* Roper Organization survey, New York, April 1992. Because the moratorium question had not been asked previously, it is not known whether the poll represents a shift in public opinion on this issue.

2. Lawrence Auster, "Our Disappearing Common Culture: The Forbidden Topic," *National Review,* April 27, 1992, pp. 42–44.

3. See James Bornemeier, "Most Favor U.S. Immigration Freeze, Polls Say," *Los Angeles Times,* May 20, 1992, p. A-16; and John Dillin, "U.S. Welcome Mat

Showing Wear," *Christian Science Monitor,* May 20, 1992, p. 8. Both newspapers gave the FAIR news conference prominent coverage.

4. Otis L. Graham, Jr., and Roy Beck, "To Help Inner City, Cut Flow of Immigrants," *Los Angeles Times,* May 19, 1992, p. B-7.

5. Lawrence Harrison, "America and Its Immigrants," *National Interest,* no. 28 (Summer 1992): 37–46. This article was the companion piece to an essay titled "The Post-Modern State," by James Kurth; together, the two were listed under the heading "Is America Still a Nation?"

6. Daniel James, "Bar the Door," *New York Times,* July 25, 1992.

7. M. S. Forbes, Jr., "We Need More People," *Forbes,* February 9, 1987, p. 25.

8. *Wall Street Journal,* July 3, 1986, p. 16. Three years later, the newspaper again appealed for higher immigration in an impassioned editorial, "The Rekindled Flame" (July 3, 1989, p. 6), which invoked the poem by Emma Lazarus.

9. "Democrats for Vitality," *Wall Street Journal,* October 1, 1990, p. A-14; and "Immigration Victories," *Wall Street Journal,* October 29, 1990.

10. "The Honest Solution," *New Republic,* April 1, 1985, p. 20.

11. Julian Simon, "The Case for Greatly Increased Immigration," *Public Interest,* no. 102 (Winter 1991): 89–103.

12. Jack Miles, "Immigration and the New American Dilemma," *Atlantic,* October 1992.

13. Paul Kennedy, *The Rise and Fall of the Great Powers* (New York: Random House, 1987).

14. See, for example, Norman C. Saunders, "Defense Spending in the 1990's: The Effects of Deeper Cuts," *Monthly Labor Review* 113, no. 10 (October 1990): 3–15. See also Congressional Budget Office, *The Economic Effect of Reduced Defense Spending* (Washington, D.C.: Government Printing Office, February 1992). Both studies, applying econometric models, found that the aggregate economic effects of defense cuts are minor. However, there is a substantial (and adverse) impact on communities with defense-related industries or facilities.

15. The impact of Spanish immigration has been summarized as follows: "The expulsion of Jews, the only citizens with economic ability, sealed the fate of the Coastline empire before it was born." M. Batista y Roca, "The Hispanic Kingdoms and the Catholic Kings," chapter 11 in *The New Cambridge Modern History,* vol. 1, ed. G. R. Potter (Cambridge: Cambridge University Press, 1957), p. 338.

16. Kennedy, *Rise and Fall of the Great Powers,* p. 531.

17. Vernon M. Briggs, *Immigration Policy and the American Labor Force* (Baltimore: Johns Hopkins University Press, 1984), pp. 257–60.

18. The two additional categories are "special immigrants" such as ministers (up to 10,000 visas) and immigrants who will create ten or more jobs for Americans by investing $1 million (or more). As of late 1992, fewer than one hundred visas had been issued to investors. The low demand is attributable primarily to American tax laws, which tax income earned worldwide.

19. During the 1980s, the vast majority of less-skilled workers who immigrated legally to the United States were admitted as immediate relatives of U.S. citizens,

as other relatives of U.S. citizens, or as immediate relatives of alien residents. Because this pattern is expected to continue, there is little need to admit additional lower-skill immigrants based on their occupations. One of the exceptions would be provisions for admitting those who can provide live-in child care. The shortfall between the supply of legalized less-skilled workers and the demand for such workers has been met by illegal aliens.

20. Hugh Windsor, "McDougall Wins Battle to Increase Immigration," *Toronto Globe and Mail,* October 24, 1990.

21. Roberto Suro, "1986 Amnesty Law Seen as Failing to Slow Alien Tide," *New York Times,* June 18, 1989, p. A-1.

22. Paul O. Flaim, "How Many New Jobs since 1982: Data from Two Surveys Differ," *Monthly Labor Review* 112, no. 8 (August 1989): 10–15.

23. As of May 1991, there were only 11, 472 applications for legalization from Koreans, 4,443 from Taiwanese, and 11,284 from mainland Chinese. These numbers represent less than 1 percent of all applicants for the legalization program. See U.S. Department of Justice, *1990 Statistical Yearbook of the Immigration and Naturalization Service* (Washington, D.C.: Government Printing Office, December 1991), Table 22, p. 94.

24. Michael Fix and Paul T. Hill, *Enforcing Employer Sanctions under IRCA: Challenges and Strategies* (Washington, D.C.: Rand Corporation and Urban Institute, 1990), p. 107. See also Michael Fix, ed., *The Paper Curtain: Employer Sanctions' Implementation, Impact, and Reform* (Washington, D.C.: Urban Institute Press, 1991).

25. Peter H. Schuck, "Immigration Law and Policy in the 1990s," *Yale Law and Policy Review* 7, no. 1 (1989): 1–19.

26. Private communication with Peter H. Schuck, June 15, 1989.

27. For example, a commission appointed by Congress in 1987 to study the issues concluded that such assistance would help to stem the flow of illegal workers. The commission concluded that "mutually beneficial economic development would obviate the need for enforcement of immigration laws." See "Unauthorized Migration: An Economic Development Response," report of the Commission for the Study of International Migration and Cooperative Economic Development, Washington, D.C., July 1990. It seems unrealistic, however, to expect economic development policies to create conditions that would significantly reduce the earnings differential between the United States and most other nations in the Western Hemisphere.

28. Alan Dowty, *Closed Borders: The Contemporary Assault on Freedom of Movement* (New Haven: Yale University Press, 1987).

Index